Lecture Notes in Computer Science   **10231**

Commenced Publication in 1973
Founding and Former Series Editors:
Gerhard Goos, Juris Hartmanis, and Jan van Leeuwen

More information about this series at http://www.springer.com/series/7408

Olga Kouchnarenko · Ramtin Khosravi (Eds.)

Formal Aspects of Component Software

13th International Conference, FACS 2016
Besançon, France, October 19–21, 2016
Revised Selected Papers

 Springer

Editors
Olga Kouchnarenko 🆔
Université Bourgogne Franche-Comté
Besançon
France

Ramtin Khosravi
University of Tehran
Tehran
Iran

ISSN 0302-9743   ISSN 1611-3349   (electronic)
Lecture Notes in Computer Science
ISBN 978-3-319-57665-7   ISBN 978-3-319-57666-4   (eBook)
DOI 10.1007/978-3-319-57666-4

Library of Congress Control Number: 2017938157

LNCS Sublibrary: SL2 – Programming and Software Engineering

Printed on acid-free paper

This Springer imprint is published by Springer Nature
The registered company is Springer International Publishing AG
The registered company address is: Gewerbestrasse 11, 6330 Cham, Switzerland

Preface

The component-based software development approach has emerged as a promising paradigm to cope with the complexity of present-day software systems by bringing sound engineering principles into software engineering. However, many challenging conceptual and technological issues still remain in this area, theoretically as well as practically. Moreover, the advent of cloud computing, cyber-physical systems, and of the Internet of Things has brought to the fore new dimensions, such as quality of service, reconfiguration, and robustness to withstand inevitable faults, which require established concepts to be revisited and new ones to be developed in order to meet the opportunities offered by those architectures.

That was emphasized by the program of FACS 2016. Several sessions and invited talks were devoted to formal analysis and model-based development, whereas a practical session focused on applications and experience. Security aspects were present, too, in particular at an invited talk. Finally, the last two sessions dealt with operations on components.

A total of 14 papers successfully passed the review process, showing that component-based development is still an active research field.

March 2017

Olga Kouchnarenko
Ramtin Khosravi

Organization

Program Committee

Farhad Arbab	CWI and Leiden University, The Netherlands
Kyungmin Bae	Carnegie Mellon University, USA
Luis Barbosa	Universidade do Minho, Portugal
Simon Bliudze	EPFL, Switzerland
Sergiy Bogomolov	IST Austria
Borzoo Bonakdarpour	McMaster University, Canada
Christiano Braga	Universidade Federal Fluminense, Brazil
Roberto Bruni	Università di Pisa, Italy
Carlos Canal	University of Málaga, Spain
Ivana Cerna	Masaryk University, Czeck Republic
Hung Dang Van	UET, Vietnam National University, Hanoi, Vietnam
Cynthia Disenfeld	University of Toronto, Canada
Ramtin Khosravi	University of Tehran, Iran
Olga Kouchnarenko	University of Franche-Comté, France
Zhiming Liu	Southwest University, China
Markus Lumpe	Swinburne University of Technology, Australia
Eric Madelaine	Inria, France
Hernan Melgratti	Universidad de Buenos Aires, Argentina
Mohammadreza Mousavi	Halmstad University, Sweden
Peter Ölveczky	University of Oslo, Norway
Wojciech Penczek	ICS PAS and Siedlce University, Poland
Michel Reniers	Eindhoven University of Technology, The Netherlands
Romain Rouvoy	University of Lille/Inria/IUF, France
Eric Rutten	Inria, France
Gwen Salaun	Grenoble INP, Inria, LIG, France
Francesco Santini	Università di Perugia, Italy
Bernhard Schaetz	TU München, Germany
Marjan Sirjani	Reykjavik University, Iceland
Frits Vaandrager	Radboud University Nijmegen, The Netherlands
Tao Yue	Simula, Norway
Naijun Zhan	Institute of Software, Chinese Academy of Sciences, China

Additional Reviewers

Bagheri, Maryam
Bayha, Andreas
Benes, Nikola
Chen, Yu-Fang
Faghih, Fathiyeh
Giorgetti, Alain
Goessler, Gregor
Héam, Pierre-Cyrille
Jafari, Ali
Kanav, Sudeep
Khamespanah, Ehsan
Knapik, Michał

Lu, Hong
Madeira, Alexandre
Mateescu, Radu
Mens, Irini-Eleftheria
Mikučionis, Marius
Peureux, Fabien
Pradhan, Dipesh
Ribeiro, Rodrigo
Weber, Jean-François
Ye, Lina
Zhang, Huihui
Zhao, Hengjun

Abstracts of Invited Papers

Formal Models and Analysis for Self-adaptive Cyber-Physical Systems

(Extended Abstract)

Holger Giese

Hasso Plattner Institute at the University of Potsdam, Potsdam, Germany
holger.giese@hpi.uni-potsdam.de

In this extended abstract, we will analyze the current challenges for the envisioned Self-Adaptive Cyber-Physical Systems. In addition, we will outline our results to approach these challenges with SMARTSOS, a generic approach based on extensions of graph transformation systems employing open and adaptive collaborations and models at runtime for trustworthy self-adaptation, self-organization, and evolution of the individual systems and the system-of-systems level taking the independent development, operation, management, and evolution of these systems into account.

From Formal Methods to Software Components: Back to the Future?

Kung-Kiu Lau

School of Computer Science, The University of Manchester,
Manchester, M13 9PL, UK
kung-kiu.lau@manchester.ac.uk

Abstract. Looking back at the past, I believe Formal Methods and Component-based Software Engineering have missed opportunities to synergise. Looking forward to the future, I believe even more strongly that this synergy will be crucial for developing Software Engineering techniques that tackle scale and complexity. In this position paper I outline the fundamentals of my belief, in terms of existing work and future challenges.

From Devices to Data: Testing the IoT

Franck Le Gall

Easy Global Market, 1200 Route des Lucioles, 06560 Valbonne, France
franck.le-gall@eglobalmark.com
http://www.eglobalmark.com

Abstract. This paper provides an extended abstract of the FACS 2016 invited call on IoT testing.

Introduction

The internet of Things paradigm relies on innovative applications transversally deployed over vertical domains. However, the situation today is still fragmented with the need for an end user to handle different applications to access information from different providers, missing the expected value from transversal deployment. Answering that concern, many standards are developing around the world which now lead to a complex ecosystem in which interoperability of solutions must be ensured [1]. In addition, IoT is handling huge amount of data, threatening users privacy while control capacity of actuators raise the security level requirement. For these reasons, appropriate verification and testing of IoT solutions become a prerequisite to any field deployment. Formal methods such as Model Based Testing (MBT) approach provide an appropriate answer and experiences learnt from on-going European research and standardisation activities have been presented during an invited talk.

Compliance to Standards and Specifications

FIWARE [3] is an ecosystem providing APIs and open-source implementation for lightweight and simple means to gather, publish, query and subscribe context-based, real-time information. This independent community includes more than 60 cities in the OASC alliance who adopt FIWARE NGSI API.

oneM2M [2] was established to develop a single horizontal platform for the exchange and sharing of M2M/IoT data among all applications. oneM2M is creating a distributed software layer which provides a framework for interworking with different technologies.

Both platforms define RESTful interfaces and from their specifications, behavioural models have been made. Such models are typically built using UML modelling with constraints defined with OCL. A commercial tool [4] has been used to generate test suites from the model. Two execution environments were built 1. To demonstrate in the case of FIWARE, the possible integration of the execution platform, as a webservice, within a Jenkins based continuous integration process and 2. in oneM2M using a normalised execution environment based on the TTCN-3 language [5], popular in the telecom word.

Use of MBT allows increasing both test coverage in comparison with manual approaches and traceability with implemented standards specifications. However, in both projects, the acceptance of functional testing is still to be accepted within the test communities as seen as complex.

Security Test

The ARMOUR project [6] co-funded by the European Commission under the Horizon 2020 program provides duly tested, benchmarked and certified Security and Trust solutions for evaluation of large-scale IoT deployments. It has defined 7 experiments each focused on a different part of an IoT tool chain going from device to data platform. In that project, a methodology based on formal methods has been proposed for security testing. A list of vulnerability patterns has been produced and allowed to derive corresponding test patterns. Here again, a model based testing approach has been chosen allowing testing of security functions by modelling of test purposes related to each experiment. A strong innovation brought by MBT is the integration of the individual models into a meta model allowing end to end security testing of the deployed solution. An offline model driven fuzzing approach is added at that stage to go beyond security functions testing and identify additional vulnerabilities which may arise from faulty implementations. Results from that project are already being contributed to the oneM2M standardisation alliance.

Conclusions and Future Outlook

In addition to compliance and security testing, new challenges are now raised by the need to test interoperability at the semantic layer level. Some initial developments have been made [7] but will require intensified efforts over the coming years. The presented projects take place in a stream of multi-year support from the European Commission toward Internet of Things. This support has been extended in the current H2020 workprogramme which now explicitly asks for verification and testing as part of its open call [8].

References

1. Alliance for IoT Innovation - Working Group 3, IoT standardisation landscape, version 2.6 (2016)
2. oneM2M. http://www.onem2m.org
3. FIWARE. http://www.fiware.org

4. Smartesting CertifyIT. http://www.smartesting.com
5. ETSI'S official TTCN-3 homepage, http://www.ttcn-3.org
6. H2020 ARMOUR. http://www.armour-project.eu/
7. Cousin P.: White Paper on flexible approach for semantic validation in the context of Internet of Things, October 2016
8. H2020 Call IoT-03-2017: R&I on IoT integration and platforms. http://ec.europa.eu/research/participants/portal/desktop/en/opportunities/h2020/topics/iot-03-2017.html

Contents

Tool Papers

Applications and Experiences Papers

Invited Papers

Formal Models and Analysis for Self-adaptive Cyber-physical Systems

(Extended Abstract)

Holger Giese[(⊠)]

Hasso Plattner Institute at the University of Potsdam, Potsdam, Germany
holger.giese@hpi.uni-potsdam.de

In the past advanced technological products and facilities employed more and more information and communication technology to enhance their functionality and quality. Therefore, already a decade ago software played an increasingly important role in the control and operation of many technical systems such as electrical and mechanical devices, complex products, or technical processes in industry. This trend towards software-intensive and embedded systems resulted in astonishing observation that, for example, the technology company Siemens employed in 2005 more software developers than Microsoft [1]. In addition, we could observe that advanced technological sectors such as the automotive industry had started major efforts to address software quality and software integration issues (cf. AUTOSAR [18]).

This development lead in recent years to the emergence of Cyber-Physical Systems (CPS) [3,20], which often include System of Systems (SoS) [13,20] aspects and may be also Ultra-Large Scale Systems (ULSS) [15] that are highly distributed. Nowadays, these CPS are in addition expected to exhibit adaptive and anticipatory behavior when operating in highly dynamic environments and interfacing with the physical world leading to Self-Adaptive CPS. Therefore, appropriate modeling and analysis techniques to address such Self-Adaptive CPS are required that support a mix of models from a multitude of disciplines such as software engineering, control engineering, and business process engineering (c.f. [2,20]).

In this extended abstract, we will analyze the current challenges for the envisioned Self-Adaptive CPS. In addition, we will outline our results to approach these challenges with SMARTSOS [10] a generic approach based on extensions of graph transformation systems employing open and adaptive collaborations and models at runtime for trustworthy self-adaptation, self-organization, and evolution of the individual systems and the system-of-systems level taking the independent development, operation, management, and evolution of these systems into account.

For these Self-Adaptive CPS the following main needs can be identified: Support for operational and managerial independence for subsystems is needed, as the subsystems of a CPS are often operated independent from each other without global coordination and therefore no centralized management decisions are possible and instead possibly conflicting local decisions have to be coordinated. Support for dynamic architecture and openness is needed, as the CPS must be

© Springer International Publishing AG 2017
O. Kouchnarenko and R. Khosravi (Eds.): FACS 2016, LNCS 10231, pp. 3–9, 2017.
DOI: 10.1007/978-3-319-57666-4_1

able to dynamically adapt/absorb structural deviations and must support that subsystems may join or leave over time in a not pre-planned manner. The CPS must scale for local systems or networked resp. large-scale systems of systems. They must support the integration of the physical, cyber, (and social) dimension, support the adaptation at the system and system of system level, allow the independent evolution of the systems and joint evolution the system of system, and must be sufficiently resilient at the system of system level.

An analogy often employed in the context of highly distributed, adaptive, and resilient systems like the considered Self-Adaptive CPS are ant colonies that operate as a superorganism that combines information processing of many ants and their interaction with the environment at the physical level (using stigmergy as coordination mechanism). In the famous "asymmetric binary bridge experiment", there are path (bridges) from the ant colony to a food source. It can be observed that initially both options will be taken with the same probability by the ants. Then, over time the higher concentration of the pheromones on the shorter path will result in an increase of its usage, while the lower concentration of the pheromones on the longer path will result in a decrease of its usage. The higher concentration of pheromones on the shorter path will make it more likely that an ant choses this shorter one and positive feedback will amplify this effect and thus finally the longer path will only be used seldom anymore. However, there also exists phenomena such as "ant mill" where a whole colony of ants is caught in cycling once the colony has by accident started to do so. All ants will starve as they do not find any new food following the scheme. But they simply do not have any strategy to avoid this.

Consequently, the envisioned class of systems cannot be simply addressed by borrow ideas from superorganisms in nature, as behavior such as the ant mil would be not acceptable for an engineered system even if they are possible only for rather unexpected circumstances (rare events). It is surprising that "nature" did not come up with design solutions that are more resilient even though evolution has operated for ages. However, there is also a solution in nature we can observe in more complex forms of life that have more advanced adaptation capabilities also including to reflect on itself and its goals. By reflecting on the behavior of the colony as a superorganism and compare it to its goals, an ant colony could have detected that their standard behavior requires a temporary adjustment to escape the ant mill. However, an ant colony lacks the required reflection capabilities, while more complex forms of life can reflect on their own behavior and how successful it is to achieve its goals to some extent. Consequently, we argue that we need in fact Self-Adaptive CPS that are capable of advanced forms of self-awareness w.r.t. goals [16] to be able to handle problems due to unexpected circumstances.

The need for adaptation has different sources: On the one hand, "Adaptation is needed to compensate for changes in the mission requirements" [15]. On the other hand, "The vision [...] is that of open, ubiquitous systems of coordinated computing and physical elements which interactively adapt to their context" [3]. This need for adaptation requests for systems that "are capable of learning, dynamically and automatically reconfigure themselves and cooperate with other

CPSs" [3]. Therefore, the challenge is to develop systems with adaptation capable of adaptation at the system level as well at the level of the system-of-systems.

An option to achieve the required capability of adaption including self-awareness w.r.t. goals, are self-adaptive systems [8], which make systems self-aware, context-aware, and requirements-aware using some form of reflection and therefore enable systems to adjust their structure/behavior accordingly, as well as self-organization, which results in the capability of a group of systems to organize their structure/behavior without a central control to achieve required behavior resp. structures in form of emergent behavior. From an engineering perspective, a spectrum from centralized top-down self-adaptation to decentralized bottom-up self-organization with many intermediate forms (e.g. partial hierarchies) exists and a proper design requires to identify the right compromise between both extremes. A crucial element for the reflection and self-awareness are runtime models [22–24] that are linked by a causal relation to the software and/or context such that self-adaptation can operate at a higher level of abstraction. Here generic runtime models allow to capture and handle many possible changes such that the adaptation adjust the core software accordingly.

Besides adaptation there is also the need for integration of the physical, cyber, (and social) dimension, which is particularly challenging as there are (1) problems to integrate models as different models of computation are employed and (2) leaky abstractions caused by lack of composability across system dimensions, which therefore result in intractable interactions, unpredictable system level behavior, and the problem that full system verification does not scale (cf. [19]).

One option to approach the integration of the physical, cyber, and social dimension is multi-paradigm modeling [14]. It enables to use different domain-specific models with different models of computation for different modeling aspects and can be employed at the system level to combine all necessary models for a system as well as at the system-of-systems level to combine all necessary models for a system-of-systems. It requires, however, that for employed model combinations a suitable semantic integration is known and supported by tools. These combinations of multiple paradigms then result in hybrid behavior covering continuous behavior and discrete behavior in real-time and probabilistic behavior as required for physical system on the one hand and discrete behavior often ignoring time with non-determinism as employed for cyber components of the system on the other hand.

It is further expected that the system "fulfill stringent safety, security and private data protection regulations" [3]. Due to the scale of the system, often also "the capability of a system [...] to absorb the disruption, recover to an acceptable level of performance, and sustain that level for an acceptable period of time" (Resilient Systems Working Group, INCOSE) is required. This resilience, which "is the attribute of a system [...] that makes it less likely to experience failure and more likely to recover from a major disruption" [21] further includes the physical and control elements (via layers of idealization), the software elements (via layers of abstraction), and the horizontal and vertical composition of layers.

Formal models and analysis at development- and run-time are an option to approach the required resilience. However, such formal model and analysis techniques must support also integration and adaptation. Consequently, formal models must support the following characteristics: Compositionality for key properties, support for dynamic structures, suitable abstraction, support for hybrid behavior including non-deterministic behavior, support for reflection via runtime models, support for the incremental extensions of models, and support for probabilistic behavior.

In our own work, we approached the formal modeling of the considered advanced form of Self-Adaptive CPS by extensions of graph transformation systems (GTS) [17]. GTS with attributes can already encode models and their linking and thus allow to combine service-oriented architecture, self-adaptive/self-organization, and runtime models with evolving structures.

Graphs and graph transformations encoding the concepts of the Service-Oriented Architecture (SOA) supporting dynamic architecture and openness can be employed for Self-Adaptive CPS that must be able to dynamically adapt/absorb structural deviations and must support that subsystems may join or leave over time in a not pre-planned manner. In addition, SOA permits Self-Adaptive CPS that scale for local systems or networked resp. large-scale systems of systems.

Self-adaptive and self-organization can be described by a graph of links between the components resp. systems that evolve/reconfigure accordingly to graph transformations and in case of reflection most models can be described by such a graph as well. Also, runtime models can be described by a dynamic graph of models and links between them and thus also reflection on models can be captured.

A need that is in contrast not supported by GTS with attributes are the integration of the physical, cyber, (and social) dimension. Thus, we developed Timed GTS [5] and Hybrid GTS [6] that support hybrid behavior and non-deterministic behavior as well as Probabilistic GTS [12] that provide probabilistic behavior in form of probabilistic decisions. However, a combination of both directions is missing.

In our SMARTSOS [10] we in addition tackle based on our results for Hybrid resp. Timed GTS also compositionality, abstraction, reflection for models, and incremental extensions. However, the approach inherits the limitations of Hybrid resp. Timed GTS concerning probabilistic behavior concerning the integration.

Even more challenging is the situation for formal analysis, which is key as we must assure resilience for complex sequence properties and even ensemble properties such as stability for hybrid probabilistic infinite state systems with structural dynamics.

For Hybrid resp. Time GTS model checking is limited to very small finite state spaces. Our own approach for checking inductive invariants for GTS [4], Timed GTS [5], and Hybrid GTS [6] covers infinite state models, however, it can support only state properties of limited complexity and does not cover complex sequence properties or ensemble properties. The model checking for Probabilistic

GTS [12] covers only very restricted probabilistic sequence properties for finite state systems of at most moderate size. Techniques for a combination of hybrid and probabilistic behavior with structural dynamics do not even exist nowadays.

To summarize, Self-Adaptive CPS require the capability of self-awareness w.r.t. goals to be able to handle problems due to unexpected circumstances such that models must be able to evolve (runtime models), systems must reflect on itself (self-aware w.r.t. goals), and must adapt/self-adapt/learn. Therefore, existing formal models and analysis approaches for CPS are no longer applicable for these Self-Adaptive CPS as they do not cover reflection/adaptation as well as the design and verification of such Self-Adaptive CPS.

Graph transformation systems encoding models and their linking allow to combine service-oriented architecture, self-adaptive/self-organization, and runtime models with evolving structures and have been extended in several directions such that are potentially a suitable basis for a solid foundation for Self-Adaptive CPS. As example in our SMARTSOS approach [10] extending ideas from [7,9,11] we support collaborations that allow system-of-systems level self-organization, system-of-systems structural dynamics, and runtime knowledge exchange. The runtime models and via collaborations shared runtime models enabled self-adaptation of the systems. Compositional verification seems to be a first element for the resilience of the Self-Adaptive CPS.

However, there also remain some serious limitations: At first the suggested model is a rather strong idealization. We argue here that if such an idealization is wrong, likely also related less idealized design will fail as well. Furthermore, also more accurate explicit runtime models can be used at the cost of making verification much harder (e.g., by storing overlapping information redundantly). In addition, the formal model requires that a strong separation into collaborations is possible to support the compositional analysis. Finally, any approach based on formal models and analysis relies on the validity/trustworthiness of the employed models and development-time models as well as run-time models may become invalid over time. However, runtime models may also in certain bounds preserve validity by employing learning based on monitored data to adhere to the characteristics of the original even though the original may change over time.

References

1. Achatz, R.E.: Keynote: optimizing the software development in industry (exemplified for Siemens). In: Liggesmeyer, P., Pohl, K., Goedicke, M. (eds.) Software Engineering 2005, March 8-11, 2005 in Essen. LNI 64 GI (2005). (German)
2. Brooks, C., Cheng, C., Feng, T.H., Lee, E.A., von Hanxleden, R.: Model engineering using multimodeling. In: 1st International Workshop on Model Co-Evolution and Consistency Management (MCCM 2008), September 2008
3. Broy, M., Cengarle, M.V., Geisberger, E.: Cyber-physical systems: imminent challenges. In: Calinescu, R., Garlan, D. (eds.) Monterey Workshop 2012. LNCS, vol. 7539, pp. 1–28. Springer, Heidelberg (2012). doi:10.1007/978-3-642-34059-8_1

4. Becker, B., Beyer, D., Giese, H., Klein, F., Schilling, D.: Symbolic invariant verification for systems with dynamic structural adaptation. In: Proceedings of the 28th International Conference on Software Engineering (ICSE), Shanghai, China. ACM Press (2006)

5. Becker, B., Giese, H.: On safe service-oriented real-time coordination for autonomous vehicles. In: Proceedings of 11th International Symposium on Object/component/service-oriented Real-time distributed Computing (ISORC), pp. 203–210. IEEE Computer Society Press, 5–7 May 2008

6. Becker, B., Giese, H.: Cyber-physical systems with dynamic structure: towards modeling and verification of inductive invariants. Technical report, 64, Hasso Plattner Institute at the University of Potsdam, Germany (2012)

7. Burmester, S., Giese, H., Münch, E., Oberschelp, O., Klein, F., Scheideler, P.: Tool support for the design of self-optimizing mechatronic multi-agent systems. Int. J. Softw. Tools Technol. Transf. (STTT) **10**(3), 207–222 (2008). Springer Verlag

8. Cheng, B.H.C., et al.: Software engineering for self-adaptive systems: a research roadmap. In: Cheng, B.H.C., Lemos, R., Giese, H., Inverardi, P., Magee, J. (eds.) Software Engineering for Self-Adaptive Systems. LNCS, vol. 5525, pp. 1–26. Springer, Heidelberg (2009). doi:10.1007/978-3-642-02161-9_1

9. Giese, H., Henkler, S., Hirsch, M.: A multi-paradigm approach supporting the modular execution of reconfigurable hybrid systems. Trans. Soc. Model. Simul. Int. SIMULATION **87**(9), 775–808 (2011)

10. Giese, H., Vogel, T., Wätzoldt, S.: Towards smart systems of systems. In: Dastani, M., Sirjani, M. (eds.) FSEN 2015. LNCS, vol. 9392, pp. 1–29. Springer, Cham (2015). doi:10.1007/978-3-319-24644-4_1

11. Giese, H., Schäfer, W.: Model-driven development of safe self-optimizing mechatronic systems with MechatronicUML. In: Cámara, J., Lemos, R., Ghezzi, C., Lopes, A. (eds.) Assurances for Self-Adaptive Systems. LNCS, vol. 7740, pp. 152–186. Springer, Heidelberg (2013). doi:10.1007/978-3-642-36249-1_6

12. Krause, C., Giese, H.: Probabilistic graph transformation systems. In: Ehrig, H., Engels, G., Kreowski, H.-J., Rozenberg, G. (eds.) ICGT 2012. LNCS, vol. 7562, pp. 311–325. Springer, Heidelberg (2012). doi:10.1007/978-3-642-33654-6_21

13. Maier, M.W.: Architecting principles for systems-of-systems. Syst. Eng. **1**(4), 267–284 (1998). John Wiley - Sons Inc

14. Mosterman, P.J., Vangheluwe, H.: Computer automated multi-paradigm modeling in control system design. IEEE Trans. Control Syst. Technol. **12**, 65–70 (2000)

15. Northrop, L., et al.: Ultra-Large-Scale Systems: The Software Challenge of the Future. Software Engineering Institute, Carnegie Mellon University, Pittsburgh (2006)

16. Kounev, S., et al.: The notion of self-aware computing. In: Kounev, S., Kephart, J.O., Milenkoski, A., Zhu, X. (eds.) Self-Aware Computing Systems, pp. 3–16. Springer, Cham (2017). doi:10.1007/978-3-319-47474-8_1

17. Rozenberg, G. (ed.): Handbook of Graph Grammars and Computing by Graph Transformation. Foundations, vol. 1. World Scientific, River Edge (1997)

18. Scharnhorst, T., Heinecke, H., Schnelle, K.-P., Fennel, H., Bortolazzi, J., Lundh, L., Heitkämper, P., Leflour, J., Maté, J.-L., Nishikawa, K.: AUTOSAR - challenges and achievements 2005. In: Proceedings of the 12th International Conference Electronics Systems for Vehicles, pp. 395–408, Baden-Baden, Germany, October 2005

19. Sztipanovits, J.: Model integration and cyber physical systems: a semantics perspective. In: Butler, M., Schulte, W. (eds.) FM 2011. LNCS, vol. 6664, pp. 1–1. Springer, Heidelberg (2011). doi:10.1007/978-3-642-21437-0_1

20. Sztipanovits, J., Koutsoukos, X., Karsai, G., Kottenstette, N., Antsaklis, P., Gupta, V., Goodwine, B., Baras, J., Wang, S.: Toward a science of cyber-physical system integration. Proc. IEEE **100**(1), 29–44 (2012)
21. Valerdi, R., Axelband, E., Baehren, T., Boehm, B., Dorenbos, D., Jackson, S., Madni, A., Nadler, G., Robitaille, P., Settles, S.: A research agenda for systems of systems architecting. Int. J. Syst. Syst. Eng. **1**(1–2), 171–188 (2008)
22. Vogel, T., Neumann, S., Hildebrandt, S., Giese, H., Becker, B.: Model-driven architectural monitoring and adaptation for autonomic systems. In: Proceedings of the 6th International Conference on Autonomic Computing and Communications (ICAC 2009), Barcelona, Spain. ACM, 15–19 June 2009
23. Vogel, T., Neumann, S., Hildebrandt, S., Giese, H., Becker, B.: Incremental model synchronization for efficient run-time monitoring. In: Ghosh, S. (ed.) MODELS 2009. LNCS, vol. 6002, pp. 124–139. Springer, Heidelberg (2010). doi:10.1007/978-3-642-12261-3_13
24. Vogel, T., Giese, H.: A language for feedback loops in self-adaptive systems: executable runtime megamodels. In: Proceedings of the 7th International Symposium on Software Engineering for Adaptive and Self-Managing Systems (SEAMS 2012), pp. 129–138. IEEE Computer Society, June 2012

From Formal Methods to Software Components: Back to the Future?

Kung-Kiu Lau(✉)

School of Computer Science, The University of Manchester,
Manchester M13 9PL, UK
kung-kiu.lau@manchester.ac.uk

Abstract. Looking back at the past, I believe Formal Methods and Component-based Software Engineering have missed opportunities to synergise. Looking forward to the future, I believe even more strongly that this synergy will be crucial for developing Software Engineering techniques that tackle scale and complexity. In this position paper I outline the fundamentals of my belief, in terms of existing work and future challenges.

1 The Future?

Any engineering discipline is based on: (i) a well-established underlying theory; (ii) standard parts or *components* for building systems; and (iii) tools for *constructing systems* from components, and for *verifying systems*. So it would seem logical to conclude that Component-based Software Engineering (CBSE) and Formal Methods (FM) are the essential ingredients for Software Engineering.

As software becomes ever more pervasive (witness the Internet of Things), the challenge facing Software Engineering nowadays is how to tackle ever increasing scale and complexity, while guaranteeing safety. Is CBSE + FM up to the challenge? Is CBSE + FM addressing the challenge? To answer in the affirmative, I believe we need to accomplish two things: (i) compositional construction; and (ii) compositional verification.

2 Compositional Construction

Compositional construction is what CBSE sets out to achieve. The general picture of CBSE is depicted in Fig. 1. The basic idea is that components should pre-exist, i.e. they should be built independently from specific systems and deposited in a repository. Repository components can be reused in many different systems constructed by composing the components.

Whilst a generic component (Fig. 2(a)) is a unit of composition with provided and required services, commonly used components fall into three main categories: (i) objects (Fig. 2(b)); (ii) architectural units (Fig. 2(c)); and (iii) encapsulated components (Fig. 2(d)). Composition mechanisms (Fig. 3) used by these categories are respectively: (i) direct message passing (method call); (ii) indirect message passing (port connection); (iii) coordination (exogenous composition).

© Springer International Publishing AG 2017
O. Kouchnarenko and R. Khosravi (Eds.): FACS 2016, LNCS 10231, pp. 10–14, 2017.
DOI: 10.1007/978-3-319-57666-4_2

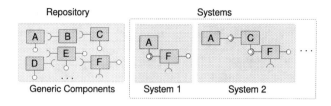

Fig. 1. CBSE: compositional construction.

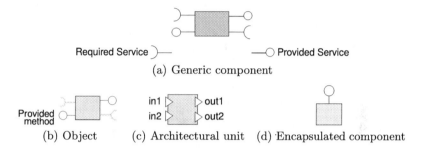

Fig. 2. Types of components.

Components	Provided services	Required services	Composition mechanism
Objects	Methods	——	Method call
Architectural units	Out-ports	In-ports	Port connection
Encapsulated components	Methods	*None*	Exogenous composition

Fig. 3. Composition mechanisms.

The desiderata for compositional construction are embodied in the *idealised component life cycle* [1], illustrated in Fig. 4. Apart from the use of pre-existing components from a repository, the key desiderata include composition in both the design phase and the deployment phase;[1] since maximum composition equates to maximum reuse.

2.1   Component Models

For compositional construction, components and their composition mechanisms [5] have to be defined properly. We advocate to do so in a *component model* [9,10]. Figure 5 shows a taxonomy of current component models with respect to the idealised component life cycle. Categories 1–4 do not support composition in both design and deployment phases. Category 5 does, but has only a lone member, namely X-MAN [2,7,8,12], that we have defined and implemented. X-

---

[1] Run-time composition, or dynamic reconfiguration, is also meaningful, though it may be harder to define, implement and verify.

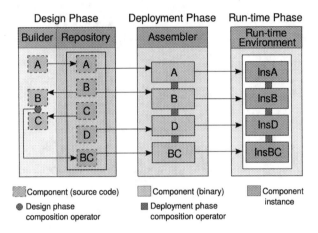

Fig. 4. Idealised component life cycle.

MAN achieves compositional construction, but it currently lacks tool support for compositional verification [3].

3   Compositional Verification

With compositional construction, we should be able to accomplish compositional verification, i.e. hierarchical, bottom-up, verification of component-based systems whereby the smallest (atomic) components at the lowest level are verified first, and their verification is reused, i.e. not repeated, in the verification of a composite at the next level up.

This is illustrated in Fig. 6, which shows the W model [6] for component-based development life cycles: component life cycle and system life cycle, and how they intersect. The W model supports compositional verification. Component verification is done in the component life cycle when components are developed for the repository, independent of specific systems. Compositional verification is done when a specific system has been assembled from already verified repository components. By reusing the verification of sub-components at successive levels of composition, instead of verifying the complete system as a monolith, compositional verification should be able to scale to large complex systems which are beyond the capability of current verification techniques and tools.

4   Back to the Future?

Looking back, I advocated synergy between FM and CBSE [4] at the early stages of the International CBSE Symposium. In my opinion, hitherto this synergy has not really materialised, or at least what little there is has not been effective. According to [11], there has been little FM activity at the CBSE symposium. I

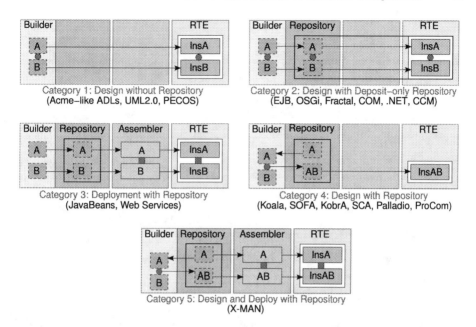

Fig. 5. Idealised component life cycle: taxonomy of component models.

surmise the converse is true of CBSE activity at FM conferences – maybe even FACS?

Looking forward to the future, I strongly believe that this synergy will be crucial for developing Software Engineering techniques that are not only truly engineering techniques as in traditional engineering disciplines, but can also tackle scale and complexity. In other words, this synergy can provide not only an engineering (compositional) approach to software construction from standard parts, but also compositional reasoning, which together can tackle ever increasing scale and complexity in software systems and their V&V.

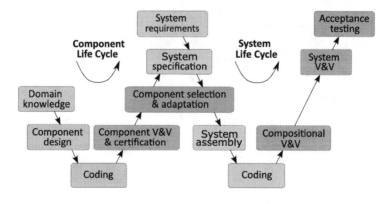

Fig. 6. The W model.

References

1. Broy, M., Deimel, A., Henn, J., Koskimies, K., Plasil, F., Pomberger, G., Pree, W., Stal, M., Szyperski, C.: What characterizes a software component? Softw. Concepts Tools **19**(1), 49–56 (1998)
2. di Cola, S., Tran, C., Lau, K.-K.: A graphical tool for model-driven development using components and services. In: Proceedings of 41st Euromicro Conference on Software Engineering and Advanced Applications (SEAA) 2015, pp. 181–182 (2015)
3. He, N., Kroening, D., Wahl, T., Lau, K.-K., Taweel, F., Tran, C., Rümmer, P., Sharma, S.: Component-based design and verification in X-MAN. In: Proceedings of Embedded Real Time Software and Systems (2012)
4. Lau, K.-K.: Component certification and system prediction: is there a role for formality? In: Crnkovic, I., Schmidt, H., Stafford, J., Wallnau, K. (eds.) Proceedings of the Fourth ICSE Workshop on Component-based Software Engineering, pp. 80–83. IEEE Computer Society Press (2001)
5. Lau, K.-K., Rana, T.: A taxonomy of software composition mechanisms. In: Proceedings of 36th EUROMICRO Conference on Software Engineering and Advanced Applications, pp. 102–110. IEEE (2010)
6. Lau, K.-K., Taweel, F., Tran, C.: The W model for component-based software development. In: Proceedings of 37th EUROMICRO Conference on Software Engineering and Advanced Applications, pp. 47–50. IEEE (2011)
7. Lau, K.-K., Tran, C.: X-MAN: an MDE tool for component-based system development. In: Proceedings of 38th EUROMICRO Conference on Software Engineering and Advanced Applications, pp. 158–165. IEEE (2012)
8. Lau, K.-K., Velasco Elizondo, P., Wang, Z.: Exogenous connectors for software components. In: Heineman, G.T., Crnkovic, I., Schmidt, H.W., Stafford, J.A., Szyperski, C., Wallnau, K. (eds.) CBSE 2005. LNCS, vol. 3489, pp. 90–106. Springer, Heidelberg (2005). doi:10.1007/11424529_7
9. Lau, K.-K., Wang, Z.: Software component models. IEEE Trans. Softw. Eng. **33**(10), 709–724 (2007)
10. Lau, K.-K., Wang, Z., di Cola, S., Tran, C., Christou, V.: Software component-models: past, present and future. In: Tutorial at COMPARCH 2014 Conference, 30 June 2014, Lille, France (2014)
11. Maras, J., Lednicki, L., Crnkovic, I.: 15 years of CBSE symposium - impact on the research community. In: Proceedings of the 15th International ACM SIGSOFT Symposium on Component-Based Software Engineering, pp. 61–70. ACM (2012)
12. Elizondo, P.V., Lau, K.-K.: A catalogue of component connectors to support development with reuse. J. Syst. Softw. **83**, 1165–1178 (2010)

Full Research Papers

A Core Model for Choreographic Programming

Luís Cruz-Filipe[✉] and Fabrizio Montesi

University of Southern Denmark, Odense, Denmark
{lcf,fmontesi}@imada.sdu.dk

Abstract. Choreographic Programming is a paradigm for developing concurrent programs that are deadlock-free by construction, by programming communications declaratively and then synthesising process implementations automatically. Despite strong interest on choreographies, a foundational model that explains which computations can be performed with the hallmark constructs of choreographies is still missing.

In this work, we introduce Core Choreographies (CC), a model that includes only the core primitives of choreographic programming. Every computable function can be implemented as a choreography in CC, from which we can synthesise a process implementation where independent computations run in parallel. We discuss the design of CC and argue that it constitutes a canonical model for choreographic programming.

1 Introduction

Programming concurrent and distributed systems is hard, because it is challenging to predict how programs executed at the same time in different computers will interact. Empirical studies reveal two important lessons: (i) while programmers have clear intentions about the order in which communication actions should be performed, tools do not adequately support them in translating these wishes to code [21]; (ii) combining different communication protocols in a single application is a major source of mistakes [20].

The paradigm of Choreographic Programming [22] was introduced to address these problems. In this paradigm, programmers declaratively write the communications that they wish to take place, as programs called *choreographies*. Choreographies are descriptions of concurrent systems that syntactically disallow writing mismatched I/O actions, inspired by the "Alice and Bob" notation of security protocols. An EndPoint Projection (EPP) can then be used to synthesise implementations in process models, which faithfully realise the communications given in the choreography and are guaranteed to be deadlock-free by construction even in the presence of arbitrary protocol compositions [6,25].

So far, work on choreographic programming focused on features of practical value – including web services [5], multiparty sessions [6,8], modularity [24], and runtime adaptation [12]. The models proposed all come with differing domain-specific syntaxes, semantics and EPP definitions (e.g., for channel mobility or runtime adaptation), and cannot be considered minimal. Another problem, arguably a consequence of the former, is that choreographic programming is

© Springer International Publishing AG 2017
O. Kouchnarenko and R. Khosravi (Eds.): FACS 2016, LNCS 10231, pp. 17–35, 2017.
DOI: 10.1007/978-3-319-57666-4_3

meant for implementation, but we still know little of what can be computed with the code obtained from choreographies (*choreography projections*). The expressivity of the aforementioned models is evaluated just by showing some examples.

In this paper, we propose a canonical model for choreographic programming, called Core Choreographies (CC). CC includes only the core primitives that can be found in most choreography languages, restricted to the minimal requirements to achieve the computational power of Turing machines. In particular, local computation at processes is severely restricted, and therefore nontrivial computations must be implemented by using communications. Therefore, CC is both representative of the paradigm and simple enough to analyse from a theoretical perspective. Our technical development is based on a natural notion of function implementation, and the proof of Turing completeness yields an algorithm for constructing a choreography that implements any given computable function. Since choreographies describe concurrent systems, it is also natural to ask how much parallelism choreographies exhibit. CC helps us in formally defining parallelism in choreographies; we exemplify how to use this notion to reason about the concurrent implementation of functions.

However, analysing the expressivity of choreographies is not enough. What we are ultimately interested in is what can be computed with choreography projections, since those are the terms that represent executable code. However, the expressivity of choreographies does not translate directly to expressivity of projections, because EPP is typically an incomplete procedure: it must guarantee deadlock-freedom, which in previous models is obtained by complex requirements, 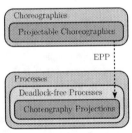 e.g., type systems [5,6]. Therefore, only a subset of choreographies (projectable choreographies) can be used to synthesise process implementations. The EPPs of such projectable choreographies form the set of choreography projections, which are deadlock-free processes (see figure on the right).

The main technical contribution of this paper is showing that the set of projectable choreographies in CC is still Turing complete. Therefore, by EPP, the set of corresponding choreography projections is also Turing complete, leading us to a characterisation of a Turing complete and deadlock-free fragment of a process calculus (which follows the same minimal design of CC). Furthermore, the parallel behaviour observed in CC choreographies for function implementations translates directly to parallel execution of the projected processes.

More importantly, the practical consequence of our results is that CC is a simple common setting for the study of foundational questions in choreographies. This makes CC an appropriate foundational model for choreographic programming, akin to λ-calculus for functional programming and π-calculus for mobile processes. As an example of such foundational questions, we describe how the standard communication primitive of label selection can be removed from CC without altering its computational power, yielding a truly minimal choreography language wrt computation called Minimal Choreographies (MC). However, doing so eliminates the clean separation between data and behaviour in message exchanges, which makes the resulting choreography hard to read. Thus, in a practical application of our work, CC would be the better candidate as frontend language for programmers, and MC could be used as an intermediate step in a compiler. A key technical advantage of this methodology is that it bypasses the need for the standard notion of merging [5], which is typically one of the most complicated steps in EPP. Our EPP for MC enjoys an elegant definition.

Structure of the paper. CC is defined in Sect. 2. In Sect. 3, we introduce Stateful Processes (SP), our target process model, and an EPP procedure from CC to SP. We show that CC and its set of choreography projections are Turing complete in Sect. 4. In Sect. 5, we show that all primitives of CC except for label selections are necessary to achieve Turing completeness; we then introduce MC (the fragment of CC without label selections) and prove both that it is Turing complete and that removing or weakening any of its primitives breaks this property. In Sect. 6, we discuss the implications of our work for other choreography languages. Related work and discussion are given in Sect. 7. Full definitions and proofs are in [9].

2   Core Choreographies

We introduce Core Choreographies (CC), define function implementation and parallel execution of choreographies, and prove some key properties of CC.

Syntax. The syntax of CC is as follows, where C ranges over choreographies.

$$C ::= \eta; C \mid \text{if } \mathsf{p} \overset{\leftarrow}{=} \mathsf{q} \text{ then } C_1 \text{ else } C_2 \mid \text{def } X = C_2 \text{ in } C_1 \mid X \mid \mathbf{0}$$

$$\eta ::= \mathsf{p}.e \rightarrow \mathsf{q} \mid \mathsf{p} \rightarrow \mathsf{q}[l] \qquad e ::= \varepsilon \mid \mathsf{c} \mid \mathsf{s} \cdot \mathsf{c} \qquad l ::= \mathrm{L} \mid \mathrm{R}$$

We use two (infinite) disjoint sets of names: processes $(\mathsf{p}, \mathsf{q}, \ldots)$ and procedures $(X, \ldots)$. Processes run in parallel, and each process stores a value – a string of the form $\mathsf{s} \cdots \mathsf{s} \cdot \varepsilon$ – in a local memory cell. Each process can access its own value, but it cannot read the contents of another process (no data sharing). Term $\eta; C$ is an interaction between two processes, read "the system may execute η and proceed as C". An interaction η is either a value communication – $\mathsf{p}.e \rightarrow \mathsf{q}$ – or a label selection – $\mathsf{p} \rightarrow \mathsf{q}[l]$. In $\mathsf{p}.e \rightarrow \mathsf{q}$, p sends its local evaluation of expression e to q, which stores the received value. Expressions are either the constant ε, the value of the sender (written as c), or an application of the successor operator to c. In $\mathsf{p} \rightarrow \mathsf{q}[l]$, p communicates label l (either L or R) to q. In a conditional if $\mathsf{p} \overset{\leftarrow}{=} \mathsf{q}$ then C_1 else C_2, q sends its value to p, which checks if the received value is equal to its own; the choreography proceeds as C_1, if that is the case, or as C_2, otherwise. In value communications, selections and conditionals, the two interacting processes must be different (no self-communications). Definitions and invocations of recursive procedures are standard. The term $\mathbf{0}$, also called *exit point*, is the terminated choreography.

Semantics. The semantics of CC uses reductions of the form $C, \sigma \to C', \sigma'$. The total state function σ maps each process name to its value. We use v, w, ... to range over values: $v, w, \ldots :: = \varepsilon \mid \mathsf{s} \cdot v$. Values are isomorphic to natural numbers via $\lceil n \rceil = \mathsf{s}^n \cdot \varepsilon$. The reduction relation $\to$ is defined by the rules given below and closed under structural precongruence $\preceq$.

$$\frac{v = e[\sigma(\mathsf{p})/\mathsf{c}]}{\mathsf{p}.e \text{ -> } \mathsf{q}; C, \sigma \to C, \sigma[\mathsf{q} \mapsto v]} \; \lfloor C | \mathrm{Com} \rfloor \qquad \frac{i = 1 \text{ if } \sigma(\mathsf{p}) = \sigma(\mathsf{q}), \; i = 2 \text{ o.w.}}{\text{if } \mathsf{p} \overset{\leftarrow}{=} \mathsf{q} \text{ then } C_1 \text{ else } C_2, \sigma \to C_i, \sigma} \; \lfloor C | \mathrm{Cond} \rfloor$$

$$\frac{}{\mathsf{p} \text{ -> } \mathsf{q}[l]; C, \sigma \to C, \sigma} \; \lfloor C | \mathrm{Sel} \rfloor \qquad \frac{C_1, \sigma \; \to \; C_1', \sigma'}{\text{def } X = C_2 \text{ in } C_1, \sigma \; \to \; \text{def } X = C_2 \text{ in } C_1', \sigma'} \; \lfloor C | \mathrm{Ctx} \rfloor$$

These rules formalise the intuition presented earlier. In the premise of $\lfloor C | \mathrm{Com} \rfloor$, we write $e[\sigma(\mathsf{p})/\mathsf{c}]$ for the result of replacing c with $\sigma(\mathsf{p})$ in e. In the reductum, $\sigma[\mathsf{q} \mapsto v]$ denotes the updated state function σ where q now maps to v. The key rule defining the structural precongruence is $\lfloor C | \mathrm{Eta\text{-}Eta} \rfloor$, allowing non-interfering actions to be executed in any order.

$$\lfloor C | \mathrm{Eta\text{-}Eta} \rfloor \qquad \text{if} \quad \mathsf{pn}(\eta) \cap \mathsf{pn}(\eta') = \emptyset \quad \text{then} \quad \eta; \eta' \; \equiv \; \eta'; \eta$$

Function $\mathsf{pn}(C)$ returns the set of all process names occurring in C, and $C \equiv C'$ stands for $C \preceq C'$ and $C' \preceq C$. The other rules for $\preceq$ are standard, and support recursion unfolding and garbage collection of unused definitions.

Remark 1 (Label Selection). To the reader unfamiliar with choreographies, the role of selection – p -> $\mathsf{q}[l]$ – may be unclear at this point. They are crucial in making choreographies projectable, as we anticipate with the choreography if $\mathsf{p} \overset{\leftarrow}{=} \mathsf{q}$ then $(\mathsf{p}.\mathsf{c}$ -> $\mathsf{r}; 0)$ else $(\mathsf{r}.\mathsf{c}$ -> $\mathsf{p}; 0)$. Here, p checks whether its value is the same as that of q. If so, p communicates its value to r; otherwise, it is r that communicates its value to p. Recall that processes are assumed to run independently and share no data. Here, p is the only process that knows which branch of the conditional should be executed. However, r also needs to know this information, since it must behave differently. Intuitively, we need to propagate p's decision to r, which is achieved with selections: if $\mathsf{p} \overset{\leftarrow}{=} \mathsf{q}$ then $(\mathsf{p}$ -> $\mathsf{r}[\mathrm{L}]; \mathsf{p}.\mathsf{c}$ -> $\mathsf{r}; 0)$ else $(\mathsf{p}$ -> $\mathsf{r}[\mathrm{R}]; \mathsf{r}.\mathsf{c}$ -> $\mathsf{p}; 0)$. Now, p tells r about its choice by sending a different label. This intuition will be formalised in our definition of EndPoint Projection in Sect. 3. The first choreography we presented (without label selections) is not projectable, whereas the second one is.

Theorem 1. *If C is a choreography, then either $C \preceq \mathbf{0}$ (C has terminated) or, for all σ, $C, \sigma \to C', \sigma'$ for some C' and σ' (C can reduce).*

The semantics of CC suggests a natural definition of computation. We write $\to^*$ for the transitive closure of $\to$ and $C, \sigma \not\to^* \mathbf{0}$ for $C, \sigma \not\to^* \mathbf{0}, \sigma'$ for any σ'.

Definition 1. *A choreography C implements a function $f : \mathbb{N}^n \to \mathbb{N}$ with input processes $p_1, \ldots, p_n$ and output process q if, for all $x_1, \ldots, x_n \in \mathbb{N}$ and for every state σ s.t. $\sigma(p_i) = \ulcorner x_i \urcorner$:*

- *if $f(\tilde{x})$ is defined, then $C, \sigma \to^* \mathbf{0}, \sigma'$ where $\sigma'(q) = \ulcorner f(\tilde{x}) \urcorner$;*
- *if $f(\tilde{x})$ is undefined, then $C, \sigma \not\to^* \mathbf{0}$.*

By Theorem 1, in the second case C, σ must reduce infinitely (diverge).

Sequential composition and parallelism. The results in the remainder use choreographies with only one exit point (a single occurrence of $\mathbf{0}$). When C has a single exit point, we write $C \,\fatsemi\, C'$ for the choreography obtained by replacing $\mathbf{0}$ in C with C'. Then, $C \,\fatsemi\, C'$ behaves as a "sequential composition" of C and C'.

Lemma 1. *Let C have one exit point, C' be a choreography, $\sigma, \sigma', \sigma''$ be states.*

1. *If $C, \sigma \to^* \mathbf{0}, \sigma'$ and $C', \sigma' \to^* \mathbf{0}, \sigma''$, then $C \,\fatsemi\, C', \sigma \to^* \mathbf{0}, \sigma''$.*
2. *If $C, \sigma \not\to^* \mathbf{0}$, then $C \,\fatsemi\, C', \sigma \not\to^* \mathbf{0}$.*
3. *If $C, \sigma \to^* \mathbf{0}, \sigma'$ and $C', \sigma' \not\to^* \mathbf{0}$, then $C \,\fatsemi\, C', \sigma \not\to^* \mathbf{0}$.*

Structural precongruence gives $C \,\fatsemi\, C'$ fully parallel behaviour in some cases. Intuitively, C_1 and C_2 run in parallel in $C_1 \,\fatsemi\, C_2$ if their reduction paths to $\mathbf{0}$ can be interleaved in any possible way. Below, we write $C \xrightarrow{\tilde{\sigma}}^* \mathbf{0}$ for $C, \sigma_1 \to C_2, \sigma_2 \to \cdots \to \mathbf{0}, \sigma_n$, where $\tilde{\sigma} = \sigma_1, \ldots, \sigma_n$, and $\widetilde{\sigma(p)}$ for the sequence $\sigma_1(p), \ldots, \sigma_n(p)$.

Definition 2. *Let $\tilde{p}$ and $\tilde{q}$ be disjoint. Then, $\tilde{\sigma}$ is an interleaving of $\widetilde{\sigma_1}$ and $\widetilde{\sigma_2}$ wrt $\tilde{p}$ and $\tilde{q}$ if $\tilde{\sigma}$ contains two subsequences $\widetilde{\sigma'_1}$ and $\widetilde{\sigma'_2}$ such that:*

- $\widetilde{\sigma'_2} = \tilde{\sigma} \setminus \widetilde{\sigma'_1}$;
- $\widetilde{\sigma'_1(p)} = \widetilde{\sigma_1(p)}$ *for all $p \in \tilde{p}$, and* $\widetilde{\sigma'_2(q)} = \widetilde{\sigma_2(q)}$ *for all $q \in \tilde{q}$;*
- $\widetilde{\sigma(r)}$ *is a constant sequence for all $r \notin \tilde{p} \cup \tilde{q}$.*

Definition 3. *Let C_1 and C_2 be choreographies such that $\mathsf{pn}(C_1) \cap \mathsf{pn}(C_2) = \emptyset$ and C_1 has only one exit point. We say that C_1 and C_2 run in parallel in $C_1 \,\fatsemi\, C_2$ if: whenever $C_i \xrightarrow{\tilde{\sigma}_i}^* \mathbf{0}$, then $C_1 \,\fatsemi\, C_2 \xrightarrow{\tilde{\sigma}}^* \mathbf{0}$ for every interleaving $\tilde{\sigma}$ of $\tilde{\sigma}_1$ and $\tilde{\sigma}_2$ wrt $\mathsf{pn}(C_1)$ and $\mathsf{pn}(C_2)$.*

Theorem 2. *Let C_1 and C_2 be choreographies such that $\mathsf{pn}(C_1) \cap \mathsf{pn}(C_2) = \emptyset$ and C_1 has only one exit point. Then C_1 and C_2 run in parallel in $C_1 \,\fatsemi\, C_2$.*

Example 1. We present examples of choreographies in CC, writing them as macros (syntax shortcuts). We use the notation $\mathrm{M}(params) \stackrel{\Delta}{=} C$, where M is the name of the macro, *params* its parameters, and C its body.

The macro $\mathrm{INC}(p, t)$ increments the value of p using an auxiliary process t.

$$\mathrm{INC}(p, t) \quad \stackrel{\Delta}{=} \quad p.c \to t;\ t.(s \cdot c) \to p;\ \mathbf{0}$$

Using INC, we write a macro $\mathrm{ADD}(p, q, r, t_1, t_2)$ that adds the values of p and q and stores the result in p, using auxiliary processes r, t_1 and t_2. We follow the intuition as in low-level abstract register machines. First, t_1 sets the value of r to zero, and then calls procedure X, which increments the value of p as many times as the value in q. In the body of X, r checks whether its value is the same as q's. If so, it informs the other processes that the recursion will terminate (selection of L); otherwise, it asks them to do another step (selection of R). In each step, the values of p and r are incremented using t_1 and t_2. The compositional usage of INC is allowed, as it has exactly one exit point.

$$\text{ADD}(p, q, r, t_1, t_2) \overset{\Delta}{=}$$

$$\text{def } X = \text{if } r \overset{\leftarrow}{=} q \text{ then } r \to p[\text{L}]; r \to q[\text{L}]; r \to t_1[\text{L}]; r \to t_2[\text{L}]; \mathbf{0}$$

$$\text{else } r \to p[\text{R}]; r \to q[\text{R}]; r \to t_1[\text{R}]; r \to t_2[\text{R}]; \text{INC}(p, t_1) \,\mathring{,}\, \text{INC}(r, t_2) \,\mathring{,}\, X$$

$$\text{in } t_1.\varepsilon \to r; X$$

By Theorem 2, the calls to $\text{INC}(p, t_1)$ and $\text{INC}(r, t_2)$ can be executed in parallel. Indeed, applying rule $\lfloor\text{C}|\text{Eta-Eta}\rfloor$ for $\preceq$ repeatedly we can check that:

$$\underbrace{p.c \to t_1; \ t_1.(s \cdot c) \to p;}_{\text{expansion of INC}(p, t_1)} \underbrace{r.c \to t_2; \ t_2.(s \cdot c) \to r;}_{\text{expansion of INC}(r, t_2)} X$$

$$\preceq \underbrace{r.c \to t_2; \ t_2.(s \cdot c) \to r;}_{\text{expansion of INC}(r, t_2)} \underbrace{p.c \to t_1; \ t_1.(s \cdot c) \to p;}_{\text{expansion of INC}(p, t_1)} X$$

Definition 3 and Theorem 2 straightforwardly generalise to an arbitrary number of processes. We provide an example of such parallel behaviour in Theorem 6.

3   Stateful Processes and EndPoint Projection

We present Stateful Processes (SP), our target process model, and show how to synthesise process implementations from choreographies in CC.

Syntax. The syntax of SP is reported below. Networks (N, M) are either the inactive network $\mathbf{0}$ or parallel compositions of processes $p \rhd_v B$, where p is the name of the process, v its stored value, and B its behaviour.

$$B ::= q!\langle e \rangle; B \ \mid \ p?; B \ \mid \ q \oplus l; B \ \mid \ p\&\{l_i : B_i\}_{i \in I} \quad \mid \quad N, M ::= p \rhd_v B \ \mid \ \mathbf{0} \ \mid \ N \mid M$$

$$\mid \mathbf{0} \mid \text{if } c \overset{\leftarrow}{=} q \text{ then } B_1 \text{ else } B_2 \ \mid \ \text{def } X = B_2 \text{ in } B_1 \ \mid \ X$$

Expressions and labels are as in CC. A send term $q!\langle e \rangle; B$ sends the evaluation of expression e to q, proceeding as B. Term $p?; B$, the dual receiving action, stores the value received from p in the process executing the behaviour, proceeding as B. A selection term $q \oplus l; B$ sends l to q. Dually, a branching term $p\&\{l_i : B_i\}_{i \in I}$ receives one of the labels l_i and proceeds as B_i. A process offers either: a single branch (labeled L or R); or two branches (with distinct labels). In a conditional if $c \overset{\leftarrow}{=} q$ then B_1 else B_2, the process receives a value from process q and compares it with its own value to choose the continuation B_1 or B_2. The other terms (definition/invocation of recursive procedures, termination) are standard.

Semantics. The reduction rules for SP are mostly standard, from process calculi. The key difference from CC is that execution is now distributed over processes. We report the key rules for synchronisation:

$$\frac{u = e[v/c]}{p \triangleright_v q!\langle e \rangle; B_1 \mid q \triangleright_w p?; B_2 \;\rightarrow\; p \triangleright_v B_1 \mid q \triangleright_u B_2} \; \lfloor S|Com \rfloor$$

$$\frac{j \in I}{p \triangleright_v q \oplus l_j; B \mid q \triangleright_w p\&\{l_i : B_i\}_{i \in I} \;\rightarrow\; p \triangleright_v B \mid q \triangleright_w B_j} \; \lfloor S|Sel \rfloor$$

$$\frac{i = 1 \text{ if } v = e[w/c], \quad i = 2 \text{ otherwise}}{p \triangleright_v \text{ if } c \overset{\leftarrow}{=} q \text{ then } B_1 \text{ else } B_2 \mid q \triangleright_w p!\langle e \rangle; B' \;\rightarrow\; p \triangleright_v B_i \mid q \triangleright_w B'} \; \lfloor S|Cond \rfloor$$

Rule $\lfloor S|Com \rfloor$ follows the standard communication rule in process calculi. A process p executing a send action towards a process q can synchronise with a receive-from-p action at q; in the reduct, q's value is updated with the value sent by p, obtained by replacing the placeholder c in e with the value of p. Rule $\lfloor S|Sel \rfloor$ is selection from session types [15], with the sender selecting one of the branches offered by the receiver. In rule $\lfloor S|Cond \rfloor$, p (executing the conditional) acts as a receiver for the value sent by the process whose value it wants to read (q). All other rules are standard (see [9]), and use a structural precongruence that supports: recursion unfolding, garbage collection of terminated processes and unused definitions, and associativity and commutativity of parallel composition.

As for CC, we can define function implementation in SP.

Definition 4. *A network N implements* a function $f : \mathbb{N}^n \to \mathbb{N}$ *with input processes* $p_1, \ldots, p_n$ *and output process* q *if* $N \preceq (\prod_{i \in [1,n]} p_i \triangleright_{v_i} B_i) \mid q \triangleright_w B' \mid N'$ *and, for all* $x_1, \ldots, x_n \in \mathbb{N}$:

- *if* $f(\tilde{x})$ *is defined, then* $N(\tilde{x}) \to^* q \triangleright_{\ulcorner f(\tilde{x}) \urcorner} \mathbf{0}$;
- *if* $f(\tilde{x})$ *is not defined, then* $N(\tilde{x}) \not\to^* \mathbf{0}$.

where $N(\tilde{x})$ *is a shorthand for* $N[\widetilde{\ulcorner x_i \urcorner / v_i}]$, *the network obtained by replacing in N the values of the input processes with the arguments of the function.*

Projection. We now define an EndPoint Projection (EPP) from CC to SP.

We first discuss the rules for projecting the behaviour of a single process p, a partial function $[\![C]\!]_p$ defined by the rules in Fig. 1. All rules follow the intuition of projecting, for each choreography term, the local action performed by the process that we are projecting. For example, for a communication term $p.e \rightarrow q$, we project a send action for the sender p, a receive action for the receiver q, or just the continuation otherwise. The rule for selection is similar. The rules for projecting recursive definitions and calls assume that procedure names have been

$$[\![\mathsf{p}.e \rightarrow \mathsf{q}; C]\!]_r = \begin{cases} \mathsf{q}!\langle e \rangle; [\![C]\!]_r & \text{if } r = \mathsf{p} \\ \mathsf{p}?; [\![C]\!]_r & \text{if } r = \mathsf{q} \\ [\![C]\!]_r & \text{o.w.} \end{cases} \qquad [\![\mathsf{p} \rightarrow \mathsf{q}[l]; C]\!]_r = \begin{cases} \mathsf{q} \oplus l; [\![C]\!]_r & \text{if } r = \mathsf{p} \\ \mathsf{p}\&\{l : [\![C]\!]_r\} & \text{if } r = \mathsf{q} \\ [\![C]\!]_r & \text{o.w.} \end{cases}$$

$$[\![\mathsf{if}\ \mathsf{p} \stackrel{\leftarrow}{=} \mathsf{q}\ \mathsf{then}\ C_1\ \mathsf{else}\ C_2]\!]_r = \begin{cases} \mathsf{if}\ c \stackrel{\leftarrow}{=} \mathsf{q}\ \mathsf{then}\ [\![C_1]\!]_r\ \mathsf{else}\ [\![C_2]\!]_r & \text{if } r = \mathsf{p} \\ \mathsf{p}!\langle c \rangle; ([\![C_1]\!]_r \sqcup [\![C_2]\!]_r) & \text{if } r = \mathsf{q} \\ [\![C_1]\!]_r \sqcup [\![C_2]\!]_r & \text{o.w.} \end{cases} \qquad [\![\mathbf{0}]\!]_r = \mathbf{0}$$

$$[\![\mathsf{def}\ X^{\tilde{\mathsf{p}}} = C_2\ \mathsf{in}\ C_1]\!]_r = \begin{cases} \mathsf{def}\ X = [\![C_2]\!]_r\ \mathsf{in}\ [\![C_1]\!]_r & \text{if } r \in \tilde{\mathsf{p}} \\ [\![C_1]\!]_r & \text{o.w.} \end{cases} \qquad [\![X^{\tilde{\mathsf{p}}}]\!]_r = \begin{cases} X & \text{if } r \in \tilde{\mathsf{p}} \\ \mathbf{0} & \text{o.w.} \end{cases}$$

Fig. 1. Minimal Choreographies, Behaviour Projection.

annotated with the process names appearing inside the body of the procedure, in order to avoid projecting unnecessary procedure code (see [5]).

The rule for projecting a conditional is more involved, using the partial merging operator $\sqcup$ to merge the possible behaviours of a process that does not know which branch will be chosen. Merging is a homomorphic binary operator; for all terms but branchings it requires isomorphism, e.g.: $\mathsf{q}!\langle e \rangle; B \sqcup \mathsf{q}!\langle e \rangle; B' = \mathsf{q}!\langle e \rangle; (B \sqcup B')$. Branching terms can have unmergeable continuations, as long as they are guarded by distinct labels. In this case, merge returns a larger branching including all options (merging branches with the same label):

$$\mathsf{p}\&\{l_i : B_i\}_{i \in J} \sqcup \mathsf{p}\&\{l_i : B'_i\}_{i \in K} =$$
$$\mathsf{p}\&\big(\{l_i : (B_i \sqcup B'_i)\}_{i \in J \cap K} \cup \{l_i : B_i\}_{i \in J \setminus K} \cup \{l_i : B'_i\}_{i \in K \setminus J}\big)$$

Merging explains the role of selections in CC, common in choreography models [2,5,6,12,16,25]. Recall the choreographies from Remark 1. In the first one, the behaviour of r cannot be projected because we cannot merge its different behaviours in the two branches of the conditional (a send with a receive). The second one is projectable, and the behaviour of r is $[\![C]\!]_r = \mathsf{p}\&\{\mathsf{L} : \mathsf{p}?; \mathbf{0}, \ \mathsf{R} : \mathsf{p}!\langle c \rangle; \mathbf{0}\}$.

Definition 5. *Given a choreography C and a state σ, the* endpoint projection *of C and σ is the parallel composition of the projections of the processes in C:*
$$[\![C, \sigma]\!] = \textstyle\prod_{\mathsf{p} \in \mathsf{pn}(C)} \mathsf{p} \triangleright_{\sigma(\mathsf{p})} [\![C]\!]_\mathsf{p}.$$

Since the σs are total, $[\![C, \sigma]\!]$ is defined for some σ iff $[\![C, \sigma']\!]$ is defined for all other σ'. In this case, we say that C is *projectable*.

EPP guarantees the following operational correspondence.

Theorem 3. *Let C be a projectable choreography. Then, for all σ:*

Completeness: *If $C, \sigma \rightarrow C', \sigma'$, then $[\![C, \sigma]\!] \rightarrow\succ [\![C', \sigma']\!]$;*
Soundness: *If $[\![C, \sigma]\!] \rightarrow N$, then $C, \sigma \rightarrow C', \sigma'$ for some σ', with $[\![C', \sigma']\!] \prec N$.*

The *pruning relation* $\prec$ [5,6] deletes branches introduced by merging when no longer needed; $N \succ N'$ means $N' \prec N$. Pruning does not alter the behaviour of a network: eliminated branches are never selected, as shown in [5,12,18]. As a consequence of Theorems 1 and 3, choreography projections never deadlock.

Theorem 4. *Let $N = [\![C, \sigma]\!]$ for some C and σ. Then, either $N \preceq \mathbf{0}$ (N has terminated), or $N \to N'$ for some N' (N can reduce).*

Choreography Amendment. An important property of CC is that all unprojectable choreographies can be made projectable by adding some selections. We annotate recursion variables as for EPP, assuming that $\mathsf{pn}(X^{\tilde{p}}) = \{\tilde{p}\}$.

Definition 6. *Given C in CC, the transformation $\mathsf{Amend}(C)$ repeatedly applies the following procedure until no longer possible, starting from the innermost subterms in C. For each conditional subterm if $\mathsf{p} \overset{\leftarrow}{=} \mathsf{q}$ then C_1 else C_2 in C, let $\tilde{r} \subseteq (\mathsf{pn}(C_1) \cup \mathsf{pn}(C_2))$ be the largest set such that $[\![C_1]\!]_r \sqcup [\![C_2]\!]_r$ is undefined for all $\mathsf{r} \in \tilde{r}$; then if $\mathsf{p} \overset{\leftarrow}{=} \mathsf{q}$ then C_1 else C_2 in C is replaced with:*

if $(\mathsf{p} \overset{\leftarrow}{=} \mathsf{q})$ then $(\mathsf{p} \mathbin{\text{->}} \mathsf{r}_1[\mathrm{L}]; \cdots ; \mathsf{p} \mathbin{\text{->}} \mathsf{r}_n[\mathrm{L}]; C_1)$ else $(\mathsf{p} \mathbin{\text{->}} \mathsf{r}_1[\mathrm{R}]; \cdots ; \mathsf{p} \mathbin{\text{->}} \mathsf{r}_n[\mathrm{R}]; C_2)$

From the definitions of Amend, EPP and the semantics of CC, we get:

Lemma 2. *For every choreography C:*

Completeness: $\mathsf{Amend}(C)$ *is defined;*
Projectability: *for all σ, $[\![\mathsf{Amend}(C), \sigma]\!]$ is defined;*
Correspondence: *for all σ, $C, \sigma \to^* C', \sigma'$ iff $\mathsf{Amend}(C), \sigma \to^* \mathsf{Amend}(C'), \sigma'$.*

Example 2. Applying Amend to the first choreography in Remark 1 yields the second choreography in the same remark. Thanks to merging, amendment can also recognise some situations where additional selections are not needed. For example, in the choreography $C = $ if $\mathsf{p} \overset{\leftarrow}{=}$ q then $(\mathsf{p}.(\mathsf{s} \cdot \mathsf{c}) \mathbin{\text{->}} \mathsf{r}; \mathbf{0})$ else $(\mathsf{p}.(\mathsf{c}) \mathbin{\text{->}} \mathsf{r}; \mathbf{0})$, r does not need to know the choice made by p, as it always performs the same input action. Here, C is projectable and $\mathsf{Amend}(C) = C$.

4 Turing Completeness of CC and SP

We now move to our main result: the set of choreography projections of CC (the processes synthesised by EPP) is not only deadlock-free, but also capable of computing all partial recursive functions, as defined by Kleene [17], and hence Turing complete. To this aim, the design and properties of CC give us a considerable pay off. First, by Theorem 3, the problem reduces to establishing that a projectable fragment of CC is Turing complete. Second, by Lemma 2, this simpler problem is reduced to establishing that CC is Turing complete regardless of projectability, since any unprojectable choreography can be amended to one that is projectable and computes the same values. We also exploit the concurrent semantics of CC and Theorem 2 to parallelise independent sub-computations (Theorem 6).

Our proof is in line with other traditional proofs of computational completeness [11,17,27], where data and programs are distinct. This differs from other proofs of similar results for, e.g., π-calculus [26] and λ-calculus [1], which encode data as particular programs. The advantages are: our proof can be used to build choreographies that compute particular functions; and we can parallelise independent sub-computations in functions (Theorem 6).

Partial Recursive Functions. Our definition of the class of partial recursive functions $\mathcal{R}$ is slightly simplified, but equivalent to, that in [17], where it is shown to be the class of computable functions. $\mathcal{R}$ is defined inductively as follows.

Unary zero: $Z \in \mathcal{R}$, where $Z : \mathbb{N} \to \mathbb{N}$ is s.t. $Z(x) = 0$ for all $x \in \mathbb{N}$.
Unary successor: $S \in \mathcal{R}$, where $S : \mathbb{N} \to \mathbb{N}$ is s.t. $S(x) = x + 1$ for all $x \in \mathbb{N}$.
Projections: If $n \geq 1$ and $1 \leq m \leq n$, then $P_m^n \in \mathcal{R}$, where $P_m^n : \mathbb{N}^n \to \mathbb{N}$ is
s.t. $P_m^n(x_1, \ldots, x_n) = x_m$ for all $x_1, \ldots, x_n \in \mathbb{N}$.
Composition: if $f, g_i \in \mathcal{R}$ for $1 \leq i \leq k$, with each $g_i : \mathbb{N}^n \to \mathbb{N}$ and $f : \mathbb{N}^k \to \mathbb{N}$,
then $h = C(f, \tilde{g}) \in \mathcal{R}$, where $h : \mathbb{N}^n \to \mathbb{N}$ is defined by composition from f
and $g_1, \ldots, g_k$ as: $h(\tilde{x}) = f(g_1(\tilde{x}), \ldots, g_k(\tilde{x}))$.
Primitive recursion: if $f, g \in \mathcal{R}$, with $f : \mathbb{N}^n \to \mathbb{N}$ and $g : \mathbb{N}^{n+2} \to \mathbb{N}$, then
$h = R(f, g) \in \mathcal{R}$, where $h : \mathbb{N}^{n+1} \to \mathbb{N}$ is defined by primitive recursion from
f and g as: $h(0, \tilde{x}) = f(\tilde{x})$ and $h(x_0 + 1, \tilde{x}) = g(x_0, h(x_0, \tilde{x}), \tilde{x})$.
Minimization: If $f \in \mathcal{R}$, with $f : \mathbb{N}^{n+1} \to \mathbb{N}$, then $h = M(f) \in \mathcal{R}$, where
$h : \mathbb{N}^n \to \mathbb{N}$ is defined by minimization from f as: $h(\tilde{x}) = y$ iff (1) $f(\tilde{x}, y) = 0$
and (2) $f(\tilde{x}, y)$ is defined and different from 0 for all $z < y$.

Encoding Partial Recursive Functions in CC. All functions in $\mathcal{R}$ can be implemented in CC, in the sense of Definition 1. Given $f : \mathbb{N}^n \to \mathbb{N}$, we denote its implementation by $[\![f]\!]^{\tilde{p} \mapsto q}$, where $\tilde{p}$ and q are parameters. All choreographies we build have a single exit point, and we combine them using the sequential composition operator $\,\overset{\circ}{,}\,$ from Sect. 2. We use auxiliary processes $(r_0, r_1, \ldots)$ for intermediate computation, and annotate the encoding with the index ℓ of the first free auxiliary process name $([\![f]\!]_\ell^{\tilde{p} \mapsto q})$. To alleviate the notation, the encoding assigns mnemonic names to these processes and their correspondence to the actual process names is formalised in the text using $\pi(f)$ for the number of auxiliary processes needed for encoding $f : \mathbb{N}^n \to \mathbb{N}$, defined by

$$\pi(S) = \pi(Z) = \pi(P_m^n) = 0 \qquad\qquad \pi(R(f, g)) = \pi(f) + \pi(g) + 3$$
$$\pi(C(f, g_1, \ldots, g_k)) = \pi(f) + \sum_{i=1}^{k} \pi(g_i) + k \qquad \pi(M(f)) = \pi(f) + 3$$

For simplicity, we write $\tilde{p}$ for $p_1, \ldots, p_n$ (when n is known) and $\{A_i\}_{i=1}^n$ for $A_1 \,\overset{\circ}{,}\, \ldots \,\overset{\circ}{,}\, A_n$. We omit the selections needed for projectability, as they can be inferred by amendment; we will discuss this aspect formally later.

The encoding of the base cases is straightforward.

$$[\![Z]\!]_\ell^{p \mapsto q} = p.\varepsilon \rightarrow q \qquad [\![S]\!]_\ell^{p \mapsto q} = p.(s \cdot c) \rightarrow q \qquad [\![P_m^n]\!]_\ell^{\tilde{p} \mapsto q} = p_m.c \rightarrow q$$

Composition is also simple. Let $h = C(f, g_1, \ldots, g_k) : \mathbb{N}^n \to \mathbb{N}$. Then:

$$[\![h]\!]_\ell^{\tilde{p} \mapsto q} = \left\{ [\![g_i]\!]_{\ell_i}^{\tilde{p} \mapsto r_i'} \right\}_{i=1}^k \,\overset{\circ}{,}\, [\![f]\!]_{\ell_{k+1}}^{r_1', \ldots, r_k' \mapsto q}$$

where $r_i' \doteq r_{\ell+i-1}$, $\ell_1 = \ell + k$ and $\ell_{i+1} = \ell_i + \pi(g_i)$. Each auxiliary process r_i' connects the output of g_i to the corresponding input of f. Choreographies obtained inductively use these process names as parameters; name clashes are prevented by increasing ℓ. By definition of $\overset{\circ}{,}$ $[\![g_{i+1}]\!]$ is substituted for the (unique) exit point of $[\![g_i]\!]$, and $[\![f]\!]$ is substituted for the exit point of $[\![g_k]\!]$. The resulting choreography also has only one exit point (that of $[\![f]\!]$). Below we discuss how to modify this construction slightly so that the g_is are computed in parallel.

For the recursion operator, we need to use recursive procedures. Let $h = R(f, g) : \mathbb{N}^{n+1} \to \mathbb{N}$. Then, using the macro INC from Example 1 for brevity:

$$[\![h]\!]_\ell^{p_0, \ldots, p_n \mapsto q} = \quad \text{def } T = \text{if } (r_c \overset{\leftarrow}{=} p_0) \text{ then } (q'.c \to q; \; 0)$$
$$\text{else } [\![g]\!]_{\ell_g}^{r_c, q', p_1, \ldots, p_n \mapsto r_t} \,\overset{\circ}{,}\, r_t.c \to q'; \; \text{INC}(r_c, r_t) \,\overset{\circ}{,}\, T$$
$$\text{in } [\![f]\!]_{\ell_f}^{p_1, \ldots, p_n \mapsto q'} \,\overset{\circ}{,}\, r_t.\varepsilon \to r_c; \; T$$

where $q' = r_\ell$, $r_c = r_{\ell+1}$, $r_t = r_{\ell+2}$, $\ell_f = \ell + 3$ and $\ell_g = \ell_f + \pi(f)$. Process r_c is a counter, q' stores intermediate results, and r_t is temporary storage; T checks the value of r_c and either outputs the result or recurs. Note that $[\![h]\!]$ has only one exit point (after the communication from r to q), as the exit points of $[\![f]\!]$ and $[\![g]\!]$ are replaced by code ending with calls to T.

The strategy for minimization is similar, but simpler. Let $h = M(f) : \mathbb{N}^n \to \mathbb{N}$. Again we use a counter r_c and compute successive values of f, stored in q', until a zero is found. This procedure may loop forever, either because $f(\tilde{x}, x_{n+1})$ is never 0 or because one of the evaluations itself never terminates.

$$[\![h]\!]_\ell^{p_1, \ldots, p_{n+1} \mapsto q} = \text{def } T = [\![f]\!]_{\ell_f}^{p_1, \ldots, p_n, r_c \mapsto q'} \,\overset{\circ}{,}\, r_c.\varepsilon \to r_z;$$
$$\text{if } (r_z \overset{\leftarrow}{=} q') \text{ then } (r_c.c \to q; \; 0) \text{ else } \left(\text{INC}(r_c, r_z) \,\overset{\circ}{,}\, T \right)$$
$$\text{in } r_z.\varepsilon \to r_c; \; T$$

where $q' = r_\ell$, $r_c = r_{\ell+1}$, $r_z = r_{\ell+2}$, $\ell_f = \ell + 3$ and $\ell_g = \ell_f + \pi(f)$. In this case, the whole if-then-else is inserted at the exit point of $[\![f]\!]$; the only exit point of this choreography is again after communicating the result to q.

Definition 7. *Let $f \in \mathcal{R}$. The* encoding *of f in CC is $[\![f]\!]^{\tilde{p} \mapsto q} = [\![f]\!]_0^{\tilde{p} \mapsto q}$.*

Main Results. We prove that our construction is sound by induction.

Theorem 5. *If $f : \mathbb{N}^n \to \mathbb{N}$ and $f \in \mathcal{R}$, then, for every k, $[\![f]\!]_k^{\tilde{p} \mapsto q}$ implements f with input processes $\tilde{p} = p_1, \ldots, p_n$ and output process q.*

Let $\text{SP}^{\text{CC}} = \{ [\![C, \sigma]\!] \mid [\![C, \sigma]\!] \text{ is defined} \}$ be the set of the projections of all projectable choreographies in CC. By Theorem 4, all terms in SP^{CC} are deadlock-free. By Lemma 2, for every function f we can amend $[\![f]\!]$ to an equivalent projectable choreography. Then SP^{CC} is Turing complete by Theorems 3 and 5.

Corollary 1. *Every partial recursive function is implementable in* SP^{CC}.

We finish this section by showing how to optimize our encoding and obtain parallel process implementations of independent computations. If h is defined by composition from f and $g_1, \ldots, g_k$, then in principle the computation of the g_is could be completely parallelised. However, $[\![\,]\!]$ does not fully achieve this, as $[\![g_1]\!], \ldots, [\![g_k]\!]$ share the processes containing the input. We define a modified variant $\{\!\{\,\}\!\}$ of $[\![\,]\!]$ where, for $h = C(f, g_1, \ldots, g_k)$, $\{\!\{h\}\!\}_\ell^{\tilde{\mathrm{p}} \mapsto \mathrm{q}}$ is

$$\left\{ \mathrm{p}_j.\mathrm{c} \rightarrow \mathrm{p}_j^i \right\}_{1 \le i \le k, 1 \le j \le n} \, \, \overset{\circ}{\scriptstyle 9} \, \left\{ \{\!\{g_i\}\!\}_{\ell_i}^{\tilde{\mathrm{p}}^i \mapsto r'_i} \right\}_{i=1}^{k} \, \, \overset{\circ}{\scriptstyle 9} \, \{\!\{f\}\!\}_{\ell_{k+1}}^{r'_1, \ldots, r'_k \mapsto \mathrm{q}}$$

with a suitably adapted label function ℓ. Now Theorem 2 applies, yielding:

Theorem 6. *Let* $h = C(f, g_1, \ldots, g_k)$. *For all* $\tilde{\mathrm{p}}$ *and* q, *if* $h(\tilde{x})$ *is defined and* σ *is such that* $\sigma(\mathrm{p}_i) = \ulcorner x_i \urcorner$, *then all the* $\{\!\{g_i\}\!\}_{\ell_i}^{\tilde{\mathrm{p}}^i \mapsto r'_i}$ *run in parallel in* $\{\!\{h\}\!\}^{\tilde{\mathrm{p}} \mapsto \mathrm{q}}$.

This parallelism is preserved by EPP, through Theorem 3.

5 Minimality in Choreography Languages

We now discuss our choice of primitives for CC, showing it to be a good candidate core language for choreographic programming. We analyse each primitive of CC. Recall that Turing completeness of CC is a pre-requisite for the Turing completeness of choreography projections. In many cases, simplifying CC yields a decidable termination problem (thus breaking Turing completeness). We discuss these cases first, and then proceed to a discussion on label selection.

Minimality in CC. Removing or simplifying the following primitives makes termination decidable.

– Exit point – **0**: without it, no choreography terminates.
– Value communication – p.e –> q: without it, values of processes cannot be changed, and termination becomes decidable. The syntax of expressions is also minimal: ε (zero) is the only terminal; without c values become statically defined, while without s no new values can be computed; in either case, termination is decidable.
– Recursion – def $X = C_2$ in C_1 and X: without it, all choreographies trivially terminate. The terms are minimal: they support only tail recursion and definitions are not parameterised.

Theorem 7. *Let* C *be a choreography with no conditionals. Then, termination of* C *is decidable and independent of the initial state.*

More interestingly, limiting processes to evaluating only their own local values in conditions makes termination decidable. Intuitively, this is because a process can only hold a value at a time, and thus no process can compare its current value to that of another process anymore.

Theorem 8. *If the conditional is replaced by* if $\mathsf{p.c} = v$ then C_1 else C_2, *where v is a value, and rule* $\lfloor C | Cond \rfloor$ *by* $\dfrac{i = 1\ if\, \sigma(\mathsf{p}) = v,\ \ i = 2\ otherwise}{\text{if } \mathsf{p.c} = v \text{ then } C_1 \text{ else } C_2, \sigma\ \ \to\ \ C_i, \sigma}$, *then termination is decidable.*

Label selection. The argument for including label selections in CC is of a different nature. As the construction in Sect. 4 shows, selections are not needed for implementing computable functions in CC; they are used only for obtaining projectable choreographies, via amendment. We now show that we can encode selections introduced by amendment using the other primitives of CC, thereby eliminating the need for them from a purely computational point of view.

We denote by Minimal Choreographies (MC) the fragment of CC that does not contain label selections. We can therefore view amendment as a function from MC into the subset of projectable CC choreographies. Recall that the definition of amendment guarantees that selections only occur in branches of conditionals, and that they are always paired and in the same order (see Definition 6). The fragment of CC obtained by amending choreographies in MC is thus:

$$C ::= \mathsf{p}.e \to \mathsf{q}; C \mid \text{if } \mathsf{p} \overset{\leftarrow}{=} \mathsf{q} \text{ then } S(\mathsf{p}, \tilde{r}, \mathrm{L}, C_1) \text{ else } S(\mathsf{p}, \tilde{r}, \mathrm{R}, C_2) \mid \mathsf{def}\ X = C_2\ \mathsf{in}\ C_1 \mid X \mid \mathbf{0}$$

Term $S(\mathsf{p}, \tilde{r}, l, C)$ denotes a series of selections of label l from p to all processes in the list $\tilde{r}$. Formally, $S(\mathsf{p}, \emptyset, l, C) = C$ and $S(\mathsf{p}, \mathsf{r} : \tilde{r}, l, C) = \mathsf{p} \to \mathsf{r}[l]; S(\mathsf{p}, \tilde{r}, l, C)$.

Definition 8. *Let C be obtained by amending a choreography in MC. The encoding $(\!| C |\!)^+$ of C in MC uses processes $\mathsf{p}, \mathsf{p}^\bullet$ for each $\mathsf{p} \in \mathsf{pn}(C)$ and a special process z, and is defined as $(\!| C |\!)^+ = \mathsf{p}.\varepsilon \to \mathsf{z}; (\!| C |\!)$, with $(\!| C |\!)$ defined in Fig. 2.*

$(\!| \mathbf{0} |\!) = \mathbf{0}$ $(\!| \mathsf{p}.e \to \mathsf{q}; C |\!) = \mathsf{p}.e \to \mathsf{q}; (\!| C |\!)$ $(\!| \mathsf{def}\ X = C_2\ \mathsf{in}\ C_1 |\!) = \mathsf{def}\ X = (\!| C_2 |\!)\ \mathsf{in}\ (\!| C_1 |\!)$

$(\!| X |\!) = X$ $(\!| \text{if } \mathsf{p} \overset{\leftarrow}{=} \mathsf{q} \text{ then } C_1 \text{ else } C_2 |\!) = \text{if } \mathsf{p} \overset{\leftarrow}{=} \mathsf{q} \text{ then } (\!| C_1, C_2 |\!)_1 \text{ else } (\!| C_1, C_2 |\!)_2$

$(\!| C_1, C_2 |\!) = \langle (\!| C_1 |\!), (\!| C_2 |\!) \rangle$ if C_1 and C_2 do not begin with a selection

$(\!| \mathsf{p} \to \mathsf{q}[\mathrm{L}]; C_1, \mathsf{p} \to \mathsf{q}[\mathrm{R}]; C_2 |\!) =$

$\Big\langle \mathsf{q.c} \to \mathsf{q}^\bullet; \mathsf{p}.\varepsilon \to \mathsf{q}; \text{if } \mathsf{q} \overset{\leftarrow}{=} \mathsf{z} \text{ then } \mathsf{q}^\bullet.\mathsf{c} \to \mathsf{q}; (\!| C_1, C_2 |\!)_1 \text{ else } \mathsf{q}^\bullet.\mathsf{c} \to \mathsf{q}; (\!| C_1, C_2 |\!)_2,$

$\qquad \mathsf{q.c} \to \mathsf{q}^\bullet; \mathsf{p.sc} \to \mathsf{q}; \text{if } \mathsf{q} \overset{\leftarrow}{=} \mathsf{z} \text{ then } \mathsf{q}^\bullet.\mathsf{c} \to \mathsf{q}; (\!| C_1, C_2 |\!)_1 \text{ else } \mathsf{q}^\bullet.\mathsf{c} \to \mathsf{q}; (\!| C_1, C_2 |\!)_2 \Big\rangle$

Fig. 2. Elimination of selections from amended choreographies.

The definition of $(\!| C |\!)$ exploits the structure of amended choreographies, where selections are always paired at the top of the two branches of conditionals. It is immediate that $|\mathsf{pn}((\!| C |\!)^+)| = 2|\mathsf{pn}(C)| + 1$ (the extra process is z). Let $|C|$ be the size of the syntax tree of C. Then, $|(\!| C |\!)^+| \leq 2^{|C|}$, and in the worst case we get exponential growth. However, EPP collapses all branches of conditionals, hence projections do not grow exponentially: $|[\![(\![C\!]\!)^+]\!]_{q\bullet}| \leq |[\![(\![C\!]\!)^+]\!]_q| \leq 3|[\![C]\!]_q|$ for every $q \in pn(C)$.

Theorem 9. *For every choreography C in MC, $[\![(\![\mathsf{Amend}(C)\!]\!)]\!]$ is defined.*

It is straightforward to prove that C and $(\![\mathsf{Amend}(C)\!]\!)$ behave exactly in the same way when we only observe communications between the original processes – except that label selections are replaced by regular messages.

Lemma 3. *If $C, \sigma \to C', \sigma'$ and σ^+ is such that $\sigma^+(p) = \sigma(p)$ for $p \in pn(C)$ and $\sigma^+(z) = \varepsilon$, then $(\![\mathsf{Amend}(C)\!]\!), \sigma^+ \to^* (\![C'\!]\!), \sigma'^+$ for some σ'^+ similarly related to σ'. Conversely, if $(\![\mathsf{Amend}(C)\!]\!), \sigma^+ \to C', \sigma'$, then $C, \sigma \to C'', \sigma''$ where $C', \sigma' \to^* (\![\mathsf{Amend}(C'')\!]\!), \sigma''^+$.*

Corollary 2. *With the notation of the previous lemma, if $C, \sigma \to^* C', \sigma'$, then $(\![\mathsf{Amend}(C)\!]\!)^+, \sigma^+ \to^* (\![\mathsf{Amend}(C')\!]\!), \sigma'^+$.*

As a consequence, the set $\mathrm{SP}^{\mathrm{MC}} = \{[\![C, \sigma]\!] \mid C \text{ in MC and } [\![C, \sigma]\!] \text{ is defined}\}$ of projections of minimal choreographies is also Turing complete.

Corollary 3. *Every partial recursive function is implementable in SP^{MC}.*

Since choreographies in MC do not have selections, process projections of choreographies in MC never have branchings. This means that, in the case of MC, the merging operator $\sqcup$ used in EPP is exactly syntactic equality (since the only nontrivial case was that of branchings). Consequently, we can replace the rule for projecting conditionals with a simpler one:

$$[\![\text{if } p \overset{\leftarrow}{=} q \text{ then } C_1 \text{ else } C_2]\!]_r = \begin{cases} \text{if } c \overset{\leftarrow}{=} q \text{ then } [\![C_1]\!]_r \text{ else } [\![C_2]\!]_r & \text{if } r = p \\ p!\langle c \rangle; [\![C_1]\!]_r & \text{if } r = q \text{ and } [\![C_1]\!]_r = [\![C_2]\!]_r \\ [\![C_1]\!]_r & \text{if } r \notin \{p, q\} \text{ and } [\![C_1]\!]_r = [\![C_2]\!]_r \end{cases}$$

The advantages of eliminating selections are thus a simpler choreography language, a simpler definition of EPP (without merging), and a simpler process language (without selection and branching). The main drawback is that eliminating a selection needed for projectability makes the choreography exponentially larger and requires the addition of extra processes and communications; this significantly changes the structure of the choreography, potentially making it unreadable. Selections are also present in virtually all choreography models [2,5,6,12,16,25], therefore we believe that a core model such as CC should have them (in addition to the drawback we mentioned).

Our results suggest the viability of a particular implementation strategy for choreographic programming. Programmers could write choreographies without label selections, and then our results could be used to translate these choreographies to process implementations in a simple language that does not include label communications, thus simplifying the target language. The exponential growth of the intermediate choreography representation can be bypassed by using shared data structures for the syntax tree, since the generated choreographies contain a lot of duplicate terms.

However, this implementation removes an important ability provided in CC and all other standard choreography calculi: deciding at which point of execution selections should be performed. In more expressive languages than CC, processes can perform complex internal computations [10]. For example, assume that p had to assign tasks to other two processes r and s based on a condition. In one case, r would run a slow task and s a fast one; otherwise, r would run a fast task and s a slow one. In this case, p should begin by sending a selection to the process with the slow task and then by sending it the necessary data for its computation, before it sends the selection to the process with the fast task.

6   CC and Other Languages

CC is representative of the body of previous work on choreographic programming, where choreographies are used for implementations, for example [5,6,8,12,24,28]. All the primitives of CC can be encoded in such languages. Thus, we obtain a notion of function implementation for these languages, induced by that for CC, for which they are Turing complete. For the model in [6], we formalise this result in [9]. Below, we discuss the significance of our results for the cited languages.

Differently from CC, other choreography languages typically use channel-based communications (as in the π-calculus [26]). Communications via process references as in CC can be encoded by assigning a dedicated channel to each pair of processes [9]. For example, the calculus in [6], which we refer to as Channel Choreographies (ChC), features an EPP targeting the session-based π-calculus [2]. ChC is a fully-fledged calculus aimed at real-world application that has been implemented as a choreographic programming framework (the Chor language [8]). Our formal translation from CC to ChC (given in [9]) shows that many primitives of ChC are not needed to achieve Turing completeness, including: asynchronous communications, creation of sessions and processes, channel mobility, parameterised recursive definitions, arbitrary local computation, unbounded memory cells at processes, multiparty sessions. While useful in practice, these primitives come at the cost of making the formal treatment of ChC very technically involved. In particular, ChC (and its implementation Chor) requires a sophisticated type system, linearity analysis, and definition of EPP to ensure correctness of projected processes. These features are not needed in CC. Using our encoding from CC to ChC, we can repeat the argument in Sect. 4 to characterise a fragment of the session-based π-calculus from [2] that contains only deadlock-free terms and is Turing complete. ChC has also been translated to the Jolie programming language [14,23], whence our reasoning also applies to the latter and, in general, to service-oriented languages based on message correlation.

The language WS-CDL from W3C [28] and the formal models inspired by it (e.g., [5]) are very similar to ChC and a similar translation from CC could be formally developed, with similar implications as above. The same applies to the choreography language developed in [12], which adds higher-order features to choreographies in terms of runtime adaptation. Finally, the language of compositional choreographies presented in [24] is an extension of ChC and therefore our translation applies directly. This implies that adding modularity to choreographies does not add any computational power, as expected.

7 Related Work and Discussion

Register Machines. The computational primitives in CC recall those of the Unlimited Register Machine (URM) [11], but CC and URM differ in two main aspects. First, URM programs contain go-to statements, while CC supports only tail recursion. Second, in the URM there is a single sequential program manipulating the cells, whereas in CC computation is distributed among the various cells (the processes), which operate concurrently.

Simulating the URM is an alternative way to prove Turing completeness of CC. However, our proof using partial recursive functions is more direct and gives an algorithm to implement any function in CC, given its proof of membership in $\mathcal{R}$. It also yields the natural interpretation of parallelisation stated in Theorem 6. Similarly, we could establish Turing completeness of CC using only a bounded number of processes. However, such constructions encode data using Gödel numbers, which is not in the spirit of our declarative notion of function implementation. They also restrict concurrency, breaking Theorem 6.

Multiparty Sessions and Types. The communication primitives in CC recall those of protocols for multiparty sessions, e.g., in Multiparty Session Types (MPST) [16] and conversation types [4]. These protocols are not meant for computation, as in choreographic programming (and CC); rather, they are types used to verify that sessions (e.g., π-calculus channels) are used accordingly to their respective protocol specifications. For such formalisms, we know of a strong characterisation result: a variant of MPST corresponds to communicating finite state machines [3] that respect the property of multiparty compatibility [13]. To the best of our knowledge, this is the first work studying the expressivity of choreographic programming (choreographies for implementations).

Full β-reduction and Nondeterminism. Execution in CC is nondeterministic due to the swapping of communications allowed by the structural precongruence $\preceq$. This recalls full β-reduction for λ-calculus, where sub-terms can be evaluated whenever possible. However, the two mechanisms are actually different. Consider the choreography $C \overset{\Delta}{=}$ p.c -> q; q.ε -> r; 0. If CC supported full β-reduction, we should be able to reduce the second communication before the first one, since there is no data dependency between the two. Formally, for some $\sigma: C, \sigma \rightarrow$ p.c -> q; 0, $\sigma[r \mapsto \varepsilon]$. However, this reduction is disallowed by our semantics: rule $\lfloor C|Eta\text{-}Eta \rfloor$ cannot be applied because q is present in both communications. This difference is a key feature of choreographies, stemming from their practical origins: controlling sequentiality by establishing causalities using process identifiers is important for the implementation of business processes [28]. For example, imagine that the choreography C models a payment transaction and that the message from q to r is a confirmation that p has sent its credit card information to q; then, it is a natural requirement that the second communication happens only after the first. Note that we would reach the same conclusions even if we adopted an asynchronous messaging semantics for SP, since the first action by q is a blocking input.

While execution in CC can be nondeterministic, computation results are deterministic as in many other choreography languages [6,7,24]: if a choreography terminates, the result will always be the same regardless of how its execution is scheduled (recalling the Church–Rosser Theorem for the λ-calculus). Nondeterministic computation is not necessary for our results. Nevertheless, it can be easily added to CC. Specifically, we could augment CC with the syntax primitive $C_1 \oplus^p C_2$ and the reduction rule $C_1 \oplus^p C_2 \rightarrow C_i$ for $i = 1, 2$. Extending SP with an internal choice $B_1 \oplus B_2$ and our definition of EPP is straightforward: in SP, we would also allow $B_1 \oplus B_2 \rightarrow B_i$ for $i = 1, 2$, and define $[\![C_1 \oplus^p C_2]\!]_r$ to be $[\![C_1]\!]_r \oplus [\![C_2]\!]_r$ if r = p and $[\![C_1]\!]_r \sqcup [\![C_2]\!]_r$ otherwise.

Merging and Amendment. Amendment was first studied in [19] for a simple language with finite traces (thus not Turing complete). Our definition is different, since it uses merging for the first time.

Actors and Asynchrony. Processes in SP communicate by using direct references to each other, recalling actor systems. However, there are notable differences: communications are synchronous and inputs specify the intended sender. The first difference comes from minimality: asynchrony would add possible behaviours to CC, which are unnecessary to establish Turing completeness. We leave an investigation of asynchrony in CC to future work. The second difference arises because CC is a choreography calculus, and communication primitives in choreographies typically express both sender and receiver.

Acknowledgements. We thank Hugo Torres Vieira and Gianluigi Zavattaro for their useful comments. Montesi was supported by CRC (Choreographies for Reliable and efficient Communication software), grant no. DFF–4005-00304 from the Danish Council for Independent Research.

References

1. Barendregt, H.: The Lambda Calculus: Its Syntax and Semantics, 2nd edn. North Holland, Amsterdam (1984)
2. Bettini, L., Coppo, M., D'Antoni, L., De Luca, M., Dezani-Ciancaglini, M., Yoshida, N.: Global progress in dynamically interleaved multiparty sessions. In: Breugel, F., Chechik, M. (eds.) CONCUR 2008. LNCS, vol. 5201, pp. 418–433. Springer, Heidelberg (2008). doi:10.1007/978-3-540-85361-9_33
3. Brand, D., Zafiropulo, P.: On communicating finite-state machines. J. ACM **30**(2), 323–342 (1983)
4. Caires, L., Vieira, H.T.: Conversation types. Theor. Comput. Sci. **411**(51–52), 4399–4440 (2010)

5. Carbone, M., Honda, K., Yoshida, N.: Structured communication-centered programming for web services. ACM Trans. Program. Lang. Syst. **34**(2), 8 (2012)
6. Carbone, M., Montesi, F.: Deadlock-freedom-by-design: multiparty asynchronous global programming. In: Giacobazzi, R., Cousot, R., (eds.) POPL, pp. 263–274. ACM (2013)
7. Carbone, M., Montesi, F., Schürmann, C.: Choreographies, logically. In: Baldan, P., Gorla, D. (eds.) CONCUR 2014. LNCS, vol. 8704, pp. 47–62. Springer, Heidelberg (2014). doi:10.1007/978-3-662-44584-6_5
8. Chor. Programming Language. http://www.chor-lang.org/
9. Cruz-Filipe, L., Montesi, F.: Choreographies, computationally. CoRR, abs/1510.03271 (2015)
10. Cruz-Filipe, L., Montesi, F.: Choreographies, divided and conquered. CoRR, abs/1602.03729 (2016, Submitted)
11. Cutland, N.J.: Computability: An Introduction to Recursive Function Theory. Cambridge University Press, Cambridge (1980)
12. Dalla Preda, M., Gabbrielli, M., Giallorenzo, S., Lanese, I., Mauro, J.: Dynamic choreographies – safe runtime updates of distributed applications. In: Holvoet, T., Viroli, M. (eds.) COORDINATION 2015. LNCS, vol. 9037, pp. 67–82. Springer, Cham (2015). doi:10.1007/978-3-319-19282-6_5
13. Deniélou, P.-M., Yoshida, N.: Multiparty compatibility in communicating automata: characterisation and synthesis of global session types. In: Fomin, F.V., Freivalds, R., Kwiatkowska, M., Peleg, D. (eds.) ICALP 2013. LNCS, vol. 7966, pp. 174–186. Springer, Heidelberg (2013). doi:10.1007/978-3-642-39212-2_18
14. Gabbrielli, M., Giallorenzo, S., Montesi, F.: Applied choreographies. CoRR, abs/1510.03637 (2015)
15. Honda, K., Vasconcelos, V.T., Kubo, M.: Language primitives and type discipline for structured communication-based programming. In: Hankin, C. (ed.) ESOP 1998. LNCS, vol. 1381, pp. 122–138. Springer, Heidelberg (1998). doi:10.1007/BFb0053567
16. Honda, K., Yoshida, N., Carbone, M.: Multiparty asynchronous session types. In: Necula, G.C., Wadler, P., (eds.) POPL, pp. 273–284. ACM (2008)
17. Kleene, S.C.: Introduction to Metamathematics. North-Holland Publishing Co., Amsterdam (1952)
18. Lanese, I., Guidi, C., Montesi, F., Zavattaro, G.: Bridging the gap between interaction- and process-oriented choreographies. In: Cerone, A., Gruner, S., (eds.) SEFM, pp. 323–332. IEEE (2008)
19. Lanese, I., Montesi, F., Zavattaro, G.: Amending choreographies. In: Ravara, A., Silva, J., (eds.) WWV 2013. EPTCS, vol. 123, pp. 34–48 (2013)
20. Leesatapornwongsa, T., Lukman, J.F., Shan, L., Gunawi, H.S.: TaxDC: a taxonomy of non-deterministic concurrency bugs in datacenter distributed systems. In: ASPLOS, pp. 517–530. ACM (2016)
21. Shan, L., Park, S., Seo, E., Zhou, Y.: Learning from mistakes: a comprehensive study on real world concurrency bug characteristics. In: ASPLOS, pp. 329–339. ACM (2008)
22. Montesi, F.: Choreographic Programming. Ph. D. thesis, IT University of Copenhagen (2013). http://fabriziomontesi.com/files/choreographic_programming.pdf
23. Montesi, F., Guidi, C., Zavattaro, G.: Service-oriented programming with Jolie. In: Bouguettaya, A., Sheng, Q.Z., Daniel, F. (eds.) Web Services Foundations, pp. 81–107. Springer, Heidelberg (2014)

24. Montesi, F., Yoshida, N.: Compositional choreographies. In: D'Argenio, P.R., Melgratti, H.C. (eds.) CONCUR 2013. LNCS, vol. 8052, pp. 425–439. Springer, Heidelberg (2013). doi:10.1007/978-3-642-40184-8_30
25. Qiu, Z., Zhao, X., Cai, C., Yang, H.: Towards the theoretical foundation of choreography. In: Williamson, C.L., Zurko, M.E., Patel-Schneider, P.F., Shenoy, P.J., (eds.) WWW, pp. 973–982. ACM (2007)
26. Sangiorgi, D., Walker, D.: The π-Calculus: A Theory of Mobile Processes. Cambridge University Press, Cambridge (2001)
27. Turing, A.M.: Computability and λ-definability. J. Symb. Log. **2**(4), 153–163 (1937)
28. W3C WS-CDL Working Group: Web services choreography description language version 1.0 (2004). http://www.w3.org/TR/2004/WD-ws-cdl-10-20040427/

Checking Business Process Evolution

Pascal Poizat[1,2(⊠)] , Gwen Salaün[3], and Ajay Krishna[3]

[1] Université Paris Lumières, Univ Paris Ouest, Nanterre, France
pascal.poizat@lip6.fr
[2] Sorbonne Universités, UPMC Univ Paris 06, CNRS, LIP6 UMR7606, Paris, France
[3] University of Grenoble Alpes, Inria, LIG, CNRS, Grenoble, France

Abstract. Business processes support the modeling and the implementation of software as workflows of local and inter-process activities. Taking over structuring and composition, evolution has become a central concern in software development. We advocate it should be taken into account as soon as the modeling of business processes, which can thereafter be made executable using process engines or model-to-code transformations. We show here that business process evolution needs formal analysis in order to compare different versions of processes, identify precisely the differences between them, and ensure the desired consistency. To reach this objective, we first present a model transformation from the BPMN standard notation to the LNT process algebra. We then propose a set of relations for comparing business processes at the formal model level. With reference to related work, we propose a richer set of comparison primitives supporting renaming, refinement, property- and context-awareness. Thanks to an implementation of our approach that can be used through a Web application, we put the checking of evolution within the reach of business process designers.

1 Introduction

Context. A business process is a structured set of activities, or tasks, that is used to create some product or perform some service. BPMN [16,24] has become the standard notation for business processes. It allows one to model these processes as sequences of tasks, but also as more complex workflows using different kinds of gateways. There are now plenty of frameworks supporting BPMN modeling, *e.g.*, Activiti, Bonita BPM, or the Eclipse BPMN Designer. Most of them accept BPMN 2.0 (BPMN for short in the rest of this paper) as input and enable one to execute it using business process engines.

Modern software exhibits a high degree of dynamicity and is subject to continuous evolution. This is the case in areas such as autonomic computing, pervasive or self-adaptive systems, where parts of the system components may have to be removed or added in reaction to some stimulus. This is also the case for more mainstream software, *e.g.*, when developed using an agile method.

In this paper, we focus on software development based on BPMN. We suppose some application has been developed from a BPMN model and in order to evolve this application one wants first to evolve the BPMN model. This is sensible to

© Springer International Publishing AG 2017
O. Kouchnarenko and R. Khosravi (Eds.): FACS 2016, LNCS 10231, pp. 36–53, 2017.
DOI: 10.1007/978-3-319-57666-4_4

keep the application and the model consistent, either for documentation purposes or because one follows a model at runtime approach (executing business processes on process engines being a specific case of this).

Objective. Given two BPMN business processes, we want to support the (human) process designer in the evolution activity with automated verification techniques to check whether the evolved process satisfies desired properties with reference to the original process version. The designer should have different kinds of verifications at hand for different kinds of evolutions one can perform on a business process. These verifications will enable the designer to understand the impact of evolution and, if necessary, support the refinement of an incorrect evolution into a correct one.

Approach. Since BPMN has only an informal semantics, we have first to define a model transformation into a formal model that could ground the different needed verifications. For this we choose to transform BPMN processes into LNT [4] process algebraic descriptions. Using the LNT operational semantics, we can retrieve Labelled Transition Systems (LTSs) which are a formal model with rich tool support. Then we define a set of atomic evolution verifications based on LTS equivalences and LTS pre-orders originating from concurrency theory. These can be applied iteratively to get feed-back on the correctness of evolutions and perform changes on business processes until satisfaction. Our approach is completely automated in a tool we have developed, VBPMN, that designers may use through a Web application to check process evolution [1]. It includes an implementation of our BPMN to LNT transformation, and relies on a state-of-the-art verification tool-box, CADP [13], for computing LTS models from LNT descriptions and for performing LTS-level operations and atomic analysis actions used in our evolution verification techniques. We have applied our approach and tool support to many examples for validation purposes. Thanks to the use of a modular architecture in VBPMN, other workflow-based notations, such as UML activity diagrams [20] or YAWL workflows [28], could be integrated to our framework.

Organization. Section 2 introduces BPMN and our running example. Section 3 presents the process algebra and the formal model transformation we use to give a translational semantics to BPMN process. We then build on this to present and formalize in Sect. 4 our different notions of business process evolution. Section 5 gives details on the implementation of our approach in a tool and discusses results of experiments performed with it. We present related work in Sect. 6 and we conclude in Sect. 7.

2   BPMN in a Nutshell

In this section, we give a short introduction on BPMN. We then present the running example we will use for illustration purposes in the rest of this paper.

BPMN is a workflow-based graphical notation (Fig. 1) for modeling business processes that can be made executable either using process engines (*e.g.*, Activiti, Bonita BPM, or jBPM) or using model transformations into

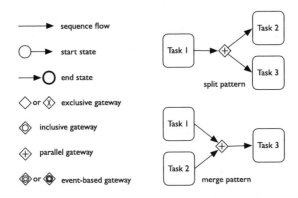

Fig. 1. BPMN notation (Part of)

executable languages (*e.g.*, BPEL). BPMN is an ISO/IEC standard since 2013 but its semantics is only described informally in official documents [16,24]. Therefore, several attempts have been made for providing BPMN with a formal semantics, *e.g.*, [10,18,22,25,33]. In this paper, we abstract from the features of BPMN related to data and we focus on the core features of BPMN, that is, its control flow constructs, which is the subset of interest with respect to the properties we propose to formally analyze in this paper. More precisely, we consider the following categories of workflow nodes: *start* and *end event*, *tasks*, and *gateways*.

Start and end events are used to denote respectively the starting and the ending point of a process. A task is an abstraction of some activity and corresponds in practice, *e.g.*, to manual tasks, scripted tasks, or inter-process message-based communication. In our context, we use a unique general concept of task for all these possibilities. Start (end, resp.) events must have only one outgoing (incoming, resp.) flow, and tasks must have exactly one incoming and one outgoing flow. Gateways are used, along with sequence flows, to represent the control flow of the whole process and in particular the task execution ordering. There are five types of gateways in BPMN: *exclusive, inclusive, parallel, event-based* and *complex gateways*. We take into account all of them but for complex gateways, which are used to model complex synchronization behaviors especially based on data control. An exclusive gateway is used to choose one out of a set of mutually exclusive alternative incoming or outgoing branches. It can also be used to denote looping behaviors as in Fig. 5. For an inclusive gateway, any number of branches among all its incoming or outgoing branches may be taken. A parallel gateway creates concurrent flows for all its outgoing branches or synchronizes concurrent flows for all its incoming branches. For an event-based gateway, it takes one of its outgoing branches based on events (message reception) or accepts one of its incoming branches. If a gateway has one incoming branch and multiple outgoing branches, it is called a *split* (gateway). Otherwise, it should have one outgoing branch and multiple incoming branches, and it is called a *merge* (gateway). In this paper, we assume processes where we have an exact split→merge

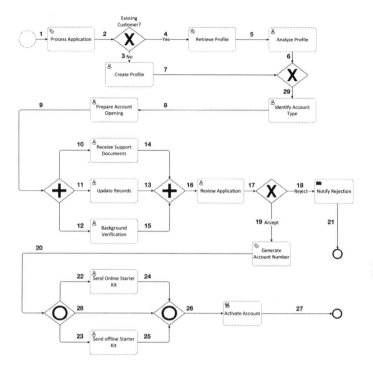

Fig. 2. Bank account opening process in BPMN. Sequence flow identifiers (used for the encoding in Fig. 3) are given as textual annotations.

correspondence for inclusive gateways. We also suppose that BPMN processes are syntactically correct. This can be enforced using a BPMN designer, *e.g.,* the Activiti BPM platform, Bonita BPM, or the Eclipse BPMN Designer.

Example. We use as running example the opening of a bank account depicted in Fig. 2. This process starts by retrieving information about the customer (exclusive gateway, top part). Then, the type of account is identified and several documents need to be delivered (parallel gateway, middle part). Finally, the account creation is rejected or accepted, and in the latter case, some information is sent to the customer (inclusive gateway, bottom part) and the account is activated.

3   From BPMN to LTS

We present in this section a translational semantics from BPMN to LTSs, obtained through a model transformation from BPMN to the LNT process algebra, LNT being equipped with an LTS semantics.

3.1   LNT

LNT [4] is an extension of LOTOS, an ISO standardized process algebra [15], which allows the definition of data types, functions, and processes. LNT processes are built from actions, choices (select), parallel composition (par), looping behaviors (loop), conditions (if), and sequential composition (;). The communication between the process participants is carried out by rendezvous on a list of synchronized actions included in the parallel composition (par).

The use of a process algebra such as LNT is preferred over the direct use of LTS (*i.e.*, the definition of a BPMN to LTS transformation) since this yields a simpler, high-level and more declarative transformation. Thanks to the LTS semantics of process algebras, one can use thereafter the rich set of tools existing for LTS-based verification. The choice of LNT over other process algebras has been guided by the availability of the CADP [13] toolbox, which comes with a very comprehensive set of verification tools, including ones supporting the implementation of the various checks presented in the sequel.

3.2   From BPMN to LNT

We present here the encoding into LNT of the BPMN constructs that we support. The main idea is to encode as LNT processes all BPMN elements involved in a process definition, that is, the nodes (tasks, gateways), which correspond to the behavior of the BPMN process, initial/end events, and sequence flows, which encode the execution semantics of the process. Finally, all these independent LNT processes are composed in parallel and synchronized in order to respect the BPMN execution semantics. For instance, after execution of a node, the corresponding LNT process synchronizes with the process encoding the outgoing flow, which then synchronizes with the process encoding the node appearing at the end of this flow, and so on.

Table 1 presents the encoding patterns for the main BPMN constructs. The actions corresponding to the flows (incf, outf, etc.) will be used as synchronization points between the different BPMN elements. The begin and finish actions in the initial/end events are just used to trigger and terminate, respectively, these events. The actions used in task constructs (*e.g.*, task) will be the only ones to appear in the final LTS. All other synchronizations actions will be hidden because they do not make sense from an observational point of view. Both the sequence flow and the task construct are enclosed within an LNT loop operator since these elements can be repeated several times if the BPMN process exhibits looping behaviors. We do not present the encoding of communication/interaction messages in Table 1 because they are translated similarly to tasks.

The parallel gateway is encoded using the par LNT operator, which corresponds in this case to an interleaving of all flows. The exclusive gateway is encoded using the select LNT operator, which corresponds to a nondeterministic choice among all flows. The event-based gateway is handled in the same way as the exclusive gateway, hence it is not presented here.

The semantics of inclusive gateways is quite intricate [5]. We assume here that each inclusive merge gateway has a corresponding inclusive split gateway. The inclusive gateway uses the select and par operators to allow all possible combinations of the outgoing branches. Note the introduction of synchronization points (s_i), which are necessary to indicate to the merge gateway the behavior

Table 1. Encoding patterns in LNT for the main BPMN constructs

BPMN construct	BPMN notation	LNT encoding
Initial event	◯ outf →	begin ; outf
End event	incf →◯	incf ; finish
Sequence flow	→	**loop begin ; finish end loop**
Task	incf → [task] outf →	**loop** incf ; task ; outf **end loop**
Parallel gateway (split)	incf ⬦+ outf1 / outf2 / outf3	incf ; **par** outf1 || outf2 || outf3 **end par**
Parallel gateway (merge)	incf1 / incf2 ⬦+ outf / incf3	**par** incf1 || incf2 || incf3 **end par** ; outf
Exclusive gateway (split)	incf ⬦X outf1 / outf2 / outf3	incf ; **select** outf1 [] outf2 [] outf3 **end select**
Exclusive gateway (merge)	incf1 / incf2 ⬦X outf / incf3	**select** incf1 [] incf2 [] incf3 **end select** ; outf
Inclusive gateway (split)	incf ⬦◯ outf1 / outf2	incf ; **select** (* s_i *if one matching merge* *) outf1 ; *s1* [] outf2 ; *s2* [] **par** outf1 || outf2 **end par** ; *s3* **end select**
Inclusive gateway (merge)	incf1 / incf2 ⬦◯ outf	**select** (* s_i *if one matching split* *) *s1* ; incf1 [] *s2* ; incf2 [] *s3* ; **par** incf1 || incf2 **end par** **end select** ; outf

that was executed at the split level. Without such synchronization points, the corresponding merge does not know whether it is supposed to wait for one or several branches (and which branches in this second case).

Once all BPMN elements are encoded into LNT, the last step is to compose them in order to obtain the behavior of the whole BPMN process. To do so, we compose in parallel all the flows with all the other constructs. All flows are interleaved because they do not interact one with another. All events and nodes

```
process main [processApplication:any, createProfile:any, ...] is
  hide begin:any, finish:any, flow1_begin:any, flow1_finish:any, ... in
    par flow1_begin, flow1_finish, flow2_begin, flow2_finish, ... in
      par
        flow [flow1_begin, flow1_finish] ||...|| flow [flow29_begin, flow29_finish]
      end par
    ||
      par
        init [begin,flow1_begin]
      || final [flow21_finish, finish] || final [flow27_finish, finish]
      || task [flow1_finish, processApplication, flow2_begin] || task [...] || ...
      || xorsplit [flow2_finish, flow3_begin, flow4_begin]
      || xormerge [flow6_finish, flow7_finish, flow29_begin]
      end par
    end par
  end hide
end process
```

Fig. 3. Main LNT process for the bank account opening process

(start/end events, tasks, gateways) are interleaved as well for the same reason. Then both sets are synchronized on flow sequences (flowXX actions). These additional actions are finally hidden because they should not appear as observable actions and will be transformed into internal transitions in the resulting LTS. Each process call is accompanied with its alphabet, that is, the list of actions used in that process. For instance, each call of a flow process comes with a couple of actions corresponding to the initiation and termination of the flow.

Example. The translation of the bank account opening process in LNT results in several processes. The main process is given in Fig. 3. Process actions of the form flowXX correspond to the encoding of flows, *e.g.*, flow2_finish, flow3_begin, and flow4_begin for the flows 2, 3, and 4 that are connected to the first split exclusive gateway. The corresponding LTS is shown in Fig. 4.

4   Comparing Processes

In this section, we formally define several kinds of comparisons between BPMN processes. Their analysis allows one to ensure that the evolution of one process into another one is satisfactory.

Notation. LNT processes are denoted in italics, *e.g.*, p, and BPMN processes are denoted using a bold fond, *e.g.*, **b**. In the sequel, we denote with $||p||$ the semantic model of an LNT process p, that is the LTS for p. Further, we denote the BPMN to LNT transformation introduced in the previous section using Θ, and the application of it to a BPMN process **b** using $\Theta(\mathbf{b})$. Accordingly, $||\Theta(\mathbf{b})||$ denotes the LTS for this process. As far as the comparisons are concerned, we suppose we are in the context of the evolution of a BPMN process **b** into a BPMN process **b**′, denoted by **b** --→ **b**′.

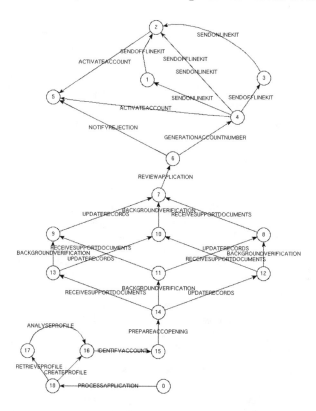

Fig. 4. LTS formal model for the bank account opening process

4.1 Conservative Evolution

Our first comparison criterion is quite strong. Given an evolution **b** --→ **b′**, it ensures that the observable behavior of **b** is exactly preserved in **b′**. It supports very constrained refactorings of BPMN processes such as grouping or splitting parallel or exclusive branches (*e.g.*, $\langle\!\mathbf{\otimes}\!\rangle(\langle\!\mathbf{\otimes}\!\rangle(\mathbf{a}, \mathbf{b}), \mathbf{c}) \overset{\text{---}\rightarrow}{\underset{\leftarrow\text{---}}{}} \langle\!\mathbf{\otimes}\!\rangle(\mathbf{a}, \mathbf{b}, \mathbf{c})$ where $\langle\!\mathbf{\otimes}\!\rangle(x_1, \ldots, x_n)$ denotes a balanced exclusive split-merge). At the semantic level, several behavioral equivalences could be used. We have to deal with internal transitions introduced by hiding (see Sect. 3.2). Hence, we chose to use branching equivalence [30], denoted with $\overset{\text{br}}{\equiv}$, since it is the finest equivalence notion in presence of such internal transitions.

Definition 1 *(Conservative Evolution). Let* **b** *and* **b′** *be two processes,* **b** --→ **b′** *is a conservative evolution iff* $\| \Theta(\mathbf{b}) \| \overset{\text{br}}{\equiv} \| \Theta(\mathbf{b}') \|$.

4.2   Inclusive and Exclusive Evolution

In most cases, one does not want to replace a business process by another one having exactly the same behavior. Rather, one wants to be able to add new functionalities in the process, without interfering with the existing ones. A typical example is adding new choices, *e.g.*, ⊕(a, b) --→ ⊕(a, b, c), or evolving an existing one, *e.g.*, ⊕(a, b) --→ ⊕(a, ⊗(b, c)). So here, we ground on a preorder relation rather than on an equivalence one, ensuring that, given b --→ b′, all observable behaviors that were in b are still in b′. For this we rely on the branching preorder [30], denoted by $\overset{br}{<}$.

Definition 2 *(Inclusive Evolution). Let* b *and* b′ *be two processes,* b --→ b′ *is an inclusive evolution iff* $\| \Theta(\mathbf{b}) \| \overset{br}{<} \| \Theta(\mathbf{b}') \|$.

Similarly, one may refine a process by implementing only a part of it. Here, in b --→ b′, one does not want that b′ exposes any additional behavior that is outside what is specified in b. This is a reversed form of inclusive evolution.

Definition 3 *(Exclusive Evolution). Let* b *and* b′ *be two processes,* b --→ b′ *is an exclusive evolution iff* $\| \Theta(\mathbf{b}') \| \overset{br}{<} \| \Theta(\mathbf{b}) \|$.

The duality between inclusive and exclusive evolution is usual when one formalizes the fact that some abstract specification a is correctly implemented into a more concrete system c. For some people, this means that at least all the behaviors expected from a should be available in c. Taking the well-known "coffee machine" example, if a specification requires that the machine is able to deliver coffee, an implementation delivering either coffee or tea (depending on the people interacting with it) is correct. For others, *e.g.*, in the testing community, an implementation should not expose more behaviors than what was specified.

4.3   Selective Evolution

Up to now, we have supposed that all tasks in the original process were of interest. Still, one could choose to focus on a subset of them, called tasks of interest. This gives freedom to change parts of the processes as soon as the behaviors stay the same for the tasks of interest. For this, we define selective evolution up to a set of tasks T. Tasks that are not in this set will be hidden in the comparison process. Formally, this is achieved with an operation $[T]$ on LTSs, which, given an LTS l, hides any transition whose label is not in T by changing this label to τ (it becomes an *internal* transition). Again, here we can rely on branching equivalence to deal with these internal transitions.

Definition 4 *(Selective Conservative Evolution). Let* b *and* b′ *be two processes, and* T *be a set of tasks,* b --→ b′ *is a selective conservative evolution with reference to* T *iff* $\| \Theta(\mathbf{b}') \| [T] \overset{br}{\equiv} \| \Theta(\mathbf{b}) \| [T]$.

A specific interesting case of selective evolution is when the set of tasks of interest corresponds exactly to the tasks of the original process. This lets the designer add new behaviors not only in a separate way (as with inclusive evolution) but also within the behaviors of the original process. For example, $\mathbf{a}; \mathbf{b} \dashrightarrow \bigoplus(\mathbf{a}, \mathbf{log}); \mathbf{b}$, that is a way to log some information each time $\mathbf{a}$ is done is not an inclusive evolution but is a selective conservative evolution with reference to $\{\mathbf{a}, \mathbf{b}\}$. Accordingly to selective conservative evolution, we can define selective inclusive evolution (respectively selective exclusive evolution) by using the branching preorder, $\overset{br}{<}$, instead of $\overset{br}{\equiv}$.

4.4   Renaming and Refinement

One may also want to take into account renaming when checking an evolution $\mathbf{b} \dashrightarrow \mathbf{b}'$. For this we use a relabelling relation $R \subseteq T_{\mathbf{b}} \times T_{\mathbf{b}'}$, where $T_{\mathbf{b}}$ (respectively $T_{\mathbf{b}'}$) denotes the set of tasks in $\mathbf{b}$ (respectively $\mathbf{b}'$). Applying a relabelling relation R to an LTS l, which is denoted by $l \lhd R$, consists in replacing in l any transition labelled by some t in the domain of R by a transition labelled by $R(t)$.

To take into account task renaming in any of the above-mentioned evolutions, we just have to perform the equivalence (or preorder) checking up to relabelling in the formal model for $\mathbf{b}$. For example, $\mathbf{b} \dashrightarrow \mathbf{b}'$ is a conservative evolution up to a relabelling relation R for $\mathbf{b}$ and $\mathbf{b}'$ iff $\| \Theta(\mathbf{b}) \| \lhd R \overset{br}{\equiv} \| \Theta(\mathbf{b}') \|$.

Sometimes renaming is not sufficient, *e.g.*, when evolution corresponds to the refinement of a task by a workflow. We define a refinement rule as a couple (t, W), noted $t \dashrightarrow W$[1], where t is a task and W a workflow. A set of refinement rules, or refinement set, $\mathcal{R} = \bigcup_{i \in 1...n} t_i \dashrightarrow W_i$ is valid if there are no multiple refinements of the same task ($\forall i, j \in 1...n, i \neq j \Rightarrow t_i \neq t_j$) and if no refinement rule has in its right-hand part a task that has to be refined ($\forall i, j \in 1...n$, $t_i \notin W_j$). These constraints enforce that refinements do not depend on the application ordering of refinement rules, *i.e.*, they are deterministic.

To take into account refinement in evolution, a pre-processing has to be performed on the source process. For example, given that $\mathbf{b} \blacktriangleleft \mathcal{R}$ denotes the replacement in $\mathbf{b}$ of t_i by W_i for each $t_i \dashrightarrow W_i$ in $\mathcal{R}$, $\mathbf{b} \dashrightarrow \mathbf{b}'$ is a conservative evolution up to a refinement set $\mathcal{R}$ iff $\| \Theta(\mathbf{b} \blacktriangleleft \mathcal{R}) \| \overset{br}{\equiv} \| \Theta(\mathbf{b}') \|$.

4.5   Property-Aware Evolution

A desirable feature when checking evolution is to be able to focus on properties of interest and avoid in-depth analysis of the workflows. This gives the freedom to perform changes (including some not possible with the previous evolution relations) as long as the properties of interest are preserved. Typical properties are deadlock freedom or safety and liveness properties defined over the alphabet of process tasks and focusing on the functionalities expected from the process

---

[1] The $\dashrightarrow$ symbol is overloaded since a refinement rule is an evolution at the task level.

under analysis. Such properties are written in a temporal logic supporting actions and, to make the property writing easier, the developer can rely on well-known patterns as those presented in [11].

Definition 5 *(Property-Aware Evolution). Let* $\mathbf{b}$ *and* $\mathbf{b}'$ *be two processes,* T *be a set of tasks, and* ϕ *be a formula defined over* T, $\mathbf{b}$ --→ $\mathbf{b}'$ *is a property-aware evolution with respect to* ϕ *iff* $\| \Theta(\mathbf{b}) \| \models \phi \Rightarrow \| \Theta(\mathbf{b}') \| \models \phi$.

4.6   Context-Aware Evolution

A process is often used in the context of a collaboration, which in BPMN takes the form of a set of processes ("pool lanes") communicating via messages. When evolving a process $\mathbf{b}$, one may safely make changes as soon as they do not have an impact on the overall system made up of $\mathbf{b}$ and these processes. To ensure this, we have to compute the semantics of $\mathbf{b}$ communicating on a set of interactions I (a subset of its tasks) with the other processes that constitute the context of $\mathbf{b}$. We support two communication modes: synchronous or asynchronous. For each mode m we have an operation $\times_I^m$, where $\| \Theta(\mathbf{b}) \| \times_I^m \| \Theta(\mathbf{c}) \|$ denotes the LTS representing the communication on a set of interactions I between $\mathbf{b}$ and $\mathbf{c}$. For synchronous communication, $\times_I^m$ is the LTS synchronous product [2]. For asynchronous communication, $\times_I^m$ is achieved by adding a buffer to each process [3]. Here, to keep things simple, we will suppose without loss of generality, that a context is a single process $\mathbf{c}$.

Definition 6 *(Context-Aware Conservative Evolution). Let* $\mathbf{b}$, $\mathbf{b}'$, *and* $\mathbf{c}$ *be three processes,* $\mathbf{c}$ *being the context for* $\mathbf{b}$ *and* $\mathbf{b}'$, m *be a communication mode* $(m \in \{\text{sync}, \text{async}\})$, *and* I *be the set of interactions taking place between* $\mathbf{b}$ *and* $\mathbf{c}$, $\mathbf{b}$ --→ $\mathbf{b}'$ *is a context-aware conservative evolution with reference to* $\mathbf{c}$, m, *and* I *iff* $\| \Theta(\mathbf{b}) \| \times_I^m \| \Theta(\mathbf{c}) \| \stackrel{br}{\equiv} \| \Theta(\mathbf{b}') \| \times_I^m \| \Theta(\mathbf{c}) \|$.

Accordingly, we may define context-aware inclusive and exclusive evolution, or combine them with renaming and refinement.

Example. We introduce in Fig. 5 a revised version of the bank account opening process presented in Fig. 2. In this new process, if the application is rejected, additional information may be asked to the customer. This is achieved adding a split exclusive gateway and a task "request additional info".

The two versions of the bank account opening process are not conservative because all traces including the task "request additional info" are present only in the new version of the process. However, both versions are related with respect to the inclusive/exclusive evolution notions. The new version includes all possible executions of the former one (the opposite is false) while incorporating new traces (those including "request additional info").

If we make another update to our process by taking the task "receive support documents" out of the parallel gateway (central part of the original process given in Fig. 5). This slight modification is shown in Fig. 6. In this case, both versions

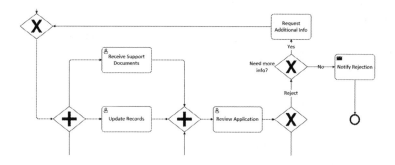

Fig. 5. Bank account opening process in BPMN (V2, partial view)

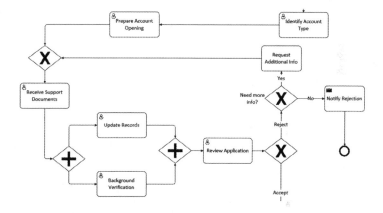

Fig. 6. Bank account opening process in BPMN (V3, partial view)

(V2 and V3) of the process are not conservative, because V3 is more restrictive and V2 exhibits behavior, *e.g.*, the trace "process application", "create profile", "identify account", "prepare opening", and "background verification", which does not appear in V3. However, all behaviors appearing in V3 are included in V2, so both versions are related *wrt.* the inclusive evolution relation.

As far as property-aware evolution is concerned, one can check for instance whether any process execution eventually terminates by a rejection notification or by an account activation. This is formalized in the MCL [23] temporal logic as shown below using box modalities and fix points. This property is actually satisfied for the original process, but not for its two extensions because in those processes a possible behavior is to infinitely request additional information.

[true* . PROCESSAPPLICATION] mu X .
        (⟨ true ⟩ true and [not (NOTIFYREJECTION or ACTIVATEACCOUNT)] X)

5   Tool Support

The goal of this section is to present the implementation of the approach presented beforehand into our VBPMN tool and some experimental results. VBPMN is available online with a set of BPMN samples [1].

5.1   Architecture

VBPMN heavily relies on model transformation as depicted in Fig. 7. The central part is a pivot language called Process Intermediate Format (PIF). We propose this format to make our approach more modular, generic, and easily extensible. PIF gathers common constructs and operators one can find in any workflow-based modeling language. The interest of such an intermediate language is that several front-end modeling languages could be used as input (*e.g.*, UML activity diagrams or YAWL workflows). Further, several analysis techniques and tools could also be connected as a back-end to the PIF format (*e.g.*, to deal with data or timed aspects of processes).

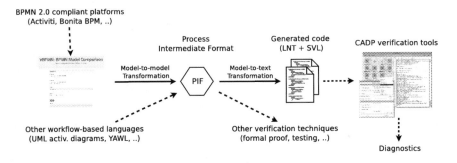

Fig. 7. Overview of VBPMN

As front-end, we integrate with BPMN editors by providing a Web application to which designers may submit the BPMN models they want to compare, together with parameters for the evolution. A model-to-model transformation is used to transform the BPMN processes to compare into PIF models. Then, a model-to-text transformation is used to generate from the PIF models two LNT encodings and a CADP verification script in the SVL language [12]. Equivalences $(\overset{br}{=})$, preorders $(\overset{br}{<})$, and relabelling ($\triangleleft$, used for renaming) are directly supported by SVL commands. Restriction to tasks of interest ($[T]$, used for selective evolution) is achieved by using the SVL command for hiding all labels but for the ones to restrict to. The communication products ($\overset{synch}{\times_I}$ and $\overset{asynch}{\times_I}$) are achieved at the LNT level by using the par operator and (for $\overset{asynch}{\times_I}$) using additional LNT processes encoding buffers. The refinement ($\blacktriangleleft$) and context-aware evolutions are not yet available in the current version of VBPMN. When one of the checks in the SVL scripts fails, one gets a witness (counter-example) that is presented in our Web application so that the designer can use it to modify the erroneous process evolution.

5.2 Experiments

We used a Mac OS laptop running on a 2.3 GHz Intel Core i7 processor with 16 GB of Memory. We carried out experiments on many examples taken from the literature or hand-crafted, and we present in Table 2 some of these results.

Table 2. Experimental results

BPMN Proc.	Size			LTS (states/transitions)		Evol.		
	Tasks	Flows	Gateways	Raw	Minimized	≡	<	>
1	6	11	2⊗	29/29	8/9	×	√	×
1'	7	15	2⊗ + 2⊕	78/118	11/14	15s		
2	4	7	1⊙	70/105	7/9	√	√	√
2'	8	14	2⊗	36/38	10/12	15s		
3	7	14	2⊗ + 2⊕	62/87	10/11	×	×	×
3'	8	16	4⊙	1,786/5,346	28/56	15s		
4	15	29	3⊗ + 2⊕ + 2⊙	469/1,002	24/34	×	√	×
4'	16	33	5⊗ + 2⊕ + 2⊙	479/1,013	26/37	15s		
5	12	24	6⊙	742,234/3,937,158	148/574	×	×	√
5'	12	24	4⊙ + 2⊗	6,394/21,762	60/152	31s		
6	20	43	6⊙ + 6⊕	4,488,843/26,533,828	347/1,450	×	√	×
6'	20	39	8⊙	4,504,775/26,586,197	348/1,481	9m31s		

Each example consists of two versions of the process (original and revised). For each version, we first characterize the size of the workflow by giving the number of tasks, sequence flows, and gateways. We show then the size (states and transitions) of the resulting LTS before and after minimization. Minimization is useful for automatically removing unnecessary internal transitions, which were introduced during the process algebra encoding but do not make sense from an observational point of view. We use branching reduction [30], which is the finest equivalence notion in presence of internal transitions and removes most internal transitions in an efficient way. Finally, the last column gives the results when comparing the LTSs for the two versions of the process using conservative, inclusive, and exclusive evolution, resp., and the overall computation time.

Examples 4 and 4' correspond to the first and second versions of our running example. Medium-size examples (e.g., examples 5 and 6) can result in quite huge LTSs involving millions of states and transitions. This is not always the case and this is due to our choice to show processes in the table containing several parallel and inclusive gateways, which result in many possible interleaved executions in the corresponding LTSs. In our database, we have much larger examples of BPMN processes in terms of tasks and gateways, which result in small LTSs (thousands of states and transitions) due to their sequential behavior. Another comment concerns the considerable drop in size of the LTSs before and after minimization. Example 3' for example goes from about 2,000 states/5,000 transitions to about 30 states/60 transitions. This drastic reduction is due to all sequence flow actions encoded in LNT for respecting the BPMN original semantics. They do not have any special meaning *per se*, and are therefore hidden and removed by reduction.

As far as computation times are concerned, we observe that the final column of Table 2 gives the overall time, that is, the time for generating both LTSs, minimizing and comparing them. The comparison time is negligible. It takes 568 s for instance for generating and minimizing both LTSs for examples 6 and 6', and only 3 s for comparing both LTSs *wrt.* the three evolution notions considered in the table. On a wider scale, computation times remain reasonable (about 10 min) even for LTSs containing millions of states and transitions.

6   Related Work

Several works have focused on providing formal semantics and verification techniques for business processes using Petri nets, process algebras, or abstract state machines, see, *e.g.*, [9, 10, 14, 18, 21, 22, 25, 26, 33, 34]. Those using process algebras for formalizing and verifying BPMN processes are the most related to the approach presented in this paper. The authors of [33] present a formal semantics for BPMN by encoding it into the CSP process algebra. They show in [34] how this semantic model can be used to verify compatibility between business participants in a collaboration. This work was extended in [32] to propose a timed semantics of BPMN with delays. In a previous work [14,25], we have proposed a first transformation from BPMN to LNT, targetted at checking the realizability of a BPMN choreography. We followed a state machine pattern for representing workflows, while we here encode them in a way close to Petri net firing semantics, which favours compositionality and is more natural for a workflow-based language such as BPMN. In [6], the authors propose a new operational semantics of a subset of BPMN focusing on collaboration diagrams and message exchange. The BPMN subset is quite restricted (no support of the inclusive merge gateway for instance) and no tool support is provided yet. Compared to the approaches above, our encoding also gives a semantics to the considered BPMN subset by translation to LNT, although it was not our primary goal. The main difference with respect to these related works is our focus on the evolution of processes and its automated analysis.

In the rest of this section, we present existing approaches for comparing several BPMN processes (or workflows). In [19], the author proposes a theoretical framework for comparing BPMN processes. His main focus is substitutability and therefore he explores various sorts of behavioral equivalences in order to replace equals for equals. This work applies at the BPMN level and aims at detecting equivalent patterns in processes. In a related line of works, [17] studies BPMN behaviors from a semantic point of view. It presents several BPMN patterns and structures that are syntactically different but semantically equivalent. This work is not theoretically grounded and is not complete in the sense that only a few patterns are tackled. The notion of equivalence is similar to the one used in [19]. The authors of [17] also overview best practices that can be used as guidelines by modelers for avoiding syntactic discrepancies in equivalent process models. Compared to our approach, this work only studies strong notions of equivalence where the behavior is preserved in an identical manner. We consider a similar notion here, but we also propose weaker notions because one can make deeper changes (*e.g.*, by introducing new tasks) and in these cases such strong equivalences cannot be preserved.

In Chap. 9 of [27], the authors study the evolution of processes from a migration point of view. They define several notions of evolution, migration, and refactoring. Our goal here is rather complementary since we have studied the impact of modifying a workflow *wrt.* a former version of this workflow on low-level formal models, but we do not propose any solutions for applying these changes on a running instance of that initial workflow. In [31], the authors address the equivalence or alignment of two process models. To do so, they check whether correspondences exist between a set of activities in one model and a set of activities in the other model. They consider Petri net systems as input and process graphs as low-level formalism for analysis purposes. Their approach resides in the identification of regions (set of activities) in each graph that can coincide with respect to an equivalence notion. They particularly study two equivalence notions, namely trace and branching equivalences. The main limit of this approach is that it does not work in the presence of overlapping correspondences, meaning that in some cases, the input models cannot be analyzed. This work shares similarities with our approach, in particular the use of low-level graph models, hiding techniques and behavioral equivalences for comparing models. Still, our approach always provides a result and considers new notions of model correspondence such as property-aware evolution.

7   Concluding Remarks

We have introduced our approach for checking the evolution of BPMN processes. To promote its adoption by business process designers, we have implemented it in a tool, VBPMN, that can be used through a Web application. We have presented different kinds of atomic evolutions that can be combined and formally verified. We have defined a BPMN to LNT model transformation, which, using the LTS operational semantics of LNT enables us to automate our approach using existing LTS verification tools. We have applied our approach to many examples for evaluation purposes. It turns out that our tool is rather efficient since it can handle quite huge examples within a reasonable amount of time.

Diagnoses are returned to the designers under the form of low-level counterexamples (LTSs). This could be enhanced by presenting this information directly on the BPMN models, *e.g.* using animation. In the implementation of our BPMN to LNT transformation, we rely on an intermediate format including the main workflow-based constructs. This paves the way for new front-end DSLs and other back-end verification techniques. Another perspective of this work is to propose quantitative analysis for comparing business processes as studied in [8,29]. Our goal is thus to consider non-functional requirements in BPMN processes, such as the throughput and latency of tasks, which can be modeled by extending LTSs with Markovian information and computed using steady-state analysis [7].

References

1. VBPMN Framework. https://pascalpoizat.github.io/vbpmn/
2. Arnold, A.: Finite Transition Systems - Semantics of Communicating Systems. Prentice Hall International Series in Computer Science. Prentice Hall, Hertfordshire (1994)
3. Brand, D., Zafiropulo, P.: On communicating finite-state machines. J. ACM **30**(2), 323–342 (1983)
4. Champelovier, D., Clerc, X., Garavel, H., Guerte, Y., Lang, F., McKinty, C., Powazny, V., Serwe, W., Smeding, G.: Reference Manual of the LNT to LOTOS Translator, Version 6.1. INRIA/VASY (2014)
5. Christiansen, D.R., Carbone, M., Hildebrandt, T.: Formal semantics and implementation of BPMN 2.0 inclusive gateways. In: Bravetti, M., Bultan, T. (eds.) WS-FM 2010. LNCS, vol. 6551, pp. 146–160. Springer, Heidelberg (2011). doi:10.1007/978-3-642-19589-1_10
6. Corradini, F., Polini, A., Re, B., Tiezzi, F.: An operational semantics of BPMN collaboration. In: Braga, C., Ölveczky, P.C. (eds.) FACS 2015. LNCS, vol. 9539, pp. 161–180. Springer, Cham (2016). doi:10.1007/978-3-319-28934-2_9
7. Coste, N., Garavel, H., Hermanns, H., Lang, F., Mateescu, R., Serwe, W.: Ten years of performance evaluation for concurrent systems using CADP. In: Margaria, T., Steffen, B. (eds.) ISoLA 2010. LNCS, vol. 6416, pp. 128–142. Springer, Heidelberg (2010). doi:10.1007/978-3-642-16561-0_18
8. de Medeiros, A.K.A., van der Aalst, W.M.P., Weijters, A.J.M.M.: Quantifying process equivalence based on observed behavior. Data Knowl. Eng. **64**(1), 55–74 (2008)
9. Decker, G., Weske, M.: Interaction-centric modeling of process choreographies. Inf. Syst. **36**(2), 292–312 (2011)
10. Dijkman, R.M., Dumas, M., Ouyang, C.: Semantics and analysis of business process models in BPMN. Inf. Softw. Technol. **50**(12), 1281–1294 (2008)
11. Dwyer, M.B., Avrunin, G.S., Corbett, J.C.: Patterns in property specifications for finite-state verification. In: Proceedings of ICSE 1999, pp. 411–420. ACM (1999)
12. Garavel, H., Lang, F.: SVL: A scripting language for compositional verification. In: Kim, M., Chin, B., Kang, S., Lee, D. (eds.) FORTE 2001. IIFIP, vol. 69, pp. 377–392. Springer, Boston, MA (2002). doi:10.1007/0-306-47003-9_24
13. Garavel, H., Lang, F., Mateescu, R., Serwe, W.: CADP 2011: A toolbox for the construction and analysis of distributed processes. STTT **2**(15), 89–107 (2013)
14. Güdemann, M., Poizat, P., Salaün, G., Dumont, A.: VerChor: A framework for verifying choreographies. In: Cortellessa, V., Varró, D. (eds.) FASE 2013. LNCS, vol. 7793, pp. 226–230. Springer, Heidelberg (2013). doi:10.1007/978-3-642-37057-1_16
15. ISO. LOTOS – A Formal Description Technique Based on the Temporal Ordering of Observational Behaviour. Technical Report 8807, ISO (1989)

16. ISO/IEC. International Standard 19510, Information technology - Business Process Model and Notation (2013)
17. Kluza, K., Kaczor, K.: Overview of BPMN model equivalences. Towards normalization of BPMN diagrams. In: Proceedings of KESE 2012, pp. 38–45 (2012)
18. Kossak, F., Illibauer, C., Geist, V., Kubovy, J., Natschläger, C., Ziebermayr, T., Kopetzky, T., Freudenthaler, B., Schewe, K.-D.: A Rigorous Semantics for BPMN 2.0 Process Diagrams. Springer, Heidelberg (2014)
19. Lam, V.: Foundation for equivalences of BPMN models. Theoret. Appl. Inform. **24**(1), 33–66 (2012)
20. Larman, C.: Applying UML and Patterns an Introduction to Object-Oriented Analysis and Design and Iterative Development. Prentice Hall, Upper Saddle River (2005)
21. Martens, A.: Analyzing web service based business processes. In: Cerioli, M. (ed.) FASE 2005. LNCS, vol. 3442, pp. 19–33. Springer, Heidelberg (2005). doi:10.1007/978-3-540-31984-9_3
22. Mateescu, R., Salaün, G., Ye, L.: Quantifying the parallelism in BPMN processes using model checking. In: Proceedings of CBSE 2014, pp. 159–168 (2014)
23. Mateescu, R., Thivolle, D.: A model checking language for concurrent value-passing systems. In: Cuellar, J., Maibaum, T., Sere, K. (eds.) FM 2008. LNCS, vol. 5014, pp. 148–164. Springer, Heidelberg (2008). doi:10.1007/978-3-540-68237-0_12
24. OMG. Business Process Model and Notation (BPMN) - Version 2.0., January 2011
25. Poizat, P., Salaün, G.: Checking the realizability of BPMN 2.0 choreographies. In: Proceedings of SAC 2012, pp. 1927–1934 (2012)
26. Raedts, I., Petkovic, M., Usenko, Y.S., van der Werf, J.M., Groote, J.F., Somers, L.: Transformation of BPMN models for behaviour analysis. In: Proceedings of MSVVEIS 2007, pp. 126–137 (2007)
27. Reichert, M., Weber, B.: Enabling Flexibility in Process-Aware Information Systems - Challenges, Methods, Technologies. Springer, Heidelberg (2012)
28. van der Aalst, W.M.P., Ter Hofstede, A.H.M.: YAWL: Yet another workflow language. Inf. Syst. **30**, 245–275 (2003)
29. van Dongen, B., Dijkman, R., Mendling, J.: Measuring similarity between business process models. In: Bellahsène, Z., Léonard, M. (eds.) CAiSE 2008. LNCS, vol. 5074, pp. 450–464. Springer, Heidelberg (2008). doi:10.1007/978-3-540-69534-9_34
30. van Glabbeek, R.J., Weijland, W.P.: Branching time and abstraction in bisimulation semantics. J. ACM **43**(3), 555–600 (1996)
31. Weidlich, M., Dijkman, R.M., Weske, M.: Behaviour equivalence and compatibility of business process models with complex correspondences. Comput. J. **55**(11), 1398–1418 (2012)
32. Wong, P.Y.H., Gibbons, J.: A relative timed semantics for BPMN. Electr. Notes Theor. Comput. Sci. **229**(2), 59–75 (2009)
33. Wong, P.Y.H., Gibbons, J.: A process semantics for BPMN. In: Proceedings of ICFEM 2008, pp. 355–374 (2008)
34. Wong, P.Y.H., Gibbons, J.: Verifying business process compatibility. In: Proceedings of QSIC 2008, pp. 126–131 (2008)

Compositionality, Decompositionality and Refinement in Input/Output Conformance Testing

Lars Luthmann[1]([⊠]), Stephan Mennicke[2], and Malte Lochau[1]

[1] Real-Time Systems Lab, TU Darmstadt, Darmstadt, Germany
lars.luthmann@es.tu-darmstadt.de
[2] Institute for Programming and Reactive Systems,
TU Braunschweig, Braunschweig, Germany

Abstract. We propose an input/output conformance testing theory utilizing Modal Interface Automata with Input Refusals (IR-MIA) as novel behavioral formalism for both the specification and the implementation under test. A modal refinement relation on IR-MIA allows distinguishing between obligatory and allowed output behaviors, as well as between implicitly underspecified and explicitly forbidden input behaviors. The theory therefore supports positive and negative conformance testing with optimistic and pessimistic environmental assumptions. We further show that the resulting conformance relation on IR-MIA, called modal-irioco, enjoys many desirable properties concerning component-based behaviors. First, modal-irioco is preserved under modal refinement and constitutes a preorder under certain restrictions which can be ensured by a canonical input completion for IR-MIA. Second, under the same restrictions, modal-irioco is compositional with respect to parallel composition of IR-MIA with multi-cast and hiding. Finally, the quotient operator on IR-MIA, as the inverse to parallel composition, facilitates decompositionality in conformance testing to solve the unknown-component problem.

Keywords: Model-based testing · Modal transition systems · Input/output conformance · Composition and decomposition in testing

1 Introduction

Formal approaches to model-based testing of component-based systems define notions of *behavioral conformance* between a *specification* and a (black-box) *implementation (under test)*, both usually given as (variations of) labeled transition systems (LTS). Existing notions of behavioral conformance may be categorized into two research directions. *Extensional* approaches define *observational*

L. Luthmann and M. Lochau—This work has been supported by the German Research Foundation (DFG) in the Priority Programme SPP 1593: Design For Future – Managed Software Evolution (LO 2198/2-1).
S. Mennicke—This work has been supported by the German Research Foundation (DFG), grant GO-671/6-2.

© Springer International Publishing AG 2017
O. Kouchnarenko and R. Khosravi (Eds.): FACS 2016, LNCS 10231, pp. 54–72, 2017.
DOI: 10.1007/978-3-319-57666-4_5

equivalences, requiring that no observer process (tester) is ever able to distinguish behaviors shown by the implementation from those allowed by the specification [9]. In contrast, *intensional* approaches rely on I/O labeled transition systems (IOLTS) from which *test cases* are derived as sequences of controllable input and observable output actions, to establish an *alternating simulation relation* on IOLTS [1,11,27]. One of the most prominent conformance testing theories, initially introduced by Tretmans in [24], combines both views on formal conformance testing into an input/output conformance (**ioco**) relation on IOLTS. Although many formal properties of, and extensions to, **ioco** have been intensively investigated, **ioco** still suffers several essential weaknesses.

- **ioco** permits *underspecification* by means of (1) unspecified input behaviors and (2) non-deterministic input/output behaviors. But, concerning (1), **ioco** is limited to *positive* testing (i.e., unspecified inputs may be implemented arbitrarily) thus implicitly relying on optimistic environmental assumptions. Also supporting *negative* testing in a pessimistic setting, however, would require a distinction between *critical* and *uncritical* unintended input behaviors. Concerning (2), **ioco** requires the implementation to exhibit *at most* output behaviors permitted by the specification. In addition, the notion of *quiescence* (i.e., observable absence of any outputs) enforces implementations to show *at least one* specified output behavior (if any). Apart from that, no explicit distinction between *obligatory* and *allowed* output behaviors is expressible in IOLTS.
- **ioco** imposes a special kind of *alternating simulation* between specification and implementation which is, in general, not a preorder, although being a crucial property for testing relations on LTS [10].
- **ioco** lacks a unified theory for input/output conformance testing in the face of component-based behaviors being compatible with potential solutions for the aforementioned weaknesses.

As all these weaknesses mainly stem from the limited expressiveness of IOLTS as behavioral formalism, we propose *Modal Interface Automata with Input Refusals (IR-MIA)* as a new model for input/output conformance testing for both the specification and the implementation under test. IR-MIA adopt Modal Interface Automata (MIA) [5], which combine concepts of Interface Automata [8] (i.e., I/O automata permitting underspecified input behaviors) and (I/O-labeled) Modal Transitions Systems [2,13,22] (i.e., LTS with distinct mandatory and optional transition relations). In particular, we exploit enhanced versions of MIA supporting both optimistic and pessimistic environmental assumptions [16] and non-deterministic input/output behaviors [5]. For the latter, we have to re-interpret the universal state of MIA, simulating every possible behavior, as *failure state* to serve as target for those unintended, yet critical input behaviors to be *refused*, i.e., non-blocking which means that the input event is received but its processing is refused by the implementation [21]. Modal refinement of IR-MIA therefore allows distinguishing between obligatory and allowed output behaviors, as well as between implicitly underspecified and explicitly forbidden input behaviors.

The resulting testing theory on IR-MIA unifies positive and negative conformance testing with optimistic and pessimistic environmental assumptions.

We further prove that the corresponding modal I/O conformance relation on IR-MIA, called **modal-irioco**, exhibits essential properties, especially with respect to component-based systems testing.

- **modal-irioco** is preserved under modal refinement and constitutes a pre-order under certain restrictions which can be obtained by a canonical input completion [23].
- **modal-irioco** is compositional with respect to parallel composition of IR-MIA with multi-cast and hiding [5].
- **modal-irioco** allows for decomposition of conformance testing, thus support-ing environmental synthesis for component-based testing in contexts [7,20], also known as the *unknown-component problem* [28]. To this end, we adapt the MIA quotient operator to IR-MIA, serving as the inverse to parallel com-position.

The remainder of this paper is organized as follows. In Sect. 2, we revisit the foundations of **ioco** testing. In Sect. 3, we introduce IR-MIA and modal refine-ment on IR-MIA and, thereupon, define **modal-irioco**, provide a correctness proof and discuss necessary restrictions to obtain a preorder. Our main results concerning compositionality and decompositionality of **modal-irioco** are pre-sented in Sects. 4 and 5, respectively. In Sect. 6, we discuss related work and in Sect. 7, we conclude the paper. Please note that all proofs and more detailed examples may be found in the accompanying technical report [18].

2   Preliminaries

The **ioco** testing theory relies on I/O-labeled transition systems (IOLTS) as behavioral formalism [24]. An IOLTS $(Q, I, O, \longrightarrow)$ specifies the *externally visible* behaviors of a system or component by means of a transition relation $\longrightarrow \subseteq Q \times (I \cup O \cup \{\tau\}) \times Q$ on a set of states Q. The set of transition labels $A = I \cup O$ consists of two disjoint subsets: set I of externally controllable/internally observable *input* actions, and set O of internally controllable/externally observable *output* actions. In figures, we use prefix *?* to mark input actions and prefix *!* for output actions, respectively. In addition, transitions labeled with *internal* actions $\tau \notin (I \cup O)$ denote silent moves, neither being externally controllable, nor observable. We write $A^\tau = A \cup \{\tau\}$, and by $q \xrightarrow{\alpha} q'$ we denote that $(q, \alpha, q') \in \longrightarrow$ holds, where $\alpha \in A^\tau$, and we write $q \xrightarrow{\alpha}$ as a short hand for $\exists q' \in Q : q \xrightarrow{\alpha} q'$ and $q \not\xrightarrow{\alpha}$, else. Furthermore, we write $q \xrightarrow{\alpha_1 \cdots \alpha_n} q'$ to express that $\exists q_0, \ldots, q_n \in Q : q = q_0 \xrightarrow{\alpha_1} q_1 \xrightarrow{\alpha_2} \cdots \xrightarrow{\alpha_n} q_n = q'$ holds, and write $q \xrightarrow{\epsilon} q'$ whenever $q = q'$ or $q \xrightarrow{\tau \cdots \tau} q'$. Additionally, by $q \xrightarrow{\alpha} q'$, we denote that $\exists q_1, q_2 : q \xrightarrow{\epsilon} q_1 \xrightarrow{\alpha} q_2 \xrightarrow{\epsilon} q'$. We further use the notations $q \xrightarrow{a_1 \cdots a_n} q'$ and $q \xrightarrow{a} (a, a_1, \ldots, a_n \in A^*)$ analogously to $q \xrightarrow{\alpha_1 \cdots \alpha_n} q'$ and $q \xrightarrow{\alpha}$. Finally, by $q_0 \xrightarrow{a_1} q_1 \xrightarrow{a_2} \cdots \xrightarrow{a_n} q_n$ we denote a *path*, where $\sigma = a_1 a_2 \ldots a_n \in A^*$ is called a *trace* (note: τ equals ϵ). We pick from an IOLTS a state and use it to identify the behavior associated with it (i.e., $q \in Q$ describes one behavior of $(Q, I, O, \longrightarrow)$). We only consider *strongly convergent* IOLTS (i.e., no infinite τ-sequences exist).

In the **ioco** testing theory, both specification s as well as a (black-box) implementation under test i are assumed to be (explicitly or implicitly) given as IOLTS. In particular, **ioco** does not necessarily require specification s to be *input-enabled*, whereas implementation i is assumed to never reject any input $a \in I$ from the environment (or tester). More precisely, **ioco** requires implementations to be *weak input-enabled* (i.e., $\forall q \in Q : \forall a \in I : q \overset{a}{\Longrightarrow}$) thus yielding the subclass of *I/O transition systems* (IOTS). Intuitively, the IOTS of implementation i *I/O-conforms* to the IOLTS of specification s if all output behaviors of i observed after any possible sequence $\sigma = \alpha_1 \cdots \alpha_n$ in s are permitted by s. In case of non-determinism, more than one state may be reachable in i as well as in s after sequence σ and therefore all possible outputs of any state in the set

$$p \textbf{ after } \sigma := \{q \in Q \mid p \overset{\sigma}{\Longrightarrow} q\}$$

have to be taken into account. Formally, set $Out(Q') \subseteq O$ denotes all output actions being enabled in any possible state $q \in Q' = p \textbf{ after } \sigma$. To further reject trivial implementations never showing any outputs, the notion of *quiescence* has been introduced by means of a special observable action δ explicitly denoting the permission of the *absence* (suspension) of any output in a state p, thus requiring an input to proceed. In particular, p is *quiescent*, denoted $\delta(p)$, iff

$$init(p) := \{\alpha \in (I \cup O \cup \{\tau\}) \mid p \overset{\alpha}{\Longrightarrow}\} \subseteq I$$

holds. Thereupon, we denote

$$Out(P) := \{\alpha \in O \mid \exists p \in P : p \overset{\alpha}{\longrightarrow}\} \cup \{\delta \mid \exists p \in P : \delta(p)\},$$

where symbol δ is used both as action as well as a state predicate. Based on these notions, I/O conformance is defined w. r. t. the set of *suspension traces*

$$Straces(s) := \{\sigma \in (I \cup O \cup \{\delta\})^* \mid p \overset{\sigma}{\Longrightarrow}\}$$

of specification s, where $q \overset{\delta}{\longrightarrow} q$ iff $\delta(q)$.

Definition 1 (ioco [24]). *Let s be an IOLTS and i an IOTS with identical sets I and O.*

$$i \textbf{ ioco } s :\Leftrightarrow \forall \sigma \in Straces(s) : Out(i \textbf{ after } \sigma) \subseteq Out(s \textbf{ after } \sigma).$$

3   Modal Input/Output Conformance with Input Refusals

IOLTS permit specifications s to be *underspecified* by means of *unspecified* input behaviors and *non-deterministic* input/output behaviors. In particular, if $q \overset{a}{\nrightarrow}$, then no proper reaction on occurrences of input $a \in I$ is specified while residing in state q. Moreover, if $q \overset{a}{\longrightarrow} q'$ and $q \overset{a}{\longrightarrow} q''$, $a \in A^\tau$, it does not necessarily follow that $q' = q''$ and if $q \overset{a'}{\longrightarrow} q'$ and $q \overset{a''}{\longrightarrow} q''$ with $a', a'' \in O$, it does not necessarily follow that $a' = a''$ (i.e., IOLTS are neither input-, nor output-deterministic). In this way, **ioco** permits, at least up to a certain degree, implementation freedom in two ways. First, in case of input behaviors being unspecified in s, **ioco** solely relies on *positive* testing principles, i.e., reactions to unspecified input behaviors are never tested and may therefore show *arbitrary* output behaviors if ever applied to i. Second, in case of non-deterministic specifications, implementation i is allowed to show *any, but at least one* of those output behaviors being permitted by s (if any), or it must be quiescent, else. These limitations of **ioco** in handling underspecified behaviors essentially stem from the limited expressive power of IOLTS. To overcome these limitations, we propose to adopt richer specification concepts from interfaces theories [22] to serve as novel formal foundation for I/O conformance testing. In particular, we replace IOLTS by a modified version of (I/O-labeled) Modal Interface Automata (MIA) with universal state [5]. Similar to IOLTS, MIA also support both kinds of underspecification but allow for explicit distinctions (1) between obligatory and allowed behaviors in case of non-deterministic input/output behaviors, and (2) between critical and non-critical unspecified input behaviors.

Concerning (1), MIA separate mandatory from optional behaviors in terms of may/must transition modality. For every *must*-transition $q \xrightarrow{a}_\Box q'$, a corresponding *may*-transition $q \xrightarrow{a}_\Diamond q'$ exists, as mandatory behaviors must also be allowed (so-called syntactic consistency). Conversely, may-transitions $q \xrightarrow{a}_\Diamond q'$ for which $q \not\xrightarrow{a}_\Box q'$ holds constitute optional behaviors. Accordingly, we call may-transitions without corresponding must-transitions *optional*, else *mandatory*.

Concerning (2), MIA make explicit input actions $a \in I$ being unspecified, yet uncritical in a certain state q by introducing may-transitions $q \xrightarrow{a}_\Diamond u$ leading to a special *universal state* u (permitting any possible behavior following that input). In contrast, unintended input actions to be rejected in a certain state are implicitly forbidden if $q \not\xrightarrow{a}_\Diamond$ holds. We alter the interpretation of unspecified input behaviors of MIA by introducing a distinct *failure state* q_Φ replacing u. As a consequence, an unspecified input $a \in I$ being uncritical if residing in a certain state q is (similar to IOLTS) implicitly denoted as $q \not\xrightarrow{a}_\Diamond$, whereas inputs $a' \in I$ being critical while residing in state q are explicitly forbidden by $q \xrightarrow{a'}_\Box q_\Phi$. We therefore enrich I/O conformance testing by the notion of *input refusals* in the spirit of refusal testing, initially proposed by Phillips for testing preorders on LTS with undirected actions [21]. Analogous to quiescence, denoting the *observable absence of any output* in a certain state, refusals therefore denote the *observable rejection of a particular input* in a certain state during testing. In this way, we unify positive testing (i.e., unspecified behaviors are ignored) and negative testing (i.e., unspecified behaviors must be rejected) with optimistic and pessimistic environmental assumptions known from interface theories [22]. In particular, we are now able to explicitly reject certain input behavior, which is not supported by **ioco**. We refer to the resulting model as *Modal Interface Automata with Input Refusals (IR-MIA)*.

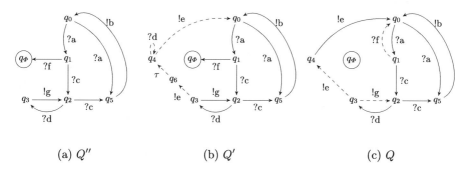

(a) Q'' (b) Q' (c) Q

Fig. 1. Sample IR-MIA

Definition 2 (IR-MIA). *A Modal Interface Automaton with Input-Refusal (IR-MIA or MIA_Φ) is a tuple $(Q, I_Q, O_Q, \longrightarrow_\Box, \longrightarrow_\Diamond, q_\Phi)$, where Q is a finite set of states with failure state $q_\Phi \in Q$, $A_Q = I_Q \cup O_Q$ is a finite set of actions with $\tau \notin A_Q$ and $I_Q \cap O_Q = \emptyset$ and for all $\gamma \in \{\Diamond, \Box\}$, $a \in A_Q \cup \{\tau\}, i \in I_Q$,*

1. $\longrightarrow_\gamma \subseteq ((Q \setminus \{q_\Phi\}) \times I_Q \times Q) \cup ((Q \setminus \{q_\Phi\}) \times (O_Q \cup \{\tau\}) \times (Q \setminus \{q_\Phi\}))$,
2. $q \xrightarrow{a}_\Box q' \Rightarrow q \xrightarrow{a}_\Diamond q'$,
3. $q \xrightarrow{i}_\Diamond q_\Phi \Leftrightarrow q \xrightarrow{i}_\Box q_\Phi$, *and*
4. $q \xrightarrow{i}_\Box q_\Phi \Rightarrow \left(\forall q'.q \xrightarrow{i}_\Diamond q' \Rightarrow q' = q_\Phi \right)$.

Property 3 ensures syntactic consistency and properties 1 and 2 together with property 4 ensure that the failure state q_Φ only occurs as target of must-transitions being labeled with input actions. Property 5 further requires consistency of refusals of specified input actions in every state (i.e., each input is either forbidden or not, but not both in a state q).

Figure 1b shows a sample IR-MIA. Dashed lines denote optional behaviors and solid lines denote mandatory behaviors. Additionally, the distinct state q_Φ depicts the failure state (i.e., input f is refused by state q_1). This example also exhibits input non-determinism (state q_0 defines two possible reactions to input a), as well as output non-determinism (state q_3 defines two possible outputs after input d).

Modal refinement provides a semantic implementation relation on MIA [5], an adapted version of modal refinement due to Larsen and Thomsen [14]. Intuitively, MIA P refines MIA Q if mandatory behaviors of Q are preserved in P and optional behaviors in P are permitted by Q. Adapted to IR-MIA, input behaviors being unspecified in Q, may be either implemented arbitrarily in P, or become forbidden after refinement. In particular, if $q \not\xrightarrow{a}_\Diamond$ holds in Q, then either $q \not\xrightarrow{a}_\Diamond$, $q \xrightarrow{a}_\Diamond q'$ (and even $q \xrightarrow{a}_\Box q'$), or $q \xrightarrow{a}_\Box q_\Phi$ holds in P, respectively.

Definition 3 (IR-MIA Refinement). *Let P, Q be MIA_Φ with $I_P = I_Q$ and $O_P = O_Q$. A relation $\mathcal{R} \subseteq P \times Q$ is an IR-MIA Refinement Relation if for all $(p, q) \in \mathcal{R}$ and $\omega \in (O \cup \{\tau\})$, with $p \neq p_\Phi$ and $\gamma \in \{\Diamond, \Box\}$, it holds that*

1. $q \neq q_{\Phi}$,
2. $q \xrightarrow{i}_{\square} q' \neq q_{\Phi}$ implies $\exists p'.p \xrightarrow{i}_{\square} \overset{\epsilon}{\Longrightarrow}_{\square} p' \neq p_{\Phi}$ and $(p',q') \in \mathcal{R}$,
3. $q \xrightarrow{\omega}_{\square} q'$ implies $\exists p'.p \overset{\hat{\omega}}{\Longrightarrow}_{\square} p'$ and $(p',q') \in \mathcal{R}$,
4. $p \xrightarrow{i}_{\lozenge} p' \wedge q \xrightarrow{i}_{\lozenge}$ implies $\exists q'.q \xrightarrow{i}_{\lozenge} \overset{\epsilon}{\Longrightarrow}_{\lozenge} q'$ and $(p',q') \in \mathcal{R}$,
5. $q \xrightarrow{i}_{\lozenge} q'$ implies $\exists p'.p \xrightarrow{i}_{\lozenge} \overset{\epsilon}{\Longrightarrow}_{\lozenge} p'$ and $(p',q') \in \mathcal{R}$, and
6. $p \xrightarrow{\omega}_{\lozenge} p'$ implies $\exists q'.q \overset{\hat{\omega}}{\Longrightarrow}_{\lozenge} q'$ and $(p',q') \in \mathcal{R}$.

State p refines state q if there exists $\mathcal{R}$ such that $(p,q) \in \mathcal{R}$. (Note: $q \overset{\hat{\omega}}{\Longrightarrow}_{\gamma} q'$ equals $q \overset{\epsilon}{\Longrightarrow}_{\gamma} \xrightarrow{\omega}_{\gamma} \overset{\epsilon}{\Longrightarrow}_{\gamma} q'$).

Clause 1 ensures that the failure state q_{Φ} can only be refined by p_{Φ}, since both suspend any subsequent behavior. Clauses 2 and 3 guarantee that mandatory behavior of Q is preserved by P. All other clauses handle optional behavior, where inputs are either refined to forbidden or mandatory inputs, and outputs are either refined to mandatory or unspecified outputs. By $P \sqsubseteq_{\Phi} Q$, we denote the existence of an IR-MIA refinement relation between P and Q.

As an example, consider IR-MIA Q and Q' in Fig. 1. $Q' \sqsubseteq_{\Phi} Q$ does not hold as the mandatory output e of q_4 in Q is not mandatory anymore in Q'. However, the other modifications in Q' are valid refinements of Q as output g of q_3 has become mandatory, and optional input f of q_1 is now refused (i.e., the transition is redirected to q_{Φ}). Additionally, inputs being unspecified in Q may be added to Q' (e.g., q_4 of Q' now accepts input d). Furthermore, internal steps may be added after inputs as well as before and after outputs under refinement (e.g., Q' has a τ step after output e in q_3). The former ensures that a refined IR-MIA may be controlled by the environment in the same way as the unrefined IR-MIA. Considering IR-MIA Q'' in Fig. 1 instead, $Q'' \sqsubseteq_{\Phi} Q$ holds. The removal of mandatory output e from q_4 is valid as q_4 is not reachable anymore after refinement.

In the context of modal I/O conformance testing, modal refinement offers a controlled way to resolve underspecification within specifications s. In addition, we also assume i to be represented as IR-MIA in order to support (partially) underspecified implementations under test as apparent in earlier phases of continuous systems and component development.

We next define an adapted version of **ioco** to operate on IR-MIA. Intuitively, a modal implementation i *I/O-conforms* to a modal specification s if all observable mandatory behaviors of s are also observable as mandatory behaviors of i and none of the observable optional behaviors of i exceed the observable optional behaviors of s. If established between implementation i and specification s, modal I/O conformance ensures for all implementations $i' \sqsubseteq_{\Phi} i$, derivable from i via modal refinement, the existence of an accompanying specification refinement $s' \sqsubseteq_{\Phi} s$ of s such that i' is I/O conforming to s'.

Similar to δ denoting observable quiescence, we introduce a state predicate φ to denote *may-failure/must-failure* states (i.e., states having may/must input-transitions leading to q_{Φ}). We therefore use φ as a special symbol to observe refusals of particular inputs in certain states of the implementation during testing. To this end, we first lift the auxiliary notations of **ioco** from IOLTS to IR-MIA, where we write $\gamma \in \{\Diamond, \Box\}$ for short in the following.

Definition 4. *Let Q be a MIA_Φ over I and O, $p \in Q$ and $\sigma \in (I \cup O \cup \{\delta, \varphi\})^*$.*

- $init_\gamma(p) := \{\mu \in (I \cup O) \mid p \xrightarrow{\mu}_\gamma\} \cup \{\varphi \mid p = p_\Phi\}$,
- *p is* may-quiescent, *denoted by $\delta_\Diamond(p)$, iff $init_\Box(p) \subseteq I$ and $p \neq p_\Phi$,*
- *p is* must-quiescent, *denoted by $\delta_\Box(p)$, iff $init_\Diamond(p) \subseteq I$ and $p \neq p_\Phi$,*
- *p is* may-failure, *denoted by $\varphi_\Diamond(p)$, iff $p = p_\Phi$ or $\exists p' \in Q : (p'' \xrightarrow{i}_\Diamond p \wedge p'' \xrightarrow{i}_\Box p)$,*
- *p is* must-failure, *denoted by $\varphi_\Box(p)$, iff $p = p_\Phi$,*
- $p \text{ \textbf{after}}_\gamma \sigma := \{p' \mid p \xRightarrow{\sigma}_\gamma p'\}$,
- $Out_\gamma(p) := \{\mu \in O \mid p \xrightarrow{\mu}_\gamma\} \cup \{\delta \mid \delta_\gamma(p)\} \cup \{\varphi \mid \varphi_\gamma(p)\}$, *and*
- $Straces_\gamma(p) := \{\sigma \in (I \cup O \cup \{\delta, \varphi\})^* \mid p \xRightarrow{\sigma}_\gamma\}$, *where $p \xrightarrow{\delta}_\gamma p$ if $\delta_\gamma(p)$, and $p \xrightarrow{\varphi}_\gamma p$ if $\varphi_\gamma(p)$.*

Hence, quiescence as well as failure behaviors may occur with both may- and must-modality. Intuitively, a state is may-quiescent if all enabled output transitions are optional, i.e., such a state *may* become quiescent under refinement. Likewise, a state p is a may-failure if there is an optional input leading to p, since this optional input may be refused under refinement.

According to **ioco**, MIA_Φ i constituting a modal implementation under test is assumed to be input-enabled. In particular, *modal input-enabledness* of IR-MIA comes in four flavors by combining weak/strong input-enabledness with may-/must-modality. Note, that $q \xrightarrow{i}_\gamma q'$ implies $q \xRightarrow{i}_\gamma q'$, $q \xRightarrow{i}_\Box q'$ implies $q \xRightarrow{i}_\Diamond q'$, and $q \xrightarrow{i}_\Box q'$ implies $q \xrightarrow{i}_\Diamond q'$.

Definition 5 (Input-Enabled IR-MIA). *MIA_Φ Q is* weak/strong *γ-input-enabled, respectively, iff for each $q \in Q \setminus \{q_\Phi\}$ it holds that $\forall i \in I : \exists q' \in Q : q \xRightarrow{i}_\gamma q'$, or $\forall i \in I : \exists q' \in Q : q \xrightarrow{i}_\gamma q'$.*

May-input-enabledness is preserved under modal refinement as optional input behaviors either remain optional, become mandatory, or are redirected to the failure state (and finally become must-input-enabled under complete refinement).

Lemma 1. *If MIA_Φ i is strong may-input-enabled then $i' \sqsubseteq_\Phi i$ is strong may-input-enabled.*

We now define a modal version of **ioco** on IR-MIA (called **modal-irioco** or **mioco$_\Phi$**), by means of alternating suspension-trace inclusion.

Definition 6 (modal-irioco). *Let s and i be MIA_Φ over I and O with i being weak may-input-enabled. i **mioco$_\Phi$** $s :\Leftrightarrow$*

1. *$\forall \sigma \in Straces_\Diamond(s) : Out_\Diamond(i \text{ \textbf{after}}_\Diamond \sigma) \subseteq Out_\Diamond(s \text{ \textbf{after}}_\Diamond \sigma)$, and*
2. *$\forall \sigma \in Straces_\Diamond(i) : Out_\Box(s \text{ \textbf{after}}_\Diamond \sigma) \subseteq Out_\Box(i \text{ \textbf{after}}_\Diamond \sigma)$.*

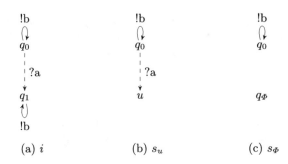

Fig. 2. Problem of modal-irioco regarding MIA with universal state.

We illustrate the intuition of **modal-irioco** by providing a concrete example. Let IR-MIA in Fig. 1b constitute implementation i and IR-MIA in Fig. 1c constitute specification s. Similar to **ioco**, Property 1 of **modal-irioco** requires all possible output behaviors of i to be permitted by s which is satisfied in this example. Property 2 of **modal-irioco** requires all mandatory outputs of s to be actually implemented as mandatory outputs in i. This property does not hold in the example as mandatory output e of q_4 in s is not mandatory in i. As a consequence, i **mioco$_\Phi$** s does not hold. The example in Fig. 1 also explains why we consider $Straces_\Diamond$ and **after$_\Diamond$** in property 2 (unlike **modal-ioco** in [15]). Otherwise, output e of q_4 in i would not be considered as mandatory output behavior because q_4 is not reachable via must-transitions. In contrast, when considering the IR-MIA in Fig. 1a as i and the IR-MIA in Fig. 1c as s, we have i **mioco$_\Phi$** s as the mandatory output e of q_4 in s is not reachable in i.

Finally, Fig. 2a, b and c illustrate the necessity for re-interpreting universal state u of MIA [5] as failure state q_Φ in IR-MIA. The IR-MIA in Fig. 2a serves as implementation i, the MIA in Fig. 2b serves as specification s_u with universal state, and the IR-MIA in Fig. 2c depicts the same specification with failure state s_Φ instead of u. Hence, i would be (erroneously) considered to be non-conforming to s_u as state u does not specify any outputs (i.e., u is quiescent). In contrast, we have i **mioco$_\Phi$** s_Φ as the reaction of i to input a is never tested, because this input is unspecified in s_Φ.

An I/O conformance testing theory is *correct* if it is *sound* (i.e., every implementation i conforming to specification s does indeed only show specified behaviors), and *complete* (i.e., every erroneous implementation i is rejected) [24]. For lifting these notions to IR-MIA, we relate **modal-irioco** to **ioco**. This way, we show compatibility of **modal-irioco** and the original **ioco** as follows.

- **modal-irioco** is *sound* if i **mioco$_\Phi$** s implies that every refinement of i conforms to a refinement of s with respect to **ioco**.
- **modal-irioco** is *complete* if the correctness of all refinements of i regarding s with respect to **ioco** implies i **mioco$_\Phi$** s, and if at least one refinement of i is non-conforming to any refinement of s, then i **mioco$_\Phi$** s does not hold.

We first have to show that **modal-irioco** is preserved under modal refinement. Although, intuitions behind both relations are quite similar, they are incomparable (cf. [18] for counter-examples). Instead, we obtain a weaker correspondence.

Theorem 1. *Let i, s be MIA_Φ, i being weak may-input-enabled and i **mioco$_\Phi$** s. Then for each $i' \sqsubseteq_\Phi i$ there exists $s' \sqsubseteq_\Phi s$ such that i' **mioco$_\Phi$** s' holds.*

Note, that we refer to the **ioco**-relation in our **modal-irioco** in Clause 1 in Definition 6. Hence, in order to relate **modal-irioco** and **ioco**, we define applications of **ioco** to IR-MIA by considering the may-transition relation as the actual transition relation.

Definition 7 (ioco on MIA_Φ). *Let i, s be MIA_Φ, i be weak may-input-enabled. Then, i **ioco** $s :\Leftrightarrow \forall \sigma \in Straces_\Diamond(s) : Out_\Diamond(i \, \mathbf{after}_\Diamond \, \sigma) \subseteq Out_\Diamond(s \, \mathbf{after}_\Diamond \, \sigma)$.*

Based on this definition, we are able to prove correctness of **modal-irioco**.

Theorem 2 (modal-irioco is correct). *Let i, s be MIA_Φ, i being weak may-input-enabled.*

1. *If i **mioco$_\Phi$** s, then for all $i' \sqsubseteq_\Phi i$, there exists $s' \sqsubseteq_\Phi s$ such that i' **ioco** s'.*
2. *If there exists $i' \sqsubseteq_\Phi i$ such that i' **ioco** s' does not hold for any $s' \sqsubseteq_\Phi s$, then i **mioco$_\Phi$** s does not hold.*

Property 1 states soundness of **modal-irioco**. However, the immediate inverse does not hold as **ioco** does not guarantee mandatory behaviors of s to be actually implemented by i (cf. [18] for a counter-example). Instead, Property 2 states completeness of **modal-irioco** in the sense that modal implementations i are rejected if at least one refinement of i exists not conforming to any refinement of specification s. Finally, we conclude that **mioco$_\Phi$** becomes a preorder if being restricted to input-enabled IR-MIA specifications.

Theorem 3. **mioco$_\Phi$** *is a preorder on the set of weak may-input-enabled MIA_Φ.*

Must-input-enabledness (and therefore may-input-enabledness) of a specification s may be achieved for any given IR-MIA by applying a behavior-preserving canonical *input completion*, while still allowing arbitrary refinements of previously unspecified inputs (instead of ignoring inputs as, e.g., achieved by *angelic completion* [25]). This construction essentially adapts the notion of *demonic completion* [10] from IOLTS to IR-MIA as follows.

Definition 8 (Demonic Completion of IR-MIA). *The* demonic completion *of MIA_Φ $(Q, I, O, \longrightarrow_\Box, \longrightarrow_\Diamond, q_\Phi)$ with $\forall q \in Q : q \xrightarrow{\tau}_\Diamond \Rightarrow q \xrightarrow{\tau}_\Box$ is a MIA_Φ $(Q', I, O, \longrightarrow'_\Box, \longrightarrow'_\Diamond, q_\Phi)$, where*

- $Q' = Q \cup \{q_\chi, q_\Omega\}$ *with* $q_\chi, q_\Omega \notin Q$, *and*
- $\longrightarrow'_\Box = \longrightarrow_\Box \cup \{(q, i, q_\chi) \mid q \in Q, i \in I, q \not\xrightarrow{i}_\Box, q \not\xrightarrow{\tau}_\Box\} \cup \{(q_\chi, \tau, q_\Omega)\} \cup \{(q_\chi, \lambda, q_\chi), (q_\Omega, \lambda, q_\Omega) \mid \lambda \in I\}$.

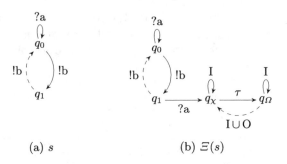

Fig. 3. Demonic completion adapted for MIA$_\Phi$ and **mioco**$_\Phi$.

$$- \longrightarrow'_\Diamond = \longrightarrow_\Diamond \cup \{(q, i, q_\chi) \mid q \in Q, i \in I, q \not\xrightarrow{i}_\Box, q \not\xrightarrow{i}_\Box\} \cup \{(q_\chi, \tau, q_\Omega)\} \cup$$
$$\{(q_\Omega, \lambda, q_\chi) \mid \lambda \in (I \cup O)\} \cup \{(q_\chi, \lambda, q_\chi), (q_\Omega, \lambda, q_\Omega) \mid \lambda \in I\}.$$

The restriction imposed by $\forall q \in Q : q \xrightarrow{\tau}_\Diamond \Rightarrow q \xrightarrow{\tau}_\Box$ is due to weak input-enabled states not being input-enabled anymore if an optional τ-transition is removed. We refer to the demonic completion of MIA$_\Phi$ s as $\Xi(s)$.

Figure 3 illustrates demonic completion. As state q_1 of s is not must-input-enabled, a must-transition for action a is added from q_1 to q_χ. The fresh states q_χ and q_Ω have outgoing must-transitions for each $i \in I$, thus being (strong) must-input-enabled. Additionally, q_χ in combination with q_Ω allow (but do not require) every output $o \in O$ (in q_χ via one silent move), such that demonic completion preserves underspecification. We conclude that this construction preserves **modal-irioco**.

Theorem 4. *Let i, s be MIA$_\Phi$ with i being weak must-input-enabled. Then i **mioco**$_\Phi$ $\Xi(s)$ if i **mioco**$_\Phi$ s.*

4   Compositionality

Interface theories are equipped with a (binary) *interleaving parallel operator* $\|$ on interface specifications to define interaction behaviors in systems composed of multiple concurrently running components [8]. Intuitively, transition $p \xrightarrow{a} p'$, $a \in O_P$, of component P synchronizes with transition $q \xrightarrow{a} q'$, $a \in I_Q$, of component Q, where the resulting synchronized action $(p, q) \xrightarrow{\tau} (p', q')$ becomes a silent move. Modal interface theories generalize parallel composition to *multi-cast* communication (i.e., one output action synchronizes with all concurrently running components having this action as input) and explicit *hiding* of synchronized output actions [22]. According to MIA, we define parallel composition on IR-MIA in two steps: (1) standard parallel product $P_1 \otimes_\Phi P_2$ on MIA$_\Phi$ P_1, P_2, followed by (2) parallel composition $P_1 \|_\Phi P_2$, removing erroneous states (p_1, p_2) from $P_1 \otimes_\Phi P_2$, where for an output action of p_1, no corresponding input is provided by p_2 (and vice versa). In addition, all states (p_1', p_2') from which erroneous states are reachable are also removed (pruned) from $P_1 \|_\Phi P_2$.

Concerning (1), we first require *composability* of P_1 and P_2 (i.e., disjoint output actions). In $P_1 \otimes_\Phi P_2$, a fresh state $p_{12\Phi}$ serves as unified failure state. The input alphabet of $P_1 \otimes_\Phi P_2$ contains all those inputs of P_1 and P_2 not being contained in one of their output sets, whereas the output alphabet of $P_1 \otimes_\Phi P_2$ is the union of both output sets. The modality γ of composed transitions $(p_1, p_2) \xrightarrow{\alpha}_\gamma (p_1', p_2')$ depends on the modality of the individual transitions.

Definition 9 (IR-MIA Parallel Product). MIA_Φ P_1, P_2 *are* composable *if* $O_1 \cap O_2 = \emptyset$. *The* parallel product *is defined as* $P_1 \otimes_\Phi P_2 = ((P_1 \times P_2) \cup \{q_{12\Phi}\}, I, O, \longrightarrow_\Box, \longrightarrow_\Diamond, p_{12\Phi})$, *where* $I =_{def} (I_1 \cup I_2) \setminus (O_1 \cup O_2)$ *and* $O =_{def} O_1 \cup O_2$, *and where* $\longrightarrow_\Box$ *and* $\longrightarrow_\Diamond$ *are the least relations satisfying the following conditions:*

(May1/Must1) $(p_1, p_2) \xrightarrow{\alpha}_\gamma (p_1', p_2)$ *if* $p_1 \xrightarrow{\alpha}_\gamma p_1'$ *and* $\alpha \notin A_2$

(May2/Must2) $(p_1, p_2) \xrightarrow{\alpha}_\gamma (p_1, p_2')$ *if* $p_2 \xrightarrow{\alpha}_\gamma p_2'$ *and* $\alpha \notin A_1$

(May3/Must3) $(p_1, p_2) \xrightarrow{a}_\gamma (p_1', p_2')$ *if* $p_1 \xrightarrow{a}_\gamma p_1'$ *and* $p_2 \xrightarrow{a}_\gamma p_2'$
    for some a

(May4/Must4) $(p_1, p_2) \xrightarrow{a}_\gamma p_{12\Phi}$ *if* $p_1 \xrightarrow{a}_\gamma p_1'$ *and* $p_2 \xslashed{\xrightarrow{a}}_\gamma$
    for some $a \in I_1 \cap A_2$

(May5/Must5) $(p_1, p_2) \xrightarrow{a}_\gamma p_{12\Phi}$ *if* $p_2 \xrightarrow{a}_\gamma p_2'$ *and* $p_1 \xslashed{\xrightarrow{a}}_\gamma$
    for some $a \in I_2 \cap A_1$.

Rules *(May1/Must1)* and *(May2/Must2)* define interleaving of transitions labeled with actions being exclusive to one of both components; whereas Rule *(May3/Must3)* synchronizes transitions with common actions, and the Rules *(May4/Must4)* and *(May5/Must5)* forbid transitions of a component labeled with inputs being common to both components, but not being supported by the other component. Concerning (2), we define $E \subseteq P_1 \times P_2$ to contain *illegal state pairs* (p_1, p_2) in $P_1 \otimes_\Phi P_2$.

Definition 10 (Illegal State Pairs). *Given a parallel product* $P_1 \otimes_\Phi P_2$, *a state* (p_1, p_2) *is a* new error *if there exists* $a \in A_1 \cap A_2$ *such that*

- $a \in O_1$, $p_1 \xrightarrow{a}_\Diamond$ *and* $p_2 \xslashed{\xrightarrow{a}}_\Box$, *or*
- $a \in O_2$, $p_2 \xrightarrow{a}_\Diamond$ *and* $p_1 \xslashed{\xrightarrow{a}}_\Box$, *or*
- $a \in O_1$, $p_1 \xrightarrow{a}_\Diamond$ *and* $p_2 \xrightarrow{a}_\Diamond p_{2\Phi}$, *or*
- $a \in O_2$, $p_2 \xrightarrow{a}_\Diamond$ *and* $p_1 \xrightarrow{a}_\Diamond p_{1\Phi}$.

The relation $E \subseteq P_1 \times P_2$ *containing* illegal state pairs *is the least relation such that* $(p_1, p_2) \in E$ *if*

- (p_1, p_2) *is a* new error, *or*
- $(p_1, p_2) \xrightarrow{\omega}_\Box (p_1', p_2')$ *with* $\omega \in (O \cup \{\tau\})$ *and* $(p_1', p_2') \in E$.

If the initial state of $P_1 \otimes_\Phi P_2$ is illegal (i.e., $(p_{01}, p_{02}) \in E$), it is replaced by a fresh initial state without incoming and outgoing transitions such that P_1 and P_2 are considered *incompatible*.

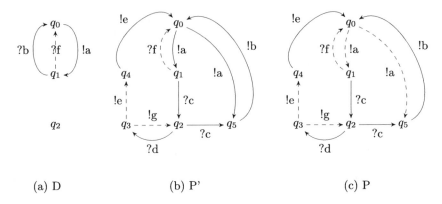

(a) D   (b) P'   (c) P

Fig. 4. Example for Parallel Composition with Multicast and Quotienting (cf. Sect. 5)

Definition 11 (IR-MIA Parallel Composition). *The parallel composition $P_1 \|_\Phi P_2$ of $P_1 \otimes_\Phi P_2$ is obtained by pruning illegal states as follows.*

- *transitions leading to a state of the form $(q_{1\Phi}, p_2)$ or $(p_1, q_{2\Phi})$ are redirected to $q_{12\Phi}$.*
- *states $(p_1, p_2) \in E$ and all unreachable states (except for $q_{12\Phi}$) and all their incoming and outgoing transitions are removed.*
- *for states $(p_1, p_2) \notin E$ and $(p_1, p_2) \xrightarrow{i}_\diamond (p_1', p_2') \in E$, $i \in I$, all transitions $(p_1, p_2) \xrightarrow{i}_\diamond (p_1'', p_2'')$ are removed.*

If $(p_1, p_2) \in P_1 \|_\Phi P_2$, we write $p_1 \|_\Phi p_2$ and call p_1 and p_2 compatible.

For example, consider $P' = Q \|_\Phi D$ (cf. Figs. 1c and 4). Here, q_0 of both Q and D have action a as common action thus being synchronized to become an output action in P' (to allow multicast communication). Action a is mandatory in P' as a is mandatory in both Q and D. In any other case, the resulting transition modality becomes optional. Further common actions (i.e., b and f) are treated similarly under composition. In contrast, transitions with actions being exclusive to Q or D are preserved under composition. As $Q \otimes_\Phi D$ contains no illegal states, no pruning is required in $P' = Q \|_\Phi D$. In contrast, assuming, e.g., one of the inputs a of Q being optional instead, then the initial state of P' would become illegal as $a \in O_D$, $p_D \xrightarrow{a}_\diamond$ and $p_Q \not\xrightarrow{a}_\Box$, and Q and D would be incompatible.

We obtain the following compositionality result for **modal-irioco** with respect to parallel composition with multicast communication.

Theorem 5 (Compositionality of modal-irioco). *Let s_1, s_2, i_1, and i_2 be MIA_Φ with i_1 and i_2 being strong must-input-enabled, and s_1 and s_2 being compatible. Then it holds that $(i_1 \mathbf{mioco}_\Phi s_1 \wedge i_2 \mathbf{mioco}_\Phi s_2) \Rightarrow i_1 \|_\Phi i_2 \mathbf{mioco}_\Phi s_1 \|_\Phi s_2$.*

Theorem 5 is restricted to must-input-enabled implementations as the input of an input/output pair has to be mandatory (otherwise leading to an illegal state). We further require *strong* input-enabledness as inputs in an input/output pair have to immediately react to outputs (otherwise, again, leading to an illegal state). In [18], it is further shown that IR-MIA parallel composition is *associative*, thus facilitating multicast communication among multiple IR-MIA components being composed in arbitrary order. In addition, it is shown in [18] that compositionality of **modal-irioco** also holds if we combine multicast parallel composition with *explicit hiding of outputs*, if specification s has no τ-steps.

5   Decompositionality

Compositionality of **modal-irioco** allows for decomposing I/O conformance testing of systems consisting of several interacting components. In particular, given two components c_1, c_2 being supposed to implement corresponding specifications s_1, s_2, then Theorem 5 ensures that if c_1 **mioco**$_\Phi$ s_1 and c_2 **mioco**$_\Phi$ s_2 holds, then $c_1 \parallel_\Phi c_2$ **mioco**$_\Phi$ $s_1 \parallel_\Phi s_2$ is guaranteed without the need for (re-)testing after composition. However, in order to benefit from this property, a mechanism is required to decompose specifications $s = s_1 \parallel_\Phi s_2$ and respective implementations $i = c_1 \parallel_\Phi c_2$, accordingly. Interface theories therefore provide quotient operators $/\!\!/$ serving as the inverse to parallel composition (i.e., if $c_1 \parallel c_2 = c$ then $c /\!\!/ c_1 = c_2$), where c_2 is often referred to as *unknown component* [28] or *testing context* [20]. We therefore adopt the quotient operator defined for MIA with universal state [5] to IR-MIA. Similar to parallel composition, the quotient operator is defined in two steps.

1. The *pseudo-quotient* $P \oslash D$ is constructed as appropriate communication partner (if exists) for a given divisor D with respect to the overall specification P.
2. The *quotient* $P /\!\!/_\Phi D$ is derived from $P \oslash D$, again, by pruning erroneous states.

For this, we require P and D to be τ-free and D to be *may-deterministic* (i.e., $d \xrightarrow{a}_\Diamond d'$ and $d \xrightarrow{a}_\Diamond d''$ implies $d' = d''$). In contrast to [5], we restrict our considerations to IR-MIA with at least one state and one may-transition. A pair P and D satisfying these restrictions is called a *quotient pair*.

Definition 12 (IR-MIA Pseudo-Quotient). *Let* $(P, I_P, O_P, \longrightarrow_\Box, \longrightarrow_\Diamond, p_\Phi)$ *and* $(D, I_D, O_D, \longrightarrow_\Box, \longrightarrow_\Diamond, d_\Phi)$ *be a* MIA_Φ *quotient pair with* $A_D \subseteq A_P$ *and* $O_D \subseteq O_P$. *We set* $I =_{def} I_P \cup O_D$ *and* $O =_{def} O_P \setminus O_D$. $P \oslash D =_{def} (P \times D, I, O, \longrightarrow_\Box, \longrightarrow_\Diamond, (p_\Phi, d_\Phi))$, *where the transition relations are defined by the rules:*

(QMay1/QMust1)	$(p,d) \xrightarrow{a}_\gamma (p',d)$	if $p \xrightarrow{a}_\gamma p' \neq p_\Phi$ and $a \notin A_D$	
(QMay2)	$(p,d) \xrightarrow{a}_\Diamond (p',d')$	if $p \xrightarrow{a}_\Diamond p' \neq p_\Phi$ and $d \xrightarrow{a}_\Box d' \neq d_\Phi$	
(QMay3)	$(p,d) \xrightarrow{a}_\Diamond (p',d')$	if $p \xrightarrow{a}_\Diamond p' \neq p_\Phi$, $d \xrightarrow{a}_\Diamond d' \neq d_\Phi$	

$$\text{and } a \notin O_P \cap I_D$$

(QMust2) $(p,d) \xrightarrow{a}_{\square} (p',d')$ if $p \xrightarrow{a}_{\square} p' \neq p_{\Phi}$ and $d \xrightarrow{a}_{\square} d' \neq d_{\Phi}$

(QMust3) $(p,d) \xrightarrow{a}_{\square} (p',d')$ if $p \xrightarrow{a}_{\Diamond} p' \neq p_{\Phi}$, $d \xrightarrow{a}_{\Diamond} d' \neq d_{\Phi}$
                                                                           and $a \in O_D$

(QMay4/QMust4) $(p,d) \xrightarrow{a}_{\gamma} (p_{\Phi}, d_{\Phi})$ if $p \xrightarrow{a}_{\gamma} p_{\Phi}$ and $d \xrightarrow{a}_{\not\square} d_{\Phi}$.

The Rules *(QMay1/QMust1)* to *(QMust3)* require $p \neq p_{\Phi}$, as the special case $p = p_{\Phi}$ is handled by rule *(QMay4/QMust4)*. Rule *(QMay1/QMust1)* concerns transitions with uncommon actions. Rule *(QMay2)* requires a mandatory transition with action in D as composition requires input transitions labeled with common actions to be mandatory (the additional requirement of Rule *(QMay3)* is stated for the same reason). Rule *(QMust3)* only requires transitions to be optional, because if $a \in O_D$ holds, then the resulting transition accepts as input a common action (which must be mandatory for the composition).

The quotient $P /\!/_{\Phi} D$ is derived from pseudo-quotient $P \oslash D$ by recursively pruning all so-called *impossible states* (p,d) (i.e., states leading to erroneous parallel composition).

Definition 13 (IR-MIA Quotient). *The set $G \subseteq P \times D$ of impossible states of pseudo-quotient $P \oslash D$ is defined as the least set satisfying the rules:*

(G1) $p \xrightarrow{a}_{\square} p' \neq p_{\Phi}$ and $d \xrightarrow{a}_{\not\square}$ and $a \in A_D$ *implies* $(p,d) \in G$

(G2) $p \xrightarrow{a}_{\square} p_{\Phi}$ and $d \xrightarrow{a}_{\Diamond}$ and $a \in O_D$ *implies* $(p,d) \in G$

(G3) $(p,d) \xrightarrow{a}_{\square} r$ and $r \in G$ *implies* $(p,d) \in G$.

The quotient $P /\!/_{\Phi} D$ *is obtained from* $P \oslash D$ *by deleting all states* $(p,d) \in G$ *(and respective transitions). If* $(p,d) \in P /\!/_{\Phi} D$, *then we write* $p /\!/_{\Phi} d$, *and quotient* $P /\!/_{\Phi} D$ *is defined.*

Rule *(G1)* ensures that for a transition labeled with a common action, there is a corresponding transition in the divisor (otherwise, the state is *impossible* and therefore removed). Rule *(G2)* ensures that a forbidden action of the specification is also forbidden in the divisor (otherwise, the state is considered *impossible*). Finally, Rule *(G3)* (recursively) removes all states from which *impossible* states are reachable.

For example, consider the quotient $Q = P /\!/_{\Phi} D$ (cf. Figs. 1c, 4a, and c). A common action becomes input action in Q if it is an input action in both P and D (e.g., f), and likewise for output actions. If a common action is output action of P and input action of D, then it becomes output of Q (e.g., b). In contrast, a common action must not be input action of P and output action of D as composing outputs with inputs always yields outputs. Actions being exclusive to P are treated similar to parallel composition, whereas D must not have exclusive actions (cf. Definition 12).

For *decomposability* to hold for **modal-irioco** (i.e., $i /\!/_{\Phi} c_i$ **mioco$_{\Phi}$** $s /\!/_{\Phi} c_s \wedge c_i$ **mioco$_{\Phi}$** $c_s \Rightarrow i$ **mioco$_{\Phi}$** s), we further require i to only have mandatory outputs as illustrated in Fig. 5: here, i **mioco$_{\Phi}$** s does not hold, although c_i **mioco$_{\Phi}$** c_s and $i /\!/_{\Phi} c_i$ **mioco$_{\Phi}$** $s /\!/_{\Phi} c_s$ holds. This is due to the fact that

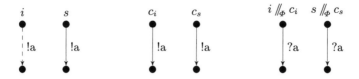

Fig. 5. Example for the necessity of mandatory outputs for i' **mioco**$_\Phi$ s' $\Rightarrow$ i **mioco**$_\Phi$ s of Theorem 6.

optional outputs combined with mandatory outputs become mandatory inputs in the quotient (as parallel composition requires inputs of an input/output pair to be mandatory). The following result ensures that the quotient operator on IR-MIA indeed serves (under the aforementioned restrictions) as the inverse to parallel composition with respect to **modal-irioco**.

Theorem 6 (Decompositionality of modal-irioco). *Let i, s, c_i, and c_s be MIA$_\Phi$ with i and c_i being weak must-input-enabled and all output behaviors of i being mandatory. Then i **mioco**$_\Phi$ s if $i \parallel_\Phi c_i$ **mioco**$_\Phi$ $s \parallel_\Phi c_s$ and c_i **mioco**$_\Phi$ c_s.*

Based on this result, **modal-irioco** supports *synthesis of testing environments* for *testing through contexts* [7,20], as well as a solution to the *unknown-component* problem [28].

6 Related Work

We discuss related work on modal conformance relations, testing equivalences, alternative formulations of, and extensions to I/O conformance testing and composition/decomposition results in I/O conformance testing.

Various interfaces theories have been presented defining *modal conformance relations* by means of different kinds of modal refinement relations [22]. Amongst others, Bauer et al. use interface automata for compositional reasoning [2], whereas Alur et al. characterize modal conformance as alternating simulation relation on interface automata [1], and Larsen et al. have shown that both views on modal conformance coincide [13]. Based on our own previous work on modal I/O conformance testing [15,17], we present, to the best of our knowledge, the first comprehensive testing theory by means of a modal I/O conformance relation. More recently, Bujtor et al. proposed testing relations on modal transition systems [6] based on (existing) test-suites, rather than being specification-based as our approach.

In contrast to I/O conformance relations, *testing equivalences* constitute a special class of (observational) equivalence relations [9,23]. One major difference to **ioco**-like theories is that actions are usually undirected, thus no distinction between (input) refusals and (output) quiescence is made as in our approach [4,21].

Concerning *alterations of and extensions to I/O conformance testing*, Veanes et al. and Gregorio-Rodríguez et al. propose to reformulate I/O conformance from suspension-trace inclusion to an alternating simulation to obtain a more fine-grained conformance notion constituting a preorder [11,27]. However, these approaches neither distinguish optional from mandatory behaviors, nor under-specified from forbidden inputs as in our approach. Heerink and Tretmans extended **ioco** by introducing so-called channels (i.e., subsets of I/O labels) for weakening the requirement of input-enabledness of implementations under test in order to also support refusal testing [12]. However, their notion of input refusals refers to a global property rather than being specific to particular states and they also do not distinguish mandatory from optional behaviors. Beohar and Mousavi extend **ioco** by replacing IOLTS with so-called *Featured Transition Systems* (FTS) and thereby enhance **ioco** to express fine-grained behavioral variability as apparent in software product lines [3]. As in our approach, FTS allow the environment to explicitly influence the presence or absence of particular transitions, whereas compositionality properties are not considered.

Concerning *(de-)compositionality in I/O conformance testing*, van der Bijl et al. present a compositional version of **ioco** with respect to synchronous parallel composition on IOTS [26], whereas Noroozi et al. consider asynchronously interacting components [19]. To overcome the inherent limitations of compositional I/O conformance testing, Daca et al. introduce alternative criteria for obtaining compositional specifications [7]. Concerning decomposition in I/O conformance testing, Noroozi et al. describe a framework for decomposition of **ioco** testing similar to our setting. However, all these related approaches neither distinguish mandatory from optional behaviors, nor support input refusals as in our approach.

7   Conclusion

We proposed a novel foundation for modal I/O-conformance testing theory based on a modified version of Modal Interface Automata with Input Refusals and show correctness and (de-)compositionality properties of the corresponding modal I/O conformance relation called **modal-irioco**. As a future work, we are interested in properties of **modal-irioco** regarding compositionality with respect to further operators on IR-MIA, such as interface conjunction [16] and asynchronous parallel composition [19]. Furthermore, we aim at generating test suites, in the spirit of Tretmans [24], exploiting the capabilities of **modal-irioco**, i.e., test cases distinguishing optional from mandatory behaviors, as well as recognizing refused inputs. In this line, we also plan to conduct a comprehensive case study showing the usefulness of the framework.

References

1. Alur, R., Henzinger, T.A., Kupferman, O., Vardi, M.Y.: Alternating refinement relations. In: Sangiorgi, D., Simone, R. (eds.) CONCUR 1998. LNCS, vol. 1466, pp. 163–178. Springer, Heidelberg (1998). doi:10.1007/BFb0055622

2. Bauer, S.S., Mayer, P., Schroeder, A., Hennicker, R.: On weak modal compatibility, refinement, and the MIO workbench. In: Esparza, J., Majumdar, R. (eds.) TACAS 2010. LNCS, vol. 6015, pp. 175–189. Springer, Heidelberg (2010). doi:10.1007/978-3-642-12002-2_15

3. Beohar, H., Mousavi, M.R.: Input-output conformance testing based on featured transition systems. In: SAC 2014, pp. 1272–1278. ACM, New York (2014)

4. Bourdonov, I.B., Kossatchev, A.S., Kuliamin, V.V.: Formal conformance testing of systems with refused inputs and forbidden actions. In: MBT 2006, pp. 83–96 (2006)

5. Bujtor, F., Fendrich, S., Lüttgen, G., Vogler, W.: Nondeterministic modal interfaces. In: Italiano, G.F., Margaria-Steffen, T., Pokorný, J., Quisquater, J.-J., Wattenhofer, R. (eds.) SOFSEM 2015. LNCS, vol. 8939, pp. 152–163. Springer, Heidelberg (2015). doi:10.1007/978-3-662-46078-8_13

6. Bujtor, F., Sorokin, L., Vogler, W.: Testing preorders for dMTS: deadlock- and the new deadlock/divergence-testing. In: ACSD 2015, pp. 60–69 (2015)

7. Daca, P., Henzinger, T.A., Krenn, W., Ničković, D.: Compositional specifications for ioco testing. In: ICST 2014, pp. 373–382 (2014)

8. de Alfaro, L., Henzinger, T.A.: Interface automata. In: ESEC, pp. 109–120. ACM (2001)

9. de Nicola, R.: Extensional equivalences for transition systems. Acta Inf. **24**(2), 211–237 (1987)

10. de Nicola, R., Segala, R.: A process algebraic view of input/output automata. Theor. Comput. Sci. **138**(2), 391–423 (1995)

11. Gregorio-Rodríguez, C., Llana, L., Martínez-Torres, R.: Input-output conformance simulation (iocos) for model based testing. In: Beyer, D., Boreale, M. (eds.) FMOODS/FORTE -2013. LNCS, vol. 7892, pp. 114–129. Springer, Heidelberg (2013). doi:10.1007/978-3-642-38592-6_9

12. Heerink, L., Tretmans, J.: Refusal testing for classes of transition systems with inputs and outputs. In: Mizuno, T., Shiratori, N., Higashino, T., Togashi, A. (eds.) Formal Description Techniques and Protocol Specification, Testing and Verification. ITIFIP, pp. 23–39. Springer, Boston, MA (1997). doi:10.1007/978-0-387-35271-8_2

13. Larsen, K.G., Nyman, U., Wąsowski, A.: Modal I/O automata for interface and product line theories. In: Nicola, R. (ed.) ESOP 2007. LNCS, vol. 4421, pp. 64–79. Springer, Heidelberg (2007). doi:10.1007/978-3-540-71316-6_6

14. Larsen, K.G., Thomsen, B.: A modal process logic. In: LICS 1988, pp. 203–210 (1988)

15. Lochau, M., Peldszus, S., Kowal, M., Schaefer, I.: Model-based testing. In: Bernardo, M., Damiani, F., Hähnle, R., Johnsen, E.B., Schaefer, I. (eds.) SFM 2014. LNCS, vol. 8483, pp. 310–342. Springer, Cham (2014). doi:10.1007/978-3-319-07317-0_8

16. Lüttgen, G., Vogler, W., Fendrich, S.: Richer interface automata with optimistic and pessimistic compatibility. Acta Inf. **52**, 1–32 (2014)

17. Luthmann, L., Mennicke, S., Lochau, M.: Towards an I/O conformance testing theory of software product lines based on modal interface automata. In: FMSPLE 2015, EPTCS, pp. 1–13 (2015)

18. Luthmann, L., Mennicke, S., Lochau, M.: Compositionality, decompositionality and refinement in input/output conformance testing - Technical report (2016). http://arxiv.org/abs/1606.09035

19. Noroozi, N., Khosravi, R., Mousavi, M.R., Willemse, T.A.C.: Synchronizing asynchronous conformance testing. In: Barthe, G., Pardo, A., Schneider, G. (eds.) SEFM 2011. LNCS, vol. 7041, pp. 334–349. Springer, Heidelberg (2011). doi:10.1007/978-3-642-24690-6_23
20. Noroozi, N., Mousavi, M.R., Willemse, T.A.C.: Decomposability in input output conformance testing. In: MBT 2013, pp. 51–66 (2013)
21. Phillips, I.: Refusal testing. Theor. Comput. Sci. 50(3), 241–284 (1987)
22. Raclet, J.-B., Badouel, E., Benveniste, A., Caillaud, B., Legay, A., Passerone, R.: A modal interface theory for component-based design. Fund. Inform. 108, 119–149 (2011)
23. Rensink, A., Vogler, W.: Fair testing. Inform. Comp. 205(2), 125–198 (2007)
24. Tretmans, J.: Test Generation with Inputs, Outputs and Repetitive Quiescence (1996)
25. Vaandrager, F.W.: On the relationship between process algebra and input/output automata. In: LICS 1991, pp. 387–398, July 1991
26. Bijl, M., Rensink, A., Tretmans, J.: Compositional testing with IOCO. In: Petrenko, A., Ulrich, A. (eds.) FATES 2003. LNCS, vol. 2931, pp. 86–100. Springer, Heidelberg (2004). doi:10.1007/978-3-540-24617-6_7
27. Veanes, M., Bjorner, N.: Alternating simulation and IOCO. STTT 14(4), 387–405 (2012)
28. Villa, T., Yevtushenko, N., Brayton, R.K., Mishchenko, A., Petrenko, A., Sangiovanni-Vincentelli, A.: The Unknown Component Problem: Theory and Applications. Springer Science & Business Media, New York (2011)

Checking Multi-view Consistency
of Discrete Systems with Respect to Periodic
Sampling Abstractions

Maria Pittou[1]([✉]) and Stavros Tripakis[1,2]

[1] Aalto University, Espoo, Finland
maria.pittou@aalto.fi
[2] University of California, Berkeley, USA

Abstract. In multi-view modeling the system under development is described by distinct models, called views, which capture different perspectives of the system. Inevitably, possible overlaps of the views may give rise to inconsistencies. Hence, it becomes essential to check for consistency among the separate views. Existing work checks view consistency of discrete systems (transition systems or finite automata) with respect to two types of abstraction functions: (1) projections of state variables, (2) projections of an alphabet of events onto a subalphabet. In this paper, we study view consistency with respect to *timing* abstractions, specifically, periodic sampling. We define the multi-view consistency problem for periodic sampling abstractions, and provide an algorithm for the problem.

1 Introduction

Designing complex systems, such as distributed, embedded, or cyber-physical systems, is a challenging task. As many of these systems are safety-critical, design by trial-and-error is not an option, and more rigorous methods such as model-based design are preferred (see [13] for an overview). In addition, the design of such systems involves several experts and stakeholders, each having their own perspective, or *view*, of the system [2,6,14]. These views are typically different kinds of models. These model cover different and potentially overlapping aspects of the system. In such a *multi-view modeling* setting, a basic problem is to check that the views are *consistent*, i.e., that they don't contradict each other [11].

In this paper we follow the multi-view modeling framework proposed in [11], where systems are sets of behaviors (often described by transition systems), and views are also sets of behaviors obtained by some kind of *abstraction* of system behaviors. Previous work studied the view consistency problem for discrete systems (transition systems or automata) with respect to two types of abstraction functions: (1) projections of state variables [11], and (2) projections of alphabet of events onto a subalphabet [10].

This work was partially supported by the Academy of Finland and the U.S. National Science Foundation (awards #1329759 and #1139138).

O. Kouchnarenko and R. Khosravi (Eds.): FACS 2016, LNCS 10231, pp. 73–91, 2017.
DOI: 10.1007/978-3-319-57666-4_6

In this work we study the multi-view consistency problem for discrete systems with respect to *timing* abstractions and in particular *periodic sampling* abstraction functions. Given a period which is a positive integer number T, the periodic sampling abstraction consists in sampling the system once every T steps. That is, given a system behavior which is a sequence of states $s_0 s_1 s_2 \cdots$, the periodic sampling w.r.t. $T = 2$ produces the abstract behavior $s_0 s_2 s_4 \cdots$.

In summary the contributions of this paper are the following: first, we define the notions of (forward and inverse) periodic sampling abstraction functions; second, we study the closure of discrete systems under these abstraction functions; third, we provide an algorithm for the multi-view consistency problem for discrete systems in the periodic sampling setting. The algorithm is *sound* in the sense that if it reports that the views are inconsistent, then an inconsistency indeed exists. However, the algorithm may fail to detect *all* inconsistencies, as it relies on a state-based reachability, and inconsistencies may also involve the transition structure of the system.

2   Related Work

The view consistency problem is a well-known problem in the engineering community. The several design teams engaged in the development process of a system obtain distinct models of the system utilizing versatile tools and modeling languages [3,12].

Existing literature mainly focus on designing architectures that combine various modeling tools or elements of the same tools [5,9,15], while a formal framework has been lacking with respect to behavioral views. [7,8] study behavioral views within the context of cyber-physical systems, in order to aid their verification rather than checking view consistency. This is the focus of the recent work [10,11] towards behavioral views. [11] offers a generic formal framework for multi-view modeling and its basic problems, since the system and views are within any global universe and most importantly they can be related by any kind of abstraction functions. The framework is instantiated for discrete systems using projection of state variables as abstraction functions, and the view consistency problem is solved. In [10] the framework is also extended to languages and automata, where abstraction functions are projections of alphabet of events onto a subalphabet.

Our work follows the setting of [10,11], but the abstraction functions studied there are different, and consist in *projections*, either of state variables, or of some events in the alphabet of events. Here we consider timing abstractions, and in particular periodic sampling abstraction functions, which to our knowledge have not been investigated earlier in the multi-view modeling context.

3   Background

Sets: Let S denote an arbitrary finite set: $|S|$ denotes its cardinality and $\mathcal{P}(S)$ denotes its powerset. Also: $\mathbb{Z}_{>0} := \{n \in \mathbb{Z} \mid n > 0\}$, $\mathbb{Z}_{\geq 0} := \{n \in \mathbb{Z} \mid n \geq 0\}$ are sets of integer numbers, and $\mathbb{B} := \{0, 1\}$ is the set of booleans.

Alphabet, Finite words, Infinite words: A finite alphabet Σ is a non-empty finite set of symbols. Σ^* is the set of all finite words over Σ and Σ^ω is the set of all infinite words over Σ. The set of all words over Σ is Σ^∞, i.e., $\Sigma^\infty = \Sigma^* \cup \Sigma^\omega$.

3.1 Automata

Nondeterministic finite automaton: A nondeterministic finite automaton (NFA for short) is a tuple $A = (Q, \Sigma, Q_0, \Delta, F)$ where Q is the finite set of states, Σ is the finite alphabet, $Q_0 \subseteq Q$ is the set of initial states, $\Delta \subseteq Q \times \Sigma \times Q$ is the transition function, and $F \subseteq Q$ is the set of final states. A path P_w of A over a finite word $w = w_0 \cdots w_{n-1} \in \Sigma^*$ is a finite sequence $P_w: (q_0, w_0, q_1) \cdots (q_{n-1}, w_{n-1}, q_n)$ such that $q_0 \in Q_0$ is the initial state and $(q_i, w_i, q_{i+1}) \in \Delta$ for every $0 \le i < n$. A path P_w of A over a finite word $w \in \Sigma^*$ is called accepting if additionally $q_n \in F$. A finite word $w \in \Sigma^*$ is accepted by A if there is an accepting path P_w of A over w. The language accepted by A, also called the behavior of A, written $L(A)$, is the set of finite words accepted by A: $L(A) = \{w \in \Sigma^* \mid \exists \text{ accepting path } P_w \text{ of } A \text{ over } w\}$.

We say that A is *deterministic* (DFA for short) iff (i) $|Q_0| = 1$ and (ii) for every $q \in Q$ and $x \in \Sigma$ there exists at most one successor state $q' \in Q$ such that $(q, x, q') \in \Delta$. We call two automata *equivalent* iff they accept the same language. It is known that every nondeterministic finite automaton can be transformed into an equivalent deterministic finite automaton [4].

Nondeterministic Muller automaton: A nondeterministic Muller automaton (NMA for short) is a tuple $A = (Q, \Sigma, Q_0, \Delta, F)$ where Q, Σ, Q_0, Δ are defined as in a NFA and $F \subseteq 2^Q$. Now an infinite path P_w of A over an infinite word $w = w_0 w_1 \cdots \in \Sigma^\omega$ is an infinite sequence $P_w: (q_0, w_0, q_1)(q_1, w_1, q_2) \cdots$ such that $q_0 \in Q_0$ is the initial state and $(q_i, w_i, q_{i+1}) \in \Delta$ for every $i \ge 0$. For every path P_w of A over an infinite word $w \in \Sigma^\omega$ we denote with $Inf(P_w)$ the set of states occurring an infinite number of times along P_w. Then, a path P_w of A over $w \in \Sigma^\omega$ is called accepting if additionally $Inf(P_w) \in F$. An infinite word $w \in \Sigma^\omega$ is accepted by A if there is an accepting path P_w of A over w. The language accepted by A, also called the behavior of A, written $L(A)$, is the set of infinite words accepted by A: $L(A) = \{w \in \Sigma^\omega \mid \exists \text{ infinite accepting path } P_w \text{ of } A \text{ over } w\}$. A deterministic Muller automaton (DMA for short) is the deterministic variant of NMA, like DFAs are deterministic NFAs. Every nondeterministic Muller automaton has an equivalent deterministic Muller automaton [1].

3.2 Multi-view Modeling

In multi-view modeling, one or more design teams obtain diverse models (views) of the same system under development, as they target capturing and analyzing different aspects of the system. For our framework we consider a system and its views as sets of behaviors [11]. There is no restriction on the behavior of the system, and we only assume that it is defined within an arbitrary global universe.

Formally, *a system S over a domain of behaviors U, is a subset of U: $S \subseteq U$*. A view is intuitively an incomplete picture of a system, and may be obtained by some kind of transformation of the system behaviors into (incomplete) behaviors in another domain. Following [11], such a transformation is defined by means of an *abstraction function $a : U \to D$*, where D is the *view domain*. A *view V over view domain D, is a subset of D: $V \subseteq D$*.

However, it is not always the case that the system S is given. Indeed, usually, only the views are available and we need to check for the existence of such a system S, which, in positive cases, is constructed from the views. The existence of S implies that the views should not have inconsistencies among them. But this raises the question of what does formally consistency mean?

Following [10,11] we define the notion of consistency. A set of views $V_1, \cdots, V_n$ over view domains $D_1, \cdots, D_n$, are *consistent with respect to a set of abstraction functions $a_1, \cdots, a_n$*, if there exists a system S over U so that $V_i = a_i(S)$, for all $i = 1, \cdots, n$. In general, we call such a system S a *witness system* to the consistency of $V_1, \cdots, V_n$. Obviously, if there is no such system, then we conclude that the views are inconsistent.

In our setting, both systems and views are finite state discrete systems, as defined in the next section, and the views are obtained by applying periodic sampling abstraction functions.

3.3   Symbolic Discrete Systems

We consider finite state discrete systems described symbolically as in [11]. The state space is described by a (finite) set of boolean variables X, resulting in 2^n states where $n = |X|$, and a *state* s over X is a function $s : X \to \mathbb{B}$. A *behavior over X* is in general a finite or infinite sequence of states over X, $\sigma = s_0 s_1 \cdots$, where s_i denotes the state at position i. We denote with $U(X)$ the set of all possible behaviors over X. Semantically, a discrete system S over X is a set of behaviors over X, i.e., $S \subseteq U(X)$.

In the sequel we give concrete (syntactic) representations of discrete systems of two kinds: first, *fully observable* systems where all variables are observable; second, *non-fully-observable* systems which also have internal, unobservable variables.

Fully-observable discrete systems: Initially we consider *fully-observable* symbolic discrete systems, i.e., systems where all variables are observable. Syntactically, a *fully-observable* discrete system (FOS for short) is defined by a triple $S = (X, \theta, \phi)$ where X is the finite set of boolean variables, θ is a boolean expression over X characterizing the set of all initial states, and ϕ is a boolean expression over $X \cup X'$, where $X' := \{x' \mid x \in X\}$ is the set of the next state variables. ϕ characterizes pairs of states (s, s') representing a transition from s to s' of S. We write $\theta(s)$ to denote that s satisfies θ. We write $\phi(s, s')$ to denote that the pair (s, s') satisfies ϕ, i.e., that there is a transition from s to s'.

A *behavior* of a FOS (X, θ, ϕ) is a finite or infinite sequence of states over X, $\sigma = s_0 s_1 \cdots$, such that σ can be generated by the FOS, i.e., such that $\theta(s_0)$ and $\forall i : \phi(s_i, s_{i+1})$. We denote by $[\![S]\!]$ the set of all behaviors of S.

Non-fully-observable discrete systems: Fully-observable systems can also be extended with a set of *internal, unobservable* state variables. For their definition we need to introduce the notion of hiding function.

Given a state s over the set of variables X and a subset $Y \subseteq X$, the *hiding function* h_Y projects s onto the set of variables Y, hence h_Y hides from s all variables in $X \backslash Y$. Then $h_Y(s)$ is defined to be the new state s', that is, $s' : Y \to \mathbb{B}$ such that $s'(x) = s(x)$ for every $x \in Y$. We extend hiding to sets of states and to behaviors. For a set of states $s = \{s_1, \cdots, s_n\}$ where $s_i : X \to \mathbb{B}$ for every $1 \leq i \leq n$, we define $h_Y(s) = \{h_Y(s_1), \cdots, h_Y(s_n)\}$. If $\sigma = s_0 s_1 \cdots$ is a behavior over X, then $h_Y(\sigma)$ is a behavior over Y defined by $h_Y(\sigma) := h_Y(s_0) h_Y(s_1) \cdots$. If $\mathcal{S}$ is a discrete system over X, then $h_Y([\![\mathcal{S}]\!]) := \{h_Y(\sigma) \mid \sigma \in [\![\mathcal{S}]\!]\}$.

Formally, a *non-fully-observable* discrete system (nFOS for short), described symbolically, is a tuple $S = (X, Z, \theta, \phi)$ where X, Z are disjoint finite sets of variables such that X describes the set of observable variables, and Z the set of internal (unobservable) variables. The initial condition θ is a boolean expression over $X \cup Z$, and the transition relation ϕ is a boolean expression over $X \cup Z \cup X' \cup Z'$.

A behavior of a nFOS $S = (X, Z, \theta, \phi)$ is a finite or infinite sequence of states over $X \cup Z$ which can be generated by $\mathcal{S}$, in the same manner as with behaviors generated by a FOS. The *observable behavior* of a behavior σ over $X \cup Z$ is the behavior $h_X(\sigma)$ over X. In what follows we denote by $[\![S]\!]$ the set of all behaviors of S (over $X \cup Z$), and by $[\![S]\!]_o$ the set of its observable behaviors (over X). If $Z = \emptyset$, i.e., the system has no internal variables, then it is a FOS. Note that for every FOS S, it holds that $[\![S]\!] = [\![S]\!]_o$.

4   Forward and Inverse Periodic Sampling Abstraction Functions

Now we would like to relate systems over $\mathcal{U}$ and views over $\mathcal{D}$, using periodic sampling abstraction functions. We define as *period* any $T \in \mathbb{Z}_{>0}$. Note that in general, we can apply the periodic sampling to the behaviors starting from the state at position $\tau = 0$ or at $\tau > 0, \tau \in \mathbb{Z}$.

Periodic sampling abstraction functions (forward): Let X be a finite set of variables. Given a domain of behaviors $\mathcal{U}(X)$ and a view domain $\mathcal{D}(X) = \mathcal{U}(X)$, a periodic sampling abstraction function from $\mathcal{U}(X)$ to $\mathcal{D}(X)$ w.r.t. period T and initial position τ, denoted by $a_{T,\tau}$, is defined by the mapping $a_{T,\tau} : \mathcal{U}(X) \to \mathcal{D}(X)$ such that for every behavior $\sigma = s_0 s_1 \cdots \in \mathcal{U}(X)$, $a_{T,\tau}(\sigma) := s'_0 s'_1 \cdots \in \mathcal{D}(X)$ where $s'_i = s_{\tau + i \cdot T}$ for every $i \geq 0$. When $\tau = 0$, instead of writing $a_{T,\tau}$ or $a_{T,0}$, we simply write a_T.

Then we lift the notion of periodic sampling abstraction function to systems. For a system $S \subseteq \mathcal{U}(X)$, we define $a_{T,\tau}(S) := \{a_{T,\tau}(\sigma) \mid \sigma \in S\}$. Since $a_{T,\tau}(S) \subseteq \mathcal{D}(X)$, $a_{T,\tau}(S)$ is a view over $\mathcal{D}(X)$. In what follows we refer to periodic sampling abstraction functions simply by periodic sampling.

Closure of discrete systems under periodic sampling: Given a nFOS $S = (X, Z, \theta, \phi)$ and periodic sampling $a_{T,\tau} : \mathcal{U}(X \cup Z) \rightarrow \mathcal{D}(X \cup Z)$, $\mathcal{D}(X \cup Z) = \mathcal{U}(X \cup Z)$, we would like to examine whether there exists a nFOS $S' = (X, Z, \theta', \phi')$ such that $[\![S']\!] = a_{T,\tau}([\![S]\!])$. Indeed, we prove closure for discrete systems S with $Z = \emptyset$ or $Z \neq \emptyset$.

Theorem 1

(a) *Given a FOS system $S = (X, \theta, \phi)$ and periodic sampling $a_{T,\tau}$, there exists a FOS system S' such that $[\![S']\!] = a_{T,\tau}([\![S]\!])$.*

(b) *Given a nFOS system $S = (X, Z, \theta, \phi)$ and periodic sampling $a_{T,\tau}$, there exists a nFOS system S' such that $[\![S']\!] = a_{T,\tau}([\![S]\!])$.*

Proof. (a) We define the FOS $S' = (X, \theta', \phi')$, where θ' contains all states over X which can be reached from some initial state of S in exactly τ steps; and ϕ' is defined as follows. Let s, s' be two states over X. Then $\phi'(s, s')$ iff S has a path from s to s' of length exactly T. Consider an arbitrary behavior $\sigma = s_0 s_1 s_2 \cdots \in [\![S]\!]$. Applying the periodic sampling $a_{T,\tau}$ to σ we obtain the behavior $a_{T,\tau}(\sigma) = s_\tau s_{\tau+T} s_{\tau+2T} \cdots$. By construction of S' we have that $\theta'(s_\tau)$ and $\phi'(s_{\tau+iT}, s_{\tau+(i+1)T})$ for every $i \geq 0$, which implies that $a_{T,\tau}(\sigma) \in [\![S']\!]$. Hence, $a_{T,\tau}([\![S]\!]) = \{a_{T,\tau}(\sigma) \mid \sigma \in [\![S]\!]\} \subseteq [\![S']\!]$. Conversely, let $\sigma' = s'_0 s'_1 s'_2 \ldots \in [\![S']\!]$. Since $\phi'(s'_0)$, by definition of S' there exists a state s_0 in S with $\theta(s_0)$ so that s'_0 can be reached from s_0 in exactly τ steps. Moreover, for σ' we have that $\phi'(s'_i, s'_{i+1})$, thus there exists a path in S from s'_i to s'_{i+1} of length exactly T for every $i \geq 0$. Then, we obtain the behavior $\sigma = s_0 s_1 s_2 \cdots \in [\![S]\!]$ where $s_{\tau+iT} = s'_i$ for every $i \geq 0$. Hence, $a_{T,\tau}(\sigma) \in a_{T,\tau}([\![S]\!])$ and $[\![S']\!] \subseteq a_{T,\tau}([\![S]\!])$ which completes our proof. The part (b) of the theorem is proved similarly.   □

Inverse periodic sampling: Consider a finite set of variables X, a domain of behaviors $\mathcal{U}(X)$ and a view domain $\mathcal{D}(X) = \mathcal{U}(X)$. Then, an inverse periodic sampling abstraction function from $\mathcal{D}(X)$ to $\mathcal{U}(X)$ w.r.t. period T and initial position τ, denoted by $a_{T,\tau}^{-1}$, is defined by the mapping $a_{T,\tau}^{-1} : \mathcal{D}(X) \rightarrow \mathcal{U}(X)$ such that for every behavior $\sigma = s_0 s_1 \cdots \in \mathcal{D}(X)$, $a_{T,\tau}^{-1}(\sigma) := \{\sigma' \mid \sigma' = s'_0 s'_1 \cdots \in \mathcal{U}(X) \text{ s.t. } s'_{\tau+i \cdot T} = s_i, i \geq 0\}$ or equivalently $a_{T,\tau}^{-1}(\sigma) := \{\sigma' \mid a_{T,\tau}(\sigma') = \sigma\}$. Moreover, for a system $S \subseteq \mathcal{U}(X)$, we define $a_{T,\tau}^{-1}(S) := \bigcup_{\sigma \in S} a_{T,\tau}^{-1}(\sigma)$. When $\tau = 0$, we simply write a_T^{-1}.

Non-closure of FOS under inverse periodic sampling: Given a FOS $S = (X, \theta, \phi)$ and inverse periodic sampling $a_{T,\tau}^{-1} : \mathcal{D}(X) \rightarrow \mathcal{U}(X)$, $\mathcal{D}(X) = \mathcal{U}(X)$, we show that there does not exist always a FOS $S' = (X, \theta', \phi')$ such that $[\![S']\!] = a_{T,\tau}^{-1}([\![S]\!])$.

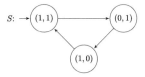

Fig. 1. FOS obtained from a_T with period $T = 2$.

Position	σ
$i = 0$	(1,1)
	$\mid$
$i = 1$	?
	$\mid$
$i = 2$	(0,1)
	$\mid$
$i = 3$	?
	$\mid$
$i = 4$	(1,0)
	$\mid$
$i = 5$	?
	$\mid$
$i = 6$	(1,1)
	$\mid$
$i = 7$	$\vdots$

Fig. 2. Incomplete behavior σ of system S'.

Example 1. Consider the FOS $S = (\{x, y\}, \theta, \phi)$ where both x and y are Boolean variables, $\theta = x \wedge y$ and $\phi = (x \wedge y \rightarrow \neg x' \wedge y') \wedge (\neg x \wedge y \rightarrow x' \wedge \neg y') \wedge (x \wedge \neg y \rightarrow x' \wedge y')$ as shown in Fig. 1. The system S has been obtained with periodic sampling a_T and period $T = 2$. In order to find a system S' such that $[\![S']\!] = a_T^{-1}([\![S]\!])$ one would have to replace each of the "?" shown in Fig. 2 with at least one state over X, so that the first 6 states in the unique behavior σ of S' would be distinct. Indeed, S' needs at least 6 distinct states, otherwise we would have to have extra transitions between the three states $(1, 1), (0, 1), (1, 0)$ shown in the figure. But adding such transitions creates loops, and results in $[\![S']\!] \neq a_T^{-1}([\![S]\!])$, which is wrong. However, having 6 distinct states is also not possible, since we only have two Boolean variables x, y, thus, only 4 possible combinations. Hence, there exists no such FOS S'.

Closure of nFOS under inverse periodic sampling: In contrast with FOS, that are not closed under inverse periodic samplings, we prove closure for nFOS, i.e., for discrete systems with internal variables.

Theorem 2. *Given a system* $S = (X, Z, \theta, \phi)$ *and inverse periodic sampling* $a_{T,\tau}^{-1} : \mathcal{D}(X \cup Z) \to \mathcal{U}(X \cup Z \cup W)$, *there exists always a non-fully-observable system* $S' = (X \cup Z, W, \theta', \phi')$ *such that* $[\![S']\!] = a_{T,\tau}^{-1}([\![S]\!])$.

Proof. Given the nFOS $S = (X, Z, \theta, \phi)$ let R denote the set of reachable states of S over $X \cup Z$. Moreover, let $|R| = n$ and consider a set of Boolean variables W such that $|W| \geq \lfloor \log_2(n \cdot (T-1) + \tau) \rfloor$ (here we assume that $T \geq 2$; if $T = 1$ then we can simply take $S' = S$). By definition we have that $\sigma \in a_{T,\tau}^{-1}([\![S]\!])$ iff $a_{T,\tau}(\sigma) \in [\![S]\!]$. Moreover, $\sigma' = a_{T,\tau}(\sigma) = s_\tau s_{\tau+T} s_{\tau+2T} \cdots$, i.e., each behavior σ' in $[\![S]\!]$ has been obtained with starting position τ and period T. The system S' has to be defined such that each behavior in $[\![S']\!]$ results from σ' by (i) adding τ transitions (or states) in the beginning of σ' and T transitions (or $T-1$ states) in between the transition $\phi(s_{\tau+iT}, s_{\tau+(i+1)T})$ for every $i \geq 0$, and by (ii) replacing each $s_{\tau+iT}$ in σ' with $s'_{\tau+iT} = h_{X \cup Z}(s_{\tau+iT})$. Since S consists of n reachable states then S' should have at least $n(T-1) + \tau$ more reachable states or equivalently $\lfloor \log_2(n \cdot (T-1) + \tau) \rfloor$ more Boolean variables. One can then obtain a nFOS S' over $X \cup Z \cup W$, where $X \cup Z$ and W denote the set of observable and unobservable variables respectively, such that $[\![S']\!] = a_{T,\tau}^{-1}([\![S]\!])$.   □

Note that the system S' of Theorem 2 is not unique. Indeed, even for each possible value of $|W|$ one obtains a family of systems S' with $[\![S']\!] = a_{T,\tau}^{-1}([\![S]\!])$.

5   Checking View Consistency W.r.t. Periodic Sampling Abstraction Functions

For this entire section, we assume that $\tau = 0$.

5.1   Views and Consistency

Views are finite-state discrete systems with or without internal variables. In our framework views are obtained applying some periodic sampling a_T, where T is the period of the periodic sampling. Thus, if $S = (X, Z, \theta, \phi)$ is a discrete system over a set of observable variables X and domain of behaviors $\mathcal{U}(X \cup Z)$, then a view obtained with periodic sampling a_T is a discrete system $V = (X, Z, \theta', \phi')$ over the same set of observable variables X and view domain $\mathcal{D}(X \cup Z) = \mathcal{U}(X \cup Z)$.

We consider views defined by nFOS and we refer to V simply as a view of S. However, this does not exclude the case where the views are described by a FOS. Indeed, FOS is a special case of nFOS and we can always assume that the set of unobservable variables is empty. Hence, the results we derive can be naturally extended also for views described by FOS. Moreover, in the rest of the paper when we compare systems or views we compare them with respect to their observable behaviors, and instead of writing for instance $[\![V]\!]_o = a_T([\![S]\!]_o)$ we simply write $[\![V]\!] = a_T([\![S]\!])$.

Note that, although each of the views is a nFOS, this does not always imply that the *witness* system is also a nFOS. This motivates to study three different variants of the consistency problem for views obtained by periodic sampling.

Problem 1. Given a finite set of nFOS $S_i = (X, W_i, \theta_i, \phi_i)$ and periodic samplings a_{T_i}, for $1 \leq i \leq n$, check whether there exists a system $\mathcal{S}$ over $\mathcal{U}(X)$ such that $a_{T_i}(\mathcal{S}) = [\![S_i]\!]$ for every $1 \leq i \leq n$.

Problem 2. Given a finite set of nFOS $S_i = (X, W_i, \theta_i, \phi_i)$ and periodic samplings a_{T_i}, for $1 \leq i \leq n$, check whether there exists an nFOS $S = (X, W, \theta, \phi)$, $W \supseteq W_1 \cup \ldots \cup W_n$, such that $a_{T_i}([\![S]\!]) = [\![S_i]\!]$ for every $1 \leq i \leq n$.

Problem 3. Given a finite set of nFOS $S_i = (X, W_i, \theta_i, \phi_i)$ and periodic samplings a_{T_i}, for $1 \leq i \leq n$, check whether there exists a fully-observable system $S = (X, \theta, \phi)$, such that $a_{T_i}([\![S]\!]) = [\![S_i]\!]$ for every $1 \leq i \leq n$.

Observe that the three problems are different, since Problem 1 asks for a *semantic* witness system, not necessarily representable as a symbolic discrete system, while Problems 2 and 3 ask for a symbolic discrete witness system with or without internal variables respectively. Obviously, a solution to Problem 3 is also a solution to Problem 2, and a solution to Problem 2 is also a solution to Problem 1. We do not yet know whether Problems 1 and 2 are equivalent, i.e., whether existence of a semantic witness implies existence of a syntactic (nFOS) witness. This is an interesting question which has to do with whether the finite-state nature of nFOS is enough to represent all possible semantic witnesses of consistent nFOS views. Example 2 that follows shows that Problems 2 and 3 are not equivalent, that is, existence of a nFOS witness does not always imply existence of a FOS witness.

Example 2. Consider the views $V_i = (\{x_i\}, \{y_i, z_i\}, \theta_i = \neg x_i \wedge \neg y_i \wedge \neg z_i, \phi_i)$ for $i = 1, 2$, where all variables are Boolean and ϕ_1, ϕ_2 are such that $[\![V_1]\!] = \{\sigma_1 = (0, 0, 0)(0, 1, 1)(0, 1, 0)(0, 0, 1), \sigma_1' = (0, 0, 0)(1, 1, 1)(1, 1, 0)(1, 0, 1)\}$ and $[\![V_2]\!] = \{\sigma_2 = (0, 0, 0)(0, 1, 1)(0, 0, 1), \sigma_2' = (0, 0, 0)(1, 1, 0)(1, 1, 1)\}$. The views V_1 and V_2 have been sampled with periods $T_1 = 2$ and $T_2 = 3$ respectively. The observable behavior of the views is shown in the form of trees in Fig. 3, along with the corresponding positions as described in the sequel. For the view V_2 which has been sampled with period $T_2 = 3$, we have that in the first position $i = 0$, V_2 is at state $x = 0$, in the next position $i = 3$, V_2 is at one of the states $x = 0$ or $x = 1$, and similarly in the last position $i = 6$. Similarly are interpreted the tree of behaviors for V_1. There exists a nFOS system S witness to the consistency of V_1 and V_2, with one observable state variable, whose observable behavior is shown in the form of a tree in the rightmost part of Fig. 3 where the $*$-state of the system denotes an arbitrary state 0 or 1. However, there does not exist any fully-observable system with a single state variable x that is a witness system to the consistency of V_1 and V_2. For instance, it is not possible to define by distinct states, the five states labelled by 0 in the positions $i = 0, 2, 3, 4, 6$, using only one Boolean variable (as it can only encode 2 states).

In the sequel we prove a Lemma that will help prove one of the main results of this paper. We firstly introduce some notation. Consider a set of views $S_1, ..., S_n$. For every $1 \leq i \leq n$ and any positive integer m let Y_i^m be the set of all states

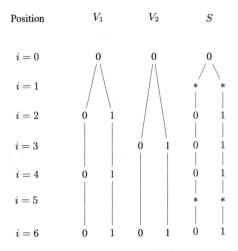

Fig. 3. Behavior trees for views V_1 and V_2 and possible nFOS witness system S.

that can be found at position m in some behavior of S_i, i.e., $Y_i^m = \{s_i \mid s_i : X \to \mathbb{B}$ occurs at position m in some behavior $\sigma \in [\![S_i]\!]\}$.

Lemma 1. *Consider a set of views $S_1, ..., S_n$ and periodic samplings a_{T_i}, for $1 \le i \le n$. If there exist $i, j \in \{1, ..., n\}$ and positive integer m multiple of $LCM(T_i, T_j)$ such that $Y_j^{m/T_j} \ne Y_i^{m/T_i}$, then $S_1, ..., S_n$ are inconsistent.*

Proof. Let $S_i = (X, W_i, \theta_i, \phi_i)$. Assume that there exist $i, j \in \{1, ..., n\}$ and positive integer m multiple of $LCM(T_i, T_j)$ such that $Y_j^{m/T_j} \ne Y_i^{m/T_i}$. W.l.o.g., suppose that there exists a state $s \in Y_i^{m/T_i} \setminus Y_j^{m/T_j}$. We would like to prove that the views $S_1, ..., S_n$ are inconsistent. Assume to the contrary that they are consistent. This implies that there exists a system $\mathcal{S}$ over $\mathcal{U}(X)$ such that $a_{T_k}(\mathcal{S}) = [\![S_k]\!]$ for every $1 \le k \le n$. Then, $a_{T_i}(\mathcal{S}) = [\![S_i]\!]$ and $a_{T_j}(\mathcal{S}) = [\![S_j]\!]$. Since there exists state $s \in Y_i^{m/T_i} \setminus Y_j^{m/T_j}$, then there exists some behavior $\sigma_i \in [\![S_i]\!]$ such that σ_i is at position m/T_i at state s. Because $a_{T_i}(\mathcal{S}) = [\![S_i]\!]$ we have that $\sigma_i \in a_{T_i}(\mathcal{S})$. By definition, $a_{T_i}(\mathcal{S}) = \{a_{T_i}(\sigma) \mid \sigma \in \mathcal{S}\}$ and because $\sigma_i \in a_{T_i}(\mathcal{S})$ then $\exists \sigma \in \mathcal{S}$ such that $a_{T_i}(\sigma) = \sigma_i$. By construction, σ is at state s at position m. Since $\sigma \in \mathcal{S}$ we have that $a_{T_j}(\sigma) \in a_{T_j}(\mathcal{S}) = [\![S_j]\!]$. Let $\sigma_j = a_{T_j}(\sigma)$. Because σ is at state s at position m, σ_j must be at the same state s at position m/T_j. This in turn implies that $s \in Y_j^m$, which is a contradiction. □

5.2   Algorithm for Detecting View Inconsistency

In this chapter we describe the steps of the algorithm for detecting inconsistencies among a finite number of views, w.r.t. periodic sampling abstraction functions. Our algorithm applies to sets of views that satisfy one of the following conditions: (i) either every view generates only infinite behaviors; (ii) or every view generates only finite behaviors. This means that we cannot have views that have both finite and infinite behaviors, and also that we cannot have some views with finite behaviors and some other views with infinite behaviors. Extending the algorithm to those cases is part of future work. Note that a view which only has finite behaviors corresponds to a transition system where all paths eventually lead to a deadlock. On the other hand, a view which only has infinite behaviors corresponds to a transition system with no reachable deadlocks.

From now on we use the term *finite automata* (FA for short) to refer to NFA or NMA, and the term *deterministic finite automata* to refer to DFA or DMA.

Our algorithm involves constructing the so called *hyper-period automaton* (HPA). The algorithm also involves a special composition operator for finite automata w.r.t. HPA called the *label-driven composition*. We define these notions next.

Hyper-period finite automaton: Consider a finite set of periods $T_1, \ldots, T_n \in \mathbb{Z}_{>0}$. Let LCM be the least common multiple operator, and let $T = LCM(T_1, \ldots, T_n)$ be the *hyper-period* of the above set of periods. Also let $M = \{0, m_1, \ldots, m_k\}$ denote the finite ordered set of multiples of $T_1, \ldots, T_n$ up to the hyper-period, i.e., with $m_k < T$. For example, let $T_1 = 2, T_2 = 3$ and $T_3 = 6$. Then, $T = LCM(T_1, T_2, T_3) = 6$ and $M = \{0, 2, 3, 4\}$.

The intuition of the hyper-period automaton is that it contains as states the elements of M and its transitions are labelled with sets of labels of the form p_{T_i}, denoting the fact that the period T_i is "active" at the corresponding time instant. The accepting states of the automaton correspond to those instants where two or more periods are "active".

We first illustrate this intuition by example, and then provide the formal definition of the hyper-period automaton.

Example 3. Consider the two periods $T_1 = 3$ and $T_2 = 2$. Then, the hyper-period automaton w.r.t. T_1, T_2, is the automaton H shown in Fig. 4. We have $H = (M, P, \{0\}, \Delta, \{0\})$ where $M = \{0, 2, 3, 4\}$, $P = \mathcal{P}(\{p_{T_1}, p_{T_2}\}) = \mathcal{P}(\{p_3, p_2\})$ ($T_1 = 3$ and $T_2 = 2$, hence $p_{T_1} = p_3$ and $p_{T_2} = p_2$), and the transition function Δ is as depicted in Fig. 4.

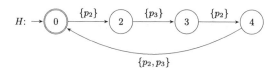

Fig. 4. HPA w.r.t. the periods 2 and 3.

The above example of HPA is simple as we only have two periods. In the sequel we provide a more interesting example which involves three periods. This example also illustrates the fact that the HPA generally has more than one accepting states.

Example 4. Consider the three periods $T_1 = 4$, $T_2 = 2$ and $T_3 = 3$. Then, the hyper-period automaton is $H = (M, P, \{0\}, \Delta, F)$ where $M = \{0, 2, 3, 4, 6, 8, 9, 10\}$, $P = \mathcal{P}(\{p_{T_1}, p_{T_2}, p_{T_3}\}) = \mathcal{P}(\{p_4, p_2, p_3\})$, $F = \{0, 4, 6, 8\}$, and the transition function Δ is as depicted in Fig. 5.

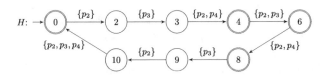

Fig. 5. HPA w.r.t. the periods 2, 3 and 4.

We now formally define the *hyper-period automaton* H w.r.t. $T_1, \ldots, T_n$ as the deterministic finite automaton $H = (M, P, \{0\}, \Delta, F)$, where:

- M is the (finite) set of states of H.
- $P = \mathcal{P}(\{p_{T_1}, \ldots, p_{T_n}\})$ is the (finite) alphabet of H, where $\{p_{T_1}, \ldots, p_{T_n}\}$ is obtained by assigning to every $i = 1, \ldots, n$ the label p_{T_i}, corresponding to the period T_i.
- Δ is defined as follows. First, let $M = \{m_0, m_1, \ldots, m_k\}$ where we assume that m_i are ordered in increasing sequence, i.e., $m_0 < m_1 < \cdots < m_k$. Note that under this assumption, m_0 must be 0. Then Δ contains exactly $k+1$ transitions (i.e., as many as the elements of M): $\Delta = \{(m_0, l_0, m_1), (m_1, l_1, m_2), \ldots, (m_k, l_k, m_0)\}$, where for $i = 0, \ldots, k$, $l_i = \{p_{T_j} \mid T_j \text{ is a divisor of } m_{i+1}\}$. Note that, as defined, Δ creates a loop starting at the initial state $m_0 = 0$, and ending at the same state, with each state in M having a unique successor as well as a unique predecessor. Given $m \in M$, let $\pi(m)$ denote the set of period labels annotating the unique incoming transition to m. For example, in the HPA of Fig. 5, $\pi(3) = \{p_3\}$ and $\pi(4) = \{p_2, p_4\}$.
- $F = \{m \in M \mid |\pi(m)| \geq 2\}$, that is, F contains all states whose (unique) incoming transition is labeled by a set containing at least two period labels.

Since H is deterministic, in the sequel we use for simplicity the notation $\Delta(s, x)$ for the transition function, i.e., to denote the unique successor state of s with symbol x.

Label-driven composition of view automata with an HPA: Suppose we want to check consistency between a set of views described as finite automata $A_1, \ldots, A_n$, w.r.t. periods $T_1, \ldots, T_n$. Our view consistency algorithm, described later in this section, relies on computing a special kind of automata composition among modified versions of $A_1, \ldots, A_n$ and the HPA H w.r.t. $T_1, \ldots, T_n$. The modified version of A_i consists essentially in labeling all transitions of A_i by its period label p_{T_i}, and then determinizing. Then, the composition with H consists in synchronizing every transition of H with the corresponding automata A_i whose period is "active" on that transition, i.e., whose label p_{T_i} belongs to the corresponding label set of the transition of H. This composition is called *label-driven composition*, and is formalized next.

Consider a set of deterministic finite automata $A_r = (Q_r, \Sigma_r, Q_{r_0}, \Delta_r, F_r)$ where $\Sigma_r = \{p_{T_r}\}$ for $1 \leq r \leq n$. Let $H = (M, P, \{0\}, \Delta, F)$ be the HPA w.r.t. $T_1, ..., T_n$ defined as above. The *label-driven composition* of $A_1, ..., A_n$ and H, denoted by $A_1 \parallel ... \parallel A_n \parallel H$, is the finite automaton $C = (Q_c, \Sigma_c, Q_{c_0}, \Delta_c, F_c)$ where $Q_c = Q_1 \times \cdots \times Q_n \times M$, $\Sigma_c = P$, $Q_{c_0} = Q_{1_0} \times \cdots \times Q_{n_0} \times \{0\}$, $F_c = Q_1 \times \cdots \times Q_n \times F$, and the transition function $\Delta_c \subseteq Q_c \times \Sigma_c \times Q_c$ is defined as follows:

$$\Delta_c = \{((q_1, \ldots, q_n, m), l, (q'_1, \ldots, q'_n, m')) \mid (m, l, m') \in \Delta \ \wedge$$
$$\forall i = 1, ..., n: \text{ if } p_{T_i} \in l \text{ then } (q_i, p_{T_j}, q'_i) \in \Delta_i, \text{ otherwise } q'_i = q_i\}.$$

Example 5. Consider the finite automata A_1, A_2 as shown in Fig. 6 and the HPA H of Fig. 4. Then, Fig. 7 depicts the label-driven composition $C = A_1 \parallel A_2 \parallel H$.

Algorithm for detecting view inconsistency: Consider a finite set of views defined by the nFOS $S_i = (X, W_i, \theta_i, \phi_i)$, and obtained by applying some periodic sampling a_{T_i} with sampling period T_i, for $i = 1, \ldots, n$, respectively.

Let $T = LCM(T_1, \ldots, T_n)$, $P = \mathcal{P}(\{p_{T_1}, \ldots, p_{T_n}\})$ and $M = \{0, m_1, \ldots, m_k\}$ denote respectively the hyper-period of periods, the labels of periods, and the ordered set of multiples of periods up to their hyper-period, as defined previously. The algorithm for detecting inconsistency among the views $S_1, \ldots, S_n$, consists of the following steps:

- **Step 1:** Construct for each S_i, $i = 1, \ldots, n$, the FA $L_i = (Q_i, \Sigma_i, Q_{i_0}, \Delta_i, F_i)$ where $Q_i = \mathbb{B}^{X \cup W_i}$, $\Sigma_i = \{p_{T_i}\}$, $Q_{i_0} = \{s \mid \theta_i(s)\}$, $F_i = \emptyset$, and $\Delta_i \subseteq Q_i \times \Sigma_i \times Q_i$ is defined such that $(s, p_{T_i}, s') \in \Delta_i$ iff $\phi_i(s, s')$.
- **Step 2:** Determinize each of the FA L_i and obtain the equivalent deterministic FA dL_i for every $i = 1, \ldots, n$.

Fig. 6. Finite automata A_1 and A_2.

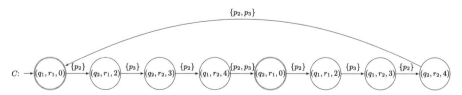

Fig. 7. The label-driven composition of automata A_1, A_2 of Fig. 6 and HPA H of Fig. 4.

- **Step 3:** Construct the hyper-period automaton H w.r.t. the periods $T_1, \ldots, T_n$.
- **Step 4:** Obtain the label-driven composition $C = (dL_1, \ldots, dL_n, H)$ w.r.t HPA H.
- **Step 5:** Let $s = (s_1, \ldots, s_n, m)$ be a state of C, and let $I_s = \{i \in \{1, ..., n\} \mid p_{T_i} \in \pi(m)\}$. The algorithm reports **inconsistency** if C contains at least one reachable state $s = (s_1, \ldots, s_n, m)$ where s_i are states of dL_i for $i = 1, \ldots, n$ respectively, and $m \in F$ is a final state of H, such that $\exists i, j \in I_s : h_X(s_i) \neq h_X(s_j)$. Otherwise, it reports **inconclusive**.

The determinization procedure at Step 2 is needed because the algorithm detects view inconsistency by comparing sets of states of where each of the given views can be at same points in time. We note that this determinization procedure does not attempt to *complete* an automaton, i.e., to add transitions with missing symbols.

In the sequel we prove that the algorithm is sound, i.e., if it reports inconsistency then the views are indeed inconsistent. We first introduce two auxiliary lemmas used for proving this fact.

Lemma 2. *Let S be a nFOS, T a period, L the FA obtained from S as in Step 1 of the algorithm above, and dL the deterministic FA obtained from L. Then every reachable state of dL is non-empty.*

Proof. The set of initial states of S, and therefore also of L, is non-empty. Therefore, the initial state of dL is a non-empty set of states of L. Recall that the alphabet of both L and dL is the singleton $\{p_T\}$. Let s be a state of dL. We show by induction that if s is a non-empty set, and (s, p_T, s') is a transition of dL, then s' is also non-empty. By definition of dL, if all elements of s are deadlocks, i.e., none of them has a transition with p_T, then no transition is added to s either (note that we do not complete the automaton dL as we mentioned above). Therefore, in order for a transition (s, p_T, s') to exist, at least one state $q \in s$ must have a transition (q, p_T, q') in L. But in that case, s' contains at least the state q', and is therefore non-empty. $\qquad\square$

We now introduce some concepts used in the lemma that follows. First, observe that the HPA H is finite and deterministic, and so is every automaton dL_i. Moreover, by definition, the label driven composition C obtained by Step **4** of the algorithm forms a *lasso*, that is, C is finite-state and every state has a unique successor state. Consider a state m of the HPA H as obtained by Step **3** of the algorithm. We define the *indices* of m, denoted by $ins(m)$, to be the ordered set of numbers $ins(m) = \bigcup_{w \geq 0} \{w \cdot LCM(T_1, \ldots, T_n) + m\}$. For instance, consider the HPA H of Example 3. Since $T_1 = 3$ and $T_2 = 2$ we have that $LCM(T_1, T_2) = 6$. Then, the indices of the state $m = 3$ is the set $ins(3) = \bigcup_{w \geq 0} \{w \cdot 6 + 3\} = \{3, 9, 15, \ldots\}$.

Now consider a reachable state $s = (q_1, \ldots, q_n, m)$ of the label driven composition C. Because C is a lasso, there is a unique acyclic path in C that reaches m.

Let ξ be the number of times that the state m of the HPA occurs in the states of this path reaching s. We define the *latent index* of s, denoted by $lin(s)$, to be the element of $ins(m)$ that occurs in position ξ in $ins(m)$. For instance, consider the label driven composition C of Example 5. For the state $s = (q_1, r_2, 3)$ of C we have that $m = 3$ and $ins(3) = \{3, 9, 15, \dots\}$ computed as above. The state $m = 3$ of the HPA H occured twice up to the state $s = (q_1, r_2, 3)$, hence $\xi = 2$. Then, the second element of $ins(m)$ is the integer 9, and thus $lin(s) = 9$. The intuition is that $lin(s)$ represents the first point in time where s appears in a behavior of the system.

Lemma 3. *Consider the label driven composition C as obtained by Step 4 of the algorithm. Let $s = (s_1, \dots, s_n, m)$ be a state of C, and let $I_s = \{i \in \{1, ..., n\} \mid p_{T_i} \in \pi(m)\}$. Then, for every $i \in I_s$, $lin(s)/T_i$ is an integer number and it holds that $s_i = Y_i^{lin(s)/T_i}$.*

Proof. Let $i \in I_s$. Then $p_{T_i} \in \pi(m)$. By definition of the HPA H, and since p_{T_i} belongs as a label in the incoming transition to m, $lin(s)$ is a multiple of the period T_i, thus $k = lin(s)/T_i$ is an integer number. We also need to show that $s_i = Y_i^k$. By definition of C, automaton dL_i has "moved" (i.e., taken a transition) k times up to state s. Thus, s_i must contain the set of all states of L_i that can be reached from an initial state after k steps. But this is exactly the set of states contained in Y_i^k. □

Theorem 3. *If the algorithm reports inconsistency then there exists no solution to Problems 1, 2, and 3.*

Proof. Assume that the algorithm reports inconsistency. Then there exists a reachable final state $(s_1, \dots, s_n, m)$ of C such that $\exists i, j \in I_s : h_X(s_i) \neq h_X(s_j)$, where s_i is a state of dL_i, s_j is a state of dL_j, and m is a final state of the HPA H. By Lemma 2 we have that $s_i \neq \emptyset$ and $s_j \neq \emptyset$. Moreover by Lemma 3 we have that $s_i = Y_i^{lin(s)/T_i}$ and $s_j = Y_j^{lin(s)/T_j}$, where $lin(s)$ is the latent index of state s. Since $h_X(s_i) \neq h_X(s_j)$ we obtain that $s_i \neq s_j$ and hence $Y_i^{lin(s)/T_i} \neq Y_j^{lin(s)/T_j}$. Then, by Lemma 1 the views $S_1, \dots, S_n$ are inconsistent. Hence, there is no solution to Problem 1, and therefore neither to Problems 2 and 3. □

The algorithm is sound, but not complete, i.e., if the algorithm reports "inconclusive" then the views can either be consistent or not. Example 6 that follows indicates this fact.

Example 6. Consider the views $V_i = (\{x_i\}, \{y_i, z_i, w_i\}, \theta_i = \neg x_i \wedge \neg y_i \wedge \neg z_i \wedge \neg w_i, \phi_i)$ for $i = 1, 2$, where all variables are Boolean and ϕ_1, ϕ_2 are such that $[\![V_1]\!]_o = \{\sigma_1 = (0)(0)(0)(0)(0), \sigma_1' = (0)(1)(1)(1)(1)\}$ and $[\![V_2]\!]_o = \{\sigma_2 = (0)(0)(1), \sigma_2' = (0)(1)(0)\}$. The views V_1 and V_2 have been sampled with periods $T_1 = 2$ and $T_2 = 4$ respectively. The observable behavior of the views is shown in the form of trees in Fig. 8. We claim that the views V_1 and V_2 are inconsistent. Assume the contrary. Then a possible witness system $\mathcal{S}$ should contain at least one behavior which at position $i = 8$ is at state $x = 0$, while at position $i = 4$ it is at state $x = 0$ (like σ_1 above), and also at least one behavior which at position $i = 8$ is at state $x = 1$ while at position $i = 4$ it is at state $x = 0$ (like σ_2). This implies that $a_{T_1}(\mathcal{S})$ or equivalently $[\![V_1]\!]_o$ should contain at least one behavior that is at position $i = 8$ at state $x = 1$ while at position $i = 4$ it is at state $x = 0$. This is not possible since $[\![V_1]\!]_o$ contains only two behaviors: σ_1 which is at state $x = 0$ at both positions $i = 4$ and $i = 8$; and σ_1' which is at state $x = 1$ at both positions $i = 4$ and $i = 8$. Therefore, V_1 and V_2 are inconsistent.

The algorithm cannot detect the inconsistency of V_1 and V_2, however, and reports "inconclusive". This is because at the common positions $0, 4, 8$ the behaviors of the views are both in the same sets of states ($\{0\}$ at position 0, and $\{0, 1\}$ at both positions 4 and 8). Hence, each of the reachable final states of the relevant label driven composition C, contains in the first 2 coordinates the same states.

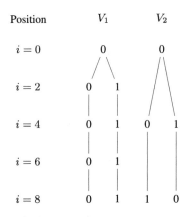

Fig. 8. Behavior trees for views V_1 and V_2.

Example 7. We provide an example run of the algorithm. Consider two views described by the FOS $S_i = (X = \{x, y\}, \theta_i = \neg x \wedge \neg y, \phi_i)$ where the definitions of ϕ_i are indicated in Fig. 9, for $i = 1, 2$. Although the two views have the same initial state and the same set of (three) reachable states, they are not identical as their transitions are different. For the remaining exposition, it helps to label the states of S_1 as $1, 2, 3$, and the states of S_2 as a, b, c. Suppose that the views have been obtained with periodic samplings a_{T_i} for $i = 1, 2$ and periods $T_1 = 2, T_2 = 3$ respectively.

Applying **Step 1** of the algorithm we obtain the finite automata L_i for each of S_i for $i = 1, 2$ respectively, as shown in Fig. 10. After the determinization **Step 2**, we obtain the deterministic automata shown in Fig. 11. The HPA H of **Step 3** coincides with the HPA shown in Fig. 4. Figure 12 shows the label driven composition $dL_1 \parallel dL_2 \parallel H$ w.r.t. H of **Step 4**. We observe that there exists a final state $(l_{123}, l_{ab}, 0)$ that $l_{123} \neq l_{ab}$. Hence, according to the **Step 5** of the view consistency algorithm, we obtain that the views S_1, S_2 are inconsistent.

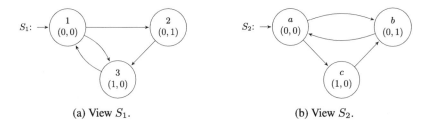

(a) View S_1.   (b) View S_2.

Fig. 9. FOS views S_1 and S_2.

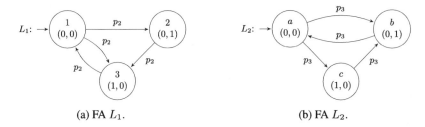

(a) FA L_1.   (b) FA L_2.

Fig. 10. Step 1: Finite automata L_1 and L_2 obtained from the views S_1 and S_2 of Fig. 9 by adding the labels p_2 and p_3 corresponding to their respective periods.

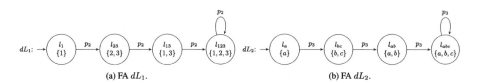

(a) FA dL_1.   (b) FA dL_2.

Fig. 11. Step 2: Deterministic FA dL_1 and dL_2 obtained by determinizing the automata L_1 and L_2 of Fig. 10.

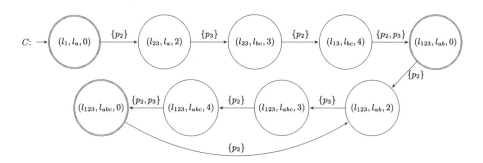

Fig. 12. Step 4: Label-driven composition $dL_1 \parallel dL_2 \parallel H$.

6   Conclusions and Future Work

Multi-view modeling is key to systems engineering, as a technique where the use of multiple models/views guides the development of a system. However, one of the crucial issues in multi-view modeling is ensuring consistency among the views. In this work we studied the view consistency problem within the formal framework of [10,11], but for a different type of abstraction functions than those studied previously. In particular, we studied view consistency w.r.t. periodic sampling abstractions.

The main future work direction is to develop a complete view consistency algorithm. It would be also interesting to answer the question whether Problems 1 and 2 are equivalent, which is currently open. Moreover, we would like to extend our results to handle Problem 3, i.e., to examine under which conditions some given views have a witness fully-observable system. Other future research includes considering other abstraction functions than projections or periodic samplings. Also part of future work is to study heterogeneous instantiations of the multi-view modeling framework, e.g., where some views are discrete, some continuous, some hybrid, and so on. In addition to these theoretical directions, ongoing work includes an implementation of the current framework and experimentation with case studies.

References

1. Baier, C., Katoen, J.-P.: Principles of Model Checking. MIT Press, Cambridge (2008)
2. Broman, D., Lee, E.A., Tripakis, S., Törngren, M.: Viewpoints, formalisms, languages, and tools for cyber-physical systems. In: 6th International Workshop on Multi-Paradigm Modeling (MPM 2012) (2012)
3. Getir, S., Grunske, L., Bernasko, C.K., Käfer, V., Sanwald, T., Tichy, M.: CoWolf – A generic framework for multi-view co-evolution and evaluation of models. In: Kolovos, D., Wimmer, M. (eds.) ICMT 2015. LNCS, vol. 9152, pp. 34–40. Springer, Cham (2015). doi:10.1007/978-3-319-21155-8_3
4. Hopcroft, J.E., Ullman, J.D.: Introduction to Automata Theory, Languages, and Computation. Addison-Wesley, New York (1990)
5. Maoz, S., Ringert, J.O., Rumpe, B.: Semantically configurable consistency analysis for class and object diagrams. CoRR, abs/1409.2313 (2014)
6. Persson, M., Törngren, M., Qamar, A., Westman, J., Biehl, M., Tripakis, S., Vangheluwe, H., Denil, J.: A characterization of integrated multi-view modeling in the context of embedded and cyber-physical systems. In: EMSOFT, pp. 10:1–10:10. IEEE (2013)
7. Rajhans, A., Krogh, B.H.: Heterogeneous verification of cyber-physical systems using behavior relations. In: HSCC 2012, pp. 35–44. ACM (2012)
8. Rajhans, A., Krogh, B.H.: Compositional heterogeneous abstraction. In: HSCC 2013, pp. 253–262. ACM (2013)
9. Rasch, H., Wehrheim, H.: Checking consistency in UML diagrams: Classes and state machines. In: Najm, E., Nestmann, U., Stevens, P. (eds.) FMOODS 2003. LNCS, vol. 2884, pp. 229–243. Springer, Heidelberg (2003). doi:10.1007/978-3-540-39958-2_16

10. Reineke, J., Stergiou, C., Tripakis, S.: Basic problems in multi-view modeling. Submitted journal version of [11]
11. Reineke, J., Tripakis, S.: Basic problems in multi-view modeling. In: Ábrahám, E., Havelund, K. (eds.) TACAS 2014. LNCS, vol. 8413, pp. 217–232. Springer, Heidelberg (2014). doi:10.1007/978-3-642-54862-8_15
12. Shah, A.A., Kerzhner, A.A., Schaefer, D., Paredis, C.J.J.: Multi-view modeling to support embedded systems engineering in SysML. In: Engels, G., Lewerentz, C., Schäfer, W., Schürr, A., Westfechtel, B. (eds.) Graph Transformations and Model-Driven Engineering. LNCS, vol. 5765, pp. 580–601. Springer, Heidelberg (2010). doi:10.1007/978-3-642-17322-6_25
13. Tripakis, S.: Compositionality in the science of system design. Proc. IEEE **104**(5), 960–970 (2016)
14. Hanxleden, R., Lee, E.A., Motika, C., Fuhrmann, H.: Multi-view modeling and pragmatics in 2020. In: Calinescu, R., Garlan, D. (eds.) Monterey Workshop 2012. LNCS, vol. 7539, pp. 209–223. Springer, Heidelberg (2012). doi:10.1007/978-3-642-34059-8_11
15. Zhao, X., Long, Q., Qiu, Z.: Model checking dynamic UML consistency. In: Liu, Z., He, J. (eds.) ICFEM 2006. LNCS, vol. 4260, pp. 440–459. Springer, Heidelberg (2006). doi:10.1007/11901433_24

Constrained Synthesis from Component Libraries

Antonio Iannopollo[1]([✉]), Stavros Tripakis[1,2],
and Alberto Sangiovanni-Vincentelli[1]

[1] EECS Department, University of California at Berkeley, Berkeley, USA
{antonio,stavros,alberto}@eecs.berkeley.edu
[2] Department of Computer Science, Aalto University, Espoo, Finland

Abstract. Synthesis from component libraries is the problem of building a network of components from a given library, such that the network realizes a given specification. This problem is undecidable in general. It becomes decidable if we impose a bound on the number of chosen components. However, the bounded problem remains computationally hard and brute-force approaches do not scale. In this paper we study scalable methods for solving the problem of bounded synthesis from libraries, proposing a solution based on the CounterExample-Guided Inductive Synthesis paradigm. Although our synthesis algorithm does not assume a specific formalism *a priori*, we present a parallel implementation which instantiates components defined as Linear Temporal Logic-based Assume/Guarantee Contracts. We show the potential of our approach and evaluate our implementation by applying it to an industrial case study.

1 Introduction

While synthesis of an implementation given formal specifications in areas such as program synthesis is a well studied problem [8,10,11,15,22,23], the application of synthesis techniques for Cyber-Physical Systems (CPS), where it is hard to completely decouple cyber and physical aspects of design, is still in its infancy. Synthesis from component libraries is the process of synthesizing a new component by composing elements chosen from a library. This type of synthesis is able to capture the complexity of CPS by restricting possible synthesis outcomes to a set of well-tested, already available components. Library-based design approaches are nowadays a *de facto* standard in many fields, such as VLSI design, where the market for Intellectual Property (IP) blocks is growing well above 3 Billion US$ [1]. On the basis of this trend the interest of system

The authors wish to acknowledge Christos Stergiou, Sanjit Seshia, and the anonymous reviewers for the useful comments. This work has been partially supported by the NSF (CCF-1139138 and CNS-1329759), by IBM and United Technologies Corporation (UTC) via the iCyPhy consortium, by TerraSwarm, one of six centers of STARnet, a Semiconductor Research Corporation program sponsored by MARCO and DARPA, and by the Academy of Finland.

© Springer International Publishing AG 2017
O. Kouchnarenko and R. Khosravi (Eds.): FACS 2016, LNCS 10231, pp. 92–110, 2017.
DOI: 10.1007/978-3-319-57666-4_7

companies on library-based design, both for hardware and software, is steadily increasing. This leads to the need of methodologies which guarantee *correct by construction* designs.

The general problem of synthesis from component libraries, where the components are state machines, is undecidable [11]. In this paper we focus on a decidable variant of the problem, presenting two variants of an algorithm, a sequential and a *parallel* one, based on the *CounterExample-Guided Inductive Synthesis* (CEGIS) paradigm [10,22]. To reduce the solution search space, this algorithm leverages designer hints and relations among components, some of them *precomputed* and stored in the libraries as additional composition rules. To the best of our knowledge, this is the first time that a concurrent synthesis algorithm is proposed for this problem, thanks to the decoupling of a solution *topology* from its semantic evaluation. Although no particular formalism is assumed *a priori*, we present an implementation of the parallel version of the algorithm (developed in a tool we call PYCO) which uses *linear temporal logic* (LTL)-based *Assume/Guarantee (A/G) Contracts* as the underlying formalism for specifying components, and exploits multiprocessor architectures to speed up synthesis. We evaluate PYCO by synthesizing a controller for an aircraft *Electrical Power distribution System* (EPS) [12]. This problem has already been studied using contracts [9,13]. In these papers, however, contracts have been used mostly for verification and to describe requirements, without playing any role in the synthesis process itself, performed using standard reactive synthesis techniques. Here, contracts collected in the component library represent controllers for a number of EPS subsystems. Our synthesis algorithm, for the first time, operates directly on those contracts to compose a controller that satisfies all the requirements.

The contributions of this paper, both theoretical and methodological, can be then summarized as: (i) definition of an algorithm for constrained synthesis from component libraries which can leverage *precomputed*, library-specific composition rules; (ii) implementation of a parallel variant of the synthesis algorithm using libraries of temporal components, defined as *A/G* Contracts; and (iii) its application to an industrial relevant case study, i.e. synthesis of a controller for an aircraft EPS. The rest of the paper is organized as follows. Section 2 provides references on background concepts and describes related works. In Sect. 3 we define the synthesis problem we tackle and analyze its complexity, proposing our solution in Sect. 4. There, we also introduce a running example used to explain in detail the problem encoding and the approach we adopt. Implementation is discussed in Sect. 5, where we also describe details of the parallel algorithm variant. In Sect. 6 we present the EPS case study and discuss empirical results. Finally, we draw conclusions in Sect. 7.

2   Previous Work

Synthesis Our work on synthesis from component libraries is inspired by two major contributions in this field. In [15], Pnueli and Rosner show that the problem of synthesizing a set of distributed finite-state controllers such that their network satisfies a given specification is undecidable. In [11], Lustig and Vardi show that the problem of synthesis from component libraries for *data-flow* composition, where the output of a component is fed to another one, is also undecidable. Thus, [15] shows that fixing the topology of the network while letting the synthesis process find the components is undecidable, while [11] shows that fixing the components while letting the synthesis process find the topology (possibly by replicating components) is also undecidable. In this paper we achieve decidability by imposing a bound on the total number of component instances, positioning our efforts in between the two approaches presented above. The general idea of synthesis from component libraries adopted here is reminiscent of the work in [8]. There, Gulwani et al. considered the problem of synthesis of finite loop-free programs from libraries of atomic program statements. Our work is different as (i) we consider a more generic concept of component (considering multiple output ports and port types) that can be also defined using temporal logic, (ii) decouple topological properties from component specification formalism, and (iii) introduce the idea, in the context of synthesis from component libraries, of applying library-specific composition rules. A recent effort in synthesis from component libraries has also been described in [3]. There, a controller is built out of library components in a *control-flow* fashion (using the terminology introduced in [11]). That approach, however, is orthogonal to ours since we focus on data-flow compositions.

Counterexample-Guided Inductive Synthesis and combination of Induction, Deduction, and Structure. CEGIS is a well known synthesis paradigm which originates from techniques of debugging using counterexamples [20] and *Counter-Example-Guided Abstraction Refinement* (CEGAR) [6]. CEGIS is an inductive synthesis approach where synthesis is the result of inferring details of the specification from I/O examples, driven by counterexamples usually provided by a constraint solver. In CEGIS an iterative algorithm, according to a certain concept class, generates candidate solutions which are processed by an oracle and either declared valid, in which case the algorithm terminates, or used as counterexamples to restrict the candidate space. Recently, a novel methodology which formalizes the combination of *Structure, Inductive and Deductive* reasoning (SID) has been proposed in [19], representing a generalization of both CEGAR and CEGIS. The approach proposed in this paper instantiate the CEGIS paradigm (not a trivial task, in general), and thus it is an implementation of the SID methodology.

Platform Based Design and A/G Contracts. Platform-Based Design (PBD) [17] is an iterative design methodology which has been successfully applied in a number of domains, including electronic and automotive design. In PBD, design is carried out as the mapping of a user defined function to a platform instance. This platform instance represents a network of interconnected components, chosen from a library. Components in PBD, together with their functionality, expose other characteristics such as composition rules and performance indices. This additional information is used to optimize the mapping process, according to both functional and non-functional specifications. In this paper, we borrow from PBD the idea that platform components can define their own composition constraints to be applied during mapping. A/G contracts, based on the more general theory of contracts [4,14,18], offer a formal framework for a rigorous application of PBD. An A/G contract describes a component as a tuple $C = (A, G)$ where A represents the assumptions that a component makes on its environment, and G represents the guarantees it provides. Contract algebra formalizes a wide set of operations to manipulate contracts, including *parallel composition* and *refinement*. In Sect. 5, we discuss the implementation of our approach for the LTL A/G contract framework, i.e., the A/G contract framework where A and G are specified as LTL formulas. Nevertheless, our solution is general and works with other compositional frameworks as well.

3   Constrained Synthesis from Component Libraries

In our framework, a *component* is a tuple $G = (I_G, O_G, \varphi_G, \sigma_G, R_G)$, where I_G is the set of input ports (or variables), O_G is the set of output ports, and φ_G is the component specification, expressed using a specific notation (e.g. an A/G Contract, or a LTL formula). I_G, O_G and φ_G are all defined over a common set of symbols, or alphabet, Σ_{IO}. $\sigma_G : I_G \cup O_G \to T$ is a function mapping ports of G to elements in T, where T is a *typeset*. A typeset is a poset consisting of a set of symbols (types) ordered by the *subtype* relation[1]. For $a, b \in T$, the notation $a \leq b$ means that a is a subtype of b. Finally $R_G = \{R_{Gi} \mid R_{Gi} \subseteq (I_G \cup O_G \times I_G \cup O_G)\}$ is a set of relations over ports in G. A library is a tuple $L = (Z, T, R_Z, R_T)$. Here $Z = \{G_1, \ldots, G_n\}$ is a finite *multiset* of components, meaning that Z might contain multiple instances of the same component. $R_Z = \{R_{Zi} \mid R_{Zi} \subseteq (\Sigma_{IO} \times \Sigma_{IO})\}$ is a set of relations over component ports in Z, while $R_T = T \times T$ is a relation over types. Sets R_G and R_Z, and relation R_T, are used by the library designer to provide additional design constraints to speed up the synthesis process, according to her domain knowledge. General *composition rules* between components, which define constraints that need to be applied no matter what a specific library defines, are collected in a set, called Q. We give more details about Q in Sect. 4.2.

Definition 1 (Topological Constraints). *With the term* Topological Constraints, *we refer to all the constraints encoded in the relations in R_G, R_Z, and R_T, together with the general composition constraints in the set Q.*

We consider the system specification $S = (I_S, O_S, \varphi_S, \sigma_S, R_S)$, that needs to be synthesized, as a component itself. In this way (through relations in R_S) a user of the synthesizer is also able to provide design hints that are specific to the problem instance, such as precise input/output interface, in terms of ports and

---

[1] Without loss of generality, here we can consider the poset T being organized as a *tree*. This is enough to obtain a simple type system with single inheritance, where all the types share the same *root type* ($\perp$).

their types, as well as additional constraints over those ports. The composition of two components $G_1 = (I_1, O_1, \varphi_1, \sigma_1, R_1)$ and $G_2 = (I_2, O_2, \varphi_2, \sigma_2, R_2)$ is a new component $G_1 \otimes G_2 = ((I_1 \cup I_2) \setminus (O_1 \cup O_2), O_1 \cup O_2, \varphi_1 \otimes \varphi_2, \sigma_1 \cup \sigma_2, R_1 \cup R_2)$, assuming that the operator $\otimes$ is defined for φ_1 and φ_2, and there is no conflict between σ_1 and σ_2. Input ports that are connected to output ports are considered outputs in the resulting composition. For instance, when input a is connected to output b, the resulting composite component only contains output b (input a "disappears" since it is going to be controlled by b). To model interactions between components (e.g. when the output of a component is the input of another one) we need to introduce the concept of connection between ports. Formally, we indicate connections between ports using the function

$$\rho : \Sigma_{IO} \times \Sigma_{IO} \rightarrow \{0, 1\}$$

Given ports a and b, we have $\rho(a, b) = 1$ if and only if, in the resulting composition, a and b will be expressed (i.e. renamed) using the same symbol[2]. Often we will refer to composition of components (and their specifications) using the notation $G_1 \otimes_\rho G_2$, where with $\otimes_\rho$ we indicate the renaming of variables of G_1 and G_2 according to ρ, followed by the usual composition operation. We also assume that the formalism used to express component specifications $\varphi_1, \ldots, \varphi_2$ includes the notion of refinement. Intuitively, if φ_1 refines φ_2, indicated with $\varphi_1 \preceq \varphi_2$, then φ_2 will always hold if φ_1 holds, i.e. φ_1 can be safely used in place of φ_2. For instance, if φ_1 and φ_2 are logic formulas, $\varphi_1 \preceq \varphi_2$ is equivalent to the implication $\varphi_1 \Rightarrow \varphi_2$. The Constrained Synthesis from Component Libraries (CSCL) problem can then be defined as:

Definition 2 (CSCL problem). *Given a system specification $S = (I_S, O_S, \varphi_S, \sigma_S, R_S)$, and a library of components $L = (Z, T, R_Z, R_T)$ where the operations of composition ($\otimes$) and refinement ($\preceq$) are defined, find a finite set of components $\{G_1, \ldots, G_N \mid G_i = (I_i, O_i, \varphi_i, \sigma_i, R_{Gi}) \in Z\}$ and a connection function ρ such that (a) $\varphi_1 \otimes_\rho \cdots \otimes_\rho \varphi_N \preceq \varphi_S$, and (b) all the topological constraints hold.*

3.1   A Combinatorial Analysis for the CSCL Problem

The CSCL problem is a hard problem. In this section, we quantify its combinatorial complexity by analyzing two simpler cases first, and then putting the results together for the general case. As in the previous section, we consider a library $L = (Z, T, R_Z, R_T)$, with finite $Z = \{G_1, \ldots, G_N\}$, and a specification $S = (I_S, O_S, \varphi_S, \sigma_S, R_S)$. Since we are interested in the worst-case scenario, in this case we assume $R_Z = R_T = R_S = R_{G_1} = \cdots = R_{G_N} = \emptyset$, and $T = \{\bot\}$ (a typeset containing only the root type). First we examine the case in which we already have a set of m *connected* components $\{G'_1, \ldots, G'_m\}$ and we want to find a single component $G_z \in Z$ such that $\varphi_z \otimes \varphi'_1 \otimes \cdots \otimes \varphi'_m \preceq \varphi_S$. Assuming N is the number of components in Z, we have N possibilities to try. Extending this

---

[2] To indicate $\rho(p, q) = 1$, we will often use the shorthand $\rho_{p,q}$, and $\neg\rho_{p,q}$ for $\rho(p, q) = 0$.

example to include $c \leq N$ unknown components is straightforward. In this case, there are $\frac{N!}{(N-c)!}$ candidate solutions. On the other hand, we have a scenario in which we still have m components $\{G'_1, \ldots, G'_m\}$, but connections among them are missing. We want to connect the components to each other, according to a certain function ρ, such that $\varphi'_1 \otimes_\rho \cdots \otimes_\rho \varphi'_m \preceq \varphi_S$. The complexity of this problem depends on the total number of ports. Assuming p being the number of ports of a component, then there are $2^{\frac{mp(mp-1)}{2}}$ possible solutions.[3] Combining together the previous two examples yields the CSCL scenario, in which we want to find both components and their connections to satisfy S. Assuming every component in our library Z has p ports, and a finite N_s as the maximum number of components in a possible solution, one can see how in this case there are $\sum_{c=1}^{N_s} \frac{N!}{(N-c)!} 2^{\frac{cp(cp-1)}{2}}$ possible solutions, where again N is number of elements in Z.

4   Encoding and Solving the CSCL Problem

We propose a solution for the CSCL problem based on the CEGIS paradigm, in which synthesis is carried out by an iterative algorithm. In each iteration two major steps are performed. In the first one, a constraint solver is invoked to provide a candidate solution, that is, a set of components and their connections. With respect to Definition 2, this first step takes care of point (b) and provides the function ρ used in point (a). To provide meaningful candidates, the solver has to make sure that all the topological constraints are satisfied. The second step satisfies point (a) of Definition 2, and it is performed interrogating a *verifier* which determines whether the candidate composition, after proper interconnection of components, refines the global specification φ_S. In this step, the choice of the verifier depends on the formalism used to specify components. For instance, a model checker could be chosen as verifier in case components are specified as state machines and the global specification is an LTL formula. We call *counterexample* a candidate composition (i.e. a set of components and their connections) which has been proven wrong by the verifier. A counterexample is used to inductively learn new constraints. These constraints include generic ones (i.e. prevent components with the same behavior of those in the counterexample to appear in future candidate compositions) and those inferred using library-specific constraints (i.e. prevent components which represent an abstraction of those in the counterexample to appear in future candidate compositions, if this information is available in the library through relations in the set R_Z).

Table 1 illustrates the CSCL algorithm. In the CSCL algorithm, the task of pruning the search space is carried out in a twofold manner. First the topological constraints drastically reduce the number of potential solutions. Note once again that some of these constraints can be *precomputed* and stored in the library through the relations in R_Z, R_T, R_S, and $R_{G_1} = \cdots = R_{G_N}$, avoiding the

---

[3] Just recall that the maximum number of edges in a graph of n nodes is $\frac{n(n-1)}{2}$. $2^{\frac{n(n-1)}{2}}$ enumerates all the subsets of those connections.

Table 1. CSCL algorithm. (STEP 1) and (STEP 2) are labels.

Algorithm 1: *CSCL*

Input: A specification $S = (I_S, O_S, \varphi_S, \sigma_S, R_S)$, a library of components $L = (Z, T, R_Z, R_T)$

Output: A set of components $H = \{G_1, \ldots, G_n\}, H \subseteq Z$, and a connection function ρ, such that $\varphi_1 \otimes_\rho \cdots \otimes_\rho \varphi_n \preceq \varphi_S$, or NULL if no solution is found

1. Initialize constraint solver and verifier, and instantiate topological constraints for problem instance
2. (STEP 1) WHILE get candidate solution $(H' = \{G_1, \ldots, G_n\}, \rho')$ from constraint solver
   (a) Build composition $G_1 \otimes_{\rho'} \cdots \otimes_{\rho'} G_n$
   (b) (STEP 2) IF the verifier checks that $\varphi_1 \otimes_{\rho'} \cdots \otimes_{\rho'} \varphi_n \preceq \varphi_S$ holds
        return $H = H'$ and $\rho = \rho'$
   (c) ELSE infer new topological constraints from counterexample (H', ρ')
3. return NULL

---

need to re-learn those constraints during the synthesis process. Second, being Z a multiset, a counterexample observed in step 2.c of the CSCL algorithm in Table 1 can be used to match multiple elements of the library, ruling out a number of possible candidate instances exponential in the number of components in the rejected candidate. For instance, if the counterexample is a composition of 4 components, and each of those components has 3 instances in Z, then adding that single counterexample will discard 3^4 erroneous candidate instances. The output of the CSCL algorithm is a finite set of components, H, and their connections, expressed as a function, ρ.

To ensure termination, the CSCL algorithm requires an implicit bound on the number of components to be used in a candidate solution. For instance, one possibility could be letting the maximum number of components in a solution be equal to the cardinality of Z. This is a problem, however, when the size of the library increases. As it will be described in Sect. 4.2, we set the maximum number of components in H to be equal to the number of outputs of the specification S. In such way, the cardinality of H is directly tied to the complexity, in terms of ports, of S. Moreover, this constraint is not too restrictive, since it is always possible to add *dummy* outputs to S to increase the maximum number of components allowed in the solution.

4.1   Running Example: Synthesize the Modulo Operation

We introduce a simple example to help understanding the CSCL algorithm and give an intuition on the formulation of the topological constraints discussed in Sect. 4.2. Our objective is to synthesize the modulo operation starting from a library of simpler arithmetic operations. In this example, the reader will have the responsibility to be the verifier. For simplicity, we assume only strictly positive integer inputs.

Let us define our library to be $L_{op} = (Z_{op}, \bot, \emptyset, \emptyset)$, where we have only one type ($\bot$) for all the ports and no additional relations over ports and types. $Z_{op} = \{add, sub, mult, div\}$ is a set containing addition, subtraction, multiplication and integer division. Every component has two inputs and one output, and its specification is the associated arithmetic operation. We assume no additional relations over ports also at component level. Thus we have:

$$add = (\{a_a, b_a\}, \{c_a\}, c_a = a_a + b_a, \{a_a, b_a, c_a\} \to \{\bot\}, \emptyset)$$
$$sub = (\{a_s, b_s\}, \{c_s\}, c_s = a_s - b_s, \{a_s, b_s, c_s\} \to \{\bot\}, \emptyset)$$
$$mult = (\{a_m, b_m\}, \{c_m\}, c_m = a_m \cdot b_m, \{a_m, b_m, c_m\} \to \{\bot\}, \emptyset)$$
$$div = (\{a_d, b_d\}, \{c_d\}, c_d = \lfloor a_d/b_d \rfloor, \{a_d, b_d, c_d\} \to \{\bot\}, \emptyset)$$

To apply the CSCL algorithm, we need to make sure the operations of composition and refinement are defined for elements in L_{op}. Here, the composition of two component specifications is the classical *function composition*, while the refinement relation can simply be the equality between functions. The specification is the component $S_{mod} = (\{x, y\}, \{z\}, z = mod(x, y), \{x, y, z\} \to \{\bot\}, \emptyset)$. Playing the role of verifier, we know that the modulo operation can be computed as $mod(x, y) = x - \lfloor x/y \rfloor \cdot y$. A composition of elements in Z_{op} that implements S_{mod} is shown in Fig. 1: $sub(x, mult(div(x, y), y))$, with connections $\rho_{b_s, c_m}, \rho_{a_m, c_d}, \rho_{x, a_s}, \rho_{x, a_d}, \rho_{y, b_d}, \rho_{y, b_m}, \rho_{z, c_s}$. Such composition is correct because, as we will see soon, it respects the topological constraint (STEP 1 of the CSCL algorithm), and because the reader, as verifier, can validate the resulting composition (STEP 2) (cf. the composition $add(x, mult(div(x, y), y))$, which is also correct according to the computation in STEP 1, but does not implement the modulo operation).

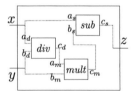

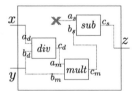

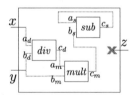

Fig. 1. Modulo operation composition from elements in L_{op} (see Sect. 4.1).

Fig. 2. Illegal composition of elements in L_{op} (a_s disconnected).

Fig. 3. Illegal composition of elements in L_{op} (z disconnected).

4.2   Topological Constraints

In this section, we discuss the topological constraints for the CSCL problem. As introduced in Sects. 3 and 4, topological constraints are a set of logic formulas defined over the library of components $L = (Z, T, R_Z, R_T)$, with components of the form $G = (I_G, O_G, \varphi_G, \sigma_G, R_G)$, and a system specification

$S = (I_S, O_S, \varphi_S, \sigma_S, R_S)$. Part of the topological constraints encode general composition rules collected in the set Q, introduced in Sect. 3. Before enumerating such constraints, it is useful to define an operator to address all the ports of all components in L:

$$\mathcal{P}_{lib} = \{p \mid \exists G \in Z : p \in I_G \cup O_G\}$$

Similarly, to address all the ports in L and the ports in the system specification S, we use:

$$\mathcal{P}_{lib \cup S} = \mathcal{P}_{lib} \cup I_S \cup O_S$$

As seen before, the result of the synthesis process is a finite set of components $H \subseteq Z$ and the connection function ρ, introduced in Sect. 3. We can then enumerate the constraints in Q as follows[4]:

- Every candidate component must control at least an output of the global specification S. Assuming N_O outputs in O_S, then trivially a solution can include at most N_O components. As already pointed out, it is possible to *relax* this constraint by adding dummy outputs to S.

$$\forall G \in H : \exists p \in O_G : \exists s \in O_S : \rho_{p,s} \tag{1}$$

Example 1. In the case of the example in Sect. 4.1, to obtain the composition showed in Fig. 1 we need to add two dummy outputs to S_{mod} (not shown in the figure). This is needed because S_{mod} has only one output port but our implementation requires three components.

- The following properties encode the semantics of our connection function. Equation 2 tells us that if for three ports p, q, w we have $\rho_{p,q}$ and $\rho_{q,w}$, then it must be also $\rho_{p,w}$.

$$\forall p, q, w \in \mathcal{P}_{lib \cup S} : \rho_{p,q} \land \rho_{q,w} \Rightarrow \rho_{p,w} \tag{2}$$

Equation 3 represents the fact that if p is connected to q, then q is also connected to p.

$$\forall p, q \in \mathcal{P}_{lib \cup S} : \rho_{p,q} \Rightarrow \rho_{q,p} \tag{3}$$

Equation 4 simply states that a port is always connected to itself.

$$\forall p \in \mathcal{P}_{lib \cup S} : \rho_{p,p} \tag{4}$$

- Two output ports of components in the library cannot be connected to each other:

$$\forall G, G' \in Z : \forall p, q \in O_G \cup O_{G'} : (p \neq q) \Rightarrow \neg \rho_{p,q} \tag{5}$$

---

[4] Here we borrow the notation typical of *first order* logic formulas, although all the formulas refer to a finite number of elements.

- Inputs of a candidate component must be connected to specification inputs or candidate component outputs (Eq. 6), while outputs of a candidate component must be connected to specification outputs or candidate component inputs (Eq. 7).

$$\forall G \in H : \forall p \in I_G : (\exists s \in I_S : \rho_{p,s}) \vee (\exists G' \in H : \exists q \in O_{G'} : \rho_{p,q}) \qquad (6)$$

$$\forall G \in H : \forall p \in O_G : (\exists s \in O_S : \rho_{p,s}) \vee (\exists G' \in H : \exists q \in I_{G'} : \rho_{p,q}) \qquad (7)$$

Example 2. Equation 5 prevents the connection of outputs of components in the library. With respect to the example in Sect. 4.1, this means enforcing $\neg \rho_{c_a,c_s}$, $\neg \rho_{c_a,c_m}$, $\neg \rho_{c_a,c_d}$, $\neg \rho_{c_s,c_m}$, $\neg \rho_{c_s,c_d}$, and $\neg \rho_{c_m,c_d}$. Equations 6 and 7 make sure that all the candidate compositions are properly connected. For instance, the composition in Fig. 2 violates Eq. 6, because a_s is not connected to any other port.

- No distinct ports of S can be connected to each other. Also in this case, this is not too restrictive. If needed, in fact, one can relax this constraint by explicitly adding a component in the library implementing the identity function.

$$\forall s, r \in I_S \cup O_S : s \neq r \Rightarrow \neg \rho_{s,r} \qquad (8)$$

- Inputs of the specification S cannot be connected to component outputs, because otherwise in the resulting composition those inputs will be treated as outputs (as seen in Sect. 3).

$$\forall s \in I_S : \forall G \in Z : \forall p \in O_G : \neg \rho_{s,p} \qquad (9)$$

- Every input of the specification S has to be connected at least to one candidate component input (Eq. 10), while every output of S has to be connected at least to one candidate component output (Eq. 11).

$$\forall s \in I_S : \exists G \in H : \exists p \in I_G : \rho_{s,p} \qquad (10)$$

$$\forall s \in O_S : \exists G \in H : \exists p \in O_G : \rho_{s,p} \qquad (11)$$

Example 3. Equations 10 and 11 ensure that there is a full mapping of specification ports into components ports. For instance, the composition in Fig. 3 violates Eq. 11 because there is an output of the specification, z, which is not connected to any component outputs.

Together with constraints in Q, topological constraints encode also rules to properly connect ports of different types, according to the subtype relation defined in Sect. 3 and considering contravariant inputs and outputs[5] (similarly to

---

[5] This means that, given two components G_1 and G_2, if G_1 has more legal inputs and less legal outputs than G_2 then G_1 can be used in place of G_2.

what described by de Alfaro and Henzinger in [2]). Moreover, they encode rules to include designer hints into the synthesis process at library (R_{G_i}s, R_T, and R_Z) and specification level (R_S). Such additional constraints, although being domain specific, can greatly reduce the solution search space and therefore synthesis time. For space reasons, however, here we omit an exhaustive enumeration of all the topological constraints, which can be derived autonomously by the reader as interesting exercise.

4.3   An Efficient Encoding for the Topological Constraints

If implemented directly, the encoding we just presented is not particularly efficient. For instance one can see how Eq. 2 represents a formula which grows cubically in the number of ports of all components in the library. The encoding we present in this section exploits a more efficient representation of component connections.

Given library $L = (Z, T, R_Z, R_T)$ and global specification $S = (I_S, O_S, \varphi_S, \sigma_S, R_S)$, we assign an *index* to all the output ports in the library and also to all the input ports of the specification S, and indicate with $\mathbb{I}$ the set containing such indices. Conversely, we associate an integer variable to every input port in the library, as well as to every output port of S. We call these variables *connection variables* and group them in the set $\mathbb{V}$. Connection variables, as the name suggests, are used to specify connections between ports, and they are *assigned* by the constraint solver in the first step of the CSCL algorithm. We use the function $\mathcal{I} : \mathcal{P}_{lib \cup S} \rightarrow \mathbb{I} \cup \{-1\}$ to retrieve the index of a given port, or -1 if the index is not defined for the port. Similarly, we use the function $\mathcal{V} : \mathcal{P}_{lib \cup S} \rightarrow \mathbb{V} \cup \{\emptyset\}$ to retrieve the connection variable of a given port, or $\emptyset$ if the connection variable is not defined for that port (e.g. input ports of S). We then map connection variables to indices using the function $\mathcal{M} : \mathbb{V} \rightarrow \mathbb{I} \cup \{-1\}$. Such encoding allows us to eliminate the expensive explicit representation of function ρ. For instance, the new encoding will represent the assertion $\rho_{p,q}$ for an input port p and output port q with the assignment $\mathcal{M}(\mathcal{V}(p)) = \mathcal{I}(q)$, also indicated, for convenience, as $\mathcal{M}(p) = \mathcal{I}(q)$. If p is not connected to any port, then $\mathcal{M}(p) = -1$. We only allow inputs from the library to be connected to outputs in the library or inputs of the specification S:

$$\forall G \in Z : \forall p \in I_G :$$
$$(\mathcal{M}(p) = -1) \vee [\exists G' \in Z : \exists q \in O_{G'} : \mathcal{M}(p) = \mathcal{I}(q)] \vee [\exists s \in I_S : \mathcal{M}(p) = \mathcal{I}(s)] \tag{12}$$

We also impose that outputs of the specification S can only be mapped to outputs from the library:

$$\forall s \in O_S : (\mathcal{M}(s) = -1) \vee (\exists G \in Z : \exists p \in O_G : \mathcal{M}(s) = \mathcal{I}(p)) \tag{13}$$

The following theorem affirms that, under the list of constraints in the set Q, the encoding presented in this section is at least as expressive as the one obtained representing ρ explicitly.

Theorem 1. *Let $\mathbf{C_1}$ be the set of connections among components in $Z \cup \{S\}$ representable by the function ρ under the set of constraints Q defined in Sect. 4.2. Let also $\mathbf{C_2}$ be the set of connections representable with the connection variables in $\mathbb{V}$ and indices in $\mathbb{I}$, constrained by Eqs. 12 and 13. Then $\mathbf{C_1} \subseteq \mathbf{C_2}$.*

Proof. We start considering only connections between ports in $\mathcal{P}_{lib}$. Given an input port p and an output port q, a connection $\rho_{p,q}$ in $\mathbf{C_1}$ (and by Eq. 3 also $\rho_{q,p}$) can be trivially be represented in $\mathbf{C_2}$ by the assignment $\mathcal{M}(p) = \mathcal{I}(q)$. If both p and q are outputs, then by Eq. 5 their connection cannot be in $\mathbf{C_1}$. If both p and q are inputs and $\rho_{p,q}$ is in $\mathbf{C_1}$, then by Eq. 6 p and q have to be connected to another output in the library or to an input of S. In either case, assume w be such port, where $\rho_{p,w}$ and $\rho_{q,w}$ are also in $\mathbf{C_1}$. Then $\mathcal{M}(p) = \mathcal{I}(w)$ and $\mathcal{M}(q) = \mathcal{I}(w)$ represent the equivalent connections in $\mathbf{C_2}$, including indirectly $\rho_{p,q}$ (because they have a reference to the same index). Consider now also ports of the specification S. Since, in $\mathbf{C_1}$, we do not allow any two ports of S being connected to each other (Eq. 8), we have only the case in which there is a connection $\rho_{s,p}$ between ports $s \in I_S \cup O_S$ and $p \in \mathcal{P}_{lib}$. If s is an input, then p has to be an input too (because of Eq. 9), and we can represent $\rho_{s,p}$ as $\mathcal{M}(p) = \mathcal{I}(s)$ in $\mathbf{C_2}$. If s is an output, then p can be either a component input or output. If p is output, then $\rho_{s,p}$ can be represented as $\mathcal{M}(s) = \mathcal{I}(p)$. If p is an input, then by Eq. 11 there must be another component output q such that $\rho_{s,q}$. By Eq. 2, then it must be also $\rho_{p,q}$. Therefore we can map these three connections in $\mathbf{C_2}$ with $\mathcal{M}(s) = \mathcal{I}(q)$ and $\mathcal{M}(p) = \mathcal{I}(q)$ (where $\rho_{S,q}$ is implicit because s and p refer to the same index). This shows that all the connections in $\mathbf{C_1}$ have an equivalent in $\mathbf{C_2}$, hence $\mathbf{C_1} \subseteq \mathbf{C_2}$.   □

Given Theorem 1, one can define additional topological constraints for the new encoding, to further shrink $\mathbf{C_2}$ and create a set $\mathbf{C_2'} = \mathbf{C_1} \cap \mathbf{C_2}$, equivalent to $\mathbf{C_1}$. For space reasons, we omit here the explicit enumeration of those constraints. We claim however that their derivation, given the constraints defined in Sect. 4.2, is rather simple. All the results in Sect. 6 are obtained using the encoding described in this section and the reformulated topological constraints.

5   Implementing the CSCL Algorithm

In this and the following sections we describe the implementation of a parallel variant of the CSCL algorithm and evaluate its capabilities and performance. We used the SMT solver Z3 [7] to find candidates satisfying the topological constraints and we chose to represent our library as a multiset of LTL-based A/G contracts. This choice is also motivated by the fact composition and refinement operations are well defined in the contract algebra. Moreover, additional concepts such as compatibility and consistency, can be leveraged to derive, before the actual synthesis process, library constraints on components composability (in the form of incompatible sets of ports stored through relations in R_Z). Lastly, but not less important, several tools are available to deal with LTL specifications. In our experiments the verifier chosen to compute refinement checks is *NuXMV* [5].

Table 2. Parallel CSCL algorithm

Algorithm 2: *Parallel CSCL*

Input: A specification $S = (I_S, O_S, \varphi_S, \sigma_S, R_S)$, a library of components $L = (Z, T, R_Z, R_T)$

Output: A set of components $H = \{G_1, \ldots, G_n\}, H \subseteq Z$, and a connection function ρ, such that $\varphi_1 \otimes_\rho \cdots \otimes_\rho \varphi_n \preceq \varphi_S$, or NULL if no solution is found

---

1. Initialize constraint solver and verifier, and instantiate topological constraints for problem instance
2. WHILE get candidate solution $(H' = \{G_1, \ldots, G_n\}, \rho')$ from constraint solver
   (a) Build composition $G_1 \otimes_{\rho'} \cdots \otimes_{\rho'} G_n$
   (b) Spawn a new verifier instance (process) to verify $\varphi_1 \otimes_{\rho'} \cdots \otimes_{\rho'} \varphi_n \preceq \varphi_S$
   (c) IF any verifier instance has signaled success
         retrieve instance and return $H = H'$ and $\rho = \rho'$
   (d) ELSE infer new topological constraints from counterexample (H', ρ')
3. Wait for all the remaining running verifier instances to terminate
4. IF any verifier instance has signaled success
         retrieve instance and return $H = H'$ and $\rho = \rho'$
5. return NULL

An efficient implementation of the CSCL algorithm has been developed using the encoding described in Sect. 4.3. Moreover, we decided to modify the CSCL algorithm to exploit multiprocessor architectures and further speed up synthesis. In what described so far, the CSCL algorithm computes a candidate solution first and then it asks the verifier to validate or discard that candidate. The verifier execution is, in general, a time consuming operation (i.e. verifying the validity of a LTL formula is a PSPACE-complete problem [16,21]). The intuition behind this version of the algorithm is that it is possible (and convenient) to interrogate several verifier instances at the same time, providing them with different candidates. The CSCL algorithm in Table 1 needs then to be modified to reject a candidate as soon as it is given to the verifier, providing the ability to retrieve an *old* candidate in case one of the many verifier instances gives a positive answer. Table 2 illustrates the parallel version of the CSCL algorithm. We call PYCO the tool resulting from the implementation of this algorithm.

6 Case Study

Figure 4 shows the simplified structure of an aircraft EPS in the form of a *single-line diagram*[6] [9,12,13]. Generators (as those on the top left and right sides of the diagram) deliver power to the loads (e.g. avionics, lighting, heating and motors) via AC and DC buses. In case of generator failures, *Auxiliary Power Units* (APUs) will provide the required power. Some buses supply loads which

---

[6] Single line diagrams are usually used to simplify the description of three-phase power systems.

are critical, therefore they cannot be unpowered for more than a predefined amount of time. Other, non-essential, buses supply loads that may be shed in the case of a fault. The power flow from sources to loads is determined by contactors, which are electromechanical switches that can be opened or closed. *Transformer Rectifier Units* (TRUs) convert and route AC power to DC buses. The goal of the controller, called *Bus Power Control Unit* (BPCU), is to react to changes in system conditions or failures and reroute power by actuating the contactors, ensuring that essential buses are adequately powered. Generators, APUs, and TRUs are components subject to failures. Our goal is to synthesize the logic of the BCPU from a set of subsystem controllers, described by a library of A/G contracts. In our model, controller inputs are Boolean variables, corresponding to the state of the various physical elements (i.e. presence or absence of faults). Controller outputs are also Boolean variables, and represent the status of the contactors in the system (open or closed). At this level of abstraction, contactors are assumed to have a negligible reaction time.

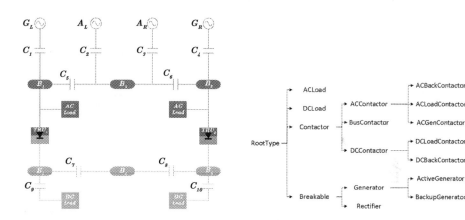

Fig. 4. Single line diagram of the EPS

Fig. 5. Tree representing the typeset used in the case study

Table 3 illustrates the set of specifications that the BPCU needs to satisfy. The first two rows describe what are the input and output variables of the EPS plant and their types, indicated in parenthesis next to the variable names (Fig. 5 shows the type tree associated to variables in the specification and library components). In total, each specification is defined over 6 input and 10 output variables. Input variables $G_L, G_R, A_L, A_R, R_L, R_R$ represent the environment event of failure of left and right generator, APU, and TRU, respectively. Output variables $C_1, \ldots, C_{10}$ represent the state of the contactors. The remaining rows of Table 3 describe a set of 9 specifications, all sharing the same assumptions. In this example, we assume from the environment that all the components do not start to operate in a faulty state (see, for instance, $\neg G_L$ in the first line of the assumptions in Table 3, referring to the left generator), and if a component breaks, then it will stay broken (specified, for the left generator, by $\Box(G_L \Rightarrow \bigcirc G_L)$). Specifications S_1 to S_4 require that if a generator or APU breaks, then it will be disconnected from the rest of the EPS in the next execution step. Note that S_1 and S_2 require also the two generators to be initially connected to the rest of the plant. S_5 requires the absence of short circuit between the two APUs, while S_6 requires the absence of short circuit between generators in case they are both healthy (after an initial setup period). Furthermore, S_7 specifies that bus B_3 needs to be isolated if no faults in generators or APUs occur. Finally, S_8 and S_9 require that DC loads need to be connected to the plant if at least one TRU is working correctly. In this example, the topological constraints include also the restriction that the variables associated to the specifications cannot be connected to each other, i.e. the failure of two EPS components needs to be associated to distinct events. These hints are encoded as a relation in R_S, not shown in Table 3.

Table 4 shows the contracts and the library-specific relations (in this example only type compatibility) in the component library. The table is divided in three sections, where the first two describe library components and the last one, on the bottom, shows the library-specific relations used to derive additional topological constraints. Every component in the library is described by its I/O variables (annotated with their types), and its specification as an A/G pair. All the components make some assumptions over the state of a certain type of EPS elements, and provide a guarantee over the state of some contactors. Consider, for instance, component B_1. It just assumes that a certain generator is not initially broken (note that the type of the input variable allows it to be connected to either a generator or an APU), and guarantees that the contactor will be always open. Clearly, B_1 is not a good candidate to satisfy either S_1 or S_2, since they require the contactor to be closed at least initially. Similarly, all the other components in the library encode a particular behavior that can be used to control parts of the EPS.

We ran all the experiments on a 2.3 GHz Intel Core i7 machine, with 8 GB of RAM, limiting the maximum number of parallel processes to 8. Figure 6 shows the observed results, in terms of execution time, running PYCO to synthesize the BPCU using two different libraries, one with 20 elements and the other with 40 (both obtained by replicating the components described in Table 4). Every bar in the histogram indicates the synthesis time for the specification subsets $\{S_1\}, \{S_1, S_2\}, \ldots, \{S_1, \ldots, S_9\}$. In both series, the increment in synthesis time is not constant between different specification sets because some specifications might have the same solution space as others, leading to similar synthesis times. We observed that the difference in synthesis times between the two series is mostly due to the initialization phase of the synthesis tool, when the library is processed and the constraint solver instantiated. For reference, a typical solution satisfying all 9 specifications included 6 components, $\{I_1, D_1, L_1, G_1, L_2, C_1\}$, for a total of 22 ports connected accordingly.

In a separate experiment, using the library with 40 elements, PYCO was been able to explore the whole solution search space invoking the verifier 108176

Table 3. Set of global specifications $S_1 \ldots S_9$ to satisfy. Assumptions are common to all the specifications

Input variables	G_L, G_R (ActiveGenerator)
	A_L, A_R (BackupGenerator)
	R_L, R_R (Rectifier)
Output variables	C_1, C_4 (ACGenContactor)
	C_2, C_3 (ACGenContactor)
	C_5, C_6 (ACBackContactor)
	C_7, C_8 (DCBackContactor)
	C_9, C_{10} (DCLoadContactor)
Assumptions (common to all)	$\neg G_L \wedge \Box(G_L \Rightarrow \bigcirc G_L) \wedge$
	$\neg G_R \wedge \Box(G_R \Rightarrow \bigcirc G_R) \wedge$
	$\neg A_L \wedge \Box(A_L \Rightarrow \bigcirc A_L) \wedge$
	$\neg A_R \wedge \Box(A_R \Rightarrow \bigcirc A_R) \wedge$
	$\neg R_L \wedge \Box(R_L \Rightarrow \bigcirc R_L) \wedge$
	$\neg R_R \wedge \Box(R_R \Rightarrow \bigcirc R_R)$
S_1	$C_1 \wedge \Box(G_L \Rightarrow \bigcirc \neg C_1)$
S_2	$C_4 \wedge \Box(G_R \Rightarrow \bigcirc \neg C_4)$
S_3	$\Box(A_L \Rightarrow \bigcirc \neg C_2)$
S_4	$\Box(A_R \Rightarrow \bigcirc \neg C_3)$
S_5	$\Box \neg(C_2 \wedge C_3)$
S_6	$\Box[(\neg G_L \wedge \neg G_R) \Rightarrow \Diamond \neg(C_5 \wedge C_6)]$
S_7	$\Box[(\neg G_L \wedge \neg A_L \wedge \neg A_R \wedge \neg G_R) \Rightarrow$ $\Diamond(\neg C_2 \wedge \neg C_3 \wedge \neg C_5 \wedge \neg C_6)]$
S_8	$\Box[\neg(R_L \wedge R_R) \Rightarrow C_9]$
S_9	$\Box[\neg(R_L \wedge R_R) \Rightarrow C_{10}]$

times. This corresponded to more than 16M rejected candidates, which did not require an explicit check thanks to the inductive learning process. Among these candidates, 386 distinct ones were satisfying all the specifications.

Figure 7 shows, instead, the effect of designer hints and library-specific constraints on synthesis time. Here synthesis is performed on smaller and simplified instances of the EPS problem, including 2, 4, 6, 10 and 16 variables, using a library with 20 elements. The graph (in logarithmic scale), shows how these constraints are critical in decreasing the overall problem complexity. In case of the instance with 16 variables, the CSCL algorithm variant without additional constraints was not able to synthesize a solution within the time bound of 10 min.

Table 4. Structure of the EPS library

Component	A$_1$	B$_1$	C$_1$	D$_1$	E$_1$
Input vars	f (Generator)	f (Generator)	f (ActiveGenerator)	f (ActiveGenerator)	f_1, f_2 (Generator)
Output vars	c (ACGenContactor)	c (ACGenContactor)	c (ACGenContactor)	c (ACGenContactor)	c (ACBackContactor)
Assumptions	$\neg f\wedge$ $\Box(f\Rightarrow\bigcirc f)$	$\neg f$	$\neg f\wedge$ $\Box(f\Rightarrow\bigcirc f)$	$\neg f\wedge$ $\Box(f\Rightarrow\bigcirc f)$	$\neg f_1\wedge\neg f_2\wedge$ $\Box(f_1\Rightarrow\bigcirc f_1)\wedge$ $\Box(f_2\Rightarrow\bigcirc f_2)$
Guarantees	$\Box(f\Rightarrow\Diamond\neg c)$	$\Box(\neg c)$	$\Box(f\Rightarrow\neg c)\wedge$ $\Box(\neg f\Rightarrow c)$	$c\wedge$ $\Box(f\Rightarrow\bigcirc\neg c)\wedge$ $\Box(\neg f\Rightarrow c)$	$\Box((f_1\vee f_2)\Rightarrow c)\wedge$ $\Box((\neg f_1\wedge\neg f_2)\Rightarrow\neg c)$

Component	F$_1$	G$_1$	H$_1$	I$_1$	L$_1$
Input vars	f_1, f_2 (BackupGenerator)	f_1, f_4 (ActiveGenerator) f_2, f_3 (BackupGenerator)	f (Rectifier)	f_1, f_2 (Rectifier)	f_1, f_2 (Rectifier)
Output vars	c_1, c_2 (ACBackContactor)	c_1, c_4 (ACBackContactor) c_2, c_3 (ACGenContactor)	c (ACLoadContactor)	c_1, c_2 (DCBackContactor)	c (DCLoadContactor)
Assumptions	$\neg f_1\wedge\neg f_2\wedge$ $\Box(f_1\Rightarrow\bigcirc f_1)\wedge$ $\Box(f_2\Rightarrow\bigcirc f_2)$	$\neg f_1\wedge\neg f_2\wedge\neg f_3\wedge\neg f_4\wedge$ $\Box(f_1\Rightarrow\bigcirc f_1)\wedge$ $\Box(f_2\Rightarrow\bigcirc f_2)\wedge$ $\Box(f_3\Rightarrow\bigcirc f_3)\wedge$ $\Box(f_4\Rightarrow\bigcirc f_4)$	$\neg f$	$\neg f_1\wedge\neg f_2$	$\neg f_1\wedge\neg f_2$
Guarantees	$\Box[(\neg f_1\wedge\neg f_2)\Rightarrow$ $(\neg c_1\wedge\neg c_2)]\wedge$ $\Box[(f_1\wedge\neg f_2)\Rightarrow$ $(\neg c_1\wedge\neg c_2)]\wedge$ $\Box[(\neg f_1\wedge f_2)\Rightarrow$ $(c_1\wedge c_2)]\wedge$ $\Box[(f_1\wedge f_2)\Rightarrow$ $(\neg c_1\wedge c_2)]$	$\Box(f_2\Rightarrow\neg c_2)\wedge$ $\Box(f_3\Rightarrow\neg c_3)\wedge$ $\Box(\neg(c_2\wedge c_3))\Rightarrow$ $\Box[(\neg f_1\wedge\neg f_4)\Rightarrow$ $(\neg c_1\wedge\neg c_2\wedge\neg c_3\wedge\neg c_4)]\wedge$ $\Box[(\neg f_1\wedge\neg f_3\wedge f_4)\Rightarrow$ $(\neg c_1\wedge\neg c_2\wedge c_3\wedge c_4)]\wedge$ $\Box[(f_1\wedge\neg f_2\wedge\neg f_4)\Rightarrow$ $(c_1\wedge c_2\wedge\neg c_3\wedge\neg c_4)]\wedge$ $\Box[(\neg f_1\wedge\neg f_2\wedge f_3\wedge f_4)\Rightarrow$ $(\neg c_1\wedge c_2\wedge\neg c_3\wedge c_4)]\wedge$ $\Box[(f_1\wedge f_2\wedge\neg f_3\wedge\neg f_4)\Rightarrow$ $(c_1\wedge\neg c_2\wedge c_3\wedge\neg c_4)]\wedge$ $\Box[(f_2\wedge f_3\wedge(f_1\vee f_4))\Rightarrow$ $(c_1\wedge\neg c_2\wedge c_3\wedge c_4)]$	$\Box(\neg f\Rightarrow c)\wedge$ $\Box(f\Rightarrow\neg c)$	$\Box[(\neg f_1\wedge\neg f_2)\Rightarrow$ $(\neg c_1\wedge\neg c_2)]\wedge$ $\Box[(f_1\vee f_2)\Rightarrow$ $(c_1\wedge c_2)]$	$\Box c$

R$_T$	{(Generator, ACGenContactor)}		R$_Z$		$\emptyset$

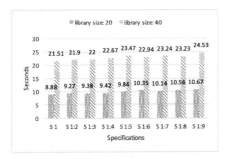

Fig. 6. Synthesis time for the EPS example, subject to increasing number of specifications

Fig. 7. Impact of types and user provided hints on synthesis time for simplified instances of the EPS example

7 Conclusion

We studied the problem of constrained synthesis from component libraries. The problem has been defined in terms of generic components subject to a number of topological constraints. These constraints include types on component ports, hints from the designer and composition rules precomputed and stored in the library. After an assessment on the complexity of the problem, we presented two variants of an algorithm based on CEGIS, a sequential and a parallel one, and evaluated its implementation with LTL-based A/G contracts on an industrial-relevant case study. Future extensions of this work include the study of algorithms to decompose complex specifications into smaller instances (to increase performance by dealing with smaller synthesis problems), the application of the synthesis technique described here to component libraries defined over multi-aspect specifications (e.g. behavioral, security, real-time specifications) and the analysis of erroneous designs and infeasible specifications in order to provide feedback to the designer on how to fix her library and obtain the intended result.

References

1. Semiconductor IP Market by Form Factor (ICs IP, SOCs IP), Design Architecture (IP cores (Hard IP, Soft IP), Standard IP, Custom IP, Processor Design), Processor Type (Microprocessor, DSP), Verification IP - Global forecast to 2022. marketsandmarkets.com (2016)
2. de Alfaro, L., Henzinger, T.A.: Interface automata. In: Proceedings of the 8th European Software Engineering Conference Held Jointly with 9th ACM SIGSOFT International Symposium on Foundations of Software Engineering, ESEC/FSE-9, pp. 109–120. ACM, New York (2001)
3. Alur, R., Moarref, S., Topcu, U.: Compositional synthesis with parametric reactive controllers. In: Proceedings of the 19th International Conference on Hybrid Systems: Computation and Control, HSCC 2016, pp. 215–224. ACM, New York (2016)
4. Benveniste, A., Caillaud, B., Ferrari, A., Mangeruca, L., Passerone, R., Sofronis, C.: Multiple viewpoint contract-based specification and design. In: Boer, F.S., Bonsangue, M.M., Graf, S., Roever, W.-P. (eds.) FMCO 2007. LNCS, vol. 5382, pp. 200–225. Springer, Heidelberg (2008). doi:10.1007/978-3-540-92188-2_9
5. Cavada, R., Cimatti, A., Dorigatti, M., Griggio, A., Mariotti, A., Micheli, A., Mover, S., Roveri, M., Tonetta, S.: The NUXMV symbolic model checker. In: Biere, A., Bloem, R. (eds.) CAV 2014. LNCS, vol. 8559, pp. 334–342. Springer, Cham (2014). doi:10.1007/978-3-319-08867-9_22
6. Clarke, E., Grumberg, O., Jha, S., Lu, Y., Veith, H.: Counterexample-guided abstraction refinement. In: Emerson, E.A., Sistla, A.P. (eds.) CAV 2000. LNCS, vol. 1855, pp. 154–169. Springer, Heidelberg (2000). doi:10.1007/10722167_15
7. de Moura, L., Bjørner, N.: Z3: an efficient SMT solver. In: Ramakrishnan, C.R., Rehof, J. (eds.) TACAS 2008. LNCS, vol. 4963, pp. 337–340. Springer, Heidelberg (2008). doi:10.1007/978-3-540-78800-3_24
8. Gulwani, S., Jha, S., Tiwari, A., Venkatesan, R.: Synthesis of loop-free programs. In: Proceedings of the 32nd ACM SIGPLAN Conference on Programming Language Design and Implementation, PLDI 2011, pp. 62–73. ACM, New York (2011)
9. Iannopollo, A., Nuzzo, P., Tripakis, S., Sangiovanni-Vincentelli, A.: Library-based scalable refinement checking for contract-based design. In: Design, Automation and Test in Europe Conference and Exhibition (DATE), pp. 1–6, March 2014
10. Jha, S., Seshia, S.A.: A theory of formal synthesis via inductive learning. CoRR abs/1505.03953 (2015)
11. Lustig, Y., Vardi, M.Y.: Synthesis from component libraries. In: Alfaro, L. (ed.) FoSSaCS 2009. LNCS, vol. 5504, pp. 395–409. Springer, Heidelberg (2009). doi:10. 1007/978-3-642-00596-1_28

12. Moir, I., Seabridge, A.: Aircraft Systems: Mechanical, Electrical and Avionics Subsystems Integration, 3rd edn. Wiley, Chichester (2008)
13. Nuzzo, P., Finn, J., Iannopollo, A., Sangiovanni-Vincentelli, A.: Contract-based design of control protocols for safety-critical cyber-physical systems. In: Design, Automation and Test in Europe Conference and Exhibition (DATE), pp. 1–4, March 2014
14. Nuzzo, P., Iannopollo, A., Tripakis, S., Sangiovanni-Vincentelli, A.: Are interface theories equivalent to contract theories? In: 2014 Twelfth ACM/IEEE International Conference on Formal Methods and Models for Codesign (MEMOCODE), pp. 104–113, October 2014
15. Pnueli, A., Rosner, R.: Distributed reactive systems are hard to synthesize. In: 31st Annual Symposium on Foundations of Computer Science, Proceedings, vol. 2, pp. 746–757, October 1990
16. Pnueli, A.: The temporal logic of programs. In: Proceedings of the 18th Annual Symposium on Foundations of Computer Science, SFCS 1977, pp. 46–57. IEEE Computer Society, Washington, DC (1977)
17. Sangiovanni-Vincentelli, A.: Quo vadis, SLD? Reasoning about the trends and challenges of system level design. Proc. IEEE 95(3), 467–506 (2007)
18. Sangiovanni-Vincentelli, A., Damm, W., Passerone, R.: Taming Dr. Frankenstein: contract-based design for cyber-physical systems. Eur. J. Control 18(3), 217–238 (2012)
19. Seshia, S.A.: Combining induction, deduction, and structure for verification and synthesis. Proc. IEEE 103(11), 2036–2051 (2015)
20. Shapiro, E.Y.: Algorithmic Program DeBugging. MIT Press, Cambridge (1983)
21. Sistla, A.P., Clarke, E.M.: The complexity of propositional linear temporal logics. J. ACM 32(3), 733–749 (1985)
22. Solar-Lezama, A., Tancau, L., Bodik, R., Seshia, S., Saraswat, V.: Combinatorial sketching for finite programs. SIGOPS Oper. Syst. Rev. 40(5), 404–415 (2006)
23. Wongpiromsarn, T., Topcu, U., Ozay, N., Xu, H., Murray, R.M.: Tulip: a software toolbox for receding horizon temporal logic planning. In: Proceedings of the 14th International Conference on Hybrid Systems: Computation and Control, HSCC 2011, pp. 313–314. ACM, New York (2011)

MARTE/pCCSL: Modeling and Refining Stochastic Behaviors of CPSs with Probabilistic Logical Clocks

Dehui Du[1(✉)], Ping Huang[1], Kaiqiang Jiang[1], Frédéric Mallet[1,2,3], and Mingrui Yang[1]

[1] Shanghai Key Laboratory of Trustworthy Computing,
East China Normal University, Shanghai, China
dhdu@sei.ecnu.edu.cn
[2] University of Nice Sophia Antipolis, I3S, UMR 7271 CNRS, Nice, France
[3] INRIA Sophia Antipolis Méditerranée, Biot, France

Abstract. Cyber-Physical Systems (CPSs) are networks of heterogeneous embedded systems immersed within a physical environment. Several ad-hoc frameworks and mathematical models have been studied to deal with challenging issues raised by CPSs. In this paper, we explore a more standard-based approach that relies on SysML/MARTE to capture different aspects of CPSs, including structure, behaviors, clock constraints, and non-functional properties. The novelty of our work lies in the use of logical clocks and MARTE/CCSL to drive and coordinate different models. Meanwhile, to capture stochastic behaviors of CPSs, we propose an extension of CCSL, called pCCSL, where logical clocks are adorned with stochastic properties. Possible variants are explored using Statistical Model Checking (SMC) via a transformation from the MARTE/pCCSL models into Stochastic Hybrid Automata. The whole process is illustrated through a case study of energy-aware building, in which the system is modeled by SysML/MARTE/pCCSL and different variants are explored through SMC to help expose the best alternative solutions.

Keywords: Cyber-physical systems · MARTE · pCCSL · Stochastic hybrid automata · Energy-aware building · Statistical model checking

1 Introduction

Cyber-Physical Systems (CPSs) combine digital computational systems with surrounding physical processes and can be viewed as a network of embedded systems where a (large) number of computational components are deployed within a physical environment [25]. Each component collects information about and offers services to its environment (e.g., environmental monitoring, health-care monitoring and traffic control). This information is processed either within the component, in the network or at a remote location (e.g., a base station), or in any combination of these. The prominent characteristic of CPSs is that they have to meet a

© Springer International Publishing AG 2017
O. Kouchnarenko and R. Khosravi (Eds.): FACS 2016, LNCS 10231, pp. 111–133, 2017.
DOI: 10.1007/978-3-319-57666-4_8

multitude of quantitative constraints, e.g., timing constraints, energy consumption, memory usage, communication bandwidth, QoS, and often with uncertain environment or user behaviors. So how to model and verify CPSs still remains a challenging problem. Now CPSs are spreading in numerous applications with a large societal impact, ranging from automotive systems, manufacturing, medical devices, automated highway systems (AHS) [17], air traffic control systems [37], personal and medical devices [22], Smart Grids and Smart Building, etc.

In the literature we find that both a variety of engineering modeling languages (lots of them are UML/SysML/MARTE-based) and a bunch of formal models (e.g., timed automata, hybrid automata, Petri nets, synchronous languages) provide a good support for formal verification. However, the integration of industry standards with verification frameworks is still in its infancy. For instance, a classical flow consists in adorning a UML state machine with some annotations and then transforming it into a timed automata for verification. We intend to go further by combining together several models of various kinds to cover heterogeneous aspects of the systems before transforming them into a language amenable to verification. While several frameworks inspired by Ptolemy [31] address the important issue of heterogeneity, most of them propose an ad-hoc environment and notation, while here we start from UML/SysML/MARTE models. The aim of our work is to facilitate the modeling CPSs with standard-based modeling language.

We consider that the UML, as a general-purpose language, provides a variety of models to cover lots of aspects of CPSs, structural aspects with structured classifiers and components, state-based models with state machines and dataflow models with activities. Because we target embedded systems, we use the MARTE profile, which appears as the best choice [8] for a UML-based solution. In particular we focus on its subprofiles covering time, allocation, non-functional properties (NFP) (like power or energy consumption) and Performance Analysis Modeling (PAM). Because CPSs combine discrete and continuous aspects, we follow the lead of other works [32] and combine MARTE with SysML. In particular, we use SysML parametrics to capture the equations that link the energy to time and power.

As in any UML-based models, the relationships among models and the consistency is of paramount importance. We claim that logical clocks [23], just like tagged structures [24], provide a good abstraction to link different models together. Indeed, logical clocks can be used as activation conditions [3] of different models. Clock constraints then define a coordination model to constrain the joint execution of these models. The time subprofile of MARTE extends the UML with logical clocks that can then be used to control the different interactions between the models, e.g., the relationships between a state transition and a part in a structured classifier, or the start of an action and the sampling step to integrate the energy and compute the power consumption, but also relationships between UML and SysML models.

While MARTE extends UML with the notion of logical clock, its companion language CCSL [1] offers a syntax to build clock constraints. CCSL as a declarative language helps build a specification that can be refined when new constraints from the environment, or the platform or the application become available. There may be several implementations that satisfy a CCSL specification, a classical approach [15] consists in defining a policy (e.g., non-deterministic choice or as soon as possible) to decide which solution to retain. Another solution, which is explored here, consists in extending CCSL with stochastic constructs and probability. Such constructs help pick one solution instead of another one by giving the likelihood that a clock ticks.

Once the SysML/MARTE model is built, we propose to analyze the resulting model through a transformation to Stochastic Hybrid Automata and to use Statistical Model Checking (SMC) [6,27,33,39] to explore different solutions. To illustrate our approach, we take the example of a energy-aware building and show how to explore and compare alternative solutions.

Our contributions are (1) to propose an extension of CCSL, called pCCSL, with stochastic constructs and probability to drive the exploration of alternative solutions when building clock specifications; (2) To show how pCCSL specifications can augment UML/SysML/MARTE models to link together several models; (3) To propose a structural transformation into SHA according to the semantics of pCCSL so as to perform evaluation on the alternative solutions with statistical model checking, which helps designers refine system models. The whole process is illustrated on the example of an energy-aware building.

The remainder of this paper is organized as follows. Section 2 introduces CCSL and our proposed extension, pCCSL. Section 3 introduces our case study and makes a joint use of UML, SysML and MARTE to capture different aspects of this model. Section 4 proposes some transformation rules to transform MARTE/pCCSL into SHA. Finally we position our work with respect to related works before concluding and discussing possible future extensions.

2   pCCSL: The Probabilistic Extensions of CCSL

2.1   Syntax of pCCSL

We first recall the basic constructs of CCSL [1] and then further describe the proposed extensions (see Fig. 1).

Core constructs of CCSL. A specification is made of clock relations and declarations. Relations prevent some clocks from ticking depending on configurations. Declarations are meant to declare new clocks, either to capture events of the system or to build intermediate clocks based on other ones. The two basic CCSL relations are *subclocking* and *causality*. The former one is inspired by synchronous languages and prevents one clock (the subclock) from ticking when its superclock cannot tick. The superclock is said to be coarser and the subclock is finer than the other one. The latter one is akin to the causality relation in event structures. It prevents a clock (the effect) from ticking when another clock (its cause) has not ticked. The cause is said to be faster than the effect (which is then slower). This typically represents first-in-first-out (FIFO) constructs, e.g., one cannot read a data before it has been written. The other relations (*precedence, synchrony, exclusion*) are derived.

When declaring a clock, one can specify (if required) how it is related to other clocks. This is done using *clock definitions*, e.g., *filters*, or *expressions*.

Filters allow for precisely defining a subclock based on its superclock. For instance, a *PeriodicFilter* makes one clock tick every p ticks of its superclock. The *Select* expression selects an interval (possibly not closed) of ticks to the superclock at which the subclock ticks.

Function-expression builds a new clock based on two (or more clocks). *Union* builds the coarsest clock that is a super clock of two other clocks, whereas *Intersection* builds the finest subclock of two clocks. *Inf* (resp. *Sup*) builds the slowest (resp. fastest) clock that is faster (resp. slower) than two clocks.

The *Sampling* takes a triggering and sampling clock and builds the fastest clock slower than the triggering clock and subclock of a sampling clock.

One can also declare a period and optionally a jitter for clock making reference to an ideal physical clock. This information related to physical time is not used in CCSL clock calculus but is a mere annotation to display results with a scale that is meaningful to the user.

$\langle specification \rangle ::= \{ (\langle relation \rangle)^* (\langle declarations \rangle)^* \}$

$\langle relation \rangle ::= \text{c} \subseteq \text{c} [\text{ 'rate:' } \langle nat \rangle \text{ '/' } \langle nat \rangle] \text{ (subclocking)}$
    $| \quad \text{c '<=' c} [\text{ 'size:' } \langle nat \rangle] \text{ (causality)}$
    $| \quad \text{c '<' c} [\text{ 'size:' } \langle nat \rangle] \text{ (precedence)}$
    $| \quad \text{c '=' c (synchrony)}$
    $| \quad \text{c '\#' c (exclusion)}$

$\langle declaration \rangle ::= \text{'Clock' c} [\langle definition \rangle]$

$\langle definition \rangle ::= \text{'is' } \langle expression \rangle$
    $| \quad \langle filter \rangle$
    $| \quad \text{'period' } \langle real \rangle [\text{'jitter' } \langle real \rangle]$
    $| \quad \text{'with probability' } \langle prob \rangle$
    $| \quad \text{'with distribution' } \langle real \rangle [\text{ c }]$

$\langle expression \rangle ::= \text{'0' } | \text{ '1'}$
    $| \quad \text{c } \langle operator \rangle \text{ c}$

$\langle filter \rangle ::= \text{c}$
    $| \quad \text{'every' } \langle nat \rangle \text{ c}$
    $| \quad \text{':=' c} [\text{'from' } \langle nat \rangle] [\text{'to' } \langle nat \rangle]$

$\langle operator \rangle ::= \text{'inf' } | \text{ 'sup'}$
    $| \quad \text{'inter' } | \text{ 'union' } | \text{ 'minus'}$
    $| \quad \text{'sampledBy'}$

$\langle nat \rangle ::= \text{(* natural number constant *)}$

$\langle prob \rangle ::= \text{(* real number between 0 and 1 *)}$

Fig. 1. Grammar of pCCSL

Proposed extensions for pCCSL. The grammar of pCCSL is shown in Fig. 1. There are three proposed extensions marked with red fonts. The first consists in adding a *rate* parameter to the subclock relation. It specifies the rate at which the subclock ticks compared to its superclock. It corresponds to a probability for the subclock to tick when its superclock ticks. This is an intermediate solution between saying nothing, which may imply that the subclock never ticks, and completely deciding when the subclock ticks, with a filtering expression for instance.

The second proposed extension consists in assigning a *probability* to a clock, to replace an expression. Rather than giving a deterministic expression that says when the clock may or cannot tick, we give the probability that the clock ticks. As we show later, the consistent integration of this probabilistic clock with the semantics of the other relations is not trivial and requires some particular caution. However, this is useful to help CCSL clock calculus picking one solution instead of another one when several solutions are possible.

The third and last extension consists in giving a parameter λ to control when a clock ticks or not. The lambda parameter makes a clock tick according to an exponential distribution. The probability that the clock ticks at the time less than x is $1 - e^{-\lambda x}$. x here is either relative to the ticks of another clock or, if no reference clock is provided, relative to an absolute ideal physical-time clock. In the latter case, the information is a mere annotation only used to interpret the ticking of the clock according to an ideal physical time reference but is not used in the clock calculus process.

Note that these three extensions cannot add new solutions, they are just meant to reduce the set of solutions in case of several possible solutions. The probability and distribution constructs help us decide on the likelihood for a clock to tick (when allowed by the other constraints).

2.2 Semantics of pCCSL

A constraint specification $spec = \langle C, Cons \rangle$, is a tuple where C is a set of clock names and $Cons$ is a set of constraints. The semantics of each individual constraint is given by a special form of transition system called clock-labeled transition systems.

Definition 1 (Labeled Transition System). *A labeled transition system (lts) is a structure $\langle S, A, \longrightarrow \rangle$ consisting of a set S (of elements, s, called states), a set A of labels, and a transition relation $\longrightarrow \subseteq S \times A \times S$. $s \xrightarrow{a} s'$ is used to denote $(s, a, s') \in \longrightarrow$.*

A clock-labeled transition system is a lts where each label is a set of clocks. From each state, there are maximum 2^n outgoing transitions, where $n = |C|$ is the number of clocks. Each transition corresponds to a particular *configuration* of ticking clocks. Transition systems may have an infinite number of states.

Definition 2 (Clock-Labeled Transition System). *A clock-labeled transition system (clts) is a structure $\langle S, C, \longrightarrow \rangle$ where $\langle S, 2^C, \longrightarrow \rangle$ is a labelled transition system.*

To capture the semantics of the proposed extension we extend the clts by adding a probability to each transition.

Definition 3 (Probabilistic CLTS). *A probabilistic clock-labeled transition system (pclts) is a clts with an extended transition relation* $\longrightarrow \subseteq S \times 2^C \times P \times S$, *where* $P \subseteq \mathbb{Q}$ *is a real number between 0 and 1 (i.e., a probability).*

For a given transition $t = (s, \Gamma, p, s') \in \longrightarrow$, $\pi(t) = p$ denotes the probability p that the transition t is fired.

For a pclts $\langle S, C, \longrightarrow \rangle$, we call $s^\bullet$ the set of all transitions whose source is s:

$$s^\bullet = \{(s, \Gamma, p, s') \in \longrightarrow\}$$

Note that $s^\bullet$ can never be empty since it is always possible to do nothing in CCSL, i.e., $(s, \emptyset, p, s)$ is always in $\longrightarrow$ for all $s \in S$ and for some value p.

Given a clock $c \in C$, let us call $s_c^\bullet$ the set of all transitions whose source is s and such that the clock c ticks:

$$s_c^\bullet = \{(s, \Gamma, p, s') \in \longrightarrow \mid c \in \Gamma\}$$

For a pclts to be well-formed, it must satisfy the two following conditions:

$$\forall s \in S, \sum_{t \in s^\bullet} \pi(t) = 1 \tag{1}$$

$$\forall s \in S, \forall c \in C, \sum_{t \in s_c^\bullet} \pi(t) = p_c \tag{2}$$

In Eq. 2, for each clock $c \in C$, the probability p_c is either manually assigned by the user with a declaration 'Clock c probability p', or derived using the rate in a subclocking relation or assigned to the default value $1/|s^\bullet|$ otherwise.

A 'normal' clts can be seen as a probabilistic clts where all the probabilities are assigned with default values $1/|s^\bullet|$ for all the states $s \in S$.

Subclocking and synchrony. Let $a, b \in C$ be two clocks and $r \in \mathbb{Q}$ a real number such that $0 \leq r \leq 1$. The *subclocking* relation (see Fig. 2(a)), $b \subseteq a$ rate r is defined as a pclts $\langle \{s0\}, \{a, b\}, \longrightarrow_\subseteq \rangle$, such that $\longrightarrow_\subseteq = \{(s0, \{\}, 1 - p_a, s0), (s0, \{a, b\}, p_a * r, s0), (s0, \{a\}, p_a * (1 - r), s0)\}$, where $p_a \in \mathbb{Q}$ is the probability assigned to clock a. Let us note that Eq. 1 is satisfied since $\sum_{t \in s0^\bullet} \pi(t) = (1 - p_a) + (p_a * r) + (p_a * (1 - r)) = 1$. Equation 2 is also satisfied since $\sum_{t \in s0_b^\bullet} \pi(t) = p_a * r = p_b$ and $\sum_{t \in s0_a^\bullet} \pi(t) = (p_a * r) + (p_a * (1 - r)) = p_a$.

If no probability was assigned then the default is $2/3$. If no rate is assigned, then r defaults to $1/2$. With default values, each one of the three transitions has a probability of $1/3$, i.e., each transition has the same probability to be fired. The transition $\{b\}$ however has a probability of 0 since it would contradict the subclocking relation.

Note that if both the probability of a is given and the rate of b relative to a is given, then $p_b = p_a * r$. In any other cases, the specification is ill-formed.

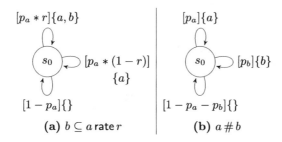

Fig. 2. pclts for subclocking and exclusion

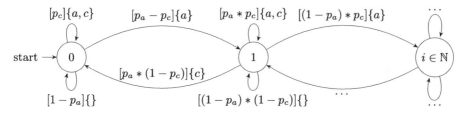

Fig. 3. pCCSL causality (infinite state pclts): $a \leq c$

The synchrony constraint is a special case of subclock defined as follows $a = b \equiv b \subseteq a$ rate 1, which implies $p_a = p_b$.

The exclusion constraint (see Fig. 2(b)), $a \# b$ is defined similarly using the following transition relation $\longrightarrow_\# = \{(s_0, \{\}, 1 - p_b - p_a, s_0), (s_0, \{b\}, p_b, s_0), (s_0, \{a\}, p_a, s_0)\}$. Again the two consistency rules are satisfied.

Causality. Let $a, c \in C$ be two clocks. The *causality* relation (see Fig. 3), $a \leq c$ is defined as a pclts $\langle \mathbb{N}, \{a, c\}, \longrightarrow_\leq \rangle$, such that $\longrightarrow_\leq = \bigcup_{i \in \mathbb{N}} s_i$, where $\mathbb{N}$ is the set of natural numbers, $s_0 = \{(0, \{\}, 1 - p_a, 0), (0, \{a, c\}, p_c, 0), (0, \{a\}, p_a - p_c, 0)\}$, and for all $i \in \mathbb{N}, i > 0$, $s_i = \{(i, \{\}, (1 - p_a) * (1 - p_c), i), (i, \{a, c\}, p_a * p_c, i), (i, \{a\}, p_a * (1 - p_c), i + 1), (i, \{c\}, (1 - p_a) * p_c, i - 1)\}$. $p_a, p_c \in \mathbb{Q}$ are the probabilities assigned to clocks a and c respectively.

Note that whatever the values of p_a and p_c, then a will occur more frequently than c since c cannot occur alone in state 0 and to reach state 0, a and c must have occurred exactly the same number of times.

When a size is associated with the causality constraint, then the transition system becomes finite and is such that the number of states equals to $size + 1$. With size 1, there are two states, with size 2 there are three states and so on.

The *precedence* is very similar to *causality* except that in state 0 the simultaneous occurrence of a and c is forbidden. The whole semantics of the operators is available in [30] and we just give here the ones used in this paper and that have been extended with stochastic constructs.

2.3 Composition

Each constraint is expressed as a clts and a specification is then captured as the synchronized product [2] of all the clts. The process for standard CCSL constraints is explained in detail in [30].

With the proposed extensions, for each clts $L = \langle S, C, \longrightarrow_L \rangle$ that results from the synchronized product and such that C is the union of all the clocks of all the composed clts, we derive a pclts $P = \langle S, C, \longrightarrow_P \rangle$ such that the two consistency rules (Eqs. 1 and 2) are satisfied.

For instance, let us consider the following pCCSL specification:

1. Clock a with probability p_a
2. Clock $b \subseteq a$ rate: r
3. Clock $a \leq c$ size: 1

The semantics of each constraint is captured with a clts which are then composed through a synchronized product. Then the probabilities are added to the transitions resulting in the pclts shown in Fig. 4.

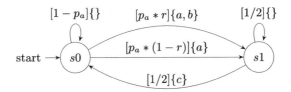

Fig. 4. Example of composition through synchronized product

Note that Eq. 1 is satisfied since $\sum_{t \in s0^\bullet} \pi(t) = (1 - p_a) + (p_a * (1 - r)) + (p_a * r) = 1$ and $\sum_{t \in s1^\bullet} \pi(t) = 1/2 + 1/2 = 1$. Equation 2 is also satisfied since $\sum_{t \in s0_a^\bullet} \pi(t) = (p_a * (1 - r)) + (p_a * r) = p_a$ and $\sum_{t \in s0_b^\bullet} \pi(t) = p_a * r = p_b$. Since the probability of c is not given and c is the only clock that can tick from state $s1$ then the outgoing transitions are assigned with the default value $1/2$ since $|s1^\bullet| = 2$.

3 Modeling and Refining Energy-Aware Building with MARTE/pCCSL

This section describes the application of MARTE/pCCSL to a hybrid system case, which addresses the control problem of the temperature of rooms in a given building with limited heaters. With MARTE/pCCSL, we can flexibly model every part of the system in multi-views (structure, equation, behavior, and clock constraints) with quite loose coupling between them. MARTE facilitates the modeling of Time and Non Functional Properties (NFP, here energy and temperature), and pCCSL provides precise and probabilistic time control through definition and constraints of logical clocks used between abstract specification and its refinements to help us expose the best alternative solutions. Next we briefly introduce the case of energy-aware building and then present its SysML/MARTE/pCCSL models in multi-views.

3.1 Energy-Aware Building Setup

As a starting point, consider a setup proposed by [11] as an extension of the challenging benchmark for hybrid systems model-checkers addressed in [20]. The case consists of a building layout with temperature dynamics, autonomous heaters and a central controller deciding which room gets a heater. The room temperature dynamics is described by a differential equation:

$$T_i' = \sum_{j \neq i} a_{i,j}(T_j - T_i) + b_i(u - T_i) + c_i h_i$$

where T_i and T_j are the temperatures in rooms i and j respectively, u is the environment temperature and h_i is equal to 1 when the heater is turned on in the room i and 0 otherwise. The building layout is encoded by an adjacency matrix a where $a_{i,j}$ is a heat exchange coefficient between rooms i and j. The heat exchange with an environment is encoded in a separate vector b, where b_i is the energy loss coefficient for room i. An energy supply from a heater is encoded as a vector c, where c_i is a power coefficient for room i. Figure 5(a) shows a building configuration instance (HEAT15 in [20]) with rooms and heaters, where the wall thickness corresponds to an isolation defined by a and b. The definition of matrix a, vectors b and c can be found in [11].

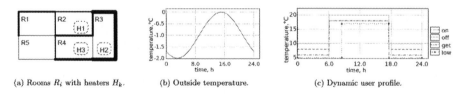

(a) Rooms R_i with heaters H_k.   (b) Outside temperature.   (c) Dynamic user profile.

Fig. 5. Representation of building layout, outside temperature and dynamic user profile

Each heater is equipped with a bang-bang controller configured to turn on the heating ($h_i := 1$) when the temperature T_i is below threshold on_i and turn off ($h_i := 0$) when the temperature T_i is greater than off_i. Whenever the heating is turned on, the heaters consume an amount of power denoted by vector pow. The central controller can switch-over the heating from one room to another. The room is said to be needing a heater if the temperature drops below its get threshold and it is said to be outside comfort zone if the temperature drops below low. To decide when the heating can be switched over, we consider a control strategy, which is based on heuristics that the temperature difference between rooms should not be too high. To be precise, if $room_i$ whose temperature $T_i \leq get_i$ has no heater while $room_j$ has a heater, the heater can move from $room_j$ to $room_i$ when the difference $T_j - T_i \geq dif_i$. To reduce the non-determinism further, we consider probabilistic choices between the possible room destinations denoted by probabilistic weights imp. The temperature thresholds for each room used above also refer to [11].

Further we propose to augment this setup with specific weather conditions and different user profiles to make a more realistic case for optimizing the energy consumption. The case [20] assumes that the environment temperature is within a range between $0°C$ and $-2°C$ without any specific dynamics. Figure 5(b) shows one daily cycle and Fig. 5(c) shows the user profile with dynamic temperature thresholds in a day. To this user profile, we have two different refinement versions, one of which is a more complex user profile with probabilistic choice that is explained later to show the usage of MARTE/pCCSL and probabilistic clock and to demonstrate how to refine the models.

3.2   MARTE/pCCSL Models of Energy-Aware Building

Structure Modeling. As described above, the structure of our energy-aware building is modeled with SysML Internal Block Diagrams shown in Fig. 6. *BuildingContext* represents the whole context that consists of five rooms and a central controller as well as the environment such as weather. *Room* represents the common template of five rooms, each of which contains a *heater*, a *TempSensor*, and a *UserProfile* for user-defined temperature conditioning thresholds. We limit the maximum number of heaters turned on at a time to three, though each room has a heater. Each part in the energy-aware building is stereotyped by *clock* that means their behaviors should be controlled by certain clock constraints (specified in pCCSL). For instance, *controller* monitors the information of *rooms* with the constraint $monitor = sensor_i$ (i is from 1 to 5), representing that monitor clock in *controller* and sensor clock of each *room* is synchronous. Besides such discrete control behavior, continuous behavior such as temperature change of each *room* as well as outside environment (*weather*) is constrained by clock, that is, continuous behavior is discretized by clocks. We use several *nfpTypes* to define related variables like *Weather.T* and *Room.T* as *NFP_Temperature*, *Heater.energy* as *NFP_Energy*, *Heater.power* as *NFP_Power* so that NFP properties like *unit* can be used. Several *nfpTypes* are imported from MARTE Library (*NFP_Energy* and *NFP_Power*), and *NFP_Temperature* is defined by us using MARTE constructs (units, dimension and nfpType stereotypes). The definition is simple and similar to most *nfpTypes* defined in MARTE Library, so we do not discuss the details.

Time/Clock Domain. Figure 7 shows the time domain of the whole system. Seven clocks are defined to constrain the time of the system and three of them are defined as probabilistic ones with the keyword **rate**. We define a new *clockType* called *BuildingClock* which serves as a base time of the whole system. *BuildingClock* is discrete and owns a read-only attribute *resolution*. *sysClk, hour, stepClk*

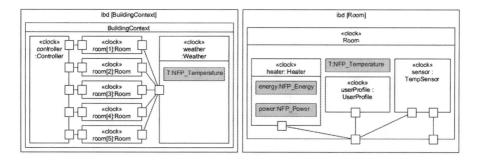

Fig. 6. Structure of an energy-aware building (Internal Block Diagram)

are three instances of *BuildingClock* with their own time units and resolutions for different usage. *sysClk* with high resolution (0.01 s) is used in precise control process; *hour* with low resolution (1h = 3600 s) is used to specify user profile. *stepClk* is similar to *sysClk*, but is mainly used for discretizing continuous behavior. Then we import *idealClk* from MARTE TimeLibrary to constrain our clock instances with pCCSL. Besides, we define three **probabilistic subclocks** *substepClk*, *refinehour1* and *refinehour2*. *substepClk* is the subclock of *stepClk* with rate 2/3. *refinehour1* and *refinehour2* is the subclock of *hour*, where *refinehour1* is used to describe user behaviors when the user may need to go out for meeting in the afternoon as well as *refinehour2* is used when the user will not go out and just work.

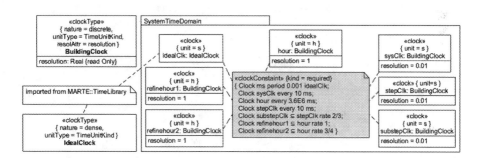

Fig. 7. Time domain of an energy-aware building

Behavior Modeling. The system behaviors specified with pCCSL specifications are shown in Fig. 8. We present these activities stereotyped by *timed-Processing*, of which the first represents monitoring and scheduling behaviors of the system and the rest represent pre-defined user behaviors (user profiles). System behavior references *sysClk* and the whole control process is triggered by a *timedEvent* called *monitorEvent* that occurs every 120 s. Each time the

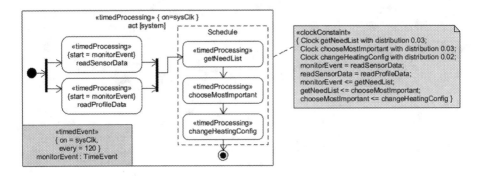

Fig. 8. Activity diagram for system behaviors

system *readSensorData* (e.g. temperature of rooms) and also *readProfileData* (e.g. whether user stays in the room or not). Then the system starts *Schedule* process made of three sequential actions: *getNeedList* (to collect need and heating information), *chooseMostImportant* (to find the room that needs to be heated most according to the strategy if more than one room is in the list), and *changeHeatingConfig* (that changes heating parameter of rooms or mode of heaters). Each action is also stereotyped by *timedProcessing* and may include complex operations implemented in code. The *chooseMostImportant* contains the code implementation of scheduling strategy described in the last subsection. The *changeHeatingConfig* contains the code that will set necessary parameters such as *Heater.on* (for denoting the running mode of heater), *HeatingVector* (for denoting the heated state of room), and *Room.cold* (for denoting the discomfort state of user) and so on. The pink part in Fig. 8 is the pCCSL specification including three kinds of constraints:

– distribution clock (e.g. *Clock getNeedList with distribution 0.03* that means *getNeedList* occurs with an exponential time delay whose parameter $\lambda = 0.03$ on this clock) to describe the possibility of the unstable performance of sensors;
– clock synchrony (e.g. *monitorEvent = readSensorData* that means *monitorEvent* coincides with *readSensorData*);
– clock causality (e.g. *getNeedList* $\leq$ *chooseMostImportant* that means *getNeedList* is always followed by *chooseMostImportant*).

Figure 9 shows us the abstract user behaviors. *userProfile_abstract* references the clock *hour* to describe the abstract possible actions of user in a day. The *newday* occurs every 24 h, representing the start of one day. User may arrive at the building between 8:00 and 9:00. The morning time lasts 4 h and the afternoon time lasts 4 h. In the middle, we have 1 h to have lunch. Having this abstract specification, we have two kinds of refined models with subclocks of *hour*.

Refinement of Behavior Models. The refinement processes are shown in Figs. 10 and 11. The refined version shown as Fig. 10 uses subclock *refinehour1*

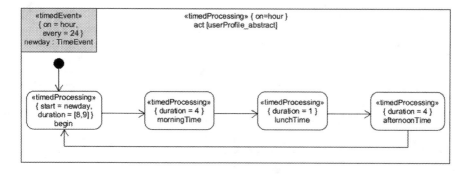

Fig. 9. Abstract activity diagram for user behaviors

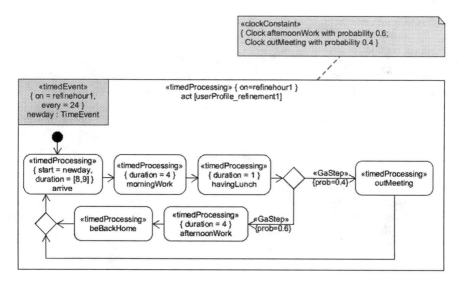

Fig. 10. Refined version 1 of activity diagram for user behaviors (refinehour1⊆hour, rate=1)

with rate 1. User arrives at the building between 8:00 and 9:00. After 4 h, user may go for lunch between 12:00 and 13:00. After lunch, user can either go on working in the building (with a probability of 0.6) or go to a meeting (with a probability 0.4). If working in the afternoon, user may leave the building after 4 h (i.e. between 17:00 and 18:00). If not, user will not go back to the building until next day. When user stays in the building, temperature thresholds are relatively higher than that when user does not, so that energy can be saved due to low temperature duration. As shown in the pink part of Fig. 10, pCCSL specifies the probabilistic clocks (e.g. *Clock outMeeting with probability 0.4* that means *outMeeting* may occur with a probability of 0.4). We also use MARTE stereotype *GaStep* from the Performance Analysis Modeling (PAM) subprofile to report that information on the UML model. The refined version shown as

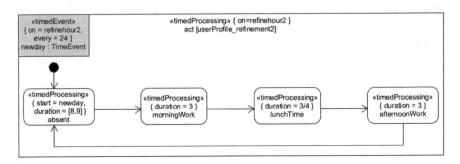

Fig. 11. Refined version 2 of activity diagram for user behaviors (refinehour2⊆hour, rate=3/4)

Fig. 11 uses subclock *refinehour2* with rate 3/4. The user doesn't need to work 8 h a day, he/she only needs to work determined time given by subclock in the morning and afternoon, and the user can leave in the rest time and we neglect it. User may also arrive at the building between 8:00 and 9:00, and then, in 4 h of morning time, according to the rate, user may work 3 h randomly and the other time is rest time (neglected). In the afternoon, user may work 3 h randomly, too. Thus, as we can see, the abstract specification and its refinements are connected logically by clock *hour* and its subclock *refinehour1* and *refinehour2*. Why we use user profiles to model is that user profiles are stochastic behaviors and we can refine these behaviors. The relation between Figs. 9, 10 and 11 is that Fig. 9 is the abstract specification of user profiles, while Fig. 10 is refinement1 and Fig. 11 is the refinement2 of the abstract specification. Lay down an abstract specification of some behaviors first, and then we can refine it with probabilistic clocks to model stochastic behaviors and various solutions.

Equation Modeling. Continuous behaviors described by differential equations also play an important role. Most continuous variables need to be monitored in effective real-time control, such as **temperature** and **energy consumption** in this case. To model continuous behaviors of CPSs, the parametric models are used to present the Ordinary Differential Equations (ODE). As shown in Fig. 12, we consider four equations: *RoomTemperatureEquation* (that determines the temperature change of each room according to the adjacent room, weather, and heater), *HeaterEnergyEquation* (for monitoring energy consumption of each heater), *DiscomfortMonitorEquation* (for monitoring discomfort value of users), *WeatherEquation* (that describes outside temperature curve). The former three equations use derivatives like $d(T)/d(t)$ where t refers to the clock *substepClk* defined already as discretization step.

From this case study, we can find the reason why we use pCCSL rather than CCSL. Since pCCSL has the concept of rate, it can present the stochastic behaviors of the system effectivly and simply. CCSL does has logical time and ticks, but its tick position is certain. For instance, if A is a subclock of B and

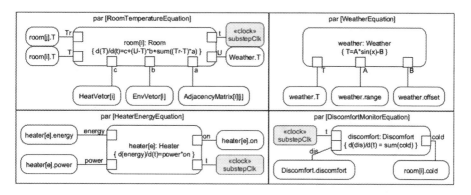

Fig. 12. Equations of continuous behavior of energy-aware building (modeled as a SysML parametrics)

A ticks every four B, then the tick positions of A must be the fist position of every four consecutive B, that is the first, the fifth, the ninth and so on. But for pCCSL, if A is a subclock of B with rate $1/4$, the tick position of A is stochastic. We can only ensure that A will tick only once in four consecutive B, but the certain position is unknown. Thus, it can be seen that pCCSL gives a global rate rather than a precise position as before, which can be used to model stochastic behaviors of CPS.

4 Transformation from MARTE/pCCSL to SHA for Evaluation

This section discusses the transformation approach from MARTE/pCCSL specification to Stochastic Hybrid Automata (SHA) used in UPPAAL-SMC [10]. The transformation mainly targets stochastic behaviors and continuous behaviors (ODE) in terms of SHA. The core elements of MARTE/pCCSL can be directly mapped to the elements of SHA. At last, we compare the energy consumption of users using UPPAAL-SMC aiming to help designers refine the design models.

4.1 Stochastic Hybrid Automata

Definition 4 (Stochastic Hybrid Automata). *A Stochastic Hybrid Automaton (SHA) H is a tuple $H = (L, l_0, X, \Sigma, E, F, I)$, where*

- *L is a finite set of locations,*
- *$l_0 \in L$ is the initial location,*
- *X is a finite set of continuous variables,*
- *Σ is a finite set of actions, and $\Sigma = \Sigma_i + \Sigma_o$, where Σ_i is the set of input actions, Σ_o is the set of output actions,*
- *E is a finite set of transitions, for each transition denoted by $(l, g, \alpha, \varphi, l'), l, l' \in L$, g is a predicate defined by R^X and action label $\alpha \in \Sigma$, φ is a binary relationship on R^X.*

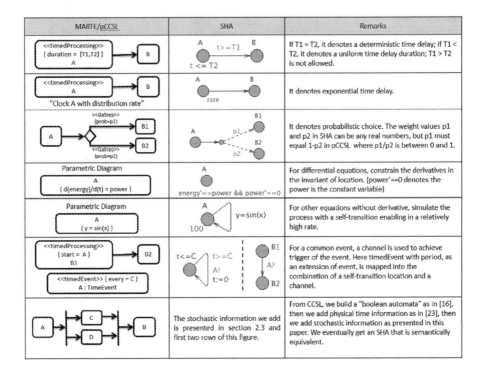

Fig. 13. Mapping rule from MARTE/pCCSL to SHA

- $F(l)$ is a time delay function for each location $l \in L$,
- I is a finite set of invariants.

UPPAAL-SMC supports the analysis of stochastic hybrid automata (SHA) that are timed automata whose clock rates can be changed to be constants or expressions depending on other clocks, effectively defining ODEs. This generalizes the model used in previous works [13,14] where only linear priced automata were handled.

Definition 5 (Semantics of SHA). *The semantics are denoted by a timed Labeled Transition System, which supports the seamlessly transformation from MARTE/pCCSL to SHA. For a SHA H, each location $(l,v) \in L \times R^X$ and $v \models I(l)$, where the transitions may be of two kinds:*

- *timed transition: $(l,v) \xrightarrow{d} (l,v')$, where $d \in \mathbb{R}_{\geq 0}$ and $v' = F(d,v)$*
- *event-triggered transition: $(l,v) \xrightarrow{\alpha} (l',v')$, which means the transition is enabled with $v \models g$ and $\varphi \in (v,v')$.*

For timed transition, the probability density distribution of delay is a uniform distribution or an exponential distribution depending on the invariant of l and $\int \mu_s(t) \cdot dt = 1$ (μ_s is the probabilistic density function). Let E_l denotes the disjunction of guards g such that $(l,g,o,-,-) \in E^j$ for some output o. Let $d(l,v)$

denotes the infimum delay and D(l,v) denotes the supremum delay, i.e. $d(l,v)=$ $inf\{d \in \mathbb{R}_{\geq 0} : v + R^j \cdot d \models E_l\}$ and $D(l,v)= sup\{d \in \mathbb{R}_{\geq 0} : v + R^j \cdot d \models I_l^j\}$. If $D(l, v)<\infty$, the probabilistic density function μ_s means a uniform distribution on $[d(l, v), D(l, v)]$. Otherwise, μ_s means an exponential distribution with rate $P(l)$, where I_l^j dosen't put an upper bound on the possible delays out of (l,v) and $P : L^j \to \mathbb{R}_{\geq 0}$ is an additional distribution rate. For action transition, the output probability function γ_s over Σ_o^j is the uniform distribution over the set $\{o : (l, g, o, -, -) \in E^j \wedge v \models g\}$ whenever this set is non-empty. The detailed semantics of SHA is referred to [13].

4.2 Transformation from MARTE/pCCSL Models to SHA

Transformation from Mode/State-based MARTE/CCSL behavior to Timed Automata (TA) has been discussed in our previous work [36]. The transformation approach to be presented in this section will reinforce it by encoding activity behavior, stochastic behavior and continuous behavior into SHA. First, we need to unify all chronometric clocks by converting all physical time units into one. For instance, if we choose the time unit of highest resolution s as the base unit, the conversion has to be conducted through multiplying all clocks in *userProfile* using the unit h by 3600. Then we can encode behaviors (modelled by Activity Diagram or State machine) with pclts according to the semantics of pCCSL. After that, we can map pclts without probabilistic time delay and choice into TA, which addresses two classes of timing constraints: deterministic delay and non-deterministic duration. For instance, the *duration* of *absent* is [8,9](h) that is mapped to an invariant ($t \leq 9$) and a guard ($t \geq 8$). Then, we add probabilistic aspects in transformed TA. For the activity who contains several actions constrained by a clock with exponential distribution, it will be mapped to an location with its exponential parameter λ equalling to the exponential distribution. When we use *GaStep* with the property *prob* to describe the probabilistic choice, it is mapped to two branches with their probabilistic weights. The mapping rules are summarized in Fig. 13. Due to the space limitation of the paper, the detailed correctness demonstration is not given here. But, the correctness of mapping is ensured with the semantics of pCCSL in [36,40].

Based on the above mapping rules, we can get corresponding SHA models. And then, we can compare and evaluate different refinement versions with Uppaal-smc to expose the best alternative one.

4.3 Evaluation with UPPAAL-SMC

With transformed SHA, we conduct evaluation experiment in Uppaal-smc. We can get a specific and quantitative analysis using SMC and the evaluation analysis results help us to expose the proper one from different refinement solutions.

To compare and evaluate energy consumption of two refined versions, the following query is used:

$$Pr[energy \leq 1000000](\langle\rangle time \geq 5 * 24)$$

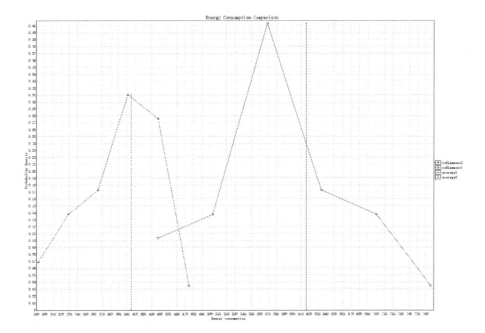

Fig. 14. Energy consumption comparison between two refinement versions

The experiment result is shown in Fig. 14. As we can see, energy consumption of refinement1 is about 50% more than that of refinement2. From the model point of view, the time of staying at the building of refinement1 is $4 + 4 * 0.6 = 6.4$ h, which is a little more than that of refinement2. Therefore, the energy consumption of refinement2 should be less than that of refinement1 and our experiment result dose confirm this. So, if we just consider energy-saving, the user profile of refinement version 2 is more suitable.

The details of our experiments can be found in https://github.com/ECNU-MODANA/AL-Modana.git.

5   Related Work

This section compares our approach to related works for (1) the modeling of Cyber-Physical Systems in general, (2) the use of MARTE to conduct various kinds of analysis, (3) the use of Statistical Model Checking along with UML-based models.

The main challenges [25] of designing CPSs resides in combining physical and computational models to deal with both the digital embedded systems, their environment and their interactions in a close-loop fashion. In [26], the author acknowledges the need to extend deterministic paradigms with probabilistic constructs to capture the unknown (and unknowable) behaviors in a more precise manner. PTides [41] is mentioned as a successful example of simulation framework that can deal with these challenges. While PTides gives an ad-hoc solution, we strive to rely on industry-standard models as a front-end. We think that UML has a large-enough acceptance in industry to be a good base, and we use some of its extensions to deal with non-functional properties (with MARTE) and systems engineering properties (Parametrics of SysML). PTides, as an analysis tool, could very well be used as a back-end provided that a semantic-preserving transformation is given.

Combining MARTE and SysML to address issues of CPSs was initially suggested in [32]. MARTE was also experimented on industrial-size case studies [16] and proved [21] first, to be up to the task, second, to require additional ad-hoc extensions depending on the kind of analysis that is targeted. MARTE has also been used standalone on academic examples to address some aspects of CPSs, notably in [29] where an extension of StateCharts is proposed and in [28] where a hybrid version is explored. MARTE is also often used for its ability to describe non-functional properties [4] or as a base to conduct performance analysis [18,38] or other sort of non-functional analysis like dependability analysis [5]. In literature [34], they use MARTE state machines to model embedded system and transform it to stochastic petri net for energy consumption estimation. In all these examples, only one model of UML is used (like state machine or sequence diagram) while this paper focuses more on finding a practical solution to combine together several UML/SysML/MARTE models. We believe that logical clocks, in a similar way than tagged systems [24], provides the good abstraction level to do that. CCSL [1] then provides a concrete syntax to handle logical clocks. While CCSL is a deterministic declarative polychronous specification language, its pCCSL extension provides new constructs to model the unknown(able) behaviors. Our proposed transformation into stochastic hybrid automata is largely inspired by our previous work to transform CCSL to timed automata [36,40] however we deal here with new operators of CCSL and with its stochastic extension.

Other works, either based on MARTE [35] or just on UML [9] also use stochastic models to analyze the energy consumption. In this case, the authors rely on Stochastic Petri Nets while in our work we use Stochastic Hybrid Automata. The key difference here again is in the use of probabilistic logical clocks to coordinate the models. However, it is rather a practical matter for us and Stochastic Petri Nets could also be used as a backend instead.

Statistical model checking is a highly scalable simulation-based approach which is useful to bound the probability of making an error by increasing the simulation effort. SMC gets widely accepted in various research areas such as software engineering, in particular for industrial applications [7,19], or even for solving problems originating from systems biology [12,22]. Inspired by our previous work [11] which particularly focuses on the analysis of energy consumption of energy-aware building case in different cases to find the most significant factors that influence energy consumption, we attempted to apply MARTE/pCCSL to this case and further evaluate NFP performance of CPSs with SMC.

6   Conclusion

This paper explores an idea of using probabilistic logical clocks in relation to UML models to capture several aspects of CPSs including the stochastic behavior of unknowable events. We believe that using industry-standard is important for a better adoption and we show how to make a consistent use of SysML and MARTE. Clocks through pCCSL are used to coordinate multi-view models. The underlying pCCSL specification is key for the semantic interpretation of models and the transformation into Stochastic Hybrid Automata.

To summarize our contributions (1) MARTE/CCSL has been extended to model stochastic behaviors. The syntax and semantics models of pCCSL are introduced; (2) To show how pCCSL specifications can augment SysML/MARTE models to link together several models and refine the abstract specification; (3) According to the semantics model of pCCSL, we present the transformation process from MARTE/pCCSL to SHA, whose aim is to perform evaluation on the alternative solutions with statistical model checking, which helps designers expose the best solution. The resulting models are analyzed with UPPAAL-SMC. The process is demonstrated on a simple case study of energy-aware building.

MARTE proposes a subprofile, called Performance Analysis Modeling (PAM), dedicated to performance analysis. We think this contribution is an important step for the integration of MARTE Time model with PAM models. Future work shall consider a more extensive use of PAM, while pCCSL may be kept as much as possible as a lower level intermediate semantic model to ease the transformation from pure UML to other formal models.

Acknowledgment. This work is partly supported by NSFC under Grant No. 61472140,61170084, NSF of Shanghai under Grant No. 14ZR1412500, and the Danish National Research Foundation Grant No. 61361136002.

References

1. André, C.: Syntax and semantics of the Clock Constraint Specification Language (CCSL). Research Report 6925, INRIA, May 2009. http://hal.inria.fr/inria-00384077/
2. Arnold, A., Point, G., Griffault, A., Rauzy, A.: The altarica formalism for describing concurrent systems. Fundam. Inform. **40**(2–3), 109–124 (1999)
3. Benveniste, A., Caspi, P., Edwards, S.A., Halbwachs, N., Le Guernic, P., de Simone, R.: The synchronous languages 12 years later. Proc. IEEE **91**(1), 64–83 (2003)
4. Berardinelli, L., Bernardi, S., Cortellessa, V., Merseguer, J.: UML profiles for non-functional properties at work: analyzing reliability, availability and performance. In: 2nd International Workshop on Non-functional System Properties in Domain Specific Modeling Languages (MoDELS/NFPinDSML), CEUR Workshop Proceedings, vol. 553. CEUR-WS.org (2009). http://ceur-ws.org/Vol-553/paper3.pdf
5. Bernardi, S., Merseguer, J., Petriu, D.C.: A dependability profile within MARTE. Softw. Syst. Model. **10**(3), 313–336 (2011). http://dx.doi.org/10.1007/s10270-009-0128-1

6. Bohlender, D., Bruintjes, H., Junges, S., Katelaan, J., Nguyen, V.Y., Noll, T.: A review of statistical model checking pitfalls on real-time stochastic models. In: Margaria, T., Steffen, B. (eds.) ISoLA 2014. LNCS, vol. 8803, pp. 177–192. Springer, Heidelberg (2014). doi:10.1007/978-3-662-45231-8_13

7. Boudjadar, A.J., David, A., Kim, J.H., Larsen, K.G., Mikucionis, M., Nyman, U., Skou, A.: Schedulability and energy efficiency for multi-core hierarchical scheduling systems. In: ERTS (2014). http://www.erts2014.org/Site/0R4UXE94/Fichier/erts2014_1A1.pdf

8. Boutekkouk, F., Benmohammed, M., Bilavarn, S., Auguin, M.: UML2.0 profiles for embedded systems and systems on a chip (SOCs). J. Object Technol. 8(1), 135–157 (2009)

9. Brosig, F., Meier, P., Becker, S., Koziolek, A., Koziolek, H., Kounev, S.: Quantitative evaluation of model-driven performance analysis and simulation of component-based architectures. IEEE Trans. Softw. Eng. 41(2), 157–175 (2015). http://dx.doi.org/10.1109/TSE.2014.2362755

10. Bulychev, P., David, A., Larsen, K.G., Mikučionis, M., Poulsen, D.B., Legay, A., Wang, Z.: UPPAAL-SMC: statistical model checking for priced timed automata. arXiv preprint arXiv:1207.1272 (2012)

11. David, A., Du, D., Larsen, K.G., Mikučionis, M., Skou, A.: An evaluation framework for energy aware buildings using statistical model checking. Sci. China Inf. Sci. 55(12), 2694–2707 (2012)

12. David, A., Larsen, K.G., Legay, A., Mikucionis, M., Poulsen, D.B., Sedwards, S.: Statistical model checker for biological systems. Int. J. Softw. Tools Technol. Transf. 17, 351–367 (2014)

13. David, A., Larsen, K.G., Legay, A., Mikučionis, M., Poulsen, D.B., Vliet, J., Wang, Z.: Statistical model checking for networks of priced timed automata. In: Fahrenberg, U., Tripakis, S. (eds.) FORMATS 2011. LNCS, vol. 6919, pp. 80–96. Springer, Heidelberg (2011). doi:10.1007/978-3-642-24310-3_7

14. David, A., Larsen, K.G., Legay, A., Mikučionis, M., Wang, Z.: Time for statistical model checking of real-time systems. In: Gopalakrishnan, G., Qadeer, S. (eds.) CAV 2011. LNCS, vol. 6806, pp. 349–355. Springer, Heidelberg (2011). doi:10.1007/978-3-642-22110-1_27

15. DeAntoni, J., Mallet, F.: TimeSquare: treat your models with logical time. In: Furia, C.A., Nanz, S. (eds.) TOOLS 2012. LNCS, vol. 7304, pp. 34–41. Springer, Heidelberg (2012). doi:10.1007/978-3-642-30561-0_4

16. Demathieu, S., Thomas, F., André, C., Gérard, S., Terrier, F.: First experiments using the UML profile for MARTE. In: 11th IEEE International Symposium on Object-Oriented Real-Time Distributed Computing (ISORC), pp. 50–57. IEEE (2008). http://dx.doi.org/10.1109/ISORC.2008.36

17. Deshpande, A., Godbole, D., Göllü, A., Varaiya, P.: Design and evaluation tools for automated highway systems. In: Alur, R., Henzinger, T.A., Sontag, E.D. (eds.) HS 1995. LNCS, vol. 1066, pp. 138–148. Springer, Heidelberg (1996). doi:10.1007/BFb0020941

18. Espinoza, H., Dubois, H., Gérard, S., Medina, J., Petriu, D.C., Woodside, M.: Annotating UML models with non-functional properties for quantitative analysis. In: Bruel, J.-M. (ed.) MODELS 2005. LNCS, vol. 3844, pp. 79–90. Springer, Heidelberg (2006). doi:10.1007/11663430_9

19. Fang, H., Shi, J., Zhu, H., Guo, J., Larsen, K.G., David, A.: Formal verification and simulation for platform screen doors and collision avoidance in subway control systems. STTT 16(4), 339–361 (2014)

20. Fehnker, A., Ivančić, F.: Benchmarks for hybrid systems verification. In: Alur, R., Pappas, G.J. (eds.) HSCC 2004. LNCS, vol. 2993, pp. 326–341. Springer, Heidelberg (2004). doi:10.1007/978-3-540-24743-2_22

21. Iqbal, M.Z., Ali, S., Yue, T., Briand, L.: Experiences of applying UML/MARTE on three industrial projects. In: France, R.B., Kazmeier, J., Breu, R., Atkinson, C. (eds.) MODELS 2012. LNCS, vol. 7590, pp. 642–658. Springer, Heidelberg (2012). doi:10.1007/978-3-642-33666-9_41

22. Jiang, Z., Pajic, M., Moarref, S., Alur, R., Mangharam, R.: Modeling and verification of a dual chamber implantable pacemaker. In: Flanagan, C., König, B. (eds.) TACAS 2012. LNCS, vol. 7214, pp. 188–203. Springer, Heidelberg (2012). doi:10.1007/978-3-642-28756-5_14

23. Lamport, L.: Time, clocks, and the ordering of events in a distributed system. Commun. ACM **21**(7), 558–565 (1978)

24. Lee, E.A., Sangiovanni-Vincentelli, A.L.: A framework for comparing models of computation. IEEE Trans. Comput. Aided Des. Integr. Circ. Syst. **17**(12), 1217–1229 (1998)

25. Lee, E.A.: Cyber physical systems: design challenges. In: 11th IEEE International Symposium on Object-Oriented Real-Time Distributed Computing (ISORC 2008), pp. 363–369. IEEE Computer Society, May 2008. http://dx.doi.org/10.1109/ISORC.2008.25

26. Lee, E.A.: The past, present and future of cyber-physical systems: a focus on models. Sensors **15**(3), 4837–4869 (2015). http://www.mdpi.com/1424-8220/15/3/4837

27. Legay, A., Delahaye, B., Bensalem, S.: Statistical model checking: an overview. In: Barringer, H., Falcone, Y., Finkbeiner, B., Havelund, K., Lee, I., Pace, G., Roşu, G., Sokolsky, O., Tillmann, N. (eds.) RV 2010. LNCS, vol. 6418, pp. 122–135. Springer, Heidelberg (2010). doi:10.1007/978-3-642-16612-9_11

28. Liu, J., Liu, Z., He, J., Mallet, F., Ding, Z.: Hybrid MARTE statecharts. Front. Comput. Sci. **7**(1), 95–108 (2013)

29. Liu, Z., Liu, J., He, J., Ding, Z.: Spatio-temporal UML statechart for cyber-physical systems. In: 17th IEEE International Conference on Engineering of Complex Computer Systems, ICECCS, pp. 137–146. IEEE Computer Society (2012). http://doi.ieeecomputersociety.org/10.1109/ICECCS.2012.36

30. Mallet, F., de Simone, R.: Correctness issues on MARTE/CCSL constraints. Sci. Comput. Program. **106**, 78–92 (2015). http://www.sciencedirect.com/science/article/pii/S0167642315000519

31. Ptolemaeus, C.: System Design, Modeling, and Simulation: Using Ptolemy II. Ptolemy.org, New York (2014)

32. Selic, B., Gerard, S.: Modeling and Analysis of Real-Time and Embedded Systems with UML and MARTE. Elsevier, Amsterdam (2013)

33. Sen, K., Viswanathan, M., Agha, G.: Statistical model checking of black-box probabilistic systems. In: Alur, R., Peled, D.A. (eds.) CAV 2004. LNCS, vol. 3114, pp. 202–215. Springer, Heidelberg (2004). doi:10.1007/978-3-540-27813-9_16

34. Shorin, D., Zimmermann, A., Maciel, P.: Transforming UML state machines into stochastic petri nets for energy consumption estimation of embedded systems. Sustain. Internet ICT Sustain. (SustainIT) **2012**, 1–6 (2012)

35. Shorin, D., Zimmermann, A.: Formal description of an approach for power consumption estimation of embedded systems. In: 24th International Workshop on Power and Timing Modeling, Optimization and Simulation, PATMOS, pp. 1–10 (2014). http://dx.doi.org/10.1109/PATMOS.2014.6951890

36. Suryadevara, J., Seceleanu, C., Mallet, F., Pettersson, P.: Verifying MARTE/CCSL mode behaviors using UPPAAL. In: Hierons, R.M., Merayo, M.G., Bravetti, M. (eds.) SEFM 2013. LNCS, vol. 8137, pp. 1–15. Springer, Heidelberg (2013). doi:10. 1007/978-3-642-40561-7_1

37. Tomlin, C., Pappas, G., Lygeros, J., Godbole, D., Sastry, S.: Hybrid control models of next generation air traffic management. In: Antsaklis, P., Kohn, W., Nerode, A., Sastry, S. (eds.) HS 1996. LNCS, vol. 1273, pp. 378–404. Springer, Heidelberg (1997). doi:10.1007/BFb0031570

38. Tribastone, M., Gilmore, S.: Automatic extraction of PEPA performance models from UML activity diagrams annotated with the MARTE profile. In: Avritzer, A., Weyuker, E.J., Woodside, C.M. (eds.) 7th International Workshop on Software and Performance, WOSP 2008, pp. 67–78. ACM (2008). http://doi.acm.org/10.1145/1383559.1383569

39. Younes, H.L.S., Simmons, R.G.: Statistical probabilistic model checking with a focus on time-bounded properties. Inf. Comput. **204**(9), 1368–1409 (2006). http://dx.doi.org/10.1016/j.ic.2006.05.002

40. Zhang, Y., Mallet, F., Chen, Y.: Timed automata semantics of spatial-temporal consistency language STeC. In: Theoretical Aspects of Software Engineering Conference, TASE, pp. 201–208. IEEE (2014). http://dx.doi.org/10.1109/TASE.2014.10

41. Zou, J., Matic, S., Lee, E.A., Feng, T.H., Derler, P.: Execution strategies for PTIDES, a programming model for distributed embedded systems. In: 15th IEEE Real-Time and Embedded Technology and Applications Symposium, RTAS, pp. 77–86. IEEE Computer Society (2009). http://dx.doi.org/10.1109/RTAS.2009.39

A Formal and Run-Time Framework for the Adaptation of Local Behaviours to Match a Global Property

Stefano Bistarelli[2], Fabio Martinelli[1], Ilaria Matteucci[1], and Francesco Santini[2(✉)]

[1] Istituto di Informatica e Telematica, IIT-CNR, Pisa, Italy
{fabio.martinelli,ilaria.matteucci}@iit.cnr.it
[2] Dipartimento di Matematica e Informatica, University of Perugia, Perugia, Italy
{bista,francesco.santini}@dmi.unipg.it

Abstract. We address the problem of automatically identifying what local properties the agents of a *Cyber Physical System* have to satisfy to guarantee a global required property ϕ. To enrich the picture, we consider properties where, besides qualitative requirements on the actions to be performed, we assume a weight associated with them: quantitative properties are specified through a weighted modal-logic. We propose both a formal machinery based on a *Quantitative Partial Model Checking* function on contexts, and a run-time machinery that algorithmically tries to check if the local behaviours proposed by the agents satisfy ϕ. The proposed approach can be seen as a run-time decomposition, privacy-sensitive in the sense agents do not have to disclose their full behaviour.

1 Introduction

The term *Cyber-Physical Systems* (*CPSs*) refers to a new generation of systems that integrate the dynamics of physical processes with those of the software and communication. Applications of CPSs include medical devices and systems, assisted living, traffic control and safety, advanced automotive systems, process control, or distributed robotics [17]. For instance, unmanned vehicles or drones encompass both the physical and cyber worlds at the same time: software, sensors, networking, and physical devices. CPSs are resource-constrained and need a high degree of automation, as the two previous examples require in fact [7,17].

The goal of the paper is to describe a formal framework that allows for opportunely finding out the properties that must be locally satisfied by each component of a CPS (or simply agent in the following), to guarantee a global required property ϕ representing a complex task a CSP has to satisfy. Such a decomposition $\langle \phi_1, \ldots, \phi_n \rangle$ is algorithmically found and tried to be satisfied at

Research supported by: "VisColla" funded by Fondazione Cassa di Risparmio di Perugia; "BitCoins" co-funded by Banca d'Italia and Cassa di Risparmio di Perugia; the H2020 EU-funded European Network for Cyber Security, NeCS, (GA #675320).

O. Kouchnarenko and R. Khosravi (Eds.): FACS 2016, LNCS 10231, pp. 134–152, 2017.
DOI: 10.1007/978-3-319-57666-4_9

run-time: each agent proposes a behaviour with the purpose to satisfy a sub-task (*i.e.*, a sub-formula, or sub-property, ϕ_i), thus trying to reduce the overall complexity into several simpler sub-tasks. Each of them can be in turn solved by more than an agent, *i.e.*, ϕ_i can be further decomposed.

In addition, we consider quantitative aspects, in order to add to the picture costs, execution times, rates and, in general, the non-functional aspects that are typical of CPS. Thus, the question is not only whether a system satisfies a task, *e.g.*, the delivery of some packages by drones, but also if the cost of enforcing this behaviour in terms of, *e.g.*, the global energy consumption of drones, or a time-limit to deliver the packages, is better than a desirable threshold t.

Sub-tasks are found through a *Quantitative Partial Model-Checking (QPMC)* function on quantitative contexts. With such QPMC function, parts of a concurrent system can be gradually removed by transforming ϕ accordingly. With respect to [15], we are now also able to accumulate (part of) the weight of removed actions into k, which represents an amount of weight that will be indeed spent to execute such removed specification; note that this removal does not affect the validity of ϕ. Not all the weight can be extracted, since non-deterministic branches may have different costs. However, such removal is anyway useful to have an estimation on the maximum weight of the remaining part, and to stop QPMC as soon as it goes beyond the imposed acceptance-threshold. Such a k will be also heuristically used to predict the best behaviour among all the possible ones of an agent. Note that, since every agent computes the QPMC function on some of its possible different behaviours, it is not required to disclose the "full" behaviour; hence, this approach also improves the privacy of agents. At run-time, each agent proposes one of its behaviours that, once pushed into a sub-formula ϕ_i, minimises k. An initiator agent collects all the proposals and checks if ϕ is satisfied with a cost better than t by the behaviour of all the agents, which contribute to a part of it. If not, the agents are required to change behaviour and adapt to the already accepted behaviours, until a solution to ϕ is found.

Privacy, complexity reduction, and a run-time approach are the key-points of our approach. The Model Checking function is "partial", hence it reduces the complexity of satisfying ϕ "agent-by-agent". This also preserves the privacy of agents, which do not need to disclose their full behaviour, but they can propose different alternatives at run-time. Agents can consequently change at run-time transparently to the framework.

The paper is organised as follows: Sect. 2 presents the necessary background-notions on c-semirings [2], the algebraic structure we use to parametrise different cost/preference metrics. In Sect. 3.1, we extend the notion of contexts [11] by presenting *quantitative contexts*, where actions are associated with a c-semiring value. In Sect. 3.3 we present a *quantitative Hennessy-Milner logic (i.e., c-HM logic)* to define properties (*i.e.*, ϕ) on quantitative contexts. Finally, to conclude the presentation of the formal side of the framework, in Sect. 3.4 we define the QPMC function. Section 4 describes instead the run-time side of the framework: it reports the pseudocode the agents have to implement to find all the single sub-behaviours. and to check if their composition satisfies ϕ. This section comes with a drone package-delivery and other examples (Sect. 1). Section 5 reports the related work, while Sect. 6 wraps up the paper with conclusions and future work.

2   C-Semirings

We introduce semirings, the core of the presented computational framework.

Definition 1 (Semiring [10]). *A commutative semiring is a five-tuple* $\mathbb{K} = \langle K, +, \times, \bot, \top \rangle$ *such that* K *is a set,* $\top, \bot \in K$, *and* $+, \times : K \times K \to K$ *are binary operators making the triples* $\langle K, +, \bot \rangle$ *and* $\langle K, \times, \top \rangle$ *commutative monoids (semigroups with identity), satisfying* i) *(distributivity)* $\forall a, b, c \in K.a \times (b+c) = (a \times b) + (a \times c)$, *and* ii) *(annihilator)* $\forall a \in A.a \times \bot = \bot$.

Definition 2 (Absorptive semirings). *Let* $\mathbb{S}$ *be a commutative semiring. An absorptive semiring verifies the absorptiveness property:* $\forall a, b \in K.a + (a \times b) = a$, *which is equivalent to* $\forall a \in S.a + \top = \top$.

Absorptive semirings are referred as *simple*, and their $+$ operator is necessarily idempotent [10]. Semirings where $+$ is idempotent are *tropical*, or *diods*.

Definition 3 (C-semiring [2]). *C-semirings are commutative and absorptive semirings. Therefore, c-semirings are tropical semirings where* $\top$ *is an absorbing element for* $+$.

The idempotency of $+$ leads to the definition of a partial ordering $\leq_K$ over the set K (K is a poset). It is defined as $a \leq_K b$ if and only if $a + b = b$, and $+$ finds the *least upper bound* (*lub*) in the lattice $\langle K, \leq_K \rangle$. This intuitively means that b is "better" than a. Therefore, we can use $+$ as an optimisation operator and always choose the best available solution.

Some more properties can be derived on c-semirings [2]: *(i)* both $+$ and $\times$ are monotone over $\leq_K$, *(ii)* $\times$ is intensive (*i.e.*, $a \times b \leq_K a$), *(iii)* $\times$ is closed (*i.e.*, $a \times b \in K$), and *(iv)* $\langle K, \leq_K \rangle$ is a complete lattice. $\bot$ and $\top$ are respectively the bottom and top elements of such lattice. When also $\times$ is idempotent, *(i)* $+$ distributes over $\times$, *(ii)* $\times$ finds the *greatest lower bound* (*glb*, or $\sqcap$) of the lattice, and *(iii)* $\langle K, \leq_K \rangle$ is a distributive lattice. $\sum$ denotes the set-wise extension of $+$.

Some c-semiring instances are: *boolean* $\langle \{F, T\}, \vee, \wedge, F, T \rangle$[1], *fuzzy* $\langle [0, 1], \max, \min, 0, 1 \rangle$, *bottleneck* $\langle \mathbb{R}^+ \cup \{+\infty\}, \max, \min, 0, \infty \rangle$, *probabilistic* $\langle [0, 1], \max, \hat{\times}, 0, 1 \rangle$ (or Viterbi semiring), *weighted* $\langle \mathbb{R}^+ \cup \{+\infty\}, \min, \hat{+}, +\infty, 0 \rangle$. Capped operators stand for their arithmetic equivalent.

Although c-semirings have been historically used as monotonic structures where to aggregate costs (and find best solutions), the need of removing values has raised in local consistency algorithms and non-monotonic algebras using

---

[1] Boolean c-semirings can be used to model crisp problems.

constraints (*e.g.*, [1]). A solution comes from *residuation theory* [4], a standard tool on tropical arithmetic that allows for obtaining a division operator via an approximate solution to the equation $b \times x = a$.

Definition 4 (Division [1]**).** *Let $\mathbb{K}$ be a tropical semiring. Then, $\mathbb{K}$ is residuated if the set $\{x \in K \mid b \times x \leq a\}$ admits a maximum for all elements $a, b \in K$, denoted $a \div b$.*

Since a complete[2] tropical-semiring is also residuated, all the classical instances of c-semiring presented above are residuated, *i.e.*, each element in K admits an "inverse", which is unique in case $\leq_K$ is a total order. For instance, the unique "inverse" $a \div b$ in the weighted semiring is defined as follows: $a \div b = \min\{x \mid b \hat{+} x \geq a\}$, which is equal to 0 if $b \geq a$, or $a \hat{-} b$ if $a > b$. Since all the previous examples of c-semirings (*e.g.*, weighted or fuzzy) are cancellative, they are uniquely invertible as well:

Definition 5 (Unique invertibility [1]**).** *Let $\mathbb{K}$ be an absorptive, invertible semiring. Then, $\mathbb{K}$ is uniquely invertible iff it is cancellative, i.e., $\forall a, b, c \in A.(a \times c = b \times c) \wedge (c \neq 0) \Rightarrow a = b$.*

Furthermore, it is also possible to consider several optimisation criteria at the same time: the Cartesian product of c-semirings is still a c-semiring, and even a lexicographic order can be modelled over multiple c-semirings [8].

3   Quantifying Properties in a Distributed Environment

In this section we focus on how we can describe the behaviour of distributed, possible partially specified systems, as well as how to express quantitative properties/constraints on such distributed systems. To this aim, we propose a variant of the notion of *context*, to enhance the one in [11] by adding a weight to tuples of actions. This allows us to quantitatively specify and analyse the behaviour of a system with some unknown parts, which have nevertheless to participate to the satisfaction of a quantitative global-property on the whole system. Furthermore, we present a quantitative Hennessy-Milner logic, proposed in [15], thus, we can specify a property on a tuple of actions, extending it to c-HM^n. Finally, we define a QPMC function allowing us to project such global constraint onto local ones that have to be locally satisfied by the subcomponents of the system.

3.1   Quantitative Contexts

The notion of *n-to-m quantitative context* is an expression describing the partial implementation of a system, denoted as $C(X_1, \ldots, X_n)$, where C denotes the known part of the system and/or how its components, $X_1, \ldots, X_n$, free variables representing the unknown ones, work together, n is the number of unknown

---

[2] $\mathbb{K}$ is complete if it is closed with respect to infinite sums, and the distributivity law holds also for an infinite number of summands [1].

components, and m is the cardinality of the output of their composition by C. This notion enhances the one given in [11] by adding weights to tuples of actions. Note that, when the dimension of the context is clear, we omit it from notation.

Definition 6 (Quantitative context). *A* quantitative context-system *is a structure* $\mathcal{C} = (\langle C_n^m \rangle_{n,m}, Act, \mathbb{K}, \langle \rightarrow_{n,m}^K \rangle_{n,m})$ *where* $\langle C_n^m \rangle_{n,m}$ *is a set of n-to-m tuple of n-to-m quantitative contexts;* $\mathbb{K} = \langle K, +, \times, \perp, \top \rangle$ *is a c-semiring; Act is a set of actions;* $Act_0 = Act \cup \{0\}$ *where* $0 \notin Act$ *is a distinguished no-action symbol,* Act_0^n *is the set of tuples of n actions in* Act_0, $\rightarrow_{n,m}^K \subseteq C_n^m \times ((Act_0^n, K) \times (Act_0^m, K)) \times C_n^m$ *is the* quantitative transduction-relation *for the n-to-m contexts satisfying* $(C, (\tilde{a}, k), (\tilde{0}, h), D) \in \rightarrow_{n,m}^K$ *if and only if* $C = D$ *and* $\tilde{a} = \tilde{0}$ *for all contexts* $C, D \in C_n^m$ ($h, k \in K$), *and* $\langle \rightarrow_{n,m}^K \rangle_{n,m}$ *is an* $\{n, m\}$-*tuple of* quantitative transduction-relations.

For $(C, (\tilde{a}, k), (\tilde{b}, h), C') \in \rightarrow_{n,m}^K$ we usually write $C \xrightarrow[(\tilde{a},k)]{(\tilde{b},h)} C'$, leaving the indices of $\rightarrow$ to be determined by the context. The informal interpretation is that the context C takes as input the set of actions $\tilde{a}$, of dimension n (cfr. $\tilde{a} = \langle a_1, \ldots, a_n \rangle$) performed with a weight k, and it returns as output $\tilde{b}$ of dimension m (cfr. $\tilde{b} = \langle b_1, \ldots, b_m \rangle$) weighted by h, finally becoming C'. If $\tilde{a}$ is 0 (*i.e.*, no action) then the context produces an output without consuming any internal action; if $\tilde{b}$ is 0 then there is not any observable transition and we omit the vector of outputs; if both $\tilde{a}$ and $\tilde{b}$ are equal to 0, then both the internal process and the external observer are not involved in the transduction. In Definitions 7 and 8, we compose contexts by means of *composition* and *product*:

Definition 7 (Composition). *Let* $\mathcal{C} = (\langle C_n^m \rangle_{n,m}, Act, \mathbb{K}, \langle \rightarrow_{n,m}^K \rangle_{n,m})$ *be a quantitative context-system. A* composition *on* $\mathcal{C}$ *is a dyadic operation* $\circ$ *on contexts such that, whenever* $C \in C_n^m$ *and* $D \in C_m^r$, *then* $D \circ C \in C_n^r$ *according to the following rule:*

$$\frac{C \xrightarrow[(\tilde{a},k)]{(\tilde{b},h)} C' \quad D \xrightarrow[(\tilde{b},h)]{(\tilde{c},w)} D'}{D \circ C \xrightarrow[(\tilde{a},k)]{(\tilde{c},w)} D' \circ C'}$$

where $\tilde{a} = \langle a_1, \ldots, a_n \rangle$, $\tilde{b} = \langle b_1, \ldots, b_m \rangle$, *and* $\tilde{c} = \langle c_1, \ldots, c_r \rangle$ *are vectors of actions, while* k, h, w *represent the weight of vector of actions* $\tilde{a}, \tilde{b}, \tilde{c}$ *respectively.*

The basic idea is that two contexts can be composed if the output of the first one (cfr. C) is exactly the same in terms of (*i*) the tuple of performed actions, (*ii*) its associated weight, with respect to the input of the second context (cfr. D). In this way, the two contexts combine their actions in such a way that the transduction of the composed context takes the input of C and its weight as input, and it returns the output of D and its weight as output.

To compose n independent processes through the same context $C \in C_n^m$ we define an *independent combination*, referred as the *product* operator of n

contexts $D_1 \times \ldots \times D_n$, where $D_i \in C^1_{m_i}$, $i = 1, \ldots, n$ and D_i is an expansion of the i'th subcomponent of C such that the cardinality m is exactly equal to the total sum of each single cardinality m_i associated with a context D_i. We consider *asynchronous* contexts, it is not required that all the components $X_1, \ldots, X_n$ contribute in a transition of the system $C(X_1, \ldots, X_n)$, *i.e.*, some X_i can perform a null action (*i.e.*, 0).

Definition 8 (Product). *Let* $\mathcal{C} = (\langle C^m_n \rangle_{n,m}, Act, \mathbb{K}, \langle \to^K_{n,m} \rangle_{n,m})$ *be a context system. A* product *on* $\mathcal{C}$ *is a context operation* $\times$, *such that whenever* $C \in C^m_n$ *and* $D \in C^s_r$ *then* $C \times D \in C^{m+s}_{n+r}$. *Furthermore, the transduction for a context* $C \times D$ *are fully characterised by the following rule:*

$$\frac{C \xrightarrow[(\tilde{a},k)]{(\tilde{b},h)} C' \quad D \xrightarrow[(\tilde{c},w)]{(\tilde{d},s)} D'}{C \times D \xrightarrow[(\tilde{a}\tilde{c},k \times w)]{(\tilde{b}\tilde{d},h \times s)} C' \times D'}$$

where juxtaposition of vectors $\tilde{a} = \langle a_1, \ldots, a_n \rangle$ *and* $\tilde{c} = \langle c_1, \ldots, c_r \rangle$ *is the vector* $\tilde{a}\tilde{c} = \langle a_1, \ldots, a_n, c_1, \ldots, c_r \rangle$, *and juxtaposition of vectors* $\tilde{b} = \langle b_1, \ldots, b_m \rangle$ *and* $\tilde{d} = \langle d_1, \ldots, d_s \rangle$ *is the vector* $\tilde{b}\tilde{d} = \langle b_1, \ldots, b_m, d_1, \ldots, d_s \rangle$. *Note that the weight of the juxtaposition of two action-vectors is just the* $\times$ *of their weights.*

The intuition behind this definition is that two contexts C and D take in input $\tilde{a}$ and $\tilde{c}$ and return as output $\tilde{b}$ and $\tilde{d}$, respectively, at the same time and both of them contribute to the evolution of the system, modelled as the product context derived from C and D. The weight associated to the product are the product of the weights of each tuple of actions. For the sake of readability, sometimes we write the combined process $C(X_1, \ldots, X_n)$ as a shorthand for $C \circ (X_1 \times \ldots \times X_n)$.

3.2   Modelling GPA as Contexts

We show how it is possible to use quantitative contexts to model the behaviour of quantitative process algebras, such as GPA [5]. In particular, transitions are labelled by pairs (a, k) where k is a quantity associated to the effect a, that we will use hereafter to model the behaviour of system's agents (see Sect. 4.2). Let us consider a fragment of GPA, *i.e.*, the prefix, non deterministic choice ($+$), and parallel ($\|$) operators.

Definition 9 (GPA syntax as contexts). *The set* $\mathcal{P}$ *of GPA processes over a countable set of transition labels Act and a semiring* $\mathbb{K}$ *is defined by the grammar:*

$$P ::= 0 \mid (a, k)^* \mid +(P, P') \mid \|(P, P')$$

where $a \in Act$, *and* $k \in K$ *(the set of values in a semiring* $\mathbb{K}$*).* $GPA(\mathbb{K})$ *denotes the set of GPA processes labelled with weights in* $\mathbb{K}$.

Process 0 describes inaction or termination; $(a, k)^*$ is a 0-to-1 quantitative context that performs a with *value* k; $+(P, P')$ is a 2-to-1 quantitative context that non deterministically behaves as either P or P'; $\|(P, P')$ is a 2-to-1 quantitative context that describes the process in which P and P' proceed concurrently when they perform complementary actions, *i.e.*, $a, \bar{a} \in Act$, and independently on all the other actions. GPA processes operators and their semantics can be expressed in terms of context $\mathcal{C}_2^1$ (see Table 1) with the help of additional operators: the *projection* Π_n^i and the *identity* I_n respectively describe the projection of the behaviour of a system on a single component, and the inaction of a system.

Table 1. Semantics of a GPA [5] context system.

Inaction:

$$C \xrightarrow[\bar{0}]{\bar{0}} C \text{ for all } C$$

Prefix:

$$(a, k)^* \xrightarrow[0]{(a,k)} I_1$$

Choice:

$$(1) + \xrightarrow[((a,k),0)]{(a,k)} \Pi_2^1 \quad (2) + \xrightarrow[(0,(a,k))]{(a,k)} \Pi_2^2 \text{ for } a \in Act$$

Projection:

$$\Pi_n^i \xrightarrow[i(\tilde{a},\tilde{k})]{(a,k)} \Pi_n^i$$

Identity:

$$I_n \xrightarrow[(\tilde{a},\tilde{k})]{(\tilde{a},\tilde{k})} I_n$$

Parallel:

$$(1) \| \xrightarrow[((a,k_a),(\bar{a},k_{\bar{a}}))]{(\tau, k_a \times k_{\bar{a}})} \| \quad (2) \| \xrightarrow[((a,k),0)]{(a,k)} \| \quad (3) \| \xrightarrow[(0,(a,k))]{(a,k)} \|$$

where $i(\tilde{a}, \tilde{k}) \in Act_0^n$ denotes that the ith component of $\tilde{a} \in Act_0^n$ is equal to a and the others are equal to 0.

3.3 Multi-action C-Semiring Hennessy-Milner Logic (c-HM^n)

The c-HM^n formulas semantics is defined on a *Multi-Labelled Transition-System*.

Definition 10 (MLTS). *A (finite) Multi-Labelled Transition-System (MLTS) is a four-tuple* $MLTS = (S, L^n, \mathbb{K}, T)$, *where* i) S *is the countable (finite) state-space,* ii) L^n *is a finite set of transition labels, where each label is a vector of labels in* L: *the label* $\langle a_1, \dots, a_n \rangle \in L^n$ *and for all* $i = 1, \dots, n$, $a_i \in L$. iii) $\mathbb{K} = \langle K, +, \times, \bot, \top \rangle$ *is a c-semiring used for the definition of transition weights, and* iv) $T : (S \times L^n \times S) \longrightarrow \mathbb{K}$ *is the transition weight-function.*

Definition 11 syntactically defines the correct formulas given over an MLTS.

Definition 11 (Syntax). *Given an MLTS* $M = \langle S, L^n, \mathbb{K}, T \rangle$, *and let* $\tilde{a} \in L^n$, *the syntax of a formula* $\phi \in \Phi_M$ *is as follows, where* $k \in K$:

$$\phi ::= k \mid \phi_1 + \phi_2 \mid \phi_1 \times \phi_2 \mid \phi_1 \sqcap \phi_2 \mid \langle \tilde{a} \rangle \phi \mid [\tilde{a}] \phi$$

The operators $+$ and $\sqcap$ (respectively the lub and glb derived from $\geq_K$ in $\mathbb{K}$), and $\times$ (still in the definition of $\mathbb{K}$) are used in place of classical logic operators $\vee$ and $\wedge$, in order to compose the truth values of two formulas together. The truth values are all the $k \in K$. In particular, while *false* corresponds to $\bot$, we can have different degrees of *true*, where "full truth" is $\top$. As a reminder, when the $\times$ operator is idempotent, then $\times$ and $\sqcap$ coincide (Sect. 2). Finally, we have the two classical modal operators, *i.e.*, "possibly" ($\langle \cdot \rangle$), and "necessarily" ($[\cdot]$).

Table 2. The semantic interpretation of c-HM. We have $\sum(\emptyset) = \bot$ and $\sqcap(\emptyset) = \top$.

$$
\begin{aligned}
\llbracket k \rrbracket(C) &= k \in K \ \ \forall C \in C_n^m & \llbracket \phi_1 + \phi_2 \rrbracket(C) &= \llbracket \phi_1 \rrbracket(C) + \llbracket \phi_2 \rrbracket(C) \\
\llbracket \phi_1 \times \phi_2 \rrbracket(C) &= \llbracket \phi_1 \rrbracket(C) \times \llbracket \phi_2 \rrbracket(C) & \llbracket \phi_1 \sqcap \phi_2 \rrbracket(C) &= \llbracket \phi_1 \rrbracket(C) \sqcap \llbracket \phi_2 \rrbracket(C) \\
\llbracket \langle \tilde{a} \rangle \phi \rrbracket(C) &= \sum_R (k_a \times \llbracket \phi \rrbracket(C')) & \llbracket [\tilde{a}] \phi \rrbracket(C) &= \sqcap_R (k_a \times \llbracket \phi \rrbracket(C'))
\end{aligned}
$$
$$
\text{where } R = \{ C' \in C_0^m \mid (C, (\tilde{a}, k_a), (0, \top), C') \in T \}
$$

The semantics of a formula ϕ is interpreted on a system of n-to-m quantitative contexts, given on top of an MLTS $M = (C_n^m, Act_0^n \times Act_0^m, \mathbb{K}, \rightarrow_{n,m}^K)$. The aim is to check the specification defined by ϕ over the behaviour of a weighted transition system M that defines the behaviour of a quantitative context. While in [11] the semantics of a formula computes the states $U \subseteq C_n^m$ that satisfy that formula, our semantics $\llbracket \rrbracket_M : (\Phi_M \times C_n^m) \longrightarrow K$ (see Table 2) computes a truth value for the same U. In particular, in the following we deal with n-ary contexts (C_0^n), hence the set of labels is $L^n = Act_0^n$. Note that we consider finite contexts C_n^m, *i.e.*, they are defined over a finite MLTS, they are not recursive, and the contexts composed with them are closed and finite as well. Hence, we consider only the set of n-to-m quantitative contexts.

In Table 2 and in the following (when clear from the context), we omit M from $\llbracket \rrbracket_M$ for the sake of readability. The semantics is parametrised over a context $C \in C_n^m$, which is used to consider only the transitions that can be fired at a given step (labelled with a vector of actions $\tilde{a}$).

In Definition 12 we rephrase the notion of satisfiability of a c-HM^n formula ϕ on a context C, by taking into account a threshold t:

Definition 12 (t-satisfiability, $\models_t$). *A context $C \in C_n^m$ quantitatively satisfies a c-HM^n formula ϕ with a threshold-value t, i.e., $C \models_t \phi$, if and only if the interpretation of ϕ on C is better/equal than t. Formally: $C \models_t \phi \Leftrightarrow t \leq_K \llbracket \phi \rrbracket_C$.*

This means that C is a model for a formula ϕ, with respect to a certain value t, if and only if the weight corresponding to the interpretation of ϕ on C is better or equal to t in the partial order $\leq_K$ defined in $\mathbb{K}$.

Remark 1. Note that, if C does not satisfy a formula ϕ then $\llbracket \phi \rrbracket_C = \bot$. Consequently, the only t such that $C \models_t \phi$ is $t = \bot$. If $\llbracket \phi \rrbracket_C \neq \bot$, then ϕ is satisfiable with a certain threshold $t \neq \bot$.

3.4 Quantitative Partial Model Checking

Here we present a QPMC function (Table 3) given with respect to the context composition-operator. The k_C in represents an amount of weight that is spent to satisfy ϕ, by considering only the actions in C. Theorem 1 states that k_C can be extracted and then composed back with $[\![\mathcal{W}(C, \phi)]\!]_P$ without changing $[\![\phi]\!]_{C(P)}$:

Table 3. A QPMC function (*i.e.*, $\mathcal{W}(C, \phi)$) for quantitative contexts; k_C corresponds to an amount of weight that can be extracted from ϕ considering the behaviour of C.

$$\mathcal{W}(C, h) = h \qquad\qquad k_{C,\phi} = \top$$

$$\mathcal{W}(C, \phi_1 \times \phi_2) = ((k_{C,\phi_1} \div k_{C,\phi}) \times \mathcal{W}(C, \phi_1)) \times ((k_{C,\phi_2} \div k_{C,\phi}) \times \mathcal{W}(C, \phi_2)) \quad k_{C,\phi} = k_{C,\phi_1} + k_{C,\phi_2}$$

$$\mathcal{W}(C, \phi_1 + \phi_2) = ((k_{C,\phi_1} \div k_{C,\phi}) \times \mathcal{W}(C, \phi_1)) + ((k_{C,\phi_2} \div k_{C,\phi}) \times \mathcal{W}(C, \phi_2)) \quad k_{C,\phi} = k_{C,\phi_1} + k_{C,\phi_2}$$

$$\mathcal{W}(C, \phi_1 \sqcap \phi_2) = ((k_{C,\phi_1} \div k_{C,\phi}) \times \mathcal{W}(C, \phi_1)) \sqcap ((k_{C,\phi_2} \div k_{C,\phi}) \times \mathcal{W}(C, \phi_2)) \quad k_{C,\phi} = k_{C,\phi_1} + k_{C,\phi_2}$$

$$\mathcal{W}(C, [\bar{a}]\phi_1) = \bigsqcap_{\substack{C \xrightarrow{(\bar{a},k_{\bar{a}})} C' \\ (\bar{b},k_{\bar{b}})}} ((k_{\bar{a}} \times k_{C',\phi_1}) \div k_{C,\phi}) \times ([\bar{b}]\mathcal{W}(C', \phi_1) \div k_{\bar{b}}) \qquad k_{C,\phi} = \sum_{C'} (k_{\bar{a}} \times k_{C',\phi_1})$$

$$\mathcal{W}(C, \langle\bar{a}\rangle\phi_1) = \sum_{\substack{C \xrightarrow{(\bar{a},k_{\bar{a}})} C' \\ (\bar{b},h_{\bar{b}})}} ((k_{\bar{a}} \times k_{C',\phi_1}) \div k_{C,\phi}) \times (\langle\bar{b}\rangle\mathcal{W}(C', \phi_1) \div k_{\bar{b}}) \qquad k_{C,\phi} = \sum_{C'} (k_{\bar{a}} \times k_{C',\phi_1})$$

Theorem 1. *Let* $\mathcal{C} = (\langle C_n^m \rangle_{n,m}, Act, \mathbb{K}, \langle\rightarrow_{n,m}^K\rangle_{n,m})$ *a quantitative context-system,* $\mathbb{K}$ *a c-semiring* $\mathbb{K} = \langle K, +, \times, \bot, \top \rangle$ *with* $k \in K$ *and* ϕ *be a c-HM^n formula and* $C \in C_n^m$ *a context, then, for any* $P \in C_0^n$, *the following holds:* $[\![\phi]\!]_{C(P)} = k_{C,\phi} \times [\![\mathcal{W}(C, \phi)]\!]_P$.

Remark 2. $k_{C,\phi}$ is extracted during the application of $\mathcal{W}(C, \phi)$ (see Table 3), and it can be useful, for instance, to immediately state that $C(P) \not\models_t \phi$ when already $k_{C,\phi} <_K t$ (see Definition 12), without also computing $[\![\mathcal{W}(C, \phi)]\!]$ to obtain the truth value of $[\![\phi]\!]_{C(P)}$ (see Theorem 1). The extraction of $k_{C,\phi}$ is correct. However, for some formulas it can be further improved: for instance, if $\phi = \phi_1 \times \phi_2$ we can extract a larger amount than what reported in Table 3, *i.e.*, $k_{C,\phi_1} \times k_{C,\phi_2}$ instead of $k_{C,\phi_1} + k_{C,\phi_2}$ Such optimisations deserve a different study and are out of the scope of this paper, but planned as future work (see Sect. 6).

Example 1. Let us consider a simple example in which we have two agents A and B that have to coordinate with the purpose to deliver two packages T and Z, respecting while some quantitative constraints. Let us consider a policy $\phi = \phi_1 + \phi_2$, where ϕ_1 and ϕ_2 represent two distinct strategies to deliver the two packages. Each (boxed) action is associated with a different weight, which can be interpreted as the energy consumption demanded to deliver such a package, or a cost in terms of capabilities to be spent in order to deliver it. The two formulas are $\phi_1 = [deliver\_T]5 \times [deliver\_Z]3$ and $\phi_2 = [deliver\_Z]6 \times [deliver\_T]4$.

Let $S(A, B) = \|(A, B)$ be the considered system. By using the QPMC function on contexts, and noting that the weight of parallel composition is equal to the product of the energy consumption of each component, $\mathcal{W}(\|, \phi) = \mathcal{W}(\|, \phi_1 + \phi_2) = ((k_{\|,\phi_1} \div k_{\|,\phi}) \times \mathcal{W}(\|, \phi_1)) + ((k_{\|,\phi_2} \div k_{\|,\phi}) \times \mathcal{W}(\|, \phi_2))$, where

$$\mathcal{W}(\|, \phi_1) = (k_{\|,\phi_1^1} \div k_{\|,\phi_1})\mathcal{W}(\|, \phi_1^1) \times (k_{\|,\phi_1^2} \div k_{\|,\phi_1})\mathcal{W}(\|, \phi_1^2),$$
$$\mathcal{W}(\|, \phi_2) = (k_{\|,\phi_2^1} \div k_{\|,\phi_2})\mathcal{W}(\|, \phi_2^1) \times (k_{\|,\phi_2^2} \div k_{\|,\phi_2})\mathcal{W}(\|, \phi_2^2),$$

$\phi_1^1 = [(deliver\_T)]5$, $\phi_1^2 = [(deliver\_Z)]3$, $\phi_2^1 = [(deliver\_Z)]6$, and $\phi_2^2 = [(deliver\_T)]4$. We suppose that the system $\|(A, B)$ is able to perform either $deliver\_T$ with weight 3, or $deliver\_Z$ with weight 6. Note that, at this step, we do not know neither which component contributes to the system behaviour, nor if the two components contribute with a different cost. Hence, we assume that both components are able to deliver both packages (T and Z), and with the same energy consumption: understanding the role of each agent is part of the adaptation algorithms in Sect. 4. The previous formula is simplified as follows:

$\mathcal{W}(\|, \phi) = (\top \times \mathcal{W}(\|, \phi_1)) + (\top \times \mathcal{W}(\|, \phi_2)) = \mathcal{W}(\|, \phi_1) + \mathcal{W}(\|, \phi_2)$ *and*

$\mathcal{W}(\|, \phi_1) = (3 \div 3)(((3 \div (3 \sqcap 3)) \times ([deliver\_T, 0]5) \div 3)) \sqcap ((3 \div (3 \sqcap 3)) \times ([0, deliver\_T]5) \div 3))$

$\qquad \times (6 \div 3)(((6 \div (6 \sqcap 6)) \times ([deliver\_Z, 0]3) \div 6)) \sqcap (((6 \div (6 \sqcap 6)) \times ([0, deliver\_Z]3) \div 6))$

$\qquad = ((([deliver\_T, 0]5) \div 3) \sqcap (([0, deliver\_T]5) \div 3)) \times (3 \times (((([deliver\_Z, 0]3) \div 6)$

$\qquad \sqcap (([0, deliver\_Z]3) \div 6)))$

$\mathcal{W}(\|, \phi_2) = (6 \div 3)(((6 \div (6 \sqcap 6)) \times ([deliver\_Z, 0]6) \div 6)) \sqcap (((6 \div (6 \sqcap 6)) \times ([0, deliver\_Z]6) \div 6))$

$\qquad \times (3 \div 3) \times (((3 \div (3 \sqcap 3)) \times ([deliver\_T, 0]4) \div 3)) \sqcap (((3 \div (3 \sqcap 3)) \times ([0, deliver\_T]4) \div 3))$

$\qquad = (3 \times (((([deliver\_Z, 0]6) \div 6) \sqcap (([0, deliver\_Z]6) \div 6)) \times ((([deliver\_T, 0]4) \div 3)$

$\qquad \sqcap (([0, deliver\_T]4) \div 3))$ *and*

$k_{\|,\phi} = 3 + 6 = \mathbf{3}$.

According to Theorem 1, we need to show that $[\![\phi]\!]_{\|(A,B)} = k_{\|,\phi} \times [\![\mathcal{W}(\|, \phi)]\!]_{A \times B}$:

$[\![\phi]\!]_{\|(A,B)} = [\![\phi_1]\!]_{\|(A,B)} + [\![\phi_2]\!]_{\|(A,B)}$

$\qquad = ([\![[deliver\_T]5 \times [deliver\_Z]3]\!]_{\|(A,B)} + [\![[deliver\_Z]6 \times [deliver\_T]4]\!]_{\|(A,B)}$

$\qquad = (3 \times 5) + (3 \times 4) = 7$ *and*

$k_{\|,\phi} \times [\![\mathcal{W}(\|, \phi)]\!]_{A \times B} = \mathbf{3} \times ((3 \times 5 \div 3) + (3 \times 4 \div 3)) = \mathbf{3} \times (5 + 4) = \mathbf{3} \times 4 = 7.$

4   Decomposition into Local Behaviours and Algorithms for the Run-Time Satisfaction of ϕ

Let us consider a distributed system in which several agents $A_1, \ldots, A_n$ have to cooperate to reach a goal. We specify such a system as a context $C(A_1, \ldots, A_n)$ where $A_1, \ldots, A_n$, even though they know the presence of each other, each A_i has to decide which behaviour wants to expose to the other in order to collaborate one another to *quantitatively satisfy* ($\models_t$, see Definition 12) a system requirement, expressed by a logic formula $\phi \in$ c-HM^n.

In this section, we consider as context an n-ary version of the GPA parallel operator, we denote with $\|^n$. The semantics interpretation of $\|^n$ is equivalent to the repeated composition of the binary parallel-operator, e.g., $\|^3(A_1, A_2, A_3)$ is equivalent to $\|(A_1, \|(A_2, A_3))^3$.

---

[3] For the sake of readability, we write $\|$ in place of $\|^2$, *i.e.*, omitting the apex.

The run-time framework in Sect. 4.1 is able to identify which are the local requirements each agent has to quantitatively satisfy in order to guarantee the satisfaction of a global property ϕ. Formally:

$$\forall A_i, \ i = 1, \ldots, n \quad (A_1 \vDash_{t_1} \phi_1 \times \ldots \times A_n \vDash_{t_n} \phi_n \Rightarrow \|^n(A_1, \ldots, A_n) \vDash_t \phi) \quad (1)$$

where $t_1, \ldots, t_n$ are the thresholds of each ϕ_i with respect to A_i, $i = \ldots, n$. The algorithms in Sect. 4.1 will find an n-tuple $\langle \phi_1, \ldots, \phi_n \rangle$ such that Eq. 1 holds.

Definition 13 (Tuple-formulas). *An n-tuple formula is $\langle \phi_1, \ldots, \phi_n \rangle$, where each ϕ_i, $i = 1, \ldots, n$, is a unary formula such that, for the context $A_1 \times \ldots \times A_n$:*

$$[\![\langle \phi_1, \ldots, \phi_n \rangle]\!]_{A_1 \times \ldots \times A_n} = [\![\langle \phi_1 \rangle]\!]_{A_1} \times \ldots \times [\![\langle \phi_n \rangle]\!]_{A_n}$$

4.1 Algorithms

In this section we focus on the run-time side of the framework. Algorithms 1 and 2 show the pseudocode of the behaviour each agent needs to implement in order to agree on the satisfaction of a given goal expressed by a c-HM^n formula ϕ. An example of the distributed computation, together with the sequence of messages exchanges among agents, is represented by Fig. 1. Afterwards, in Sect. 4.2, a more articulated example on package-delivery by drones is presented.

We suppose that a global property ϕ is received by agent A_1, for instance via an external input. We also suppose agent A_1 alone is not able to satisfy ϕ by keeping the cost below a desired threshold t, i.e., $[\![\phi]\!]_{C(A_1)} \not\geq t$. The first step

---

Algorithm 1. Pseudocode of the initiator agent.

Require: $n = |\{Agents\}|$, and a decomposed c-HM^n formula $\langle \phi_1, \ldots, \phi_n \rangle$.
1: **function** ADAPTATION($\{Agents\}, \langle \phi_1, \ldots, \phi_n \rangle$)
2:     **for all** $Agent_{i=1..n} \in \{Agents\}$ **do**
3:         Send $\langle \phi_1, \ldots, \phi_n \rangle$ to $Agent_i$
4:     **end for**   ▷ $\langle\langle \phi_1^i, \ldots, \phi_n^i \rangle, k_{Agent_i}\rangle$ is the reply from $Agent_i$
5:     **if** $\forall \phi_i, j = 1..n. \ |\phi_i^j \neq \phi_i| == 1$ **then**   ▷ Each $Agent_i$ proposes a different ϕ_i
6:         **if** $k_{Agent_1} \times \cdots \times k_{Agent_n} \times [\![\phi]\!]_{Agent_1 \times \cdots \times Agent_n} \geq t$ **then**
7:             Send Ok to all $Agent_i$ ▷ $\langle \phi_1, \ldots, \phi_n \rangle$ satisfied better than t
8:         **else**
9:             Adaptation($\{All\_Agents\}, \langle \phi_1, \ldots, \phi_n \rangle$)   ▷ Ask agents to change behaviour
10:        **end if**
11:    **else**
12:        **for all** $\forall \phi_i, j = 1..n. \ |\phi_i^j \neq \phi_i| > 1$ **do**   ▷ Find best $Agent_j$ for each clashed ϕ_i
13:            **for all** j (i fixed) **do**
14:                $k_{best} = \bot$
15:                **if** $k_{Agent_j} \geq k_{best}$ **then**
16:                    $\phi_i' = \phi_i^j$, $Agent_{best} = Agent_j$ ▷ ϕ' will be $\langle \phi_1', \ldots, \phi_n' \rangle$
17:                **end if**
18:            **end for**
19:            $\{Agents\} = \{Agents\} \setminus \{Agent_{best}\}$
20:            $\langle \phi_1, \ldots, \phi_{n-1} \rangle = \langle \phi_1, \ldots, \phi_n \rangle - \phi_i$
21:        **end for**
22:        Compose partial solution ϕ' with Adaptation($\{Agents\}, \langle \phi_1, \ldots, \phi_k \rangle$)
23:    **end if**
24: **end function**

is to contact all or some agents (such criterion is outside the scope of the paper) in range of communication, to seek for their collaboration to satisfy ϕ.

Algorithm 1 describes the behaviour of the *initiator* agent A_1, which has initially received ϕ. A_1 computes $\mathcal{W}(\|^n, \phi)$ and projects it $(=\downarrow)$ into n sub-formulas obtaining a n-tuple formula $\langle \phi_1, \ldots, \phi_n \rangle$, where $n - 1$ is the number of agents in range of communication, plus A_1 itself is equal to a total of n agents (lines 2–4 in Algorithm 1). Therefore, each ϕ_i $(i = 1..n)$ represents the sub-goal one of the agents needs to satisfy. More precisely, a ϕ_i can be also solved by more than just a single agent, if A_i in turn asks for the collaboration of more agents in its range of communication (see the example in Sect. 4.2). A_1 sends $\langle \phi_1, \ldots, \phi_n \rangle$ to all its neighbouring agents. Then A_1 collects all the replies from the contacted agents: each reply consists in the partial model checking of one ϕ_i by using one of the possible behaviours of an agent A_j: this is obtained by executing Algorithm 2 for each agent (for more details see the description of Algorithm 2 in the following). The return value of Algorithm 2 is a couple $\langle \phi'_i, k_{A_j} \rangle$. If each A_j chooses a different ϕ_i, then A only needs to check if the overall behaviour (made of different sub-behaviours) satisfies ϕ with a cost better than t, *i.e.*, $k_{A_1} \times \cdots \times k_{A_n} \times [\![\phi]\!]_{A_1 \times \ldots \times A_n} \geq t$ (lines 5–7 in Algorithm 1). Otherwise, if ϕ is not satisfied, the function in Algorithm 1 is called again with the same n-tuple formula $\langle \phi_1, \ldots, \phi_n \rangle$ (lines 8–10 in Algorithm 1): contacted agents will change their behaviour by executing again Algorithm 2.

The case more than one A_j proposes to satisfy the same ϕ_i is treated in the rest of the pseudocode in Algorithm 1, *i.e.*, from line 11 to line 23. For each sub-formula ϕ_i of $\langle \phi_1, \ldots, \phi_n \rangle$ in conflict, the candidate agent with the best extracted k_{A_j} is selected (lines 13–18). This represents a decision taken through a heuristics: k is an amount of weight that can be "safely" extracted from a formula during its partial model checking (see Remark 2) without altering its truth value (*i.e.*, its cost). Hence, it does not represent the total cost to satisfy ϕ_i, but a part of it.

Now we move to the description of Algorithm 2. In Algorithm 2, an agent B (each of the A_j in Algorithm 1) receives $\langle \phi_1, \ldots, \phi_n \rangle$, selects one its possible behaviours E (see next paragraph), and moves such description into ϕ_i, thus applying $\mathcal{W}(\phi_i, C(E))$. Then, B sends the result of the QPMC function, *i.e.*, $\langle \phi'_i, k_B \rangle$, back to A, the initiator agent. The GPA process B is described as the parallel composition of different procedures $\|^N(B', B'', \ldots B^N)$, the algorithm picks the subset of B^js that minimises the result k_B of $\mathcal{W}(\|^{|T^i|}(B^j), \phi_i)$ (lines 9–13 in Algorithm 2), according to the preference order in the chosen c-semiring, for all the possible ϕ_i in $\langle \phi_1, \ldots, \phi_n \rangle$. As already introduced, k_{B,ϕ_i} represents a minimal cost that indeed has to be paid in order to satisfy ϕ_i (considering only the actions of B).

The subset is selected in the power-set of $\{B', \ldots, B^N\}$, by restricting to all subsets of cardinality l (lines 21–24 in Algorithm 2). This parameter is initially set to 1, thus the first time returning only singleton subsets $\{\{B'\}, \ldots, \{B^N\}\}$. The motivation behind this parameter is that B tries to satisfy ϕ_i at best by first using as less actions as possible. After having tried

Algorithm 2. Pseudocode for selecting a behaviour of agent B w.r.t. $\langle \phi_1, \dots \phi_n \rangle$.

Require: Behaviour of $\|^N(B', B'', \dots B^N)$, an adaptation level l (i.e., the number of B^j in parallel), a set X of already discarded l-combinations, and an n-tuple formula $\langle \phi_1, \dots \phi_n \rangle$
1: **global** $l = 1$ ▷ adaptation level
2: **global** $T = \mathcal{P}(\{B', B'', \dots, B^N\})$ ▷ Powerset
3: **global** $X = \emptyset$ ▷ discarded combinations
4:
5: **function** $B_{HV}(\langle \phi_1, \dots \phi_n \rangle, B)$
6:     $h, k = \bot, \phi, \psi = \bot, U = \emptyset$
7:     **for all** $((T^i \in T) \wedge (T^i \not\in X) \wedge (|T^i| = l))$ **do**
8:         $E = \|^{|T^i|}(B^j) \; s.t. \; B^j \in T^i$
9:         **for all** $\phi_i \in \langle \phi_1, \dots, \phi_n \rangle$ **do**   ▷ The best k considering all ϕ_i
10:             $\langle \psi_i, h_i \rangle = \mathcal{W}(C(E), \phi_i)$ ▷ $\mathcal{W}$ in Table 3
11:         **end for**
12:         **if** $(h_i \geq k)$ **then**
13:             $k_{B.\phi_i} = h_i, \phi_i = \psi_i, U = T^i$
14:         **end if**
15:     **end for**
16:     $X \uplus U$
17:     **if** $(|X| == \binom{n}{l})$ **then**
18:         $l = l + 1, X = \emptyset$
19:     **end if**
20:     **return** $\langle \phi_1, \dots, \phi'_i, \dots, \phi_n \rangle, k_{B.\phi_i} \rangle$
21: **end function**
Ensure: $k_{B.\phi_i}$ is the best minimal cost extracted by $\mathcal{W}$ from B, an adaptation level l and all the possible ϕ_i components of $\langle \phi_1, \dots \phi_n \rangle$.

---

all the l-combinations (rejected by A), B increments l by one (e.g., with $l = 2$, all $\|^2(B', B''), \dots, \|^2(B^{N-1}, B^N)$ are checked), since ϕ_i cannot be satisfied with only smaller parts of B, and more concurrency needs to be considered.

Note that, in case an agent runs out of behaviours to propose, it can reply with inaction 0. Then, it is up to the initiator to take a decision, e.g., fail and stop, or fail and restart with a relaxed threshold.

Figure 1 depicts a possible sequence of messages exchanged among three agents, A, B, and C, by using Algorithms 1 and 2. A is the initiator agent that asks for the collaboration of neighbouring agents B and C; it sends $\langle \phi_1, \phi_2, \phi_3 \rangle$ to both of them and A itself by executing Algorithm 1. All three of them run Algorithm 2 and compute $Bhv(\langle \phi_1, \phi_2, \phi_3 \rangle, *)$ (where $*$ is $A/B/C$). While A proposes itself for the first sub-formula ϕ_1, B and C clash on the second sub-formula ϕ_2. Between the two agents, A selects C because (we suppose) $k_{C,\phi} \geq k_{B,\phi}$, and asks again to B to propose a behaviour for the remaining sub-formula ϕ_3. Then, B accomplishes to this task and returns ϕ'_3. After gathering all the returned formulas, i.e., ϕ'_1, ϕ'_2, and ϕ'_3, A finds out that $k_{A,\phi} \times k_{B,\phi} \times k_{C,\phi} \times [\![\phi]\!] \not\geq t$. Therefore, ϕ is not satisfied with a threshold better than t. For this reason, $\langle \phi_1, \phi_2, \phi_3 \rangle$ is sent again to A, B, and C. This time (see Fig. 1) the three agents propose a behaviour to satisfy a different sub-formula, i.e., respectively ϕ_3, ϕ_2, and ϕ_1. A finds out that this time $k_{A,\phi} \times k_{B,\phi} \times k_{C,\phi} \times [\![\phi]\!] \geq t$. Thus, the formula is satisfied with a cost better/equal than t: the property is satisfied, and A sends an Ok message to let B and C behave according to the selected behaviour.

The proposed algorithms extend the work in [3], where the collaboration is possible only among two agents. Indeed, here we consider the interaction of more than two agents and each agent has a partial (local) knowledge of the global system, e.g., each agent knows and cooperates only with its neighbours. For a complexity analysis of the algorithms, similar considerations can be drawn as for [3]: the worst case depends on the exponential composition of the behaviours in Algorithm 2, that is $O\binom{N}{l}$. However, indeed a solution to ϕ can be found in fewer steps (further simplifications can be adopted, see Sect. 6).

4.2 A Delivery Example with Drones

We take inspiration from the drones and packets example presented in [19]. We suppose to have three available flying drones, which receive the task to deliver two different packages at two different destinations. Besides satisfying such "crisp" global goal, we also must ensure that the global battery consumption is below a user-defined threshold t: this represents a quantitative requirement that corresponds to a major concern in CPSs [7,17].

Let us enhance Example 1 by considering three drones, *Drone1*, *Drone2*, and *Drone3*, instead of only A and B in Example 1. The scenario is represented in Fig. 2, together with other agents (*i.e.*, *Drone4* and *Drone5*) whose role will be explained in the following. The three drones need to coordinate by adapting their behaviour one another with the purpose to deliver two packages T and Z (as in Example 1). In the following of this example we adopt the weighted c-semiring, *i.e.*, $\langle \mathbb{R}^+ \cup \{+\infty\}, min, \hat{+}, +\infty, 0 \rangle$, to model battery consumption.

The actions a drone can perform are: $\{deliver\_T, deliver\_Z\}$. Each action is associated with an energy cost: for instance, the consumption to move one package from a place to another. Suppose Drone1 behaves as the *initiator* (as A in Fig. 1), while Drone2 and Drone3 are the only two agents in range of communication (as B and C in Fig. 1): they will be asked by Drone1 to collaborate in order to deliver packages T and Z. The property ϕ to be satisfied and the threshold t on the consumption are received by Drone1 as input (see Fig. 2).

We reuse the same $\phi = ([deliver\_T]5 \times [deliver\_Z]3) + ([deliver\_Z]6 \times [deliver\_T]4)$ we have proposed in Example 1 (the task is the same), while the parallel computation now is $S = \|^3(Drone1, Drone2, Drone3)$, where $Drone1 = +((deliver\_T, 2), (deliver\_Z, 7))$, $Drone2 = +((deliver\_T, 3), (deliver\_Z, 6))$, any, finally $Drone3 = +((deliver\_T, 5), (deliver\_Z, 4))$. Note that, the behaviour of each drone is described using the operators in Table 1. As the initiator agent, Drone1 sends the decomposition of ϕ to Drone2, Drone3, and itself, as represented in Fig. 1:

$$\mathcal{W}(\|^3, \phi) = \mathcal{W}(\|^3, ([deliver\_T]5 \times [deliver\_Z]3) + ([deliver\_Z]6 \times [deliver\_T]4)).$$

If $\phi_1 = [deliver\_T]5 \times [deliver\_Z]3$ and $\phi_2 = [deliver\_Z]6 \times [deliver\_T]4$, then
$$\mathcal{W}(\|^3, \phi) = ((k_{\|^3,\phi_1} \div k_{\|^3,\phi}) \times \mathcal{W}(\|^3, \phi_1)) + ((k_{\|^3,\phi_2} \div k_{\|^3,\phi}) \times \mathcal{W}(\|^3, \phi_2))$$

$$\mathcal{W}(\|^3, \phi_1) = (k_{\|^3,\phi_1^1} \div k_{\|^3,\phi_1})\mathcal{W}(\|^3, \phi_1^1) \times (k_{\|^3,\phi_1^2} \div k_{\|^3,\phi_1})\mathcal{W}(\|^3, \phi_1^2)$$
$$\mathcal{W}(\|^3, \phi_2) = (k_{\|^3,\phi_2^1} \div k_{\|^3,\phi_2})\mathcal{W}(\|^3, \phi_2^1) \times (k_{\|^3,\phi_2^2} \div k_{\|^3,\phi_2})\mathcal{W}(\|^3, \phi_2^2)$$

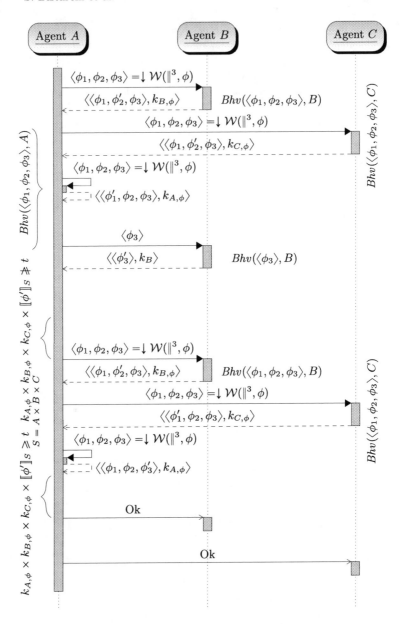

Fig. 1. An example of messages exchanged between A (the initiator), and B and C.

where $\phi_1^1 = [(deliver\_T)]5$, $\phi_1^2 = [(deliver\_Z)]3$, $\phi_2^1 = [(deliver\_Z)]6$, and $\phi_2^2 = [(deliver\_T)]4$. For each ϕ_i^j, Drone1 sends to its neighbouring drones, *i.e.*, Drone2, and Drone3, a formula similar to Eq. 1, in which both actions $deliver\_T$ or $deliver\_Z$ may be performed by one of the three drones.

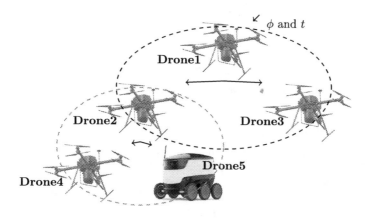

Fig. 2. The scenario in our package-delivery example: Drone1 is the initiator receiving a property ϕ and a threshold t for its satisfaction. Four other drones help to satisfy ϕ.

As soon as Drone2 receives such request, it becomes the initiator agent w.r.t. Drone4 and Drone5, asking for their collaboration in delivering package T (Fig. 2): in fact, Drone2 has low battery (*e.g.*, 1) and it is not able to move package T until destination. Hence, Drone2 acts as the initiator and sends the requirement to be satisfied, *i.e.*, $\phi = [deliver\_T]2$ to Drone4 and Drone5. They are both able to perform action $deliver\_T$ with an energy consumption of 2 and 4 respectively. In this case the defined protocol allows Drone2, Drone4, and Drone5 to adapt one another in order to deliver the package T by minimising the overall energy consumption.

$$\mathcal{W}(\|,\phi) = (k_{deliver\_T} \times \top) \div k_\phi) \times ([deliver\_T, 0]2 \div k_{deliver\_T})$$
$$\sqcap (k_{deliver\_T} \times \top) \div k_\phi) \times ([0, deliver\_T]2 \div k_{deliver\_T})$$

Then, both drones answer with $k_{Drone4,\phi} = 2$ and $k_{Drone5,\phi} = 4$. Then Drone2 selects Drone4 to cooperate with for delivering package T, with a total energy consumption of $1 \times 2 = 3$ (as a reminder, $+$ is min and $\times$ is the arithmetic plus).

Once Drone2 knows it is able to deliver T cooperating with Drone4 and spending 3, both Drone2 and Drone3 reply to Drone1 by sending back their preference. In particular, both Drone2 and Drone3 send $[0, deliver\_T, 0]$; Drone2 with $k_{Drone2} = 1 \times (3 \times 5 \div 5) = 6$, and Drone3 with $k_{Drone3} = 3 \times (5 \times 5 \div 5) = 8$. Then, according to Algorithm 1, between the two agents Drone1 selects Drone2 because $k_{Drone2,\phi} \geq_K k_{Drone3,\phi}$ ($6 \leq 8$).

After temporarily deciding who delivers package T (*i.e.*, Drone2), Drone1 simplifies the requirements asking for the satisfaction of action $deliver\_Z$ only, that is the remaining package. As in Fig. 1, the run-time framework asks only to Drone3 to deliver Z. Drone3 is able to deliver Z spending 4, and this satisfies ϕ_2 and hence, ϕ. Then the protocol successfully ends.

5   Related Work

In the literature, several works propose adaptation and negotiation protocols that allow multiple agents to cooperate and reach a goal. In the following of this section we briefly introduce some of them.

In [9,21] the authors analyse a selected list of design patterns for managing the coordination in the literature of self-organising systems. The work in [14] deals with *Security Adaptation Contracts* (*SACs*) consisting of a high-level specification of the mapping between the signature and the security policies of services, plus some temporal logic restrictions and secrecy properties to be satisfied. In [6] the authors provide a formal framework that unifies behavioural adaptation and structural reconfiguration of components; this is used for statically reasoning whether it is possible to reconfigure a system. In [18] the authors focus on automated adaptation of an agent's functionality by means of an agent factory. An agent factory is an external service that adapts agents, on the basis of a well-structured description of the software agent. Structuring an agent makes it possible to reason about an agent's functionality on the basis of its blueprint, which includes information about its configuration. In [12], Li et al. present an approach for securing distributed adaptation. A plan is synthesized and executed, allowing the different parties to apply a set of data transformations in a distributed fashion. In particular, the authors synthesise "security boxes" that wrap services. Security boxes are pre-designed, but interchangeable at run time. In [20], the *AVISPA* tool is run first to obtain the protocol of the composition, and second to verify that it preserves the desired security properties. The objective of the work in [16] is the definition of a process and tool-supported design framework to develop self-adaptive systems, which consider Belief-Desire-Intention agent models as reference architectures. The authors adopt an agent-oriented approach to explicit model system goals in requirements specification and in system architecture design.

Differently from all these works, in this paper we propose a run-time decomposition of a property, which we believe is a good choice in case of highly dynamic environments, as CPS. The novelty resides in proposing an algorithmic approach that exploits a QPMC function in order to online select the behaviour of single agents towards the satisfaction of a global property.

6   Conclusion

We have presented a formal and run-time framework where to let agents in a CPS adapt to the behaviours of other agents, with the purpose to satisfy a global property ϕ. Each agent contributes to the satisfaction of ϕ by satisfying a subproperty. To reach this goal, a QPMC function is used to push the behaviour of each agent into ϕ, thus *(i)* reducing the complexity of the satisfaction of ϕ agent-by-agent, and *(ii)* preserving the privacy of agents, which do not need to disclose their full behaviour, but they can propose different alternatives at run-time. For these reasons, Quantitative PMC [11] proves to be a powerful tool to reduce the complexity of large and complex CPS. One more advantage is that the decomposition of ϕ is accomplished at run-time: agents can consequently change through time in a way transparent to the framework. Privacy, complexity reduction, and a run-time approach are indeed the key-points of the proposal.

In the future we would like to manage infinite contexts by extending our logic to deal with fix-points; to achieve this goal; possible suggestions could come from [13]. This extension concerns more the logics and the QPMC function, since in this paper we focus on the finite behaviour of agents. Finally, Algorithms 1 and 2 can be improved to reduce the complexity of the worst case, not proposing all the possible behaviours, but refining the proposals by offering only the behaviours "close" to the asked ϕ. Finally, we also aim to improve the QPMC function in order to extract more weight (*i.e.*, in order to refine the computation of $k_{C,\phi}$ in Table 3), and define heuristics for the computation of its satisfaction.

References

1. Bistarelli, S., Gadducci, F.: Enhancing constraints manipulation in semiring-based formalisms. In: ECAI, pp. 63–67 (2006)
2. Bistarelli, S., Montanari, U., Rossi, F.: Semiring-based constraint satisfaction and optimization. J. ACM **44**(2), 201–236 (1997)
3. Bistarelli, S., Santini, F., Martinelli, F., Matteucci, I.: Automated adaptation via quantitative partial model checking. In: Proceedings of the 31st Annual ACM Symposium on Applied Computing, pp. 1993–1996. ACM (2016)
4. Blyth, T.S., Janowitz, M.E.: Residuation Theory, vol. 102. Pergamon press, Oxford (1972)
5. Buchholz, P., Kemper, P.: Quantifying the dynamic behavior of process algebras. In: Alfaro, L., Gilmore, S. (eds.) PAPM-PROBMIV 2001. LNCS, vol. 2165, pp. 184–199. Springer, Heidelberg (2001). doi:10.1007/3-540-44804-7_12
6. Cansado, A., Canal, C., Salaün, G., Cubo, J.: A formal framework for structural reconfiguration of components under behavioural adaptation. Electr. Notes Theor. Comput. Sci. **263**, 95–110 (2010)
7. Derler, P., Lee, E.A., Sangiovanni-Vincentelli, A.L.: Modeling cyber-physical systems. Proc. IEEE **100**(1), 13–28 (2012)
8. Gadducci, F., Hölzl, M., Monreale, G.V., Wirsing, M.: Soft constraints for lexicographic orders. In: Castro, F., Gelbukh, A., González, M. (eds.) MICAI 2013. LNCS (LNAI), vol. 8265, pp. 68–79. Springer, Heidelberg (2013). doi:10.1007/978-3-642-45114-0_6
9. Gardelli, L., Viroli, M., Omicini, A.: Design patterns for self-organising systems. In: Burkhard, H.-D., Lindemann, G., Verbrugge, R., Varga, L.Z. (eds.) CEEMAS 2007. LNCS (LNAI), vol. 4696, pp. 123–132. Springer, Heidelberg (2007). doi:10.1007/978-3-540-75254-7_13
10. Golan, J.: Semirings and Affine Equations Over Them: Theory and Applications. Kluwer Academic Publisher, Dordrecht (2003)
11. Larsen, K.G., Xinxin, L.: Compositionality through an operational semantics of contexts. J. Logic Comput. **1**(6), 761–795 (1991)
12. Li, J., Yarvis, M., Reiher, P.: Securing distributed adaptation. Comput. Netw. **38**(3), 347–371 (2002)

13. Lluch-Lafuente, A., Montanari, U.: Quantitative mu-calculus and CTL defined over constraint semirings. TCS **346**(1), 135–160 (2005)
14. Martín, J.A., Martinelli, F., Pimentel, E.: Synthesis of secure adaptors. J. Log. Algebr. Program. **81**(2), 99–126 (2012)
15. Martinelli, F., Matteucci, I., Santini, F.: Semiring-based specification approaches for quantitative security. In: Proceedings Thirteenth Workshop on Quantitative Aspects of Programming Languages and Systems, QAPL. EPTCS, vol. 194, pp. 95–109 (2015)
16. Morandini, M., Penserini, L., Perini, A.: Towards goal-oriented development of self-adaptive systems. In: Workshop on Software Engineering for Adaptive and Self-managing Systems, SEAMS 2008, pp. 9–16. ACM (2008)
17. Shi, J., Wan, J., Yan, H., Suo, H.: A survey of cyber-physical systems. In: 2011 International Conference on Wireless Communications & Signal Processing, WCSP 2011, pp. 1–6. IEEE (2011)
18. Splunter, S., Wijngaards, N.J.E., Brazier, F.M.T.: Structuring agents for adaptation. In: Alonso, E., Kudenko, D., Kazakov, D. (eds.) AAMAS 2001-2002. LNCS (LNAI), vol. 2636, pp. 174–186. Springer, Heidelberg (2003). doi:10.1007/3-540-44826-8_11
19. Talcott, C., Arbab, F., Yadav, M.: Soft agents: exploring soft constraints to model robust adaptive distributed cyber-physical agent systems. In: Nicola, R., Hennicker, R. (eds.) Software, Services, and Systems. LNCS, vol. 8950, pp. 273–290. Springer, Cham (2015). doi:10.1007/978-3-319-15545-6_18
20. Viganò, L.: Automated security protocol analysis with the AVISPA tool. ENTCS **155**, 69–86 (2006)
21. Wolf, T., Holvoet, T.: Design patterns for decentralised coordination in self-organising emergent systems. In: Brueckner, S.A., Hassas, S., Jelasity, M., Yamins, D. (eds.) ESOA 2006. LNCS (LNAI), vol. 4335, pp. 28–49. Springer, Heidelberg (2007). doi:10.1007/978-3-540-69868-5_3

Formal Analysis of Predictable Data Flow in Fault-Tolerant Multicore Systems

Boris Madzar[1], Jalil Boudjadar[2(✉)], Juergen Dingel[1], Thomas E. Fuhrman[3], and S. Ramesh[3]

[1] Queen's University, Kingston, Canada
[2] Aarhus University, Aarhus, Denmark
jalil@eng.au.dk
[3] General Motors R&D, Warren, MI, USA

Abstract. The need to integrate large and complex functions into today's vehicle electronic control systems requires high performance computing platforms, while at the same time the manufacturers try to reduce cost, power consumption and ensure safety. Traditionally, safety isolation and fault containment of software tasks have been achieved by either physically or temporally segregating them. This approach is reliable but inefficient in terms of processor utilization. Dynamic approaches that achieve better utilization without sacrificing safety isolation and fault containment appear to be of increasing interest. One of these approaches relies on predictable data flow introduced in PharOS and Giotto. In this paper, we extend the work on leveraging predictable data flow by addressing the problem of how the predictability of data flow can be proved formally for mixed criticality systems that run on multicore platforms and are subject to failures. We consider dynamic tasks where the timing attributes vary from one period to another. Our setting also allows for sporadic deadline overruns and accounts for criticality during fault handling. A user interface was created to allow automatic generation of the models as well as visualization of the analysis results, whereas predictability is verified using the Spin model checker.

1 Introduction

Automotive electronic control systems demand increasing computing power to accommodate the ever-growing software functionality in modern vehicles. At the same time, the trend in automotive electronic architectures is to allocate this increasing computational load to a reduced number of physical processing cores in an effort to reduce size, weight, and power consumption. These trends lead to new design challenges where an increasing number of software-based features must be grouped into tasks which must in turn be allocated to processing cores. The tasks assigned to a given processor may reflect different levels of safety-criticality (referred to as "mixed-criticality integration"). These types of mixed-criticality systems need to meet the requirements of the software processes sharing processors and resources.

© Springer International Publishing AG 2017
O. Kouchnarenko and R. Khosravi (Eds.): FACS 2016, LNCS 10231, pp. 153–171, 2017.
DOI: 10.1007/978-3-319-57666-4_10

To ensure correct operation of a critical functionality that shares processing resources with a less-critical functionality, the ISO 26262 standard for functional safety of road vehicles [1] requires mechanisms for "freedom-from-interference". Accordingly, the mapping of tasks to cores and the scheduling must take into account multiple factors such as criticality and balancing the workload while ensuring freedom from interference and fault containment.

A system whose externally-observable behavior changes only when its inputs (in terms of values or timestamps) change is said to be *predictable* [11]. Ensuring the predictability of task sets with dynamic runtime attributes and executing on multicore platforms with static analysis alone is very difficult due to the interference caused by the delays for shared resources allocation. The challenge gets even harder due to dynamic runtime and fault handling mechanisms.

Our paper introduces a formal framework for the predictability analysis of mixed criticality task sets running on a multicore platform. The framework supports window scheduling and dynamic runtime of tasks, where the attributes may vary from one window to another. It also supports fault-tolerance via runtime fault handling mechanisms. In addition to the window-based predictable data flow [6], we add support for the preservation of predictability even in cases where the scheduling constraints are violated (deadline overruns). Using this framework, we identify and implement a strategy for exhaustive verification of predictability and freedom from criticality inversion. We observe that the verification can be reduced to the checking of a specific set of fixed "edge tasks" by showing that these edge tasks never produce "tainted" (i.e., possibly not trustworthy) output. A prototype implementation to facilitate model creation, verification and result visualization is sketched.

The paper is organized as follows: Necessary background is discussed in Sect. 2. Section 3 describes how predictability can be guaranteed through limited observability. Sections 4 and 5 present, respectively, key parts of a formalization of the systems we analyze and the verification approach. Section 6 sketches the prototype and the case study we analyzed. Section 7 presents related work and Sect. 8 concludes the paper.

2   Background

Freedom-from-interference in a mixed criticality real-time system can be achieved in several ways. The most common approach segregates the different criticality levels in such a way that they are guaranteed not to interfere (run-time guarantee). Some examples of this kind of segregation include assigning each criticality level to its own processor core, assigning a fixed (though not necessarily equal) time slice to each criticality level, or a combination of the two.

The potential downside of the segregation of criticality levels is poor processor utilization. If one set of segregated tasks finishes early, the spare processor time cannot be given to another set of tasks. A common approach to setting up a task set is to assign each task a period, budget and a priority. The task's execution start, end and duration may vary within the period. Such a variability comes from several sources: inputs from the environment, sharing of the resources and the internal behavior of the task.

A potential problem with this approach, identified by Henzinger [11], is that the times at which a task reads and writes data vary in relation to the start of the period. The values visible to any given task T may change depending on its execution time and the execution order of tasks supplying T with data. Therefore, two correct executions may produce different outputs given identical input (see Fig. 1(a)), which leads to a violation of predictability.

2.1   Criticality

Tasks can be defined as belonging to different criticality levels. Following the work of [7], criticality does not need to be considered during regular (fault-free) execution. It only needs to be taken into account when a fault occurs and load-shedding must take place. Critical tasks must be prioritized over non-critical tasks, as they represent behavior that must occur to preserve important properties of the system.

Commonly, the most efficient algorithms for assigning task priorities, such as Rate Monotonic Scheduling (RMS) and Earliest Deadline First (EDF), use timing properties rather than criticality levels. Thus, a mixed strategy needs to be set up to handle both timeliness and criticality correctly: one way of doing this is through the use of zero-slack scheduling [7].

Criticality interacts with how faults are handled, as it is possible to be either more lax or more strict with faults. For instance, critical tasks may be allowed to miss their deadlines, whereas non-critical tasks would be terminated.

2.2   Zero-Slack Scheduling

The idea behind the zero-slack algorithm [7] is that the worst case execution time (WCET) of a task is often much too pessimistic when compared with the average case execution time. Any algorithm that seeks to ensure freedom from criticality inversion by using the WCET of lower-criticality tasks will under-utilize the processor. It is a much more efficient use of resources if tasks are scheduled regardless of criticality until it becomes absolutely necessary to factor criticality into a scheduling decision. Accordingly, tasks are scheduled in one of two modes: "normal" and "critical". In normal mode, criticality is ignored and an optimal scheduling strategy is used, whereas in critical mode, higher-criticality tasks are given priority. Tasks within a criticality level are scheduled as in normal mode.

The system usually executes in normal mode. The mode changes to critical when all remaining critical tasks must begin executing if they are to meet their deadlines, assuming they consume their entire execution budgets. This time point is called *zero-slack instant*. A version of this algorithm, known by Simplified Zero-Slack (ZS), uses only two criticality levels. Priorities are assigned using EDF in "normal mode", however in "critical mode" all high-criticality tasks are scheduled before all low-criticality tasks. Within a given criticality level, EDF is still used.

3   Predictability via Limited Observability

An alternative approach to manage tasks while ensuring predictability, by design, has been defined in [6,12]. This approach focuses on synchronizing data access so that a given task instance will always view the system as being in the same state regardless of when it executes within a given period (*limited observability*). This is achieved by introducing an additional constraint: each task instance must execute in its entirety within a given time window. The start (baseline) and end (deadline) of this window are defined according to the system clock, not the task's CPU time. *A snapshot of the data values is captured at the baseline, so that the task instance reads from this snapshot. Any values written by the task are not communicated to other tasks until the deadline of such a task.*

To illustrate how limited observability can be used to ensure predictability, Fig. 1 shows a system with three tasks (left to right): *T1, T2* and *T3*. Each task passes its input unchanged to the output. The tasks have periods 14, 10 and 14 and budgets 4, 4 and 3 respectively. Priorities are *T2 > T1 > T3*.

(a). Full observability   **(b). Limited observability**

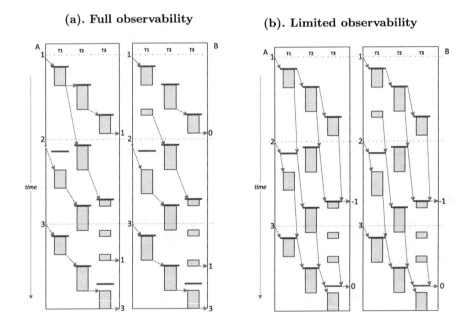

Fig. 1. Predictability via limited observability.

We consider 2 different execution scenarios *A* and *B* for each observability class (full and limited). Each execution scenario consists of 3 periods for each task. Inputs (1, 2 and 3; on the left hand column of each execution) occur at the exact same points in time for each execution. *A* displays one possible valid execution with no task violating any constraint (budget or deadline), whereas in scenario B some tasks overrun, e.g. *T1* overruns its budget during its first period. The corresponding outputs are shown to the right of each execution. Figure 1(a) does not use data access synchronization (i.e., limited observability): although there is no change in the timing or value of inputs, the outputs of A and B differ in both value and timing, as a task can hand over its output once its execution is over without waiting for the period expiry. Figure 1(b) shows how the example presented in Fig. 1(a) would behave under limited observability achieved through data access synchronization. Regardless of being overrunning or not, a task delivers its output at the end of its current period. This guarantees that the output of a given task is always delivered at the same point in time. As an example, in the execution B of Fig. 1(b) task *T1* overruns but it still delivers the output at the same point in time (end of first period) as in execution A. The priority impact can be seen during the second execution period where *T2* starts first as it is ready due its short period, after which *T1* becomes ready but it cannot preempt *T2*. *T1* waits until the current execution of *T2* terminates before it starts running. Finally, *T3* becomes ready and starts executing, however once *T2* becomes ready again it preempts it due to its higher priority. *T3* resumes early in the third period, but it gets preempted by *T1* this time.

In general, predictability should reduce the need for testing compared to the standard approach since the externally-observed behavior will not change. Limited observability ensures system predictability in case no fault occurs. In case of faulty behaviors, e.g. a deadline overrun, the system adapts its runtime to amortize the faults while maintaining the limited observability, so that it might end up being predictable despite the presence of faults (Sect. 4.2).

4   Formal Basis of Our Framework

This section introduces a formal description of the systems that can be modeled and analyzed in our framework.

4.1   System Specification

The system application we consider consists of a set of components $\{\mathcal{T}_1, .., \mathcal{T}_m\}$, each of which is a set of periodic tasks $\mathcal{T}_j = \{T_1^j, .., T_k^j\}$. Similarly, the system platform is a set $\{C_1, .., C_q\}$ of homogeneous cores, each of which (C_j) is assigned to one component (task set) $\mathcal{T}_j$.

The tasks of a given component $\mathcal{T}_j$ will be scheduled by a real-time operating system according to a scheduling function *Sched* given by:

$$Sched^j : \mathcal{T}_j \times \mathcal{T}_j \times \mathbb{R}_{\geq 0} \to \mathcal{T}_j$$

where $\mathbb{R}_{\geq 0}$ is the time domain. The function compares 2 tasks at a given time instant and returns the task having priority at that time point. It is described abstractly in order to be able to model both static and dynamic priority scheduling algorithms. The scheduling policies we have modeled in this framework are:

Earliest-Deadline First (EDF), Dynamic Deadline-Monotonic (DMS) and Simplified Zero-Slack (ZS). Throughout this paper we will focus mainly on the ZS policy as it enables to deal with faults and mixed-criticality, but DMS and EDF are manipulated in the same way.

Since each component T_j can use two execution modes (*normal* and *critical*), we distinguish two scheduling functions, $Sched_n^j$ and $Sched_c^j$, to be applied in normal and critical modes respectively. For the sake of simplicity, since components behave in the same way and cores are identical (modular design) we will only focus on one component $T = \{T_1, .., T_n\}$ running on one core C. Accordingly, all the exponent notations $(-^j)$ related to the choice of a component will be omitted. Among the tasks of a component, we identify $T_c \subseteq T$ to be the set of critical tasks.

Formally, each task is given by a period p, a budget b, a deadline d and a criticality level c. Since it is not needed to distinguish between the period and deadline of tasks in our context (assumed to have the same values), we omit deadlines and just keep the period length which must be longer than the required budget. The criticality level does not have an effect during regular operation, but can be used in an overload or fault condition to prioritize tasks for load-shedding. Following the window notion (Sect. 3) allowing for dynamic runtime, the task's attributes can vary from one period to another. Basically, a window represents one release of the task execution. Formally, the notation $w_i^j = (p, b, c)$ states the period, budget and criticality level of task T_i for the jth window. Accordingly, we represent each task T_i by a sequence of windows $W_i = (w_i^1, w_i^2, ...)$ describing its runtime. We denote the set of all potential windows by $\mathcal{W}$, and assume that there is no gap between windows i.e., the deadline of a window will be the baseline of the next window. A task execution can be scheduled anywhere within a window. The operating system stores a static lookup table containing all the possible configurations (windows) for each task. To simplify notation, we use $w.x$ to refer to the attribute x within the window structure w.

Communication between tasks is aligned to the baselines and deadlines by the operating system in a way that it is entirely transparent to the task. No matter where the task is executing within its window, it will see an identical "snapshot" taken at the baseline of the values in shared memory written by other tasks. Any changes made after the task's baseline will not be visible within the current window. Similarly, any values written to shared memory by the task will not become visible to other tasks until the deadline of the writing task. The writes to the same memory location are applied in the order of the corresponding task deadlines rather than when the data was actually written from the task point of view. If a deadline and a baseline are coincident (i.e. a write and a read of the same data in shared memory), the write is to happen before the read.

4.2   System Semantics

To simplify the semantics, we only focus on one component $T = \{T_1, .., T_n\}$ running on one core since the rest of the system behaves in the same way using the same execution rules, assuming there is no inter-component dependency. First we introduce the following variables:

– clk is a clock variable to track the global time.
– $Mode = \{Normal, Critical\}$ is the set of execution modes, and $mode$ is a variable to store the current execution mode of the system.
– $Status = \{Waiting, Running, Overrun, Done\}$ is the set of status values, whereas $status = [1..n]$ is an array used to store the current status of each task. We assume that all the status values are assigned by the operating system (assigned to the tasks), except status $Done$ which is triggered by the task itself once its execution is over.
– $curW$ is an array variable storing the current window of each task.
– $Rbudget$ is an array variable used to track the remaining budget of each task during runtime.
– $curTime$ is an array clock variable to store the start time of each period for each task. It will be used as a baseline to track when a period expires.
– $curET$ is an array variable used to measure the CPU time acquired by each task during each execution. Each variable will be set to the current time when the corresponding task is scheduled.
– $ExcessT$ is an array variable used to store the time point when a task starts overrunning its deadline.

The semantics is given in terms of a timed transition system (TTS) $\langle S, s_0, \rightarrow \rangle$ [13] where S is a set of states, s_0 is the initial state and" $\rightarrow$ " is the transition relation. Formally, $S = \mathbb{R}_{\geq 0} \times Mode \times Status^n \times \mathcal{W}^n \times \mathbb{R}^n_{\geq 0} \times \mathbb{R}^n_{\geq 0} \times \mathbb{R}^n_{\geq 0} \times \mathbb{R}^n_{\geq 0}$, $s_0 = (0, Normal, \forall i\ status(T_i) = Waiting, \forall i\ curW(T_i) = w^1_i, \forall i\ curTime(T_i) = 0, \forall i\ Rbudget(T_i) = w^1_i.b, \forall i\ curET(T_i) = 0, \forall i\ ExcessT(T_i) = 0)$ whereas transitions are given by rules **Release1**, **Release2**, **Normal**, **Critical**, **Nrml2Crit**, **Crit2Nrml** and **Overrun**. We use notation [ ] to access to the internal structure and values of each state. Updating a field, e.g. a task status, within a state s leads to a new state s' having the same values as s except for the modified field. Initially, the system is in normal mode and tasks are waiting to be scheduled. All clock variables are set to 0.

Scheduling. According to the current execution mode, the operating system schedules one of the ready tasks (having status $Waiting$) using the appropriate scheduling function, $Sched_n$ or $Sched_c$.

$$\textbf{Normal}: \frac{\forall\ s \in S, T_i \in \mathcal{T}\ |\ s.mode = Normal, s.status(T_i) = Waiting \wedge \forall T_j \in \mathcal{T}\quad Sched_n(T_i, T_j, s.clk) = T_i}{s \rightarrow s[status(T_i) := Running, curET(T_i) := clk]}$$

$$\textbf{Critical}: \frac{\forall\ s \in S, T_i \in \mathcal{T}_c\ |\ s.mode = Critical, s.status(T_i) = Waiting \wedge \forall T_j \in \mathcal{T}_c\quad Sched_c(T_i, T_j, s.clk) = T_i}{s \rightarrow s[status(T_i) := Running, curET(T_i) := clk]}$$

In both rules, the task to be scheduled (T_i) potentially preempts another task T_j (if T_j is already running). If so, the status of T_j needs to be updated to *Waiting*, and its actual remaining budget needs to be recalculated using the previous value $(Rbudget(T_j))$ and the CPU time used from its last scheduling time point until the preemption, i.e. $Rbudget(T_j) = Rbudget(T_j) - (s.clk - curET(T_j))$. We don't embed these statements in the scheduling rules just to avoid duplicating the scheduling rules for two cases: 1) CPU is free; 2) there is a lower priority task T_j currently running. The status of T_i is updated to *Running* and the current time is recorded $(curET(T_i) := clk)$ to keep track of how long T_i has been running.

Mode Switches. When the zero-slack instant is reached, the execution mode switches to *Critical* and only critical tasks are allowed to execute. Once all critical tasks are satisfied in their current windows, the mode switches back to *Normal*.

$$
\textbf{Nrml2Crit}: \frac{\forall\, s \in S, T_i \in \mathcal{T}_c \mid s.mode = Normal, T_i s.status(T_i) = Waiting \;\land\; s.curW(T_i).p + s.curTime(T_i) - s.clk \le s.Rbudget(T_i)}{s \to s[mode := Critical]}
$$

$$
\textbf{Crit2Nrml}: \frac{\forall\, s \in S, T_i \in \mathcal{T}_c \mid s.mode = Critical, s.status(T_i) \ne Waiting}{s \to s[mode := Normal]}
$$

When the remaining time of the current window, calculated from the baseline *curTime*, is less than or equal to the remaining budget of a critical task the mode switches to *Critical*. One can remark that we can predict the mode change only for the current execution windows. When all critical tasks $(\mathcal{T}_c)$ are either terminated or running, the execution mode switches back to *Normal* where tasks will be scheduled accordingly using rules **Normal** and **Critical**.

Fault Handling. There are three possible failure modes that the system can experience: task failure, budget violation and deadline violation.

Task Failure. Task failure is the most obvious failure mode: a task either incorrectly calculates its outputs or suffers other catastrophic failures e.g., unexpected termination. Handling this type of faults is beyond the scope of this work.

Budget Violation. The execution budget defined in the configuration of the execution window represents the maximum amount of time that a task consumes in correct operation. Exceeding this budget is considered a fault of the task itself (incorrect operation) or of the system integrators (incorrect execution budget).

When a violation is detected, the operating system can take one of two possible actions: either the budget violation is ignored or the offending task is terminated. Ignoring the violation is possible as the task set should not be designed to use 100% of the available processor time. Ideally, the overrun will eventually be absorbed by the available slack (idle ticks) and the system will return to normal. Terminating the task ensures that the assumptions made by the operating system continue to hold, however the behavior of the system as a whole could become wildly incorrect.

Deadline Overrun. A task *must* finish its execution before its deadline. Violating the deadline is considered a fault, but not necessarily of the task in question: it is possible that the task missed its deadline due to other tasks misbehaving, or due to an incorrect configuration.

Deadline violation is more serious than budget violation and some compensatory actions must be taken. The simplest option is to terminate the offending task. The other option is to delay the deadline until the task has finished executing. In this case, the current deadline and the next baseline are delayed until the task enters a completed state. The next deadline of the task experiencing an overrun is not delayed, rather, the next window is shortened. This guarantees that the overrunning task still sees the same snapshot of shared data at its baseline. The operating system achieves this by delaying any task's baseline and deadline occurring during the overrun, except for the overrunning task, and applies them in the same order in which they would normally occur after the overrun has completed. The next windows of these tasks are also shortened in the same way as for the overrunning task. In Fig. 2, task *T2* violates its deadline and causes a delay (dashed arrow). The baseline of task *T1* occuring within this overrun period is delayed as well. The deadline of *T1* remains at the same position relative to the original deadline (dotted arrow), with the effective size of the window reduced appropriately.

By shortening subsequent windows, it is possible that a cascade of deadline violations will be created. However, as illustrated in Fig. 3, the slack present in the system should ideally allow the overruns to be absorbed and allow the system to return to normal operation. For this mechanism to work, the system cannot operate under full load. A safety margin must be included in the system design, with more processor capacity available than is required by the tasks under normal operation. The size of this safety margin would depend on the allowable overrun.

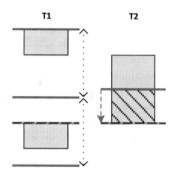

Fig. 2. Overrun delays

Having all tasks meet their deadlines is a sufficient condition for predictability, as shown by PharOS [6]. However, it is not a necessary one: if the overrun can be absorbed such that the final outputs still occur when they are supposed to, predictability can be preserved despite schedulability being violated due to the overrun.

$$\textbf{Overrun}: \frac{\forall\, s \in S, T_i \in \mathcal{T} \mid s.status(T_i) \in \{Waiting, Running\} \;\land\; s.curTime(T_i) \geq s.curW(T_i).p}{s \to s[status(T_i) := Overrun, \forall T_j \in \mathcal{T} \quad ExcessT(T_j) := clk]}$$

Rule **Overrun** describes when an overrun occurs. Basically, when a task reaches the end of its current window $curW(T_i).p$ (which coincides with the deadline) before completion an (effective) overrun case is declared. The current time clk is stored in variable $ExcessT()$ of task T_i in order to calculate the overrun duration once the task execution is done. Moreover, in order to postpone the deadlines and baselines occurring during the overrun, we also communicate the overrun start to the other running tasks $(\forall T_j \in \mathcal{T} \ ExcessT(T_j) := clk)$ so that the current window of each task will be delayed as well (fake overrun) with the same duration as for the overrunning task.

Through the release of a new window, the configuration of a task will be updated according to rule **Release1**.

$$\textbf{Release1}: \frac{\begin{array}{c} \forall \ s \in S, T_i \in \mathcal{T} \ | \ s.status(T_i) = Done, s.ExcessT(T_i) = 0 \\ \wedge \ s.curW(T_i) = w_i^x, s.curTime(T_i) = s.curW(T_i).p \\ \wedge \ \forall T_j \in \mathcal{T} \ s.status(T_j) \neq Overrun \end{array}}{\begin{array}{c} s \rightarrow s[status(T_i) := Waiting, curTime(T_i) := clk, curET(T_i) := 0, \\ curW(T_i) := w_i^{x+1}, Rbudget(T_i) := w_i^{x+1}.b] \end{array}}$$

$$\textbf{Release2}: \frac{\begin{array}{c} \forall \ s \in S, T_i \in \mathcal{T} \ | \ s.status(T_i) = Done, s.ExcessT(T_i) > 0 \\ \wedge \ s.curW(T_i) = w_i^x \end{array}}{\begin{array}{c} s \rightarrow s[curW(T_i) := w_i^{x+1}, curW(T_i).p := w_i^{x+1}.p - (clk - ExcessT(T_i)), \\ curTime(T_i) := clk, curET(T_i) := 0, Rbudget(T_i) := w_i^{x+1}.b, \\ status(T_i) := Waiting] \end{array}}$$

Rule **Release1** describes the expiry of a window w_i^x and the release of a new window w_i^{x+1} of a task T_i successfully executed during the previous window w_i^x, i.e. without missing its deadline $(s.curTime(T_i) = s.curW(T_i).p)$ and none of the other tasks is currently overrunning its own deadline. The status as well as the variables we introduced to monitor the task execution are reinitialized accordingly. When the effective overrun of a task is over, all the other postponed tasks will be released with their new windows. Rule **Release2** describes how the new window length of each task will be reduced with any overrun delay from the previous window.

In both rules **Release1** and **Release2**, one can remark that a task cannot release a new window if any other task is overrunning. This ensures that all deadlines and baselines occurring during an overrun are postponed until the overrun terminates.

5   Verification

As long as the tasks complete before their deadlines, the system described in Sect. 4 is predictable. This includes cases where execution budget violations occur. Thus, a combination of task set and fault model which is free from deadline violations is said to be schedulable and, by design, predictable [6].

The more interesting cases are those where the task set is not always schedulable. However, the task set could still be predictable: deadline violations could be absorbed by utilizing idle processor time or output values of certain tasks could be ignored in the given execution mode.

In order to be able to inject faults intentionally and verify the system's predictability accordingly, we extend the system model described in Sect. 4 with the following:

- For each task window $w_i^j = (p, b, c)$, by how much (overrun $\mathbf{o} \in \mathbb{R}_{\geq 0}$) the task will exceed its budget should it enter a fault state, i.e. $w_i^j = (p, b, c, o)$.
- We also allow for a description to be added to each task to specify how the input values are used to compute the outputs.

The final number of faults that can be absorbed depends on the length of overruns and the free time slot (λ) of the processor, i.e., $\sum_i \sum_j w_i^j.o \leq \lambda$. The analysis of predictability is performed by exhaustively checking that for each set of valid timestamped inputs, the system always produces the same set of timestamped outputs — with all possible combinations of faults allowed by the system configuration. The verification process either concludes that the system is predictable, or provides a counterexample in which the predictability is not preserved. The predictability can be analyzed using 2 approaches: direct and indirect.

5.1   Direct Approach to Analyze Predictability

The most direct approach for checking the predictability considers all possible sets of timestamped inputs, combines them with all possible failure modes, and checks that the same set of timestamped outputs is always produced for each respective set of inputs. This is not as daunting a task as it may first seem. The tasks are periodic and the number of configurations is finite. The system will eventually start to repeat previously-explored states at which point the search can stop. Additionally, as the task behavior is assumed to be correct, the range of possible inputs does not need to be fully examined. However, this approach still consumes much time and resources as well as being not cheaply implementable using Spin.

5.2   Indirect Approach to Analyze Predictability

As mentioned earlier, the system is predictable by design in no-fault cases. Therefore, to verify predictability it is necessary to analyze which behaviors the system exhibits when a fault occurs, and which of those behaviors will result in a violation of the predictability. Our approach is based on the following three observations and steps:

Inputs only Happen at Read Times. Each input/output has two parameters: a data value and time. The data value is beyond the influence of the system and is assumed to always be correct and valid. The timing of input arrival is technically beyond the control of the system as well; however, the system controls when it reads in the value of the input parameter. This is a reduction of many possible cases to one: the input can arrive anywhere between reads, but all

(a). Predictability preserved   **(b). Predictability not preserved**

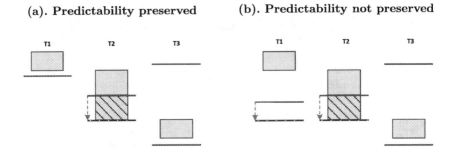

Fig. 3. Absorbing a deadline overrun

these scenarios are effectively equivalent to the input arriving at the read time. If the system is predictable with inputs that are timestamped at the read time, it is also predictable if the actual arrival times are used.

Only Monitor "edge" Task Timing. Every task set is assumed to have a task for reading input and another for writing output; these two tasks are called *edge* tasks. The edge tasks perform the input and output at their baselines and deadlines, respectively. If either the input baseline or the output baseline has to be moved to satisfy the data flow requirements, predictability is lost. Consider, e.g., Fig. 3 where *T1* is an input task, *T3* is an output task and the processing task *T2* is overrunning. The overrun can be absorbed, thus neither the baseline of the input task nor the deadline of the output task will be delayed. In Fig. 3(a), even though the baseline of *T2* gets delayed the input and output times remain unchanged, so the predictability is not violated. However, in Fig. 3(b) the predictability is violated as *T1* reads its inputs at a later time, i.e., the new baseline of *T1* occurring during the overrun of *T2* is delayed by the dashed arrow until *T2* completes.

To capture edge tasks, we introduce the following:

- We define each data $x = (v, a)$ by a value v and an arrival time (stamp) a.
- The inputs and outputs of each task T, consisting each of a set of data, are given by $T.input$ and $T.input$ respectively.
- We identify the tasks being as edges with T through function $Edge(T) = \{T_i \mid T.output \cap T_i.input \neq \emptyset\}$.

In order to maintain the predictability guaranteed by design, one needs to maintain the same relative order between the baseline/deadline of the edge tasks. In some cases, e.g. non critical settings, this can be achieved by just delaying the deadline of the faulty task as well as the baseline of its edge tasks.

Flag Outputs of Forcibly Terminated Tasks. In the most permissive operating mode, where execution budget violations are ignored and deadline violations result in delays, checking data values is not necessary as the system guarantees correct data flow by eschewing timing enforcement. However, in a more restrictive mode that involves forced task termination, e.g. hard critical systems or due to the non availability of processor free slots, the data values do need to be checked. This is done by verifying whether a task that was terminated by the operating system is involved in calculating a data value. If a terminated task was involved anywhere in the chain, the output is no longer reliable because it is not guaranteed whether the task completed the calculation successfully before being terminated. To this end, we introduce a new status *Forced* which will be assigned to any task once its misses its deadline. The termination rule is similar to rule **Overrun**, which is applicable when $s.curTime(T) \geq s.curW(T).p$ (deadline missed) and updates the status of T in the following: $status(T) := Forced$.

To check the involvement of the output of a terminated task in the calculation of other tasks data, we add a "tainted" flag to data values as they are passed between tasks. The flag is set when a task that is supposed to write a given value is forcefully terminated, and it is propagated by all other data-dependent tasks. If a tainted value is observed among the output, it results in a violation of the predictability. To flag the output of tasks, we introduce the following:

– The involvement of data x in the calculation of the output of a task T is given by predicate $Involved(x, T)$. Such a predicate can easily be derived from the functional description of tasks.
– To taint the output of a task T once it is forcibly terminated, we introduce $Taint(T.output)$ as a predicate. $Taint()$ is initially initialized to false, i.e. $\forall T,\ Taint(T.output) = false$.
– The flag function $Flag(T)$, used to propagate the taint from a forcibly terminated task T to the output of its (descendent) edge tasks, is given by:

$$Flag(T) = \begin{cases} Taint(T.output) := true & \text{If } Edge(T) = \emptyset \\ & \text{Or } (\forall T_i \in Edge(T), \forall x \in T.output\ \neg Involved(x, T_i)) \\ (Taint(T.output) := true) \wedge (Flag(T_i \mid \forall T_i \in Edge(T))) & \text{Otherwise} \end{cases}$$

The predictability violation can then simply be checked through the existence of tainted outputs. Using model checking, we quantify over all system states S by exploring all the tasks $\mathcal{T}$. Formally, the predictability is preserved if for any non forcibly terminated task the outputs are not tainted:

$$\forall s \in S\ \forall T \in \mathcal{T},\ s.status(T) \neq Forced \Rightarrow Taint(T.output) = false$$

6   Implementation and Application

Our system description has been modeled using the Promela language, allowing for verification of predictability of arbitrary task sets. The usefulness of the verifier lies in its ability to perform an exhaustive search. The verification exhaustively explores all possible executions and checks for predictability violations. If a system is not predictable, a counterexample demonstrating the violation is provided. A graphical front end was created to simplify task set definition and result parsing. This utility generates the required Promela model based on the parameters supplied by the user and pre-written skeleton code. It also parses the counterexample trail files produced by the verifier into a graphical representation of the task-to-processor assignment over time.

6.1   Spin Modifications

The counterexample trail files produced normally consist of the states and transitions visited by the verifier leading up to a state violating the predictability. This allows a trail file to be "replayed" by Spin. Within the trail file, the states are identified by their state numbers—a property internal to Spin that cannot be relied upon or (easily) determined given the source Promela model. The counterexample file becomes meaningless, as the state numbers cannot be mapped to actual behavior of the system. Even if the trail file is replayed and the source Promela statements displayed, they are meaningless to the user since the Promela code is automatically generated.

To overcome this, we have extended Spin to support state annotations using the existing Promela label syntax. Promela supports C-style labels (`label:`), used as targets for `goto` statements as well as identifying special states (`end`, `progress`, etc.). An additional special label type, `annotation`, is added. Any text included in the label is attached to the state and propagated to the generated verifier. The verifier, in turn, includes the text of these states in the trail files it produces. Annotation labels are merged and lifted when state merging happens, or within constructs that only produce one state (e.g., `dstep`) from a block of Promela code. A list of all annotations that fall within a state is included in the trail file in these cases. Meaningful data can now be extracted from the trail file.

6.2   Promela Model

The Promela model is divided into three parts: a set of tasks, the scheduler, and the environment. The task code is entirely generated by the interface, based on the user parameters. The scheduler and environment are mostly constant between different task sets, with different sections enabled and disabled via preprocessor macros depending on user inputs.

Each task is comprised of five blocks of Promela code, which are invoked at the appropriate times: initialization, baseline, deadline, execution tick and forced termination. Initialization code allows the task to push values to the global descriptor table. Baseline and deadline are called at each baseline and deadline respectively. Execution tick ("run") code is called once per every scheduling tick that the task is assigned processor time. Finally, forced termination code is called when the task needs to be terminated unexpectedly. Regular termination, if needed, is supposed to be handled by the run code.

The scheduler code is entirely deterministic—all non-deterministic choices happen within the tasks, as it is assumed that the scheduler is fault-free. This code is executed once per tick, and is responsible for updating task timing information and choosing which tasks get assigned processor time.

The environment consists mainly of the scheduler loop. It calls the task-specific code and the scheduler code at the appropriate times. The environment and scheduler together are meant to represent the operating system's role.

6.3   Interface

A cross-platform Java GUI (Fig. 4) was created to simplify creating task sets and modifying parameters. The interface allows users to enter task-specific code, as well as general parameters such as number of cores and enforcement modes. It then generates the final Promela model, automating certain repetitive tasks (e.g., inserting a task identifier in the proper places) that are too complex for the C pre-processor normally used by Spin for such purposes. Finally, if a trail file is produced, the GUI generates a visualization showing how the defined tasks were scheduled and when the predictability violation occurred. For further details regarding the implementation, we refer readers to [14].

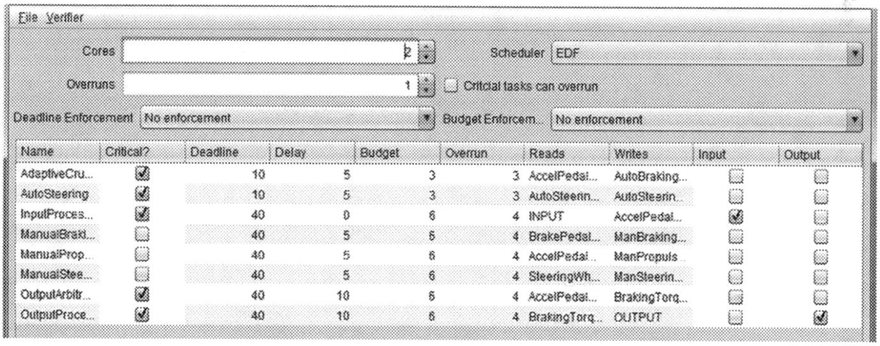

Name	Critical?	Deadline	Delay	Budget	Overrun	Reads	Writes	Input	Output
AdaptiveCru...	☑	10	5		3	3 AccelPedal...	AutoBraking...	☐	☐
AutoSteering	☑	10	5		3	3 AutoSteerin...	AutoSteerin...	☐	☐
InputProces...	☑	40	0		6	4 INPUT	AccelPedal...	☑	☐
ManualBrak...	☐	40	5		6	4 BrakePedal...	ManBraking...	☐	☐
ManualProp...	☐	40	5		6	4 AccelPedal...	ManPropuls	☐	☐
ManualStee...	☐	40	5		6	4 SteeringWh...	ManSteerin...	☐	☐
OutputArbitr...	☑	40	10		6	4 AccelPedal...	BrakingTorq...	☐	☐
OutputProce...	☑	40	10		6	4 BrakingTorq...	OUTPUT	☐	☑

Fig. 4. The Java graphical interface.

6.4   Case Study: Active Safety Demo

To show the applicability of our framework, we have analyzed a realistic example from the automotive domain. The most relevant parts of the task set description are given in Table 1. Various system configurations have been analyzed—different numbers of cores and allowable faults, along with different scheduling algorithms and enforcement modes. The size of the state space and therefore both the execution time and memory requirements increase as the number of permitted faults increases, because each fault represents a non-deterministic choice that needs to be made once per scheduling tick per task, causing a branch in the search tree. The search tree becomes very broad with many faults, but the depth remains tractable.

All optimizations performed by Spin when generating the verifier (e.g., state merging) were enabled. The performance of the verifier on some representative configurations can be seen in Fig. 5. The results shown are with critical tasks permitted to fail. Each scheduling algorithm produced broadly similar results,

Table 1. Parameters and data flow of the active safety demo task set, (C = Criticality, W = Window Size, B = Budget, O = Overrun amount, on fault). See [14] for descriptions of the values.

Task	C	W	B	O	Values read	Values written
AdaptiveCruise	Hi	10	3	3	APP BPP CO CSS TD VS	ABT APT
AutoSteering	Hi	10	3	3	ASO LMP SWA	AST
InputProcessing	Hi	40	6	4	*(Environment)*	APP ASO BPP CO CSS LMP SWA SWT TD VS
ManualBraking	Lo	40	6	4	BPP	MBT
ManualPropulsion	Lo	40	6	4	APP	MPT
ManualSteering	Lo	40	6	4	SWA	MST
OutputArbitration	Hi	40	6	4	APP ABT APT ASO AST BPP CO MBT MPT MST SWT	BT COI PT SOI ST
OutputProcessing	Hi	40	6	4	BT COI PT SOI ST	*(Environment)*

so only the results for EDF are shown. The performance of both the verifier itself and the visualization generation is very good on a modern system (Core i7, 16GB RAM), the entire process generally taking less than a second for a realistic number of faults. Further analysis results are available in [14].

Cores	Faults	States	Time	Predictable?
1	0	2178	0.010s	No
2	0	2231	0.002s	Yes
2	1	19468	0.025s	Yes
2	4	44369	0.052s	No
4	4	632906	0.682s	Yes
4	32	20055317	22.9s	Yes

Fig. 5. Analysis results of the case study.

7   Related Work

In the literature, several frameworks for the predictability analysis of real-time systems have been proposed [5,8–10,17]. However, only few proposals consider multicore platforms and dynamic attributes of tasks.

The authors of [8] presented a model-based architectural approach for improving the predictability of real-time systems. This approach is component-based and utilizes automated analysis of task and communication architectures.

The authors generate a runtime executive that can be analyzed using the MetaH language and the underlying toolset. Such a work does not deal with multicore or criticality.

Garousi *et al.* introduced a predictability analysis approach [10], for real-time systems, relying on the control flow analysis of the UML 2.0 sequence diagrams as well as the consideration of the timing and distribution information. The analysis includes resource usage, load forecasting/balancing and dynamic dependencies. Our work differs because it supports dynamic runtime and fault handling.

The authors of [3] introduced a compositional analysis enabling predictable deployment of component-based systems running on heterogeneous multi processors. The system is a composition of software and hardware models according to a specific operational semantics. Such a framework is a simulation-based analysis, thus it cannot be used as a rigorous analysis means for critical systems.

The authors of [16] defined a predictable execution model for COTS (commercial -off-the-shelf) based embedded systems. The goal is to control the use of each resource in such a way that it does not exceed its saturation limit. However, such a claim cannot always be maintained because of the non-determinism in the behavior of tasks and their environment.

The authors of [4] introduced a predictability analysis framework for real time systems given by a set of independent components running on a single core platform. Data flow is abstracted using dependability whereas predictability is compositionally analyzed through schedulability as a sufficient condition. However, simplifying the architecture to obtain a compositional analysis might not be practical for modern COTS-based embedded systems.

In [15], the authors introduce data flow graphs as a scheduling means for data flow within single core systems so that liveness and boundness are guaranteed. The schedulability analysis of data flow is then performed by translating data flow graphs to graph-based real-time tasks. A study of the applicability of such a framework for multicore systems having dynamic runtime is very interesting. In a similar way, the authors of [2] introduce a model of data flow computation to overcome the restrictions of classical data flow graphs by allowing dynamic changes during runtime. The dynamism of data flow graph is expressed by 2 parameters: the number of data required (rate) for each flow and the activation/deactivation of communications between the functional units. Compared to that, our framework considers a static topology of the data flow graph encapsulated within the dynamic runtime of tasks however the data flow timeliness can vary in accordance with faults (overruns).

8   Conclusion

In this paper, we have introduced a formal framework and model checking based approach for the predictability analysis of mixed criticality task sets running on multicore platforms. The framework supports window scheduling and dynamic tasks bahavior, and allows for failures to be handled at runtime. We formulated a system description and modeled it in Promela. A GUI was implemented to increase ease of use and Spin was extended to support the generation of visualizations. The analysis results for a realistic example are encouraging and suggest that the approach might scale to industrial settings.

We greatly simplify the analysis by observing that only monitoring "edge" tasks for delays and checking outputs for values tainted by terminated tasks is needed. Interesting future work would be to model the data flow separately from tasks behavior, in similar way to [2], to make our framework more flexible.

Acknowledgment. This work is supported by the Natural Sciences and Engineering Research Council of Canada, as part of the NECSIS Automotive Research Partnership with General Motors, IBM and Malina Software Corp.

References

1. ISO 26262-1:2011D Road vehicles-Functional safety. Technical report, ISO (2011)
2. Bebelis, V., Fradet, P., Girault, A., Lavigueur, B.: BPDF: a statically analyzable dataflow model with integer and boolean parameters. In: EMSOFT 2013, pp. 3:1–3:10. IEEE Press (2013)
3. Bondarev, E., Chaudron, M., de With, P.: Compositional performance analysis of component-based systems on heterogeneous multiprocessor platforms. In: SEAA 2006, pp. 81–91, August 2006
4. Boudjadar, A., Dingel, J., Madzar, B., Kim, J.H.: Compositional predictability analysis of mixed critical real time systems. In: Artho, C., Ölveczky, P.C. (eds.) FTSCS 2015. CCIS, vol. 596, pp. 69–84. Springer, Cham (2016). doi:10.1007/978-3-319-29510-7_4
5. Boudjadar, A., Kim, J.H., Larsen, K.G., Nyman, U.: Compositional schedulability analysis of an avionics system using UPPAAL. In: Proceedings of ICAASE 2014, pp. 140–147 (2014)
6. Chabrol, D., Aussagues, C., David, V.: A spatial and temporal partitioning approach for dependable automotive systems. In: IEEE Conference on Emerging Technologies Factory Automation, pp. 1–8 (2009)
7. de Niz, D., Lakshmanan, K., Rajkumar, R.: On the scheduling of mixed-criticality real-time task sets. In: RTSS 2009, pp. 291–300 (2009)
8. Feiler, P., Lewis, B., Vestal, S.: Improving predictability in embedded real-time systems. Technical report CMU/SEI-2000-SR-011, December 2000
9. Fredriksson, J.: Improving predictability and resource utilization in component-based embedded real-time systems. Ph.D. thesis, Mälardalen University (2008)
10. Garousi, V., Briand, L., Labiche, Y.: A unified approach for predictability analysis of real-time systems using UML-based control flow information. In: Gérard, S., Graf, S., Haugen, O., Selic, B. (eds.) MARTES 2005, Workshop on Modelling and Analysis of Real Time and Embedded Systems, with MODELS (2005). http://link.springer.com/chapter/10.1007/11663430_7
11. Henzinger, T.A.: Two challenges in embedded systems design: predictability and robustness. Philos. Trans. R. Soc. A Math. Phys. Eng. Sci. **366**, 3727–3736 (2008)
12. Henzinger, T.A., Horowitz, B., Kirsch, C.M.: Giotto: a time-triggered language for embedded programming. In: Henzinger, T.A., Kirsch, C.M. (eds.) EMSOFT 2001. LNCS, vol. 2211, pp. 166–184. Springer, Heidelberg (2001). doi:10.1007/3-540-45449-7_12

13. Henzinger, T.A., Manna, Z., Pnueli, A.: Timed transition systems. In: Bakker, J.W., Huizing, C., Roever, W.P., Rozenberg, G. (eds.) REX 1991. LNCS, vol. 600, pp. 226–251. Springer, Heidelberg (1992). doi:10.1007/BFb0031995

14. Madzar, B.: Modelling and verification of predictable data flow in real-time systems, M. Sc thesis. Queen's University Canada (2015)

15. Mohaqeqi, M., Abdullah, J., Yi, W.: Modeling and analysis of data flow graphs using the digraph real-time task model. In: Bertogna, M., Pinho, L.M., Quiñones, E. (eds.) Ada-Europe 2016. LNCS, vol. 9695, pp. 15–29. Springer, Cham (2016). doi:10.1007/978-3-319-39083-3_2

16. Pellizzoni, R., Betti, E., Bak, S., Yao, G., Criswell, J., Caccamo, M., Kegley, R.: A predictable execution model for COTS-based embedded systems. In: RTAS 2011

17. Yau, S., Zhou, X.: Schedulability in model-based software development for distributed real-time systems. In: WORDS 2002, pp. 45–52 (2002)

Reasoning About Connectors in Coq

Xiyue Zhang, Weijiang Hong, Yi Li, and Meng Sun[(✉)]

Department of Informatics and LMAM, School of Mathematical Sciences,
Peking University, Beijing, China
{zhangxiyue,wj.hong,liyi_math,sunm}@pku.edu.cn

Abstract. Reo is a channel-based exogenous coordination model in
which complex coordinators, called connectors, are compositionally built
out of simpler ones. In this paper, we present a new approach to model
connectors in Coq which is a proof assistant based on higher-order logic
and λ-calculus. The model reflects the original structure of connectors
simply and clearly. In our framework, basic connectors (channels) are
interpreted as axioms and composition operations are specified as infer-
ence rules. Furthermore, connectors are interpreted as logical predicates
which describe the relation between inputs and outputs. With such definitions provided, connector properties, as well as equivalence and refinement relations between different connectors, can be naturally formalized
as *goals* in Coq and easily proved using pre-defined *tactics*.

Keywords: Coordination language · Reo · Coq · Reasoning

1 Introduction

Modern software systems are typically distributed over large networks of computing devices, and usually the components that comprise a system do not exactly
fit together as pieces of a jigsaw puzzle, but leave significant interfacing gaps
that must somehow be filled with additional code. Compositional coordination
models and languages provide a formalization of the "glue code" that intercon-
nects the constituent components and organizes the mutual interactions among
them in a distributed processing environment, and played a crucial role for the
success of component-based systems in the past decades.

As an example, Reo [3], which is a channel-based model for exogenous coordination, offers a powerful language for implementation of coordinating component
connectors. Connectors provide the protocols that control and organize the communication, synchronization and cooperation among the components that they
interconnect. Primitive connectors, called *channels* in Reo, can be composed to
build complex connectors. Reo has been successfully applied in different application domains, such as service-oriented computing and bioinformatics [7,18].
In recent years, verifying the correctness of connectors is becoming a critical
challenge, especially due to the advent of Cloud computing technologies. The
rapid growth of size and complexity of the computing infrastructures has made

© Springer International Publishing AG 2017
O. Kouchnarenko and R. Khosravi (Eds.): FACS 2016, LNCS 10231, pp. 172–190, 2017.
DOI: 10.1007/978-3-319-57666-4_11

it more difficult to model and verify connector properties, and thus leads to less confidence on the correctness of connectors.

Several works have been done for formal modeling and verifying connectors. An operational semantics for Reo using Constraint Automata (CA) was provided by Baier et al. [6], and later the symbolic model checker Vereofy [5] was developed, which can be used to check CTL-like properties. Besides, one attractive approach is to translate from Reo to other formal models such as Alloy [12], mCRL2 [14], UTP [2,19], etc., which makes it possible to take advantage of existing verification tools. A comparison of existing semantic models for Reo can be found in [11].

In this paper, we aim to provide an approach to formally modeling and reasoning about connectors using Coq. The basic idea of our approach is to model the behavior of a connector by representing it as a logical predicate which describes the relation among the timed data streams on the input and output nodes, and to reason about connectors' properties, as well as the equivalence and refinement relations between connectors, by using proof principles and tactics in Coq. Compared with existing approaches for verifying connectors' properties [5,13,14], using Coq is especially helpful when we take infinite behavior into consideration. The coinductive proof principle makes it possible to prove connectors' properties easily while it is difficult (sometimes impossible) for other approaches (like model checking) because of the huge (or maybe infinite) number of states.

This is not a brand new idea, as we have already provided a solution for modeling Reo in Coq in [15], where connectors are represented in a constructive way, and verification is essentially based on simulations. We do believe that the approach in this paper is reasonably different from its predecessor where Coq seldom shows its real power. To be more specific, our new work has its certain advantages comparing with [15] in the following aspects:

- **Modeling Method:** We use axioms to describe basic channels and their composition operations, which is more natural on a proof-assistant platform than the simulation-based approach in [15].
- **Expression Power:** Any valid Coq expression can be used to depict properties, which is obviously more powerful than just using LTL formulas in [15]. Furthermore, support for continuous time behavior is also possible in our approach in this paper.
- **Refinement and Equivalence Checking:** In our framework, equivalence and refinement relations can be proved among different connectors, while the previous one is not capable of either equivalence or refinement checking.

The paper is organized as follows: After this general introduction, we briefly summarize Reo and Coq in Sect. 2. Section 3 shows the notion of timed data streams and some pre-defined auxiliary functions and predicates. Section 4 presents the formal modeling of basic channels and operators, as well as complex connectors. Section 5 shows how to reason about connector properties and equivalence (or refinement) relations in our framework. In Sect. 6, we concludes with some further research directions. Full source codes can be found at [1] for further reference.

2   Preliminaries

In this section, we provide a brief introduction to the coordination language Reo and Coq.

2.1   The Coordination Model Reo

Reo is a channel-based exogenous coordination model wherein complex coordinators, called connectors, are compositionally built out of simpler ones [3]. Further details about Reo and its semantics can be found in [3,4,6]. The simplest connectors are channels with well-defined behavior such as synchronous channels, FIFO channels, etc. Each channel in Reo has exactly two directed ends, with their own identities. There are two types of channel ends: source ends and sink ends. A source channel end accepts data into the channel. A sink channel end dispenses data out of the channel.

Sync   Syncdrain   FIFO1   Asyncdrain   LossySync

Fig. 1. Five types of basic channels.

The graphical notations of some basic channels are presented in Fig. 1, and their behavior can be interpreted as follows:

- **Sync:** a synchronous channel with one source end and one sink end. The pair of I/O operations on its two ends can succeed only simultaneously.
- **SyncDrain:** a synchronous channel which has two source ends. The pair of input operations on its two ends can succeed only simultaneously. All data items written to this channel are lost.
- **FIFOn:** an asynchronous channel with one source end and one sink end, and a bounded buffer with capacity n. It can accept data items from its source end. The accepted data items are kept in the internal buffer, and dispensed to the sink end in FIFO order. Especially, the FIFO1 channel is an instance of FIFOn where the buffer capacity is 1.
- **AsyncDrain:** an asynchronous channel which has two source ends. The channel guarantees that the operations on its two ends never succeed simultaneously. All data items written to this channel are lost.
- **LossySync:** a synchronous channel with one source end and one sink end. The source end always accepts all data items. If there is no matching output operation on the sink end of the channel at the time that a data item is accepted, then the data item is lost; otherwise, the channel transfers the data item exactly the same as a Sync channel, and the output operation at the sink end succeeds.

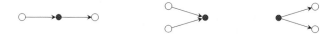

Fig. 2. Operations of channel composition.

Complex connectors are constructed by composing simpler ones via the join and hiding operations. Channels are joined together in nodes. The set of channel ends coincident on a node is disjointly partitioned into the sets of source and sink channel ends that coincide on the node, respectively. Nodes are categorized into source, sink and mixed nodes, depending on whether all channel ends that coincide on a node are source ends, sink ends or a combination of the two. The hiding operation is used to hide the internal topology of a connector. The hidden nodes can no longer be accessed or observed from outside. There are three types of operations for channel composition: flow-through, merge and replicate. Figure 2 provides the graphical representation of these operations.

2.2 The Proof Assistant Coq

Coq [9] is a widely-used proof assistant tool, where denotational formalizations (e.g. theorem and hypothesis) and operational formalizations (e.g. functions and algorithms) are naturally integrated. Moreover, it allows the interactive construction of formal proofs. The formal language used in Coq is called *Gallina*, which provides a convenient way to define both programming statements and mathematical propositions, for example:

```
(* a variable definition *)
Variables a b: nat.
(* a simple non-recursive function *)
Definition inc(a:nat) := a + 1.
(* axioms don't have to be proved *)
Axiom inc_ax: forall c:nat, inc(c) > c.
(* theorems rely on proving *)
Theorem inc_eq: forall c:nat, inc(c) = c + 1.
Proof.
   (* interactive proving based on tactics *)
   auto.
Qed.
```

As shown in this example, there are two rather different mode in Coq's interactive shell. When we start Coq, we can write declarations and definitions in a functional-programming mode. Then, when we start a *Theorem*, or *Lemma*, Coq jumps into the proving mode. We need to write different *tactics* to reduce the proving goal and finally finish the formal proof.

Furthermore, Coq is equipped with a set of well-written standard libraries. For example, as used in this paper, *List* describes the widely-used finite list structure, *Stream* provides a co-inductive definition of infinite lists, and *Reals* defines various operations and theorems on real numbers. Usually, quite a few lemmas and theorems are pre-defined in such libraries, making it substantially easier to prove our goals.

3   Basic Definitions

In this section, we briefly introduce the notion of timed data streams and some pre-defined auxiliary functions and predicates in Coq, which are used in the following sections for modeling connectors.

The behavior of a connector can be formalized by means of data-flows at its sink and source nodes which are essentially infinite sequences. With the help of the stream library in Coq, such infinite data-flows can be defined as *timed data streams*:

```
Definition Time := R.
Definition Data := nat.
(*Inductive Data : Set :=
    |Natdata : nat-> Data
    |Empty : Data.*)
Definition TD := Time * Data.
Variable Input : Stream TD.
Variable Output : Stream TD.
```

In our framework, time is represented by real numbers. Benefit from the completeness of real number system, we can express and carry out the effective operation of a quantity at any precision request. The continuity of the set of real numbers is sufficiently enough for our modeling approach. Also the continuous time model is more appropriate since it is very expressive and closer to the nature of time in the real world. Thus, the time sequence consists of increasing and diverging time moments. For simplicity, here we take the natural numbers as the definition of data, which can be easily expanded according to different application domains. The Cartesian product of time and data defines a TD object. We use the stream module in Coq to produce streams of TD objects.

Some auxiliary functions and predicates are defined to facilitate the representation of axioms for basic channels in Reo. This part can be extended for further use in different problems.

The terms "PrL" and "PrR" take a pair of values (a, b) that has Cartesian product type A × B as the argument and return the first or second value of the pair, respectively.

The following functions provide some judgment of time, which can make the description of axioms and theorems for connectors more concise and clear. "Teq" means that time of two streams are equal and "Tneq" has the opposite meaning. "Tle" ("Tgt") represents that time of the first stream is strictly less (greater) than the second stream. The judgement about equality of data is analogous to the judgement of time. The complete definition of these functions can be found at [1].

4   Formal Modeling of Basic Channels and Operators

In this section, we show how primitive connectors, i.e., channels, and operators for connector composition are specified in Coq and used for modeling of complex connectors. Then we can apply the tactics provided in Coq to reason about connector properties. Basic channels, which can be regarded as axioms of the whole framework, are specified as logical predicates illustrating the relation between the timed data streams of input and output. When we need to construct a more complex connector, appropriate composition operators are applied depending on the topological structure of the connector.

4.1   Formal Modeling of Basic Channels

We use a pair of predicates to describe the constraints on time and data, respectively, and their intersection to provide the complete specification of basic channels. This model offers convenience for the analysis and proof of connector properties. In the following, we present a few examples of the formal model of basic channels.

The simplest form of a synchronous channel is denoted by the Sync channel type. For a channel of the Sync type, a read operation on its sink end succeeds only if there is a write operation pending on its source end. Thus, the time and data of a stream flowing into the channel are exactly the same as the stream that flows out of the channel[1]. The Sync channel can be defined as follows in the Coq system:

```
Definition Sync (Input Output:Stream TD) : Prop :=
Teq Input Output /\ Deq Input Output.
```

The channel of type SyncDrain is a synchronous channel that allows pairs of write operations pending on its two ends to succeed simultaneously. All written data items are lost. Thus, the SyncDrain channel is used for synchronising two timed data streams on its two source ends. This channel type is an important basic synchronization building block for the construction of more complex connectors. The SyncDrain channel can be defined as follows:

```
Definition SyncDrain (Input Output:Stream TD) : Prop :=
Teq Input Output.
```

The channel types FIFO and FIFOn where n is an integer greater than 0 represent the typical unbounded and bounded asynchronous FIFO channels. A write to a FIFO channel always succeeds, and a write to a FIFOn channel succeeds only if the number of data items in its buffer is less than its bounded

---

[1] If we use α, β to denote the data streams that flow through the channel ends of a channel and a, b to denote the time stream corresponding to the data streams, i.e., the i-th element $a(i)$ in a denotes exactly the time moment of the occurrence of $\alpha(i)$, then we can easily obtain the specifications for different channels, as discussed in [17,19]. For example, a synchronous channel can be expressed as $\alpha = \beta \wedge a = b$.

capacity n. A read or take from a FIFO or FIFOn channel suspends until the first data item in the channel buffer can be obtained and then the operation succeeds. For simplicity, we take the FIFO1 channel as an example. This channel type requires that the time when it consumes a data item through its source end is earlier than the time when the data item is delivered through its sink end. Besides, as the buffer has the capacity 1, time of the next data item that flows in should be later than the time when the data in the buffer is delivered. We use intersection of predicates in its definition as follows:

```
Definition FIFO1(Input Output:Stream TD) : Prop :=
Tle Input Output /\ Tle Output (tl Input)
/\ Deq Input Output.
```

For a FIFO1 channel whose buffer already contains a data element e, the communication can be initiated only if the data element e can be taken via the sink end. In this case, the data stream that flows out of the channel should get an extra element e settled at the beginning of the stream. And time of the stream that flows into the channel should be earlier than time of the tail of the stream that flows out. But as the buffer contains the data element e, new data can be written into the channel only after the element e has been taken. Therefore, time of the stream that flows out is earlier than time of the stream that flows in. The channel can be represented as the intersection of several predicates as follows:

```
Definition FIFO1e(Input Output:Stream TD)(e:Data) : Prop :=
Tgt Input Output /\ Tle Input (tl Output)
/\ PrR (hd Output) = e  /\ Deq Input (tl Output).
```

In the following we choose Axiom to define LossySync and AsyncDrain because it is easier to use the coinductive expression to specify their behavior.

A LossySync channel behaves the same as a Sync channel, except that a write operation on its source always succeeds immediately. If a compatible read or take operation is already pending on the sink of a LossySync channel, the written data item is transferred to the pending operation and both succeed. Otherwise, the write operation succeeds and the data item is lost. The LossySync channel can be defined as follows:

```
Parameter LossySync: Stream TD -> Stream TD -> Prop.
Axiom LossySync_coind:
  forall Input Output: Stream TD,
  LossySync Input Output ->
    (
    (hd Output = hd Input  /\ LossySync (tl Input)(tl Output))
    \/
    LossySync(tl Input) Output
    ).
```

AsyncDrain is analogous to SyncDrain except that it guarantees that the pairs of write operations on the two channel ends never succeed simultaneously.

Similarly it only has requirements on the time of the two streams on its opposite ends, but it requires that the times of the two streams are always different. The AsyncDrain channel can be defined as follows:

```
Parameter AsyncDrain: Stream TD -> Stream TD -> Prop.
Axiom AsyncDrain_coind:
  forall Input1 Input2: Stream TD,
  AsyncDrain Input1 Input2 ->
    (~ PrL(hd Input1)  =  PrL (hd Input2) )
    /\
    ( (
      (PrL(hd Input1) < PrL (hd Input2)) /\
      AsyncDrain (tl Input1) Input2
      ) /\
      (
      (PrL(hd Input1) > PrL (hd Input2))   /\
      AsyncDrain Input1 (tl Input2)
      )
    ).
```

Defining basic channels by intersection of predicates provides the following benefits:

- Firstly, this makes the model intuitive and concise as each predicate describes a simple order relation on time or data.
- Secondly, we can easily split predicates for proofs of different properties which can make the proving process simpler.

4.2 Formal Modeling of Operators

We have just described the way to define channel types, by means of definitions in Coq. Now we start defining the composition operators for connector construction. There are three types of composition operators for connector construction, which are *flow-through*, *replicate* and *merge*, respectively.

The flow-through operator simply allows data items to flow through the junction node, from one channel to the other. We need not to give the flow-through operator a specific definition in the Coq system. For example, while we illustrate two channels *Sync(A,B)* and *FIFO1(B,C)*, a flow-through operator that acts on node *B* for these two channels has been achieved implicitly.

The replicate operator puts the source ends of different channels together into one common node, and a write operation on this node succeeds only if all the channels are capable of consuming a copy of the written data. Similar to the flow-through operator, it can be implicitly represented by the structure of connectors. For example, for two channels *Sync(A,B)* and *FIFO1(C,D)*, we can illustrate *Sync(A,B)* and *FIFO1(A,D)* in Coq instead of defining a function like *rep(Sync(A,B),FIFO1(C,D))* and the replicate operator is achieved directly by renaming *C* with *A* for the FIFO1 channel.

The merge operator is more complicated. We consider merging two channels AB and CD. When the merge operator acts on these two channels, it leads to a choice of taking from the common node that delivers a data item out of AB or CD. Similar to the definition of basic channels, we define merge as the intersection of two predicates and use recursive definition here:

```
Parameter merge:
Stream TD -> Stream TD ->Stream TD -> Prop.
Axiom merge_coind:
  forall s1 s2 s3:Stream TD,
  merge s1 s2 s3-> (
    ~ (PrL(hd s1) = PrL(hd s2)) /\
    (
      (PrL(hd s1) < PrL(hd s2)) ->
      ((hd s3 = hd s1)  /\ merge (tl s1) s2 (tl s3))
    ) /\ (
      (PrL(hd s1) > PrL(hd s2)) ->
      ((hd s3 = hd s2)  /\ merge s1 (tl s2) (tl s3))
    )
  ).
```

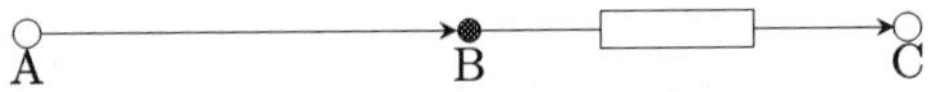

Fig. 3. A connector consisting of a Sync channel and a FIFO1 channel.

Based on the definition of basic channels and operators, more complex connectors can be constructed structurally. To show how a composite connector is constructed, we consider a simple example as shown in Fig. 3, where a FIFO1 channel is attached to the sink end of a Sync channel. Assume AB is of type Sync and BC is of type FIFO1, then we can construct the required connector by illustrating $Sync(A,B)$ and $FIFO1(B,C)$. The configuration and the functionality of the required connector can be specified using this concise method. Note that the composition operations can be easily generalized to the case of multiple nodes, where the modeling of connectors is similar. More examples can be found in Sect. 5.

5   Reasoning About Connectors

After modeling a connector in Coq, we can analyse and prove important properties of the connector. In this section, we give some examples to elucidate how to reason about connector properties and prove refinement/equivalence relations between different connectors, with the help of Coq.

5.1   Derivation of Connector Properties

The proof process of a property is as follows: the user states the proposition that needs to be proved, called a *goal*, then he/she applies commands called *tactics* to decompose this goal into simpler subgoals or solve it directly. This decomposition process ends when all subgoals are completely solved. In the following, we use some examples to illustrate our approach instead of giving all the complex technical details.

Example 1. We first consider the connector given in Fig. 3, which consists of two channels AB and BC with types Sync and FIFO1, respectively.

We use a and b to denote the time streams when the corresponding data streams flow into and out of the Sync channel AB, and c to denote the time stream for the data stream that flows out of the FIFO1 channel BC. Here we can see that a flow-through operation has acted on the mixed node B. The time when the stream flows into the FIFO1 channel BC is equal to the time when the stream flows out of the Sync channel AB. The following theorem states the property $a < c$ for this connector. The connector is based on the axioms Sync and FIFO1, which can be used as hypotheses for the proof of the theorem.

Theorem 1. $\forall A, B, C.\ Sync(A, B) \land FIFO1(B, C) \rightarrow Tle(A, C).$

In Coq, the theorem can be proved as follows:

```
Theorem test1: forall A B C,
   Sync A B /\ FIFO1 B C -> Tle A C.
Proof.
     intros. destruct H. destruct H0.
     intro n. rewrite H. apply H0.
Qed.
```

First we give the Coq system a proposition `test1` which needs to be proved. The proposition is represented by a logical expression. Table 1 shows the detailed proving steps and the feedback that the Coq system provides during the proof.

The advantages of using intersection of logical predicates to describe basic channels have emerged while proving this example. After constructing the new connector, we use "intros" to split conditions and conclusions. Then we can use "destruct" to obtain the conditions for time and data separately, and make the proving procedure much more convenient. Once the concrete conditions are obtained, using "intro" contributes to comparing each time point in a sequence element by element. Then by using "rewrite" *H*, we can make the proof a step forward with known conditions of the comparison of time a and b, and finally by "apply" *H0* we can prove the goal. This is the implementation for reasoning about the constructed connector. Note that proper selection of strategies and tactics is essential for the proof of connector properties.

Example 2. In this example, we show a more interesting connector named *alternator* which consists of three channels AB, AC and BC of type Syncdrain,

Table 1. Steps and feedbacks for proving Theorem 1

Step	Feedback
Theorem test1: *forall A B C,* *Sync A B → FIFO1 B C →* *Tle A C.*	1 subgoal: *forall A B C,* *Sync A B → FIFO1 B C → Tle A C*
intros	1 subgoal: *Tle A C* *H : Sync A B; H0 : FIFO1 B C*
destruct *H*	1 subgoal: *Tle A C* *H : Teq A B; H1 : Deq A B;* *H0 : FIFO1 B C*
destruct *H0*	1 subgoal: *Tle A C* *H : Teq A B; H1 : Deq A B;* *H0 : Tle B C; H2 : Tle C (tl B) ∧ Deq B C*
intro *n*	1 subgoal: *PrL (Str_nth n A) < PrL (Str_nth n C)* *H : Teq A B; H1 : Deq A B; H0 : Tle B C;* *H2 : Tle C (tl B)∧ Deq B C*
rewrite *H*	1 subgoal: *PrL (Str_nth n B) < PrL (Str_nth n C)* *H : Teq A B; H0 : Deq A B; H1 : Tle B C;* *H2 : Tle C (tl B)∧Deq B C;n : nat*
apply *H0*	No more subgoals

FIFO1 and Sync, respectively. With the help of this connector, we can get data from node B and A alternatively at node C. By using the axioms for the basic channels and operators of composition, we can get the connector as shown in Fig. 4(b). The two channels AC and BC are merged together at node C. Before the merge operation, the connector's structure is as shown in Fig. 4(a), which is useful in the reasoning about the alternator.

We first introduce some lemmas to facilitate the proof.

```
Lemma transfer_eq : forall s1 s2 s3 : Stream TD,
((Teq s1 s2) /\ (Teq s2 s3)) -> (Teq s1 s3).
Lemma transfer_eqtl : forall s1 s2 : Stream TD,
(Teq s1 s2) -> (Teq tl s1)) (tl s2)).
Lemma transfer_leeq : forall s1 s2 s3 : Stream TD,
((Tle s1 s2) /\ (Teq s2 s3)) -> (Tle s1 s3).
Lemma transfer_hdle : forall s1 s2 : Stream TD,
(Tle s2 s1) -> (PrL (hd s1) > PrL (hd s2)).
```

Here the replicate operation has been applied twice for the alternator: node A becomes the common source node of *Syncdrain (A,B)* and *FIFO1(A,C1)*, and node B becomes the common source node of *Syncdrain(A,B)* and *Sync(B,C2)*. Let the time streams when the data streams flow into the two source nodes A and B be denoted by a and b, and the time streams when the data streams flow out of the channels *FIFO1(A,C1)* and *Sync(B,C2)* be denoted by $c1$ and

(a) Before merge   (b) After merge

Fig. 4. Alternator

$c2$, respectively. Theorem 2 specifies the property $c2 < c1 \wedge c1 < tl(c2)$ of the connector in Fig. 4(a). The connector is based on the axioms Sync, Syncdrain and FIFO1. These three corresponding axioms are used as hypotheses for the proof of this theorem.

Theorem 2 (subtest). $\forall A, B, C1, C2.$

$$SyncDrain(A, B) \wedge FIFO1(A, C1) \wedge Sync(B, C2) \rightarrow$$
$$Tle(C2, C1) \wedge Tle(C1, tl(C2))$$

In Coq, the theorem can be proved as follows. Note that the formalizm is slightly different from the previous one. By the *section* environment, Coq is able to encapsulate hypothesises as assumptions of the theorem. So the two definitions are exactly equivalent.

```
Section Alt.
Hypothesis D1: SyncDrain A B.
Hypothesis D2: FIFO1 A C1.
Hypothesis D3: Sync B C2.
Theorem subtest:
    (Tle C2 C1)  /\  (Tle C1 (tl C2)).
```

After constructing the connector in Fig. 4(a), we use "destruct" to obtain the conditions for time and data, respectively. Since the goal we are going to prove is an intersection of logical predicates, we use "split" to obtain the single subgoals represented by logical predicates. Besides, "intros" contributes to comparing each data in a sequence element by element. Then "rewrite" and "apply" are used similarly for multiple times until the goal is proved finally. Concrete proof steps and feedbacks are specified in Table 2.

The proof of Theorem 2 for the connector in Fig. 4(a) can be used to simplify the proof for the following property of alternator.

An additional hypothesis is needed for the proof of alternator which merges $C1$ and $C2$ into a common node C. Based on the three hypotheses for channels and the additional hypothesis, the theorem of alternator is presented as the following proposition which needs to be proved:

Table 2. Steps and feedback

Step	Feedback
Theorem subtest	1 subgoal: *Tle C2 C1 ∧ Tle C1 (tl C2)*
destruct *D2*	1 subgoal: *Tle C2 C1 ∧ Tle C1 (tl C2)* *H : Tle A C1; H0 : Tle C1 (tl A) ∧ Deq A C1*
destruct *D3*	1 subgoal: *Tle C2 C1 ∧ Tle C1 (tl C2)* *H : Tle A C1; H0 : Tle C1 (tl A) ∧ Deq A C1;* *H1 : Teq B C2; H2 : Deq B C2*
destruct *H0*	1 subgoal: *Tle C2 C1 ∧ Tle C1 (tl C2)* *H : Tle A C1; H0 : Tle C1 (tl A);* *H3 : Deq A C1; H1 : Teq B C2; H2 : Deq B C2*
split	2 subgoals: *Tle C2 C1; Tle C1 (tl C2)* *H : Tle A C1; H0 : Tle C1 (tl A);* *H3 : Deq A C1; H1 : Teq B C2; H2 : Deq B C2*
intros *n*	2 subgoals: *PrL (Str_nth n C2) < PrL (Str_nth n C1); Tle C1 (tl C2)* *H : Tle A C1; H0 : Tle C1 (tl A); H3 : Deq A C1;* *H1 : Teq B C2; H2 : Deq B C2; n : nat*
rewrite ← *H1*	2 subgoals: *PrL (Str_nth n B) < PrL (Str_nth n C1); Tle C1 (tl C2)* *H : Tle A C1; H0 : Tle C1 (tl A); H3 : Deq A C1;* *H1 : Teq B C2; H2 : Deq B C2; n : nat*
rewrite ← *D1*	2 subgoals: *PrL (Str_nth n A) < PrL (Str_nth n C1); Tle C1 (tl C2)* *H : Tle A C1; H0 : Tle C1 (tl A); H3 : Deq A C1;* *H1 : Teq B C2; H2 : Deq B C2; n : nat*
apply *H*	1 subgoal: *Tle C1 (tl C2)* *H : Tle A C1; H0 : Tle C1 (tl A); H3 : Deq A C1;* *H1 : Teq B C2; H2 : Deq B C2*
intros *n*	1 subgoal: *Tle C1 (tl C2)* *H : Tle A C1; H0 : Tle C1 (tl A); H3 : Deq A C1;* *H1 : Teq B C2; H2 : Deq B C2*
rewrite ← *D4*	2 subgoals: *PrL (Str_nth n C1) < PrL (Str_nth n (tl B)); Teq B C2* *H : Tle A C1; H0 : Tle C1 (tl A); H3 : Deq A C1;* *H1 : Teq B C2; H2 : Deq B C2; n : nat*
rewrite ← *D5*	3 subgoals: *PrL (Str_nth n C1) < PrL (Str_nth n (tl A)); Teq A B; Teq B C2* *H : Tle A C1; H0 : Tle C1 (tl A); H3 : Deq A C1;* *H1 : Teq B C2; H2 : Deq B C2; n : nat*
apply *H0*	2 subgoals: *Teq A B; Teq B C2* *H : Tle A C1; H0 : Tle C1 (tl A); H3 : Deq A C1;* *H1 : Teq B C2; H2 : Deq B C2; n : nat*
apply *D1*	1 subgoal: *Teq B C2* *H : Tle A C1; H0 : Tle C1 (tl A); H3 : Deq A C1;* *H1 : Teq B C2; H2 : Deq B C2; n : nat*
apply *D3*	No more subgoals.

```
Hypothesis D4: merge C1 C2 C.
Theorem test:
hd(C) = hd(C2) /\ merge C1 (tl C2) (tl C).
Proof.
    destruct subtest.  (* ... *)
```

Here we only present the first step which shows how a proven theorem can be applied in another proof and omit the full details because of the page limitation. And it greatly simplifies the process of proving the property of alternator.

5.2   Refinement and Equivalence

A refinement relation between connectors which allows us to systematically develop connectors in a step-wise fashion, may help to bridge the gap between requirements and the final implementations. The notion of refinement has been widely used in different system descriptions. For example, in data refinement [8], the 'concrete' model is required to have *enough redundancy* to represent all the elements of the 'abstract' one. This is captured by the definition of a surjection from the former into the latter (the *retrieve map*). If models are specified in terms of pre and post-conditions, the former are weakened and the latter strengthened under refinement [10]. In process algebra, refinement is usually discussed in terms of several 'observation' preorders, and most of them justify transformations entailing *reduction of nondeterminism* (see, for example, [16]). For connectors, the refinement relation can be defined as in [19], where a proper refinement order over connectors has been established based on the implication relation on predicates.

Here we adopt the definition of refinement in [19]. Two connectors are equivalent if each one of them is a refinement of the other. In the following, we show two examples of such connector refinement and equivalence relations.

Example 3 (Refinement). Taking the two connectors in Fig. 5 into consideration, connector Q is a refinement of connector P (denoted by $P \sqsubseteq Q$).

Connector P   Connector Q

Fig. 5. Example of connector refinement

We have mentioned that newly constructed connectors can be specified as theorems. Given arbitrary input timed data stream at node A and output timed data streams at nodes C, D, essentially connector Q is a refinement of another connector P only if the behavior property of P can be derived from *theorem* Q, i.e., the property of connector Q. Intuitively, connector P enables the data written to the source node A to be asynchronously taken out via the two sink nodes C and D, but it has no constraints on the relationship between the time of the two output events. On the other hand, connector Q refines this behavior by synchronizing the two sink nodes, which means that the two output events must happen simultaneously. To be more precise, we use c,d to denote the time streams of the two outputs and a to denote the time stream of the input. Connector P satisfies condition $a < c \wedge a < d$ and connector Q satisfies $a < c \wedge a < d \wedge c = d$.

The refinement relation can be formally defined in Coq as:

```
Theorem refinement : forall A C D,
(exists B, (FIFO1 A B) /\ (Sync B C) /\ (Sync B D)) ->
(exists E, (Sync A E) /\ (FIFO1 E C) /\ (FIFO1 E D)).
```

To prove this refinement relation, we first introduce a lemma which is frequently used in the proof.

Lemma 1 (Eq). $\forall A,B$: *Stream TD. Sync $(A,B) \Leftrightarrow A=B$.*

The lemma means that *Sync(A,B)* and *A=B* can be derived from each other. Although this lemma seems to make the presence of Sync channels in connectors redundant, it is not the case for most connectors. For example, if we consider the alternator in Example 2, it can not accept any input data if we remove the synchronous channel BC and use one node for it.

By using the axioms for the basic channels and the operators of composition, we can obtain the two connectors easily. In the process of constructing the connectors, the flow-through and replicate operations act once for each connector, respectively.

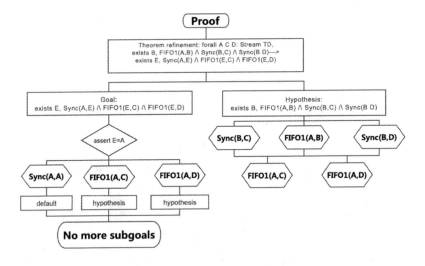

Fig. 6. Proof steps flow chart

Figure 6 shows the flow chart for the proof steps of connector refinement in this example.

We now show the specific tactics used in the proof of refinement $P \sqsubseteq Q$ for connectors P and Q in this example. We need to find a timed data stream which specifies the data-flow through node E of connector P, i.e., we need to find an appropriate E that satisfies $Sync(A, E) \land FIFO1(E, C) \land FIFO1(E, D)$.

First we employ 'intros' to acquire a simpler subgoal $\exists E_0.Sync(A, E_0) \wedge$ $FIFO1(E_0, C) \wedge FIFO1(E_0, D)$. Then we assert that $E = A$. After using 'split', we split the goal into two subgoals *Sync (A, E)* and *FIFO1 (E, C)* $\wedge$ *FIFO1 (E, D)*. And by 'rewrite' H_0 $(H_0: E = A)$, we replace the two subgoals with *Sync (A, A)* and *FIFO1 (E, C)* $\wedge$ *FIFO1 (E, D)*, respectively.

Through 'apply' Lemma 1 *(Eq)*, we have $A = A$ in place of *Sync (A, A)*. Next the tactic *reflexivity* makes the subgoal $A = A$ proved directly. Up to now, the initial subgoal *Sync (A, E)* has been achieved.

Using 'split' again, the remaining unproven subgoal is split into two subgoals *FIFO1 (E, C)* and *FIFO1 (E, D)*. After destructing the precondition three times, we succeed in obtaining three hypotheses: *H: FIFO1 (A, x); H1: Sync (x, C); H2: Sync (x, D)*. Assume x = C and then using tactics *apply Eq* and *assumption*, *assertion* $x = C$ is proved easily. Meanwhile, we get hypothesis *H3: x = C*. Via *Rewrite* $\leftarrow H3$, we bring left in place of the right side of the equation *H3: $x = C$* into *FIFO1 (E, C)* and have *FIFO1 (E, x)*. Similarly, rewrite *H0* and further we get the result *FIFO1 (A, x)* which is exactly hypothesis *H*. By using 'assumption', the second subgoal is proved already. Using substantially the same tactic steps, *FIFO1 (E, D)* can be proved. Finally, we have no more subgoals. Note that there is a new tactic 'reflexivity' used in the proof, which is actually synonymous with 'apply refl equal'. We can use it to prove that two statements are equal (Fig. 7).

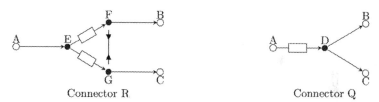

Connector R   Connector Q

Fig. 7. Example of connector equivalence

Example 4 (Equivalence). For the connector P in Example 3, we can add three more basic channels to build a new connector R which is equivalent to Q. R can be interpreted similarly based on basic channels and operators. We will omit the details for its construction here and prove the equivalence between the two connectors R and Q directly.

Equivalence relationship between the two connectors can be formalized as:

```
Theorem equivalence: forall A B C,
  (exists E F G,
    (Sync A E) /\ (FIFO1 E F) /\ (Sync F B) /\
    (FIFO1 E G) /\ (Sync G C) /\ (SyncDrain F G)
  ) <->
  (exists D,
    (FIFO1 A D) /\ (Sync D B) /\ (Sync D C)
  ).
```

The proof of this theorem has two steps. Firstly, we prove that the new connector R is a refinement of connector Q. We hope to find an appropriate D that satisfies

$$FIFO1(A, D) \wedge Sync(D, B) \wedge Sync(D, C)$$

Similar to Example 3, we first assert $D = F$, which leads to

$$FIFO1(A, F) \wedge Sync(F, B) \wedge Sync(F, C)$$

From Lemma 1, we have $Sync(A, E)$, or $A = E$. Therefore, $FIFO1(E,F)$ can be replaced by $FIFO1(A,F)$. By adopting $FIFO1(E,F)$ and $FIFO1(E,G)$, we can prove that the data sequences at F and G are equal. Similarly, data sequences at C, G and F are also equal, wrt. $Sync(G, C)$.

Further according to $Sync(G,C)$ and $Syncdrain(F,G)$, the time sequences at F and C are proved equal. With the combination of relations on time and data between F and C, we can draw the conclusion $Sync(F,C)$.

Up to now, we present a proof for $Sync(F,C)$ and $FIFO1(A,F)$ by the derivation. Besides, $Sync(F,B)$ is already declared in the assumptions. Consequently, the refinement relation has been proved.

Secondly, we prove that connector Q is a refinement of connector R. We hope to find appropriate timed data streams at E,F,G which satisfy

$$Sync(A,E) \ \wedge \ Sync(G,C) \wedge FIFO1(E,G) \wedge Sync(F,B)$$
$$\wedge \ FIFO1(E,F) \wedge Syncdrain(F,G).$$

We can directly assume $E = A$, $F = D$ and $G = D$. Now we only need to prove $Sync(A,A) \wedge Sync(D,C) \wedge FIFO1(A,D) \wedge Sync(D,B) \wedge FIFO1(A,D) \wedge Syncdrain(D,D)$, which can be easily derived from the assumptions.

6   Conclusion and Future Work

In this paper, we present a new approach to model and reason about connectors in the Coq system. The model naturally preserves the original structure of connectors. This also makes the connector description reasonably readable. We implement the proof of properties for connectors using identified techniques and tactics provided by Coq. Properties are defined in terms of predicates which provide an appropriate description of the relation among different timed data streams on the nodes of a connector. All the analysis and verification work are based on the logical framework where basic channels are viewed as axioms and composition operations are viewed as operators. As we can address the relation among different timed data streams, we can easily reason about temporal properties as well as equivalence and refinement relations for connectors.

As some of the benefits of this approach are inherited from Coq, our approach has also got some of its drawbacks as well. The main limitation is that the analysis needs much more tactics and techniques when the constructor becomes large. In the future work, we plan to enhance our framework by two different approaches. Firstly, we may try to encapsulate frequently-used proof patterns as new tactics, which may reduce lots of repetitive work. After that, automation methods may also help us to avoid tons of hand-written proof. For example, Coq provides several auto tactics to solve proof goals. With proper configuration, perhaps such tactics will work well in our framework. More attention is needed to precisely evaluate how expressive this way is for modeling temporal properties.

Acknowledgement. The work was partially supported by the National Natural Science Foundation of China under grant no. 61532019, 61202069 and 61272160.

References

1. Package of source files. https://github.com/liyi-david/reoincoq
2. Aichernig, B.K., Arbab, F., Astefanoaei, L., de Boer, F.S., Sun, M., Rutten, J.: Fault-based test case generation for component connectors. In: Proceedings of TASE 2009, pp. 147–154. IEEE Computer Society (2009)
3. Arbab, F.: Reo: a channel-based coordination model for component composition. Math. Struct. Comput. Sci. **14**(3), 329–366 (2004)
4. Arbab, F., Rutten, J.J.M.M.: A coinductive calculus of component connectors. In: Wirsing, M., Pattinson, D., Hennicker, R. (eds.) WADT 2002. LNCS, vol. 2755, pp. 34–55. Springer, Heidelberg (2003). doi:10.1007/978-3-540-40020-2_2
5. Baier, C., Blechmann, T., Klein, J., Klüppelholz, S., Leister, W.: Design and verification of systems with exogenous coordination using vereofy. In: Margaria, T., Steffen, B. (eds.) ISoLA 2010. LNCS, vol. 6416, pp. 97–111. Springer, Heidelberg (2010). doi:10.1007/978-3-642-16561-0_15
6. Baier, C., Sirjani, M., Arbab, F., Rutten, J.: Modeling component connectors in Reo by constraint automata. Sci. Comput. Program. **61**, 75–113 (2006)
7. Clarke, D., Costa, D., Arbab, F.: Modelling coordination in biological systems. In: Margaria, T., Steffen, B. (eds.) ISoLA 2004. LNCS, vol. 4313, pp. 9–25. Springer, Heidelberg (2006). doi:10.1007/11925040_2
8. de Roever, W.-P., Engelhardt, K.: Data Refinement: Model-Oriented Proof Methods and their Comparison. Cambridge University Press, New York (1998)
9. Huet, G., Kahn, G., Paulin-Mohring, C.: The coq proof assistant a tutorial. Rapport Technique, 178 (1997)
10. Jones, C.B.: Systematic Software Development Using VDM. Prentice-Hall, Upper Saddle River (1990)
11. Jongmans, S.T.Q., Arbab, F.: Overview of thirty semantic formalisms for Reo. Sci. Ann. Comp. Sci. **22**(1), 201–251 (2012)
12. Khosravi, R., Sirjani, M., Asoudeh, N., Sahebi, S., Iravanchi, H.: Modeling and analysis of Reo connectors using alloy. In: Lea, D., Zavattaro, G. (eds.) COORDINATION 2008. LNCS, vol. 5052, pp. 169–183. Springer, Heidelberg (2008). doi:10.1007/978-3-540-68265-3_11
13. Klüppelholz, S., Baier, C.: Symbolic model checking for channel-based component connectors. Sci. Comput. Program. **74**(9), 688–701 (2009)
14. Kokash, N., Krause, C., de Vink, E.: Reo+mCRL2: a framework for model-checking dataflow in service compositions. Formal Aspects Comput. **24**, 187–216 (2012)
15. Li, Y., Sun, M.: Modeling and verification of component connectors in Coq. Sci. Comput. Program. **113**(3), 285–301 (2015)

16. Roscoe, A.W.: The Theory and Practice of Concurrency. Prentice Hall, Upper Saddle River (1998)
17. Sun, M.: Connectors as designs: the time dimension. In: Proceedings of TASE 2012, pp. 201–208. IEEE Computer Society (2012)
18. Sun, M., Arbab, F.: Web services choreography and orchestration in reo and constraint automata. In: Proceedings of SAC 2007, pp. 346–353. ACM (2007)
19. Sun, M., Arbab, F., Aichernig, B.K., Astefanoaei, L., de Boer, F.S., Rutten, J.: Connectors as designs: modeling, refinement and test case generation. Sci. Comput. Program. **77**(7–8), 799–822 (2012)

(Context-Sensitivity In) Reo, Revisited

Sung-Shik T.Q. Jongmans[1,2(⊠)]

[1] School of Computer Science, Open University of the Netherlands,
Heerlen, The Netherlands
ssj@ou.nl
[2] Institute for Computing and Information Sciences,
Radboud University Nijmegen, Nijmegen, The Netherlands

Abstract. Coordination languages emerged for programming interaction protocols among components in component-based systems, in terms of *connectors*. One such language is Reo. Reo facilitates compositional construction of complex composite connectors out of simple primitive ones. Unlike the behavior of connectors in other coordination languages, the behavior of a connector in Reo may depend on whether its coordinated components are ready for I/O. Such behavior is called "context-sensitivity", and its formalization—a nontrivial problem—has received considerable attention from the community. In this paper, I study three common and historically significant primitives in Reo—context-sensitive LossySync, FIFOn, and LossyFIFOn—and prove that they have inconsistent informal semantics. Moreover, four major formal semantics of Reo do not correspond with its foremost alternative informal semantics.

1 Introduction

Background. Coordination languages have emerged for programming interaction protocols among components. One significant such language is *Reo* [1]. Reo enables compositional construction of *connectors*. Connectors are software entities that coordinate the interaction among components. Metaphorically, connectors constitute the "glue" that "sticks" components together. In this paper, I formally show that three common and historically significant Reo connectors have ambiguous semantics. This has gone unnoticed for over ten years.

Figure 1 shows six example connectors in their usual graphical Reo syntax. Briefly, a connector consists of *channels*, through which data items *flow*, and *nodes* (with meaningless names a, b, c, and d), on which channel ends *coincide*. Reo allows programmers to define their own channels, by need, with custom data-flow semantics. Nodes, in contrast to channels, come in three predefined flavors—*source nodes*, *sink nodes*, and *mixed nodes*—and have fixed data-flow semantics. Source and sink nodes constitute the *boundary nodes* of a connector and admit I/O operations from components: source nodes admit `write` operations, while sink nodes admit `take` operations. All I/O operations are blocking: until a connector is ready to accept the data item to be written to a source node, or until a connector is ready to offer a data item to be taken from a sink node,

© Springer International Publishing AG 2017
O. Kouchnarenko and R. Khosravi (Eds.): FACS 2016, LNCS 10231, pp. 191–209, 2017.
DOI: 10.1007/978-3-319-57666-4_12

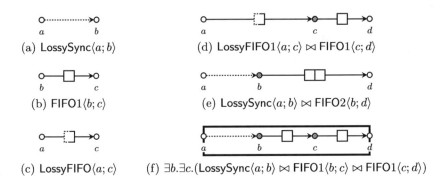

Fig. 1. Example connectors

a write or take on such a node remains *pending*. The *context* of a connector is the collection of pending I/O operations on its boundary nodes. Mixed nodes are used only for internal routing of data items (i.e., components cannot access, or perform I/O operations on, mixed nodes). A connector with mixed nodes is a *composite*; one without mixed nodes is a *primitive*. Section 2 provides details.

Connectors in Reo may exhibit *context-sensitivity* (also known as *context-dependency* or as *context-awareness*). A context-sensitive connector is a connector whose set of admissible execution steps depends on the (un)availability of pending I/O operations on its boundary nodes. A premier example of a context-sensitive connector is LossySync in Fig. 1a. Whenever a component performs a write on the source node of LossySync, if its sink node already has a pending take, LossySync behaves as a classical synchronous channel: both the write and the take synchronously complete, and the data item written to the source node is taken from the sink node in one indivisible transaction (i.e., the data item atomically flows from source to sink). In contrast, whenever a component performs a write on LossySync's source node, if its sink node does *not* have a pending take, LossySync can still accept the data item (after which the write completes), but because there is no component to offer the accepted data item to, LossySync has no choice but to *lose* that data item; LossySync does not have an internal buffer. The set of admissible execution steps of LossySync, thus, depends on whether its sink node has a pending I/O operation—this is context-sensitivity.

If a connector is not context-sensitive, it is *context-free*. An example of a context-free connector is FIFO1 in Fig. 1b. Unlike LossySync, FIFO1 has an internal 1-capacity buffer (initially empty). Whenever a component performs a write on the source node of FIFO1, and if its buffer is empty, the write completes (otherwise, the write remains pending until the buffer becomes empty), and the written data item flows into the buffer. Whenever a component performs a take on the sink node of FIFO1, and if its buffer is full, the take completes (otherwise, the take remains pending until the buffer becomes full), and the previously written data item flows out of the buffer. The set of admissible execution steps of FIFO1, thus, depends only on the state of its buffer and *not* on its context—this is context-freedomİt is straightforward to generalize FIFO1 to FIFOn, where n denotes the capacity of its buffer.

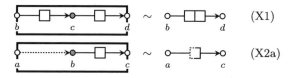

Fig. 2. Example composition axioms, graphically, where $\sim$ denotes congruence

Problem. Context-sensitivity is a powerful behavioral concept that has gained considerable attention from the Reo community. A central research topic has been to define "context-sensitive formal semantics" of Reo, which support expressing context-sensitive behavior. But, although several such semantics have been developed [6,7,11], one particular aspect of context-sensitivity has not received due attention: the consistency of [*composition axioms* for context-sensitive connectors] with [composition axioms for context-free connectors].

For instance, a typical example of a composition axiom for context-free connectors states that the composition of FIFOn and FIFOm (by connecting the sink of the former to the source of the latter) is *congruent*, in the algebraic sense, to FIFO$n+m$ [1–5]. Similarly, a premier example of a composition axiom for context-sensitive connectors states that the composition of LossySync and FIFOn is congruent to LossyFIFOn [6–8], a variant of FIFOn that loses written data items if its n-capacity buffer is full. Figure 2 shows a graphical representation of these axioms (for $n = m = 1$). A crucial question, then, is this: can these two axioms constitute a consistent axiomatic system? Answering this question—the problem addressed in this paper—is imperative, to further advance (if the answer is positive) or rebuild (if negative) Reo's theoretical foundations.

Contribution. I prove that axioms X1 and X2a in Fig. 2 constitute an inconsistent axiomatic system for Reo's informal semantics. Moreover, four major formal semantics of Reo [4–7] do not correspond with its foremost alternative informal semantics (which does not have the inconsistency).

In Sect. 2, I describe preliminaries on Reo. In Sect. 3, I prove the inconsistency result. In Sect. 4, I prove the non-correspondence results. In Sect. 5, I further discuss these results and outline the available options.

2   Preliminaries

Reo is a language for compositional construction of interaction protocols among components, manifested as *connectors* [1]. Connectors in Reo consist of *channels* and *nodes*. Figure 1 shows examples. Every channel consists of two *ends* and a constraint that relates the timing and the content of the data-flows through those ends. A channel end has one of two types: *source ends* accept data, while *sink ends* offer data. Figure 3 shows common and historically significant channels, introduced already in the first journal paper on Reo [1].

Name	Syntax	Semantics
lossysync	···············>	Atomically [accepts a data item x through its source end and either offers x through its sink end (if the connected node is ready to accept) or loses x (otherwise)].
fifo1		If its 1-capacity FIFO buffer is not full: atomically [accepts a data item x through its source end and enqueues x]. If its 1-capacity FIFO buffer is not empty: atomically [dequeues a data item x and offers x through its sink end].
fifo2		The same as fifo1, but with a 2-capacity FIFO buffer. If its buffer is simultaneously not full and not empty, both execution steps are admissible, possibly even simultaneously.
lossyfifo1		If its 1-capacity FIFO buffer is full: atomically [accepts a data item x through its source end and loses x]. Otherwise, the same as fifo1.
lossyfifo2		The same as lossyfifo1 but with a 2-capacity FIFO buffer.

Fig. 3. Name, syntax, and semantics of common channels [1]. The syntaxes for fifo1, fifo2, lossyfifo1, and lossyfifo2 indicate their number of buffered data items.

Channel ends coincide on nodes. Contrasting channels, every node behaves in the same way: repeatedly, it nondeterministically selects an available data item out of one of its coincident sink ends and replicates this data item into each of its coincident source ends. A node's nondeterministic selection and its subsequent replication constitute one atomic execution step; nodes cannot temporarily store, generate, or lose data items. A node with only coincident source ends is called a *source node*; one with only coincident sink ends is called a *sink node*; one with both coincident source ends and coincident sink ends is called a *mixed node*. Source and sink nodes constitute the *boundary nodes* of a connector. As explained already in Sect. 1, the boundary nodes of a connector admit I/O operations—writes and takes—from components. In Fig. 1, I distinguish the white boundary nodes of a connector from its shaded mixed nodes. In this figure, let symbols a, b, c, and d range over nodes (as if they are meaningless names).

Before a connector makes a global execution step, usually instigated by pending I/O operations, its channels and its nodes must have reached *consensus* about their individual behavior, to guarantee collective consistency of their local execution steps (e.g., a node cannot replicate a data item into the source end of a fifo$n$ with an already full buffer). Once consensus is reached, data-flow emerges.

A *primitive* is a connector consisting of two boundary nodes and a channel between them; a *composite* is any connector that is not a primitive. Figures 1a–c show primitives for some of the channels in Fig. 3; Figs. 1d–f show example composites. I write channel names in lowercase sans-serif font, while I write connector names in camelcase sans-serif font, optionally followed by a list of its source nodes and sink nodes, separated by a semicolon.

Through *composition*, programmers can "join" simple connectors into complex ones on their shared nodes. Essentially, the composition of two connectors is their graph-theoretic union. Note that if a shared node is a sink node in one connector, while it is a source node in another connector, that node becomes a mixed node in the composition of those connectors. Textually, I use symbol ⋈ as a binary infix operator for composition, whose operands are connector names (e.g., LossySync$\langle a; b \rangle$ ⋈ FIFO1$\langle b; c \rangle$); because composition is associative and commutative, I omit brackets in ⋈-expressions. Graphically, I use superimposition of shared nodes to represent composition of primitives, such that every connector graph denotes the composition of the primitives it consists of (e.g., Fig. 1f shows the composition of three primitives).

Through *abstraction*, programmers can "hide" mixed nodes in composites, making those nodes no longer amenable to further composition. Textually, I use symbol ∃ as a binary prefix operator for abstraction, whose first operand is a node name, and whose second operand is a connector name. Graphically, I draw a box to represent abstraction, such that all mixed nodes inside such a box are considered hidden (e.g., nodes b and c are considered hidden in Fig. 1f).

3   Inconsistency

This section consists of two subsections. In the first subsection, I informally present an example that indicates that Reo's informal semantics (for LossySync and FIFOn) is *ambiguous*. The argumentation in this first subsection, which I make formally precise in the second subsection, is based on the connectors in Figs. 1d–f, henceforth referred to as Conn[1d], Conn[1e], and Conn[1f].

Example

I start with a general statement: intuitively, abstracting a connector's mixed nodes should not affect the observable data-flows through the boundary nodes of that connector. Consequently, under the composition axioms informally stated in Sect. 1 (and shown in Fig. 2), one should expect the observable data-flows through the boundary nodes of Conn[1f] to be the same as those through the boundary nodes of Conn[1d] and Conn[1e]. In particular, under the same (traces of) write and take operations performed by their connected processes, Conn[1d], Conn[1e], and Conn[1f] should lose the same written data items.

Figure 4a shows the execution tree of Conn[1d]. At the first level of the tree, Conn[1d] has only one admissible execution step (Step 1): a write completes on the source node, causing a data item to flow into the buffer of LossyFIFO1. In Fig. 4a, this data-flow is highlighted by the purple region at the second level. Importantly, LossyFIFO1 *cannot* lose this first written data item, because its buffer is initially empty (as described in Fig. 3). After this first execution step, Conn[1d] chooses one out of three admissible execution steps:

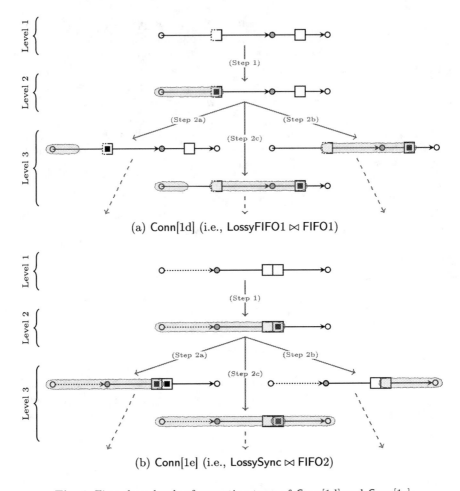

(a) Conn[1d] (i.e., LossyFIFO1 ⋈ FIFO1)

(b) Conn[1e] (i.e., LossySync ⋈ FIFO2)

Fig. 4. First three levels of execution trees of Conn[1d] and Conn[1e]

- (Step 2a) LossyFIFO1 accepts a data item written on its source node, but because its buffer is full, LossyFIFO1 *must* lose that written data item.
- (Step 2b) The data item in the buffer of LossyFIFO1 flows out of that buffer, past the mixed node, into the buffer of FIFO1. An external observer cannot directly observe this execution step, because it involves no boundary nodes.
- (Step 2c) The parallel execution of both Step 2a and Step 2b.

Step 2a and Step 2c are *truly* possible only if the source node has a pending write. If so, in fact, all three execution steps are possible, and Conn[1d] chooses one out of them *nondeterministically*. The key observation to make here, then, is that Conn[1d] can nondeterministically lose the second written data item.

Figure 4b shows the execution tree of Conn[1e]. At the first level of the tree, Conn[1e] has only one admissible execution step (Step 1): a write completes on the source node, causing a data item to flow past the mixed node, into the

$$\exists c.(\mathsf{FIFO1}\langle b; c\rangle \bowtie \mathsf{FIFO1}\langle c; d\rangle) \quad \sim \quad \mathsf{FIFO2}\langle b; d\rangle \qquad\qquad (X1)$$

$$\exists b.(\mathsf{LossySync}\langle a; b\rangle \bowtie \mathsf{FIFO1}\langle b; c\rangle) \quad \sim \quad \mathsf{LossyFIFO1}\langle a; c\rangle \qquad\qquad (X2a)$$

$$\exists b.(\mathsf{LossySync}\langle a; b\rangle \bowtie \mathsf{FIFO2}\langle b; d\rangle) \quad \sim \quad \mathsf{LossyFIFO2}\langle a; d\rangle \qquad\qquad (X2b)$$

$$\exists c.(\mathsf{LossyFIFO1}\langle a; c\rangle \bowtie \mathsf{FIFO1}\langle c; d\rangle) \quad \nsim \quad \mathsf{LossyFIFO2}\langle a; d\rangle \qquad\qquad (\overline{X3})$$

$$(C_1 \bowtie C_2) \bowtie C_3 \quad \sim \quad C_1 \bowtie (C_2 \bowtie C_3) \qquad\qquad (Y1)$$

$$C_1 \bowtie (\exists a.C_2) \quad \sim \quad \exists a.(C_1 \bowtie C_2) \text{ if } a \notin C_1 \qquad\qquad (Y2a)$$

$$(\exists a.C_1) \bowtie C_2 \quad \sim \quad \exists a.(C_1 \bowtie C_2) \text{ if } a \notin C_2 \qquad\qquad (Y2b)$$

$$\exists a.\exists b.C \quad \sim \quad \exists b.\exists a.C \qquad\qquad (Y3)$$

Fig. 5. Axioms for FIFO1, FIFO2, LossySync, LossyFIFO1, and LossyFIFO2

buffer of FIFO2. Just as LossyFIFO1 in Conn[1d], LossySync in Conn[1e] *cannot* lose this first written data item. Subsequently, Conn[1e] chooses one out of three admissible execution steps. This choice of Conn[1e], however, significantly differs from the choice of Conn[1d]: because the 2-capacity buffer of FIFO2 in Conn[1e] is not yet full—it contains only one data item—it still accepts any data item offered through the mixed node. Consequently, whenever a second `write` on the source node completes, LossySync is *not* allowed to lose the written data item but *must* offer it through the mixed node to FIFO2 (filling the latter's buffer).

To summarize, whereas Conn[1d] *can* nondeterministically lose the second written data item, Conn[1e] *cannot*. This, then, indeed makes the informal semantics of Conn[1f] ambiguous: after all, as argued for in the beginning of this subsection, one intuitively should expect the lossy behavior of Conn[1f] to be the same as the lossy behavior of *both* Conn[1d] *and* Conn[1e].

Axioms and Result

The previous example indicates that Reo's informal semantics (for LossySync and FIFOn) is ambiguous. To make this intuition formally precise, first, Fig. 5 shows a little axiomatic system for FIFO1, FIFO2, LossySync, LossyFIFO1, and LossyFIFO2, where symbol $\sim$ denotes congruence, in the algebraic sense. As before, let symbols a, b, c, and d range over nodes, let symbol C_i range over connectors, and let $a \notin C_i$ mean that node a does not occur in connector C_i.

Axiom X1 is an axiom of context-freedom (see also Sect. 1) [1,3,4]. This axiom essentially assumes "weak semantic" (i.e., it abstracts from internal steps), enforced by using abstraction in X1's formulation. In contrast, a "strong(er) semantics", without abstraction, would distinguish [the composition of FIFOn and FIFOm] from FIFO$n+m$ (i.e., the former has an internal step where a data item shifts from one buffer to the next, which the latter has not). Because Reo's informal semantics abstracts from internal behavior, we need weak semantics. This is also reflected in the fact that showing soundness of X1 is a standard example for new formal semantics of Reo (e.g., [2,5,6,8]).

Axioms X2a/b are axioms of context-sensitivity (see also Sect. 1) [6,7].

Axiom $\overline{\text{X3}}$ states that the composition of LossyFIFO1 and FIFO1 is *incongruent* to LossyFIFO2. Note that $\overline{\text{X3}}$ involves only context-free connectors. The argumentation why $\overline{\text{X3}}$ is valid follows the previous subsection. Basically, whenever LossyFIFO1 in the composite on the left-hand side of $\sim$ has a full buffer, until the data item in this buffer is transferred into the buffer of FIFO1, data items written on a are lost. Crucially, Reo's informal semantics does not state that the transfer of a data item from one buffer to the next *must* happen before data items are accepted through a; only LossyFIFO1 makes the choice between first-transferring and first-losing, nondeterministically. LossyFIFO2 on the right-hand side, in contrast, never loses the second data item written on a. $\overline{\text{X3}}$ is the result of the high *autonomy* that primitives in Reo have: LossyFIFO1 and FIFO1 have too much autonomy for them to invasively influence each other's behavior.

Finally, composition is associative (Y1), abstraction distributes over composition for unshared nodes (Y2a/b), and abstractions commute (Y3).

Intuitively, the following theorem formally establishes that connectors consisting of LossySync and FIFOn can have ambiguous semantics. In terms of the example in the previous subsection, note that Conn[1e] appears on line 2 in the derivation in the upcoming proof, Conn[1d] on line 8, and Conn[1f] on lines 4–6.

Theorem 1. *The axiomatic system in Fig. 5 is inconsistent.*

Proof. Deduce:

$$
\begin{array}{llll}
1 & & \text{LossyFIFO2}\langle a; d\rangle & \\
2 & \sim & \exists b.(\text{LossySync}\langle a; b\rangle \bowtie \text{FIFO2}\langle b; d\rangle) & \{\text{X2b}\} \\
3 & \sim & \exists b.(\text{LossySync}\langle a; b\rangle \bowtie \exists c.(\text{FIFO1}\langle b; c\rangle \bowtie \text{FIFO1}\langle c; d\rangle)) & \{\text{X1}\} \\
4 & \sim & \exists b.\exists c.(\text{LossySync}\langle a; b\rangle \bowtie (\text{FIFO1}\langle b; c\rangle \bowtie \text{FIFO1}\langle c; d\rangle)) & \{\text{Y2a}\} \\
5 & \sim & \exists b.\exists c.((\text{LossySync}\langle a; b\rangle \bowtie \text{FIFO1}\langle b; c\rangle) \bowtie \text{FIFO1}\langle c; d\rangle) & \{\text{Y1}\} \\
6 & \sim & \exists c.\exists b.((\text{LossySync}\langle a; b\rangle \bowtie \text{FIFO1}\langle b; c\rangle) \bowtie \text{FIFO1}\langle c; d\rangle) & \{\text{Y3}\} \\
7 & \sim & \exists c.(\exists b.(\text{LossySync}\langle a; b\rangle \bowtie \text{FIFO1}\langle b; c\rangle) \bowtie \text{FIFO1}\langle c; d\rangle) & \{\text{Y2b}\} \\
8 & \sim & \exists c.(\text{LossyFIFO1}\langle a; c\rangle \bowtie \text{FIFO1}\langle c; d\rangle) & \{\text{X2a}\} \\
9 & \not\sim & \text{LossyFIFO2}\langle a; d\rangle & \{\overline{\text{X3}}\} \\
\end{array}
$$

Thus: LossyFIFO2$\langle a; d\rangle \not\sim$ LossyFIFO2$\langle a; d\rangle$.   □

The axiomatic system in Fig. 5 and Theorem 1 are *general* in the sense that they are formulated at the syntactic level (i.e., in terms of connector names) rather than at the semantic level (i.e., in terms of concrete objects for connectors in a particular formal semantics). However, the axiomatic system and Theorem 1 are also *specific* in the sense that they are formulated in terms of concrete primitives instead of in terms of abstract properties (e.g., "statefulness", "context-sensitivity"). Although LossySync and FIFOn are essential in Reo, which justifies their axiomatization, lifting the axiomatic system from these concrete primitives to abstract properties as a further generalization seems worth pursuing, such that the axiomatic system in Fig. 5 can be *derived* from such a generalization. I leave such a generalization for future work.

4   Unsoundness

To resolve the inconsistency in Reo's informal semantics (Theorem 1), one should withdraw one (or more) of the axioms in Fig. 5. For the Xi-axioms, because these axioms involve concrete primitives, a withdrawal necessarily means the assertion of a negation. For instance, the composition of two FIFO1 either *is* (X1) or *is not* ($\overline{\text{X1}}$) congruent to FIFO2; leaving this unspecified would result in an unworkable situation where two implementations of Reo may behave differently.

Axioms X1 and X2a/X2b being well-established in the literature [1–8], then, the foremost resolution of the inconsistency is to negate $\overline{\text{X3}}$ into X3.

$$\exists n_2.(\mathsf{LossyFIFO1}\langle a; c\rangle \bowtie \mathsf{FIFO1}\langle c; d\rangle) \quad \sim \quad \mathsf{LossyFIFO2}\langle a; d\rangle \qquad \text{(X3)}$$

In this section, I study the consequences of this alternative informal semantics. Specifically, I show that X3 is unsound in four major formal semantics of Reo.

With "formal semantics", I mean a *formalism* (including composition/abstraction operations and congruence) *plus objects* in that formalism for the behavior of primitives. (It is possible, thus, to define two *different* formal semantics of Reo in the same formalism but with different objects for primitives [9].)

Notably, two of the four formal semantics considered in this section (those based on timed data streams and constraint automata) do not support expressing context-sensitive behavior. In these formal semantics, thus, already axioms X2a/b are unsound. This is well-known in the Reo community [6–8], though, and not up for debate here. The actual issue identified in this section is that also X3 is unsound in these two formal semantics. This is interesting, because X3 involves only context-free connectors; unsoundness of X3 can, thus, not be attributed to those semantics' lack of support for context-sensitivity.

Timed Data Streams

Reo's first formal semantics is based on *timed data streams* [2,4]. A timed data stream for a node a is a pair $(\alpha, \mathbb{A})$ consisting of two infinite sequences— "streams"—namely a *data stream* α of data items and a *time stream* $\mathbb{A}$ of monotonically increasing real numbers. Let $\alpha(i)$ and $\mathbb{A}(i)$ denote the i-th element in α and $\mathbb{A}$, and let α' and $\mathbb{A}'$ denote the tails of α and $\mathbb{A}$ (aka their *derivatives*). Also, for time streams $\mathbb{A}$ and $\mathbb{B}$, let $\mathbb{A} < \mathbb{B}$ abbreviate for $\left[\mathbb{A}(i) < \mathbb{B}(i) \textbf{ for all } i \geq 0\right]$.

Every timed data stream describes the observable data-flow through a node: a timed data stream $(\alpha, \mathbb{A})$ for a node a states that data item $\alpha(i)$ flows through a at time $\mathbb{A}(i)$, for all $i \geq 0$. Using timed data streams, then, one can define the semantics of a connector as a k-ary relation on timed data streams for its boundary nodes. Figure 6 shows examples. Figure 6a, for instance, states that a pair of timed data streams is in the relation for FIFO1, denoted by $\xmapsto{\text{FIFO1}}$, iff the data streams are equal (i.e., all data items written into a FIFO1 are eventually taken out), and the time streams "alternate" (i.e., between every two consecutive `writes` on the source node is a `take` on the sink node).

$$(\gamma, \mathbb{C}) \xrightarrow{\text{FIFO1}} (\delta, \mathbb{D}) \;\equiv\; \mathbb{C} < \mathbb{D} < \mathbb{C}' \wedge \gamma = \delta$$

(a) FIFO1$\langle c; d \rangle$

$$(\alpha, \mathbb{A}) \xrightarrow{\text{LossyFIFO1}} (\gamma, \mathbb{C}) \;\equiv\; \mathbb{A}(0) < \mathbb{C}(0) \wedge \alpha(0) = \gamma(0) \wedge (\alpha', \mathbb{A}') \xrightarrow{\text{LossyFIFO1}'} (\gamma, \mathbb{C})$$

$$(\alpha, \mathbb{A}) \xrightarrow{\text{LossyFIFO1}'} (\gamma, \mathbb{C}) \;\equiv\; \mathbb{A}(0) < \mathbb{C}(0) \wedge (\alpha', \mathbb{A}') \xrightarrow{\text{LossyFIFO1}} (\gamma', \mathbb{C})$$
$$\vee \quad \mathbb{A}(0) = \mathbb{C}(0) \wedge (\alpha', \mathbb{A}') \xrightarrow{\text{LossyFIFO1}} (\gamma', \mathbb{C}')$$
$$\vee \quad \mathbb{A}(0) > \mathbb{C}(0) \wedge (\alpha, \mathbb{A}) \xrightarrow{\text{LossyFIFO1}} (\gamma', \mathbb{C}')$$

(b) LossyFIFO1$\langle a; c \rangle$

$$(\alpha, \mathbb{A}) \xrightarrow{\text{LossyFIFO2}} (\delta, \mathbb{D}) \;\equiv\; \mathbb{A}(0) < \mathbb{D}(0) \wedge \alpha(0) = \delta(0) \wedge (\alpha', \mathbb{A}') \xrightarrow{\text{LossyFIFO2}'} (\delta, \mathbb{D})$$

$$(\alpha, \mathbb{A}) \xrightarrow{\text{LossyFIFO2}'} (\delta, \mathbb{D}) \;\equiv\; \mathbb{A}(0) < \mathbb{D}(0) \wedge \alpha(0) = \delta'(0) \wedge (\alpha', \mathbb{A}') \xrightarrow{\text{LossyFIFO2}''} (\delta, \mathbb{D})$$
$$\vee \quad \mathbb{A}(0) = \mathbb{D}(0) \wedge \alpha(0) = \delta'(0) \wedge (\alpha', \mathbb{A}') \xrightarrow{\text{LossyFIFO2}'} (\delta', \mathbb{D}')$$
$$\vee \quad \mathbb{A}(0) > \mathbb{D}(0) \wedge (\alpha, \mathbb{A}) \xrightarrow{\text{LossyFIFO2}} (\delta', \mathbb{D}')$$

$$(\alpha, \mathbb{A}) \xrightarrow{\text{LossyFIFO2}''} (\delta, \mathbb{D}) \;\equiv\; \mathbb{A}(0) < \mathbb{D}(0) \wedge (\alpha', \mathbb{A}') \xrightarrow{\text{LossyFIFO2}''} (\delta, \mathbb{D})$$
$$\vee \quad \mathbb{A}(0) = \mathbb{D}(0) \wedge (\alpha', \mathbb{A}') \xrightarrow{\text{LossyFIFO2}'} (\delta', \mathbb{D}')$$
$$\vee \quad \mathbb{A}(0) > \mathbb{D}(0) \wedge (\alpha, \mathbb{A}) \xrightarrow{\text{LossyFIFO2}'} (\delta', \mathbb{D}')$$

(c) LossyFIFO2$\langle a; d \rangle$

Fig. 6. Timed data streams semantics of FIFO1, LossyFIFO1, and LossyFIFO2

Under their timed data stream semantics, two connectors are congruent iff their relations are equal iff their relation's predicates are logically equivalent.

To compute the timed data streams semantics of a composite, one can apelational composition, denoted by $\circ$, to the relations for its constituent primitives, by taking the conjunction of those relations' predicates (composition), and by existentially quantifying timed data streams for nonboundary nodes (abstraction). An example of such conjunctions and existential quantifications appears in the proof of the following theorem. Arbab and Rutten [4], and Arbab [2], give more details and examples of Reo's timed data streams semantics.

Theorem 2. X3 *is unsound in the timed data streams semantics.*

Proof. By computing the conjunction of the predicates of $\xrightarrow{\text{LossyFIFO1}}$ and $\xrightarrow{\text{FIFO1}}$ under existential quantification of node c, derive the timed data streams semantics of $\exists c.(\text{LossyFIFO1}\langle a; c \rangle \bowtie \text{FIFO1}\langle c; d \rangle)$ as follows:

$$(\alpha, \mathbb{A}) \xrightarrow{\text{LossyFIFO1}} \circ \xrightarrow{\text{FIFO1}} (\delta, \mathbb{D})$$

$$\equiv \; \exists (\gamma, \mathbb{C}) : \mathbb{A}(0) < \mathbb{C}(0) \wedge \alpha(0) = \gamma(0) \wedge (\alpha', \mathbb{A}') \xrightarrow{\text{LossyFIFO1}'} (\gamma, \mathbb{C})$$
$$\wedge \, \mathbb{C} < \mathbb{D} < \mathbb{C}' \wedge \gamma = \delta$$

$$\equiv \qquad \mathbb{A}(0) < \mathbb{D}(0) \wedge \alpha(0) = \delta(0) \wedge \exists (\gamma, \mathbb{C}) : (\alpha', a') \xrightarrow{\text{LossyFIFO1}'} (\delta, \mathbb{C})$$
$$\wedge \, \mathbb{C} < \mathbb{D} < \mathbb{C}'$$

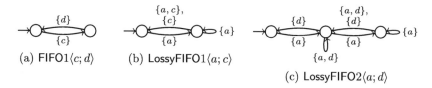

(a) FIFO1$\langle c; d \rangle$ (b) LossyFIFO1$\langle a; c \rangle$ (c) LossyFIFO2$\langle a; d \rangle$

Fig. 7. Constraint automata semantics of FIFO1, LossyFIFO1, and LossyFIFO2

Compare the derived predicate to the predicate of $\xrightarrow{\text{LossyFIFO2}}$ in Fig. 6c, and observe that it suffices to show that the existential quantification in the derived predicate, in purple, is inequivalent to the predicate of $\xrightarrow{\text{LossyFIFO2'}}$. Now, derive:

$$\exists (\gamma, \mathbb{C}) : (\alpha', \mathbb{A}') \xrightarrow{\text{LossyFIFO1'}} (\delta, \mathbb{C}) \wedge \mathbb{C} < \mathbb{D} < \mathbb{C}'$$

$$\equiv \quad \exists (\gamma, \mathbb{C}) : \mathbb{A}(0) < \mathbb{C}(0) \wedge \top \wedge (\alpha', \mathbb{A}') \xrightarrow{\text{LossyFIFO1'}} (\delta, \mathbb{C}) \wedge \mathbb{C} < \mathbb{D} < \mathbb{C}'$$

$$\vee \quad \ldots \quad \vee \quad \ldots$$

$$\equiv \quad \exists (\gamma, \mathbb{C}) : \mathbb{A}(0) < \mathbb{D}(0) \wedge \top \wedge (\alpha', \mathbb{A}') \xrightarrow{\text{LossyFIFO1'}} (\delta, \mathbb{C}) \quad \vee \quad \ldots \quad \vee \quad \ldots$$

In this derivation, the dots ("...") stand for two redundant—in this proof—disjuncts. The differences between the derived predicate and (the first disjunct in) the predicate of $\xrightarrow{\text{LossyFIFO2'}}$, in purple, are $\top$ (vs. $\alpha(0) = \delta'(0)$) and $\xrightarrow{\text{LossyFIFO1'}}$ (vs. $\xrightarrow{\text{LossyFIFO2''}}$). This means that the second written data item can be lost according to the former relation, whereas it is preserved according to the latter relation. To make this formally precise, define the following timed data streams:

$$\begin{pmatrix} \widetilde{\alpha} \\ \widetilde{\mathbb{A}} \end{pmatrix} = \begin{pmatrix} 1, & 2, & 3, & \kappa \\ 0.1, & 0.2, & 0.3, & \mathbb{K} \end{pmatrix} \qquad \begin{pmatrix} \widetilde{\delta} \\ \widetilde{\mathbb{D}} \end{pmatrix} = \begin{pmatrix} 1, & 3, & \lambda \\ 0.25, & 0.35, & \mathbb{L} \end{pmatrix}$$

such that $(\kappa, \mathbb{K}) \xrightarrow{\text{LossyFIFO1}} \circ \xrightarrow{\text{FIFO1}} (\lambda, \mathbb{L})$ (e.g., $\kappa = \lambda = \{i \mapsto 1 \mid i \geq 0\}$ and $\mathbb{K} = \{i \mapsto i + 4 \mid i \geq 0\}$ and $\mathbb{L} = \{i \mapsto i + 4.5 \mid i \geq 0\}$). Using the previously derived predicates, then, conclude $(\widetilde{\alpha}, \widetilde{\mathbb{A}}) \xrightarrow{\text{LossyFIFO1}} \circ \xrightarrow{\text{FIFO1}} (\widetilde{\delta}, \widetilde{\mathbb{D}})$, but *not* $(\widetilde{\alpha}, \widetilde{\mathbb{A}}) \xrightarrow{\text{LossyFIFO2}} (\widetilde{\delta}, \widetilde{\mathbb{D}})$, such that $\xrightarrow{\text{LossyFIFO1}} \circ \xrightarrow{\text{FIFO1}} \neq \xrightarrow{\text{LossyFIFO2}}$. Thus, the timed data streams semantics violate X3. $\square$

Constraint Automata

Reo's second formal semantics is based on *constraint automata* [5]. A constraint automaton is a tuple $(Q, \mathcal{N}, \longrightarrow, Q_0)$ consisting of a set of *states* Q, a set of *nodes* $\mathcal{N}$, a *transition relation* $\longrightarrow \subseteq Q \times 2^{\mathcal{N}} \times Q$, and a set of *initial states* Q_0.

Every transition $q \xrightarrow{N} q'$ describes an execution step of a connector, where data items synchronously flow through the nodes in N. As such, N is called the *synchronization constraint* of the transition. Originally, in addition to a synchronization constraint, every transition in a constraint automaton also carries a *data constraint*. Data constraints are logical assertions that specify which particular data items may be observed on the nodes that participate in a transition. Because data constraints do not matter in what follows, however, I omit them from the definitions (technically, I consider *port automata* [10]). Figure 7 shows examples. Figure 7a, for instance, states that initially, in its left-hand state (empty buffer), the constraint automaton for FIFO1 can make a transition in which a data item flows through node c (and into the buffer). In its right-hand state (full buffer), the constraint automaton can make a transition in which a data item flows (out of the buffer and) through node d. If there are multiple transitions between the same two states, I draw only one arrow with multiple labels, separated by a comma. In Fig. 7b, for instance, there are two transitions from the right-hand state to the left-hand state, represented by one arrow.

Under their constraint automata semantics, two connectors are congruent if their constraint automata are *bisimilar*. In the absence of data constraints, this coincides with bisimilarity on transition systems labeled with node sets [10].

To compute the constraint automata semantics of a composite, one can apply a *join operation*, denoted by $\bowtie$, and a *hide operation*, denoted by $\exists$, to the constraint automata for its constituent primitives. Let $\mathcal{A}_1 = (Q_1, \mathcal{N}_1, \longrightarrow_1, Q_{0,1})$ and $\mathcal{A}_2 = (Q_2, \mathcal{N}_2, \longrightarrow_2, Q_{0,2})$ be two constraint automata. The join of $\mathcal{A}_1$ and $\mathcal{A}_2$ is defined as $(Q_1 \times Q_2, \mathcal{N}_1 \cup \mathcal{N}_2, \longrightarrow_\bowtie, Q_{0,1} \times Q_{0,2})$, where $\longrightarrow_\bowtie$ is the smallest relation induced by the following two rules:

$$\frac{q_1 \xrightarrow{N_1}_1 q_1' \text{ and } q_2 \xrightarrow{N_2}_2 q_2' \quad q_1 \xrightarrow{N_1}_1 q_1' \text{ and } q_2 \in Q_2}{\text{and } \mathcal{N}_1 \cap N_2 = \mathcal{N}_2 \cap N_1 \qquad \text{and } \mathcal{N}_2 \cap N_1 = \emptyset}$$

$$\frac{}{(q_1, q_2) \xrightarrow{N_1 \cup N_2}_\bowtie (q_1', q_2') \qquad (q_1, q_2) \xrightarrow{N_1}_\bowtie (q_1', q_2)} \tag{1}$$

plus a symmetric version of the right-hand rule. The hide of a in a constraint automaton $\mathcal{A} = (Q, \mathcal{N}, \longrightarrow, Q_0)$ is defined as $(Q, \mathcal{N} \setminus \{n\}, \longrightarrow_\exists, Q_{0,\exists})$, where $\longrightarrow_\exists$ is the smallest relation induced by the following rules:

$$\frac{q_1 \xrightarrow{\{a\}} \cdots \xrightarrow{\{a\}} q_k \xrightarrow{N} q_{k+1} \text{ and } N \neq \{a\} \qquad q \xrightarrow{N} q' \text{ and } N \neq \{a\}}{q_1 \xrightarrow{N \setminus \{a\}}_\exists q_{k+1} \qquad\qquad q \xrightarrow{N \setminus \{a\}}_\exists q'} \tag{2}$$

and where $Q_{0,\exists} = Q_0 \cup \{q \mid q_0 \in Q_0 \text{ and } q_0 \xrightarrow{\{a\}} \cdots \xrightarrow{\{a\}} q\}$. The idea is that sequences of internal transitions *after* hiding a (i.e., $\{a\}$-labeled transitions *before* hiding a) are merged with a non-internal transition, such that only non-internal transitions remain. An example of joining and hiding appears in the proof of the following theorem. Baier et al. [5] give more details and examples of Reo's constraint automata semantics.

Theorem 3. X3 *is unsound in the constraint automata semantics.*

Proof. By applying the definitions of ⋈ and ∃, derive the constraint automata semantics of $\exists c.(\mathsf{LossyFIFO1}\langle a; c\rangle \bowtie \mathsf{FIFO1}\langle c; d\rangle)$ as follows:

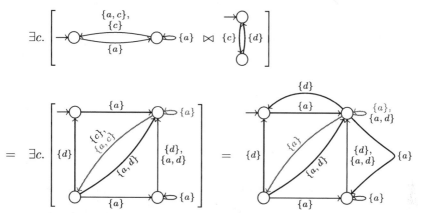

Compare the derived constraint automaton to the constraint automaton for

LossyFIFO2 in Fig. 7c, and observe that the former has transitions out of its second state, in purple, that cannot be simulated by the latter (i.e., the second written data item can be lost according to the former, whereas it is preserved according to the latter); these two constraint automata are not bisimilar. Thus, the constraint automata semantics violates X3. □

Connector Coloring

Reo's first context-sensitive formal semantics is based on *connector coloring* [7,8]. A *coloring* is a map from nodes to *colors*. A *coloring table* is a set of colorings. A *next function* is a map from [coloring table, coloring]-pairs to coloring tables.

Every coloring $\mathfrak{c}$ describes an execution step of a connector, where every node $a \in \mathrm{Dom}(\mathfrak{c})$ behaves according to color $\mathfrak{c}(a)$. For instance, $\mathfrak{c}(a) = $ ——— means that a data item flows through a, where ——— denotes the *flow color*. Another color is the *no-write color*. This color is assigned to a node a if no data item flows through a *because* a write to initiate such a flow is missing. The third and last color is, symmetrically, the *no-take color*. A coloring table describes the set of admissible execution steps of a connector in some internal state (cf. states in constraint automata); a next function describes changes in such sets as the internal state evolves (cf. transition in constraint automata). Figure 8 shows examples. Figure 8a, for instance, states that the coloring table for an empty FIFO1, t_1, has two colorings. The first coloring describes an execution step where a data item flows through node c (into the buffer), while no data item flows through node d, *because* d has no pending write (such a write should come from the FIFO1 itself, but its buffer is empty); subsequently, FIFO1 behaves according to coloring table t_2. In figures, thus, the coloring tables referenced between square brackets represent (images of) next functions. The second coloring in t_1 states

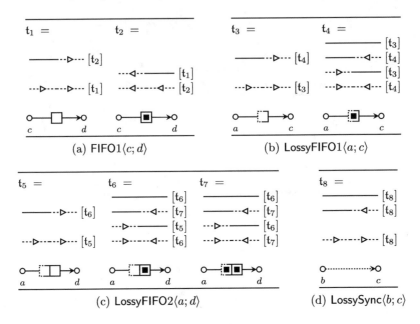

Fig. 8. Connector coloring semantics of FIFO1, LossyFIFO1, and LossyFIFO2

that a data item flows neither through c nor through d, *because* neither of these nodes has a pending `write`. In figures, thus, the no-`write` color is drawn as a dashed line with a triangle that points *toward* a sink node or *away from* a source node; conversely, the no-`take` color is drawn as a dashed line with a triangle that points *away from* a sink node or *toward* a source node. By these drawing conventions, the arrows always point away from primitives that *provide* a reason-for-no-flow, toward primitives that *require* a reason-for-no-flow.

Under their connector coloring semantics, two connectors are congruent if their next functions, coloring tables, and colorings are equal.

To compute the connector coloring semantics of a composite, one can apply *join operations* on coloring tables and next functions, denoted by $\cdot$ and $\otimes$. Although *hide operations* have later been added [8], they violate axioms Y2a/b. Let t_1 and t_2 be coloring tables. The join of t_1 and t_2 is defined as:

$$\{c_1 \cup c_2 \mid (c_1, c_2) \in t_1 \times t_2 \text{ and } \big[c_1(a) = c_2(a) \text{ for all } a \in \mathrm{Dom}(c_1) \cap \mathrm{Dom}(c_2)\big]\}$$

Let n_1 and n_2 be next functions. The join of n_1 and n_2 is defined as:

$$\{(t_1 \cdot t_2, c_1 \cup c_2) \mapsto n_1(t_1, c_1) \cdot n_2(t_2, c_2) \mid c_1 \cup c_2 \in t_1 \cdot t_2\}$$

Graphically, due to how the no-`write` and no-`take` colors are represented, joining essentially comes down to "matching flow and arrow directions". (The details are slightly more involved than this, but as the examples in this paper work also without the *flip-rule* [7], I skip the details.) An example of joining appears in the proof of the following theorem. Clarke et al. [7] and Costa [8] give more details and examples of Reo's connector coloring semantics.

Theorem 4. X3 *is unsound in the connector coloring semantics.*

Proof. By applying the definitions of · and ⊗, and by *ignoring* mixed node c (as a "poor man's hide"), derive the connector coloring semantics of $\exists c_2.(\mathsf{LossyFIFO1}\langle a; c\rangle \bowtie \mathsf{FIFO1}\langle c; d\rangle)$. Two of the four resulting coloring tables   are:

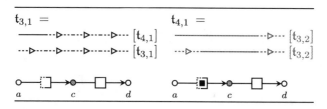

Compare the derived coloring tables to coloring tables t_5 and t_6 in Fig. 8c. Ignoring node c, observe that t_5 contains exactly the same colorings as coloring table $t_{3,1}$. However, still ignoring c, observe that t_6 contains neither of the two colorings in coloring table $t_{4,1}$. In particular, both colorings in $t_{4,1}$ state that node d has no pending **write**, while there is no such coloring in t_6 (nor can the flip-rule [7] be used to recover such a coloring in t_6). Consequently, the next function for $\exists c.(\mathsf{LossyFIFO1}\langle a; c\rangle \bowtie \mathsf{FIFO1}\langle c; d\rangle)$ and the next function for $\mathsf{LossyFIFO2}\langle a; d\rangle)$ are unequal. Thus, the connector coloring semantics violates X3. □

Guarded Automata

Another major context-sensitive formal semantics of Reo is based on *guarded automata* [6]. Guarded automata can be seen as an extension of constraint automata, where every synchronization constraint on a transition is prefixed with a *guard* γ. A guard is a boolean expression over nodes (notation: overlines for negation, juxtaposition for conjunction). A guard states which nodes *must*, and which nodes *must not*, have a pending I/O-operation for a transition to fire. For instance, guard ac means that nodes a and c each must have a pending I/O operation; guard $a\bar{c}$ means that a must, while c must not, have a pending I/O operation. Figure 9 shows examples (cf. Fig. 7).

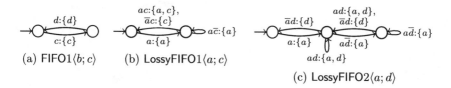

Fig. 9. Guarded automata semantics of LossyFIFO1, FIFO1, and LossyFIFO2

Under their guarded automata semantics, two connectors are congruent if their guarded automata are *bisimilar* (cf. constraint automata bisimilarity [6]).

The join and hide operations on constraint automata, $\bowtie$ and $\exists$, are extended to handle guards as follows. In the premise of the left-hand rule in (1), N_1 and N_2 are prefixed with guards γ_1 and γ_2, while in its conclusion, $N_1 \cup N_2$ is prefixed with guard $\gamma_1 \gamma_2$. In the premise of the right-hand rule in (1), N_1 is prefixed with a guard γ_1, while in its conclusion, N_1 is prefixed with guard $\gamma_1 \gamma_{q_2}^\sharp$. Here, $\gamma_{q_2}^\sharp$ stands for [the negation of [the disjunction of [the guards of the transitions from state q_2]]]. Additionally, an extra condition "$\gamma \not\Rightarrow \overline{ab}$" needs to be satisfied in both rules; I mention this here for completeness, but refer to Bonsangue et al. for details and a motivation [6, Definition 4.11 and Sect. 6.5]. In the premise of the rules in (2), $\{a\}$ and N are prefixed with guards a and γ, while in its conclusion, $N \setminus \{a\}$ is prefixed with guard γ. Originally, the join operation on guarded automata was split into two suboperations [6]: *product* and *synchronization*. For simplicity, I merged these operations together. An example of joining and hiding appears in the proof of the following theorem. Bonsangue et al. [6] give more details and examples of Reo's guarded automata semantics.

Theorem 5. X3 *is unsound in the guarded automata semantics.*

Proof. By applying the definitions of $\bowtie$ and $\exists$, derive the guarded automata semantics of $\exists c.(\mathsf{LossyFIFO1}\langle a; c \rangle \bowtie \mathsf{FIFO1}\langle c; d \rangle)$ as follows:

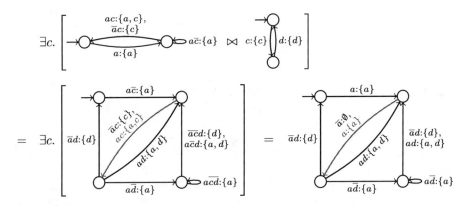

Compare this guarded automaton to the guarded automaton for LossyFIFO2 in Fig. 9c, and observe that the former has transitions out of its second state, in purple, that cannot be simulated by the latter (i.e., the second written data item can be lost according to the former, whereas it is preserved according to the latter); these two guarded automata are not bisimilar. Thus, the guarded automata semantics violates X3.   □

5   Discussion

I set out to study whether axioms for context-free and context-sensitive connectors can yield a consistent axiomatic system. To this end, I axiomatized Reo's informal semantics, including axioms for the common and historically significant primitives FIFOn (context-free) and LossySync (context-sensitive). I subsequently showed that the resulting axiomatic system (Fig. 5) is inconsistent (Theorem 1). In practice, this makes programming connectors with LossySync and FIFOn unworkable, as the semantics of such connectors can be ambiguous.

To resolve the inconsistency, one should withdraw one (or more) of the axioms (Sect. 4). X1 and X2a/X2b being well-established in the literature [1–8], the foremost resolution of the inconsistency is to negate $\overline{\text{X3}}$ into X3. The resulting alternative axiomatic system is, however, unsound in Reo's four major formal semantics—timed data streams, constraint automata, connector coloring, and guarded automata—henceforth called "The Major Four" (Theorems 2–5). Moreover, as composition operations in other formal semantics of Reo are essentially similar to those in The Major Four, I expect the alternative axiomatic system to be unsound in most of these, too.

The unsoundness of X3 in The Major Four at the same time entails that $\overline{\text{X3}}$ is sound in these formal semantics. Consequently, *some* step other than 8–9 in the proof of Theorem 1 has to fail in each of The Major Four (otherwise, $\sim$ is irreflexive). In the timed data streams semantics and the constraint automata semantics, as they do not support context-sensitivity, axioms X2a/b are unsound; steps 1–2 and 7–8 consequently fail. The connector coloring semantics and the guarded automata semantics, in contrast, *do* support context-sensitivity. On closer inspection, it turns out that axioms Y2a/b are unsound in these two formal semantics. The details are intricate and beyond this paper's scope.

(Aside: nothing is inherently wrong with, or inconsistent about, the *formalisms* of timed data streams/constraint automata/connector coloring/guarded automata. X3 is unsound only in their current *use* as formal semantics of Reo. An open question is whether one can construct new formal semantics using these existing formalisms in which X3 is sound, by defining new—perhaps complexer—objects for the behavior of primitives, different from the current ones. Jongmans et al. have done something similar to this before [9].)

Beside negating $\overline{\text{X3}}$, one can also negate X2a/b into $\overline{\text{X2a}}/\overline{\text{b}}$, thereby asserting that the composition of LossySync and FIFO1 is incongruent to LossyFIFO1. This, however, implies forsaking the notion of context-sensitivity. One can also negate X1 into $\overline{\text{X1}}$. This has the same consequence as negating $\overline{\text{X3}}$: X1 is sound in all formal semantics of Reo that I know of, so $\overline{\text{X1}}$ is unsound. Moreover, forsaking the composability of small buffers into large buffers seems undesirable. Finally, one can withdraw one of the Yi-axioms. However, losing associativity of composition, distributivity of abstraction, or commutativity of abstractions seems unworkable—or at least highly impractical—in practice, too.

Summarizing, the Reo community has three options: a practically unworkable language (withdraw none/Y1/Y2a/b/Y3), a language without context-sensitivity (withdraw X2a/b), or a language with context-sensitivity but whose four major formal semantics do not correspond with the informal semantics (withdraw X1/$\overline{\text{X3}}$). The identification of these options is this paper's main contribution.

Theory aside, the results presented in this paper have practical consequences, too. Over the past years, progress has been made in compiling Reo connectors into executable code, heavily based on their formal semantics. In one of its simplest forms, the generated code is run as a distributed system of communicating processes for all nodes and channels (essentially without abstraction). To reduce communication overhead, an important class of optimizations works by composing certain nodes and channels already at compile-time (so that fewer processes remain at run-time). In particular, it is more efficient to run *one* FIFOn instead of (a distributed system of) n FIFO1. As a consequence of Theorem 1, however, doing so is unsound (unless we consider a restricted subset of Reo). So, until the inconsistency in Reo's informal semantics is resolved, one cannot efficiently use context-sensitive connectors for construction of real software systems in practice.

We should therefore rethink Reo's informal semantics to remove the inconsistency and develop corresponding formal semantics. Possible approaches include:

- Assert X3 instead of $\overline{X3}$. To achieve this in Reo's informal semantics, we may dictate that every connector always makes internal steps until only observable steps are possible, *after* every observable step. Formally, this should be enforced by redefining the current abstraction operations.
- Allow FIFOn to accept a data item into its buffer and dispense a data item out of its buffer *in the same step*. Moussavi et al. already presented a formal semantics that supports this variant of FIFOn [11]. Curiously, however, axiom X1 seems unsound in the guarded automata semantics for such a variant of FIFOn. This needs to be studied in more detail.

Acknowledgments. I thank Farhad Arbab for his constructive comments on the results in this paper, which helped me improve their presentation. I also thank the anonymous reviewers for their very helpful comments.

References

1. Arbab, F.: Reo: a channel-based coordination model for component composition. Math. Struct. Comp. Sci. **14**(3), 329–366 (2004)
2. Arbab, F.: Abstract behavior types: a foundation model for components and their composition. Sci. Comput. Program. **55**(1–3), 3–52 (2005)
3. Arbab, F., Mavaddat, F.: Coordination through channel composition. In: Arbab, F., Talcott, C. (eds.) COORDINATION 2002. LNCS, vol. 2315, pp. 22–39. Springer, Heidelberg (2002). doi:10.1007/3-540-46000-4_6
4. Arbab, F., Rutten, J.J.M.M.: A coinductive calculus of component connectors. In: Wirsing, M., Pattinson, D., Hennicker, R. (eds.) WADT 2002. LNCS, vol. 2755, pp. 34–55. Springer, Heidelberg (2003). doi:10.1007/978-3-540-40020-2_2
5. Baier, C., Sirjani, M., Arbab, F., Rutten, J.: Modeling component connectors in Reo by constraint automata. Sci. Comput. Program. **61**(2), 75–113 (2006)
6. Bonsangue, M., Clarke, D., Silva, A.: A model of context-dependent component connectors. Sci. Comput. Program. **77**(66), 685–706 (2012)
7. Clarke, D., Costa, D., Arbab, F.: Connector colouring I: synchronisation and context dependency. Sci. Comput. Program. **66**(3), 205–225 (2007)

8. Costa, D.: Formal models for component connectors. Ph.D. thesis, Vrije Universiteit Amsterdam (2010)
9. Jongmans, S.-S.T.Q., Krause, C., Arbab, F.: Encoding context-sensitivity in Reo into non-context-sensitive semantic models. In: Meuter, W., Roman, G.-C. (eds.) COORDINATION 2011. LNCS, vol. 6721, pp. 31–48. Springer, Heidelberg (2011). doi:10.1007/978-3-642-21464-6_3
10. Koehler, C., Clarke, D.: Decomposing port automata. In: Proceedings of SAC 2009, pp. 1369–1373. ACM (2009)
11. Mousavi, M.R., Sirjani, M., Arbab, F.: Specification, simulation, and verification of component connectors in Reo. Technical report CSR-0415, Eindhoven University of Technology (2004)

Validated Test Models for Software Product Lines: Featured Finite State Machines

Vanderson Hafemann Fragal[1](✉), Adenilso Simao[1],
and Mohammad Reza Mousavi[2]

[1] Institute of Mathematics and Computer Sciences - ICMC,
University of São Paulo, São Paulo, Brazil
vanderson.hafemann@hh.se
[2] Centre for Research on Embedded Systems - CERES,
Halmstad University, Halmstad, Sweden

Abstract. Variants of the finite state machine (FSM) model have been extensively used to describe the behaviour of reactive systems. In particular, several model-based testing techniques have been developed to support test case generation and test case executions from FSMs. Most such techniques require several validation properties to hold for the underlying test models. In this paper, we propose an extension of the FSM test model for software product lines (SPLs), named featured finite state machine (FFSM). As the first step towards using FFSMs as test models, we define feature-oriented variants of basic test model validation criteria. We show how the high-level validation properties coincide with the necessary properties on the product FSMs. Moreover, we provide a mechanised tool prototype for checking the feature-oriented properties using satisfiability modulo theory (SMT) solver tools. We investigate the applicability of our approach by applying it to both randomly generated FFSMs as well as those from a realistic case study (the Body Comfort System). The results of our study show that for random FFSMs over 16 independent non-mandatory features, our technique provides substantial efficiency gains for the set of proposed validity checks.

Keywords: Formal modelling · Model validation · Software Product Line · Finite State Machine

1 Introduction

Motivation. Different forms of finite state machines (FSMs) have been extensively used as the fundamental semantic model for various behavioural specification languages and design trajectories. In particular, several test case generation techniques have been developed for hardware and software testing based on FSMs;

The work of V. Hafemann has been partially supported by the Science Without Borders project number 201694/2015-8.

The work of M.R. Mousavi has been partially supported by the Swedish Research Council award number: 621-2014-5057 and the Swedish Knowledge Foundation project number 20140312.

© Springer International Publishing AG 2017
O. Kouchnarenko and R. Khosravi (Eds.): FACS 2016, LNCS 10231, pp. 210–227, 2017.
DOI: 10.1007/978-3-319-57666-4_13

an overview of these techniques can be found in [7,16,18]. All FSM-based testing techniques require the underlying test models to satisfy some basic validation criteria such as connectedness and minimality.

Software Product Lines (SPLs) [19] are used for systematic reuse of artefacts and are effective in mass production and customisation of software. However, testing large SPLs demand substantial effort, and effective reuse is a challenge. Model-Based Testing (MBT) approaches need to be adapted to the SPL domain (see [26] for a survey of existing approaches).

There are a few recent attempts [23,33] to extend the FSM-based testing techniques to SPLs, mostly using the delta-oriented approach to SPL modelling. We are not aware of any prior work that addresses the basic test model validation criteria for SPLs at the family-wide level. The present paper aims at bridging this gap. To this end, we first propose a product-line extension of FSMs, named Featured Finite State Machine (FFSM). An FFSM unifies the test models of the valid product configurations in a family into a single model. Our aim is to extend FSM-based test case generation techniques [27,31] to generate test suites for groups of SPL products. As the first step to this end, we define feature-oriented family-based validation criteria that coincide with the necessary conditions of such test case generation techniques at the product level.

Our family-based validation criteria are implemented in a tool using Java and the Z3 [25] tool. A case study from the automotive domain concerning the Body Comfort System [20] was performed to show the applicability of our criteria and tool. Our research question is: *How large does an FFSM have to be in order to save time in the validation of the FFSM instead of its valid product FSMs?* To this end, we performed an empirical study on randomly generated FFSMs with various parameters. The results indicate that for random FFSMs with over 10 independent non-mandatory features, we have substantial efficiency gains for the set of proposed validity checks.

Contributions. The main contributions of this paper are summarised below:

1. Proposing family-based validation criteria for FSM-based test models and proving them to coincide with their product-based counterparts, and
2. Implementing efficient family-based validation techniques and investigating their applicability by applying them to a large set of examples.

Also as a carrier for these contributions, we propose a feature-oriented extension of FSMs.

Organisation. The remainder of this paper is organised as follows. Section 2 presents some preliminary notions and concepts regarding SPL testing and FSMs. Section 3 describes the FFSM formalism, the proposed validation properties, and the associated theoretical results. Section 4 provides an overview of the implementation used for property checking in Java and Z3. Section 5 illustrates the experimental study and the analysis of results. Section 6 provides an overview of the related works and a comparison among the relevant approaches in the literature. Section 7 concludes the paper and presents the directions of our future work.

2   Background

This section recapitulates the basic concepts and definitions of SPLs and FSMs that we are going to use through the rest of the paper.

2.1   Software Product Lines

A feature is an atomic unit used to differentiate the products of an SPL. Let F be the set of features. A product p is defined by a set of features $p \subseteq F$. The feature structure can be represented by a feature diagram [29]. In a feature diagram, some notational conventions are used to represent commonalities and variabilities of an SPL (e.g., mandatory, optional, and alternative features). To illustrate the concepts throughout the paper, we use the following SPL.

Example 1. The Arcade Game Maker (AGM) [30] can produce arcade games with different game rules. The objective of the player in any game is to get more points. Figure 1 shows the feature diagram of AGM. There are three alternative features for the game rule (Brickles, Pong and Bowling) and one optional feature (Save) to save the game.

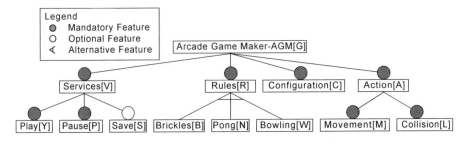

Fig. 1. AGM feature model (adapted from [30]).

In general, not all combinations of features are valid. Dependencies and constraints on feature combinations reduce the power set $\mathcal{P}(F)$ of all potential feature combinations to a subset of valid products $P \subseteq \mathcal{P}(F)$ [2,12]. A feature constraint is a propositional formula generated by interpreting the elements of the set F as propositional variables. We denote by $B(F)$ the set of all feature constraints.

A product configuration ρ of a product $p \in P$ is the feature constraint that uses all features of F, where all features in p are true, i.e., $\rho = (\bigwedge_{f \in p} f) \wedge (\bigwedge_{f \notin p} \neg f)$. We denote by Λ the set of all valid product configurations. Given a feature constraint $\chi \in B(F)$, a product configuration $\rho \in \Lambda$ satisfies χ (denoted by $\rho \vDash \chi$), if the assertion $\rho \wedge \chi$ is not false.

Consider a feature model FM, let F be a set of features extracted from FM. Given $F = \{Y, S\}$, we know from the FM that feature Play[Y] is mandatory and Save[S] is optional; an example feature constraint involving both features is $(Y \wedge \neg S) \in B(F)$, which specifies the products in which Y is included and S is excluded.

2.2   Finite State Machine

The classic Finite State Machine (FSM) formalism is often used due to its simplicity and rigour for systems such as communication protocols and reactive systems [7]. In this study, we use the following definition of FSM.

Definition 1. *An FSM M is a 5-tuple* (S, s_0, I, O, T)*, where S is a finite set of* states *with the* initial state s_0*, I is a finite set of* inputs*, O is a finite set of* outputs*, and T is a set of* transitions $t = (s, x, o, s') \in T$*, where* $s \in S$ *is the source state,* $x \in I$ *is the input label,* $o \in O$ *is the output label, and* $s' \in S$ *is the target state.*

Given an input sequence $\alpha = (x_1, ..., x_k), x_i \in I, 1 \leq i \leq k$*, a* path *from state* s_1 *to* s_{k+1} *exists when there are transitions* $t_i = (s_i, x_i, o_i, s_{i+1}) \in T$*, for each* $1 \leq i \leq k$*. A path* v *is a 5-tuple* $(s_1, \alpha, \tau, \beta, s_{k+1})$*, where*

1. $s_1 \in S$ *is the source state where the path begins,*
2. $\alpha \in I^*$ *is the defined input sequence,*
3. $\tau \in T^*$ *is the transition sequence, i.e.,* $\tau = (t_1, ..., t_k)$*,*
4. $\beta \in O^*$ *is the output result, i.e.,* $\beta = (o_1, ..., o_k)$
5. $s_{k+1} \in S$ *is the target state where the path ends.*

Notation $\Omega(s)$ *is used to denote all paths that start on state* $s \in S$*.* Ω_M *is used to denote* $\Omega(s_0)$*.*

Test case generation methods such as the *Harmonised State Identification* (HSI) [27] method, and the *Fault Coverage-Driven Incremental* (P) [31] method require FSMs with some of the semantic properties defined below.

Definition 2. *The following validation properties are defined for FSMs:*

1. **Deterministic:** *if two transitions leave a state with a common input, then both transitions reach the same state, i.e.,* $\forall_{(s,x,o,s'),(s,x,o',s'') \in T} \bullet s' = s''$*;*
2. **Complete** *(required only by some algorithms): every state has one transition for each input, i.e.,* $\forall_{s \in S, x \in I} \bullet \exists_{o \in O, s' \in S} \bullet (s, x, o, s') \in T$*;*
3. **Initially Connected:** *there is a path to every state from the initial state, i.e.,* $\forall_{s \in S} \exists_{\alpha \in I^*, \tau \in T^*, \beta \in O^*} \bullet (s_0, \alpha, \tau, \beta, s) \in \Omega_M$*;*
4. **Minimal:** *all pairs of states are distinguishable, i.e.,* $\forall_{s_a, s_b \in S} \bullet \exists_{(s_a, \alpha, \tau_a, \beta_a, s'_a) \in \Omega(s_a), (s_b, \alpha, \tau_b, \beta_b, s'_b) \in \Omega(s_b)} \bullet \beta_a \neq \beta_b$*.*

Example 2. There are six possible products that can be derived from the AGM FM. The FSM M_1 of the first configuration is presented in Fig. 2. This test model is an abstracted version of the design model where observable events are represented by inputs and the correspondent outputs. The inputs are in-game commands, while the outputs 0 and 1 are abstract captured responses. We selected the Pong[N] rule and discarded the Save[S] option represented by $\rho_1 = (G \wedge V \wedge R \wedge C \wedge A \wedge M \wedge L \wedge Y \wedge P \wedge N \wedge \neg B \wedge \neg W \wedge \neg S) \in \Lambda$. It is straightforward to check that M_1 is a deterministic, complete, initially connected and minimal FSM.

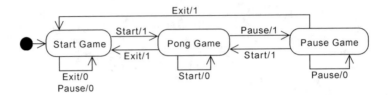

Fig. 2. FSM of the first product configuration of AGM.

3   Featured Finite State Machines

A Featured Finite State Machine (FFSM) is an extension of a Finite State Machine (FSM) by annotating states and transitions with feature constraints.

This Section presents the basic definitions for FFSMs, followed by the notion of product derivation, and the high-level validation properties required for test case generators.

3.1   Basic Definitions

The simplified syntax (with conditions) of an FFSM is defined as follows.

Definition 3. *An FFSM is a 7-tuple* $(F, \Lambda, C, c_0, Y, O, \Gamma)$, *where*

1. F *is a finite set of features,*
2. Λ *is the set of* product configurations,
3. $C \subseteq S \times B(F)$ *is a finite set of* conditional states, *where S is a finite set of state labels, $B(F)$ is the set of all feature constraints, and C satisfies the following condition:*

$$\forall_{(s,\varphi)\in C} \bullet \exists_{\rho\in\Lambda} \bullet \rho \models \varphi$$

4. $c_0 = (s_0, true) \in C$ *is the* initial conditional state,
5. $Y \subseteq I \times B(F)$ *is a finite set of* conditional inputs, *where I is the set of input labels,*
6. O *is a finite set of* outputs,
7. $\Gamma \subseteq C \times Y \times O \times C$ *is the set of conditional transitions satisfying the following condition:*

$$\forall_{((s,\varphi),(x,\varphi''),o,(s',\varphi'))\in\Gamma} \bullet \exists_{\rho\in\Lambda} \bullet \rho \models (\varphi \wedge \varphi' \wedge \varphi'')$$

The components of FFSM are self-explanatory; the above-given two conditions ensure that every conditional state and every transition is present in at least one valid product of the SPL. A conditional transition from conditional state c to c' with conditional input y and output o is represented by quadruple $t = (c, y, o, c')$, or alternatively by $c \xrightarrow[o]{y} c'$.

Example 3. Figure 3 shows the FFSM for the AGM SPL. The notation of a conditional state in the model is $s(\varphi) \equiv (s, \varphi) \in C$, the transition line by

$x(\varphi)/o \equiv \overset{(x,\varphi)}{\underset{o}{\rightarrow}} \in Y \times O$, and the operators of feature constraints are denoted by & (and), || (or), and ! (not). Omitted feature conditions mean that the condition is true, i.e., for states $s \equiv (s, true) \in C$, and transitions $\overset{x}{\underset{o}{\rightarrow}} \equiv \overset{(x,true)}{\underset{o}{\rightarrow}}$.

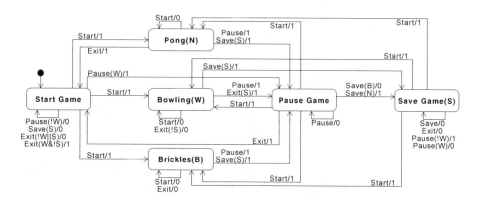

Fig. 3. FFSM for the AGM SPL.

Next, we define auxiliary definitions on FFSMs that are used to describe transfer sequences; they are subsequently used in expressing the FFSM validation properties.

Definition 4. *Given a conditional input sequence* $\delta = (y_1, ..., y_k), y_i \in Y, 1 \leq i \leq k$, *a* conditional path *from conditional state* c_1 *to* c_{k+1} *exists when there are conditional transitions* $t_i = (c_i, y_i, o_i, c_{i+1}) \in \Gamma$, *for each* $1 \leq i \leq k$. *A conditional path* σ *is a 6-tuple* $(c_1, \delta, \nu, \gamma, \omega, c_{k+1})$, *where*

1. $c_1 \in C$ *is the conditional state where the path begins,*
2. $\delta \in \dot{Y}^*$ *is the conditional input sequence,*
3. $\nu \in \Gamma^*$ *is the conditional transition sequence, i.e.,* $\nu = (t_1, ..., t_k)$,
4. $\gamma \in O^*$ *is the output result, i.e.,* $\gamma = (o_1, ..., o_k)$
5. $\omega \in B(F)$ *is the resulting path condition, i.e.,* $\omega = (\varphi_1, ...\varphi_{k+1}) \wedge (\theta_1, ..., \theta_k), y_i = (x_i, \theta_i), c_i = (s_i, \varphi_i)$
6. $c_{k+1} \in C$ *is the conditional state where the path ends.*

Notation $\Theta(c)$ *is used to denote the set of all conditional paths that start at conditional state* $c \in C$. Θ_{FF} *is used to denote* $\Theta(c_0)$.

We also define a valid transfer sequence that is used to transfer the machine from one conditional state to another.

Definition 5. *Given two conditional states* $c, c' \in C$, *a conditional input sequence* $\delta \in Y^*$ *is a valid* transfer sequence *if there are at least one path* $(c, \delta, \nu, \gamma, \omega, c') \in \Theta(c)$ *and one product that satisfies the path condition, i.e.,* $\exists_{\rho \in \Lambda} \bullet \rho \vDash \omega$.

Example 4. Consider the FFSM of Fig. 3. Note that a transfer sequence $\delta = (Start, Pause)$ of a conditional path $(StartGame, \delta, (StartGame \overset{Start}{\underset{1}{\rightarrow}}$ $Brickles(B), Brickles(B) \overset{Pause}{\underset{1}{\rightarrow}} PauseGame), (1,1), (B), PauseGame) \in \Theta_{FF}$ has a transfer condition $\omega = (B)$ and only two products can satisfy ω, namely, $\rho_5 = (G \wedge V \wedge R \wedge C \wedge A \wedge M \wedge L \wedge Y \wedge P \wedge B \wedge \neg N \wedge \neg W \wedge \neg S) \in \Lambda$ and $\rho_6 = (G \wedge V \wedge R \wedge C \wedge A \wedge M \wedge L \wedge Y \wedge P \wedge B \wedge S \wedge \neg N \wedge \neg W) \in \Lambda$. Thus, ω is not satisfied by valid product $\rho_1 = (G \wedge V \wedge R \wedge C \wedge A \wedge M \wedge L \wedge Y \wedge P \wedge N \wedge \neg B \wedge \neg W \wedge \neg S)$.

3.2 Product Derivation

We define a product derivation operator, reminiscent of the operator in [4], that is parameterised by feature constraints. Given a feature constraint, the product derivation operator reduces an FFSM into an FSM representing the selection of products.

Definition 6. *Given a feature constraint $\phi \in B(F)$ and an FFSM $FF = (F, \Lambda, C, c_0, Y, O, \Gamma)$, if exactly one product $\rho \in \Lambda$ satisfies ϕ, i.e., $\exists!_{\rho \in \Lambda} \bullet \rho \vDash \phi$, then the product derivation operator Δ_ϕ induces an FSM $\Delta_\phi(FF) = (S, s_0, I, O, T)$, where:*

1. $S = \{s | (s, \varphi) \in C \wedge \rho \vDash (\varphi \wedge \phi)\}$ *is the set of states;*
2. $s_0 = s, c_0 = (s, \varphi) \in C$ *is the initial state;*
3. $T = \{(s, x, o, s') | (s, \varphi) \overset{(x,\varphi'')}{\underset{o}{\rightarrow}} (s', \varphi') \in \Gamma \wedge \rho \vDash (\varphi \wedge \varphi' \wedge \varphi'' \wedge \phi)\}$ *is the set of transitions.*

The set of all valid products of FF is the set of all induced FSMs. Figure 3 shows the FFSM generated for the AGM SPL that can induce six products. Using the feature constraint $\phi = N \wedge \neg S$ the FFSM is projected into the FSM presented in Fig. 2.

3.3 Validation Properties

To adopt FFSMs as test models, first, we need to validate the product-line-based specification with properties used for FSMs. Next, we define the high-level counterparts of the four basic properties, namely, determinism, completeness, initially connected-ness, and minimality, and show that they coincide with the aforementioned properties for their valid FSM products.[1]

Definition 7. *An FFSM FF is* **deterministic** *if for all conditional states when exists two enabled conditional transitions with the same input for a product ρ, then both transitions lead to the same state, i.e.,* $\forall_{(s,\varphi) \overset{(x,\varphi')}{\underset{o}{\rightarrow}} (s',\varphi_a), (s,\varphi) \overset{(x,\varphi'')}{\underset{o}{\rightarrow}} (s'',\varphi_b) \in \Gamma} \bullet \forall_{\rho \in \Lambda} \bullet \rho \nvDash (\varphi \wedge \varphi' \wedge \varphi'' \wedge \varphi_a \wedge \varphi_b) \vee s' = s''.$

---

[1] Due to space limitation proof sketches are provided below; detailed proofs of correctness for these properties is available at http://ceres.hh.se/mediawiki/Vanderson_Hafemann.

Next, we state and prove that an FFSM is deterministic when all its valid product FSMs are deterministic.

Theorem 1. *An FFSM FF is deterministic if and only if all derived product FSMs $\Delta_\phi(FF)$ are deterministic.*

Proof. We break the bi-implication in the thesis into two implications and prove each by contradiction. For the implication from left to right, assume that FFSM FF is deterministic, but there is a derived FSM $\Delta_\phi(FF)$ for a product ρ which is non-deterministic; we obtain a contradiction. Let FFSM $FF = (F, \Lambda, C, c_0, Y, O, \Gamma)$ be deterministic and a derived FSM $\Delta_\phi(FF) = (S, s_0, I, O, T)$ be non-deterministic for a product $\rho \in \Lambda$ on state $s \in S$. As $\Delta_\phi(FF)$ is non-deterministic, then by the negation of Definition 2 item 1 there is an input $x \in I$ such that two transitions $(s, x, o, s'), (s, x, o, s'') \in T$ reach different states $s' \neq s''$. By Definition 6 item 3 if $\Delta_\phi(FF)$ has two transitions (s, x, s') and (s, x, o, s''), then both were induced from conditional transitions $(s, \varphi) \xrightarrow[o]{(x, \varphi')} (s', \varphi_a), (s, \varphi) \xrightarrow[o]{(x, \varphi'')} (s'', \varphi_b) \in \Gamma$ of FF and $\rho \models (\varphi \wedge \varphi' \wedge \varphi_a \wedge \varphi_b)$. However, FF is deterministic and by Definition 7 the condition $\rho \not\models (\varphi' \wedge \varphi'' \wedge \varphi_a \wedge \varphi_b) \vee s' = s''$ holds for all pairs of conditional transitions, which is a contradiction as there is a pair of conditional transitions that the negation of the condition $\rho \models (\varphi \wedge \varphi' \wedge \varphi_a \wedge \varphi_b) \wedge (s' \neq s'')$ also holds.

Likewise, for the implication right to left, assume that $\Delta_\phi(FF)$ is deterministic for ρ, but FF is non-deterministic; we obtain a contradiction. Let $FF = (F, \Lambda, C, c_0, Y, O, \Gamma)$ be non-deterministic on conditional state $(s, \varphi) \in C$, $\rho \models \varphi$, and $\Delta_\phi(FF) = (S, s_0, I, O, T)$ is deterministic for ρ. As FF is non-deterministic, then by the negation of Definition 7 there is an input $x \in I$ such that two conditional transitions $(s, \varphi) \xrightarrow[o]{(x, \varphi')} (s', \varphi_a), (s, \varphi) \xrightarrow[o]{(x, \varphi'')} (s'', \varphi_b) \in \Gamma$ are satisfied by $\rho \models (\varphi \wedge \varphi' \wedge \varphi_a \wedge \varphi_b)$ and reach different states $s' \neq s''$. As $\rho \models \phi$ and by Definition 6 item 3 each transition of FF that satisfies ϕ is induced to $\Delta_\phi(FF)$, thus $(s, x, o, s'), (s, x, o, s'') \in T$. However, $\Delta_\phi(FF)$ is deterministic and by Definition 2 item 1 the condition $s' = s''$ is true for all pairs of transitions $(s, x, o, s'), (s, x, o, s'') \in T$, which is a contradiction as there is a pair of transitions $(s, x, o, s'), (s, x, o, s'') \in T$ such $(s' \neq s'')$. $\square$

Definition 8. *An FFSM FF is* complete *if for all conditional states in a product there is an outgoing valid transition for each and every input, i.e.,*
$$\forall_{(s,\varphi) \in C} \bullet \forall_{\rho \in \Lambda} \bullet \forall_{x \in I} \bullet \rho \not\models \varphi \vee \exists_{(s,\varphi) \xrightarrow[o]{(x, \varphi'')} (s', \varphi') \in \Gamma} \bullet \rho \models \varphi' \wedge \varphi''.$$

Next, we state and prove that an FFSM is complete when all its valid product FSMs are complete.

Theorem 2. *An FFSM is complete if and only if all derived product FSMs are complete.*

Proof. We break the bi-implication in the thesis into two implications and prove each by contradiction. For the implication left to right, assume that FFSM FF

is complete, but there is a derived FSM $\Delta_\phi(FF)$ for a product ρ which is non-complete; we obtain a contradiction. Let FFSM $FF = (F, \Lambda, C, c_0, Y, O, \Gamma)$ be complete and a derived FSM $\Delta_\phi(FF) = (S, s_0, I, O, T)$ be non-complete for a product $\rho \in \Lambda$ on state $s \in S$ for input $x \in I$. As $\Delta_\phi(FF)$ is non-complete, then, by the negation of Definition 2 item 2 there is no transition $(s, x, o, s') \in T$ on s with input x. By Definition 8 if FF is complete, then for all products $\rho \in \Lambda$ that satisfies a conditional state $(s, \varphi) \in C \wedge \rho \models \varphi$ and for all inputs $x \in I$ there are conditional transitions $(s, \varphi) \xrightarrow[o]{(x, \varphi'')} (s', \varphi') \in \Gamma$ such $\rho \models \varphi' \wedge \varphi''$. However, by Definition 6 item 3 every conditional transition $(s, \varphi) \xrightarrow[o]{(x, \varphi'')} (s', \varphi') \in \Gamma$ in FF that satisfies $\rho \models \phi$ induces a transition $(s, x, o, s') \in T$ in $\Delta_\phi(FF)$, which is a contradiction as $\Delta_\phi(FF)$ does not have a transition $(s, x, o, s') \in T$ on state s for input x.

Likewise, for the implication right to left, assume that $\Delta_\phi(FF)$ is complete for ρ, but FF is non-complete; we obtain a contradiction. Let $FF = (F, \Lambda, C, c_0, Y, O, \Gamma)$ be non-complete on conditional state $(s, \varphi) \in C$ for input $x \in I$, $\rho \models \varphi$, and $\Delta_\phi(FF) = (S, s_0, I, O, T)$ is complete for ρ. As FF is non-complete, then by the negation of Definition 8 on conditional state $(s, \varphi) \in C$ there is no conditional transition $(s, \varphi) \xrightarrow[o]{(x, \varphi'')} (s', \varphi') \in \Gamma$ with input $x \in I$ for FF, or it exists but is not satisfied $\rho \not\models \varphi' \wedge \varphi''$. By Definition 6 item 3 if a conditional transition $(s, \varphi) \xrightarrow[o]{(x, \varphi'')} (s', \varphi')$ does not exist in FF, or it exists but $\rho \not\models \varphi' \wedge \varphi''$, then there is no transition $(s, x, o, s') \in T$ induced in $\Delta_\phi(FF)$. However, $\Delta_\phi(FF)$ is complete and by Definition 2 item 2 for all states $s \in S$ and for all inputs $x \in I$ there are transitions $(s, x, o, s') \in T$, which is a contradiction as there is no transition $(s, x, o, s') \in T$ in $\Delta_\phi(FF)$ for state s and input x. □

Definition 9. *An FFSM FF is* initially connected *if there exist transfer sequences from the initial conditional state to every conditional state for every satisfiable product, i.e.,* $\forall_{c=(s, \varphi) \in C} \bullet \forall_{\rho \in \Lambda} \bullet \rho \models \varphi \implies \exists_{(c_0, \delta, \nu, \gamma, \omega, c) \in \Theta_{FF}} \bullet \rho \models \omega.$

Next, we state and prove that an FFSM is initially connected when all its valid product FSMs are initially connected.

Theorem 3. *An FFSM is initially connected if and only if all derived product FSMs are initially connected.*

Proof. We break the bi-implication in the thesis into two implications and prove each by contradiction. For the implication left to right, assume that FFSM FF is initially connected, but there is a derived FSM $\Delta_\phi(FF)$ for a product ρ which is non-initially connected; we obtain a contradiction. Let FFSM $FF = (F, \Lambda, C, c_0, Y, O, \Gamma)$ be initially connected and a derived FSM $\Delta_\phi(FF) = (S, s_0, I, O, T)$ be non-initially connected for a product $\rho \in \Lambda$ on state $s_k \in S$. As $\Delta_\phi(FF)$ is non-initially connected, then, by the negation of Definition 2 item 3 there is no path $\upsilon \in \Omega_{\Delta_\phi(FF)}$ to s_k from the initial state s_0. By Definition 9 if FF is initially connected, then there is a path $\sigma_k \in \Theta_{FF}$

to every conditional state $(s_k, \varphi_k) \in C$ from the initial conditional state c_0, and ρ satisfies the path condition ω. However, by Definition 5 every conditional transition $(s_i, \varphi_i) \overset{(x_i, \varphi_i')}{\underset{o}{\rightarrow}} (s_{i+1}, \varphi_{i+1}) \in \Gamma$, $0 \le i \le k$ forms a path to reach (s_k, φ_k) which is satisfied by ρ. As $\rho \models \phi$, and by Definition 6 item 3 every conditional transition $(s_i, \varphi_i) \overset{(x_i, \varphi_i')}{\underset{o}{\rightarrow}} (s_{i+1}, \varphi_{i+1}) \in \Gamma$ is induced to $(s_i, x_i, o, s_{i+1}) \in T$ that forms a path to reach s_k, which is a contradiction as there is no path for $\upsilon \in \Omega_{\Delta_\phi(FF)}$ to reach state s_k.

Likewise, for the implication right to left, assume that $\Delta_\phi(FF)$ is initially connected for ρ, but FF is non-initially connected; we obtain a contradiction. Let $FF = (F, \Lambda, C, c_0, Y, O, \Gamma)$ be non-initially connected on conditional state $(s, \varphi) \in C$, $\rho \models \varphi$, and $\Delta_\phi(FF) = (S, s_0, I, O, T)$ is initially connected for ρ. As FF is non-initially connected, then by the negation of Definition 9 there is no path $\sigma \in \Theta_{FF}$ to reach (s_k, φ_k) from the initial conditional state c_0. By Definition 2 item 3 if $\Delta_\phi(FF)$ is initially connected, then there is a path $\upsilon \in \Omega_{\Delta_\phi(FF)}$ to reach every state $s \in S$ from the initial state s_0. As $\rho \models \phi$, and by Definition 6 item 3 every transition $(s_i, x_i, o, s_{i+1}) \in T$ was induced from a conditional transition $(s_i, \varphi_i) \overset{(x_i, \varphi_i')}{\underset{o}{\rightarrow}} (s_{i+1}, \varphi_{i+1}) \in \Gamma$ and $\rho \models \varphi_i \wedge \varphi_i' \wedge \varphi_{i+1}$ that forms a path to reach (s_k, φ_k), which is a contradiction as there is no path $\sigma \in \Theta_{FF}$ to reach (s_k, φ_k).   □

Definition 10. *An FFSM FF is* minimal *if for all pairs of conditional states of all satisfiable products there are common valid transfer sequences that distinguish both conditional states, i.e.,* $\forall_{c_a = (s_a, \varphi_a), c_b = (s_b, \varphi_b) \in C} \bullet \forall_{\rho \in \Lambda} \bullet \rho \models \varphi_a \wedge \varphi_b \Rightarrow \exists_{(c_a, \delta, \nu_a, \gamma_a, \omega_a, c_a') \in \Theta(c_a), (c_b, \delta, \nu_b, \gamma_b, \omega_b, c_b') \in \Theta(c_b)} \bullet \gamma_a \ne \gamma_b \wedge \rho \models (\omega_a \wedge \omega_b).$

Next, we state and prove that an FFSM is minimal when all its valid product FSMs are minimal.

Theorem 4. *An FFSM is minimal if and only if all derived product FSMs are minimal.*

Proof. We break the bi-implication in the thesis into two implications and prove each by contradiction. For the implication left to right, assume that FFSM FF is minimal, but there is a derived FSM $\Delta_\phi(FF)$ for a product ρ which is non-minimal; we obtain a contradiction. Let FFSM $FF = (F, \Lambda, C, c_0, Y, O, \Gamma)$ be minimal and a derived FSM $\Delta_\phi(FF) = (S, s_0, I, O, T)$ be non-minimal for a product $\rho \in \Lambda$ on states $s_a, s_b \in S$. As $\Delta_\phi(FF)$ is non-minimal, then, by the negation of Definition 2 item 4 there is no common input sequence $\alpha \in I^*$ of two paths $\upsilon_a \in \Omega(s_a), \upsilon_b \in \Omega(s_b)$ that distinguish states s_a and s_b. By Definition 10 if FF is minimal, then for every pair of conditional states $c_a = (s_{a_0}, \varphi_{a_0}), c_b = (s_{b_0}, \varphi_{b_0}) \in C$ and for all products $\rho \in \Lambda$ that satisfy the condition $\varphi_{a_0} \wedge \varphi_{b_0}$ there are two paths with a common a distinguishing sequence $\delta \in Y^*$ and ρ also satisfies both path conditions $\omega_a \wedge \omega_b$. However, by Definition 5 every pair of conditional transitions $(s_{a_i}, \varphi_{a_i}) \overset{(x_i, \varphi_i')}{\underset{o}{\rightarrow}} (s_{a_{i+1}}, \varphi_{a_{i+1}}), (s_{b_i}, \varphi_{b_i}) \overset{(x_i, \varphi_i'')}{\underset{o'}{\rightarrow}}

$(s_{b_{i+1}}, \varphi_{b_{i+1}}) \in \Gamma$, $0 \leq i \leq k$ of the distinguishing sequence δ is satisfied by ρ. As $\rho \vDash \phi$, and by Definition 6 item 3 every pair of conditional transitions $(s_{a_i}, \varphi_{a_i}) \overset{(x_i, \varphi_i')}{\underset{o}{\to}} (s_{a_{i+1}}, \varphi_{a_{i+1}}), (s_{b_i}, \varphi_{b_i}) \overset{(x_i, \varphi_i'')}{\underset{o'}{\to}} (s_{b_{i+1}}, \varphi_{b_{i+1}}) \in \Gamma$ is induced to $(s_{a_i}, x_i, o, s_{a_{i+1}}), (s_{b_i}, x_i, o', s_{b_{i+1}}) \in T$ in $\Delta_\phi(FF)$ that distinguishes s_a and s_b, which is a contradiction as there is no distinguishing sequence $\alpha \in I^*$ for states s_a and s_b.

Likewise, for the implication right to left, assume that $\Delta_\phi(FF)$ is minimal for ρ, but FF is non-minimal; we obtain a contradiction. Let $FF = (F, \Lambda, C, c_0, Y, O, \Gamma)$ be non-minimal on conditional state $c_a = (s_{a_0}, \varphi_{a_0}), c_b = (s_{b_0}, \varphi_{b_0}) \in C$, $\rho \vDash \varphi$, and $\Delta_\phi(FF) = (S, s_0, I, O, T)$ is minimal for ρ. As FF is non-minimal, then by the negation of Definition 10 there is no common input sequence $\delta \in Y^*$ that distinguish conditional states c_a and c_b. By Definition 2 item 4 if $\Delta_\phi(FF)$ is minimal, then there are two paths with a common a distinguishing sequence $\alpha \in I^*$ for every pair of states s_a and s_b. As $\rho \vDash \phi$, and by Definition 6 item 3 every pair of transitions $(s_{a_i}, x_i, o, s_{a_{i+1}}), (s_{b_i}, x_i, o', s_{b_{i+1}}) \in T$ were induced from $(s_{a_i}, \varphi_{a_i}) \overset{(x_i, \varphi_i')}{\underset{o}{\to}} (s_{a_{i+1}}, \varphi_{a_{i+1}}), (s_{b_i}, \varphi_{b_i}) \overset{(x_i, \varphi_i'')}{\underset{o'}{\to}} (s_{b_{i+1}}, \varphi_{b_{i+1}}) \in \Gamma$ and ρ satisfies both conditional paths that distinguishes c_a and c_b, which is a contradiction as there is no distinguishing sequence $\delta \in Y^*$ for c_a and c_b.   □

4   Implementation

It is well-known that feature models can be translated into propositional formulas; see, e.g., [2,10]. This translation enables mechanising the analysis of feature-based specifications using existing logic-based tools, such as SAT solvers. In our approach the Z3 tool [25] was used to check propositional formulas for FFSM properties.

We implemented a tool in Java to parse and process FFSMs in an adapted version of KISS format [14] and subsequently generate assertions in the SMT format that correspond to the initial syntactical checks on the FFSM definition (Definition 3) and the semantic FFSM validation properties in Sect. 3.3.

To check the initial FFSM conditions on the FFSM of Fig. 3, we: (i) transform the feature model of Fig. 1 into a propositional formula; and (ii) generate assertions to check feature constraints of conditional states and transitions. Subsequently, we check the validity conditions on the generated propositional formulae. The validation process is progressive, starting with validating conditional states and transitions, and proceeding with checking determinism, completeness, initially connected and then minimality.

Example 5. Figure 4 presents parts of the generated SMT files to check validity of conditional states and completeness, where: (a) all features are declared as Boolean variables: (b) the root mandatory and also the feature model propositional formula are asserted; (c) conditional states Brickles(B) and Save(S) are verified; and (d) a completeness check on the conditional state Save(S) for input Pause is verified (see Fig. 3). To check conditional states we combine and execute parts (a), (b), and (c), while to check completeness (a), (b), and (d) are combined and executed. In the end, for every $(check - sat)$ command we have an answer that we connect back to Java.

In Z3, push and pop commands are used to temporarily set the context (e.g., with assertions), and once a verification goal is discharged the context can be reset. The $(check - sat)$ command is used to evaluate the assertions which returns $(sat$ or $unsat)$. If a conditional state check yields $unsat$, then there is no product that will ever have this state and hence, the FFSM is invalid.

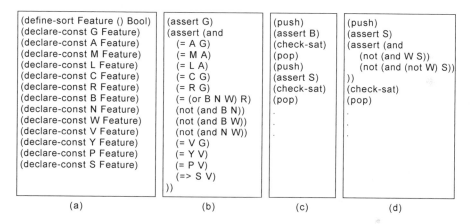

(a)   (b)   (c)   (d)

Fig. 4. SMT file generated to check some conditional states and part of the completeness property.

5   Experimental Study

To evaluate the applicability and the efficiency of our approach, we conducted an experiment to evaluate and compare the time required to check properties of FFSMs with the Product by Product (PbP) approach. Our research question is: *How large does an FFSM have to be in order to save time in validation of the FFSM instead of its valid product FSMs?* In the future, we plan to use the same setup (extended with more case studies), to evaluate the test case generation methods on FFSMs.

5.1   Experimental Setup

The setup of our experiment consists of generating random FFSMs varying the number of conditional states from 8 to 70. Every FFSM uses different types of feature models and the arrangement of the features (structure) defines the

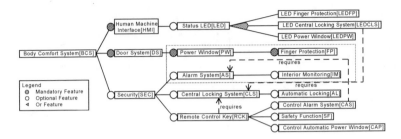

Fig. 5. Reduced feature model of BCS.

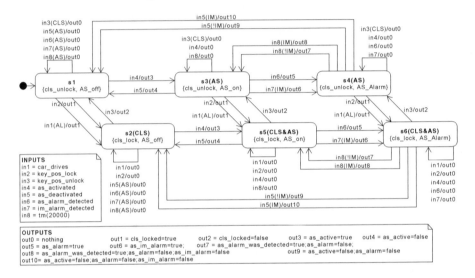

Fig. 6. FFSM for AS and CLS.

number of configurations. Initially, we manually inspected a large sample of generated FFSMs, their underlying FSMs and their validation times.

We also modeled the Body Comfort System (BCS) that is used on the VW Golf SPL [20] to reduce the threats to validity and contrast the results from randomly generated (F)FSMs with their real-world counterparts. The original BCS system has 19 non-mandatory features and can have 11616 configurations. In order to manage its complexity, we picked a subset of the feature model (without unresolved dependencies) with 13 non-mandatory features and 8 independent features at the leafs of the feature model. (We plan to introduce hierarchy into our models and treat the complete example in the future.)

Figure 5 shows the feature model of a selected part of features for the BCS. Figure 6 shows the FFSM for a small part of this specification featuring the Alarm System (AS) with an optional Interior Monitoring (IM) function; and (ii) the Central Locking System (CLS) with an optional Automatic Locking

(AL) function. This FFSM turns out to be deterministic, complete, initially connected and minimal.

The implementation of our experiments is explained in Sect. 4. We also implemented a random generator for feature models and (F)FSMs. We designed the random generator to map features to conditional states of the FFSMs. The number of conditional states is hence designed to be proportional to the number of features. We used FeatureIDE [32] to visualise and inspect the feature models and gain insight into the complexity with respect to their structure. The running environment used Windows 7 (64 bit) on an Intel processor i5-5300U at 2.30 GHz.[2]

5.2   Analysis and Threats to Validity

The collected data after running our experiments is visualised in Fig. 7. The total validation time is calculated in milliseconds, and we stopped our experiments around 2 million milliseconds (approximately 30 min) for 68 non-mandatory features when checking FFSMs.

As an immediate observation, we noticed that the number of non-mandatory features is the dominant factor in the complexity of validation time in both approaches. This was an early observation that was verified by inspecting several data points and resulted in the way we visualised the data in Fig. 7.

Additionally, the FSM-based analysis (the product-by-product approach) is very sensitive to the structure of the feature model: the number of independent optional features (optional features appearing in different branches of the feature model) play a significant role in the number of products and hence, the validation time. Thus, we classified the FSM-based data regarding the relative number of

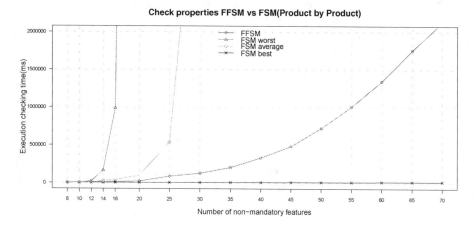

Fig. 7. Execution time for each case per number of non-mandatory features.

---

[2] The experiment package for Eclipse IDE can be found in http://ceres.hh.se/mediawiki/Vanderson_Hafemann.

independent non-mandatory features in Fig. 7; the worst-case time is where all the non-mandatory features are independent; the average case is where half of the non-mandatory features are independent, and the best case is where all non-mandatory features are dependent (form a line in the feature model).

To summarise, we conclude that for random SPLs with more than 16 independent non-mandatory features, the FSM-based approach fails to perform within a reasonable amount of time (e.g., ca. 30 min), while the FFSM-based approach scales well (regardless of the feature model structure) for up to 70 non-mandatory features.

Regarding our BCS case study, we have obtained similar results regarding the difference between the FFSM and the FSM-based approaches. Namely, for the resulting FFSM with 13 non-mandatory features (of which 8 are independent) and 50 conditional states, the validation takes approx. 500 s ($\tilde{\ }$8 min) while for its 384 configurations (FSMs) we have approx. 700 s ($\tilde{\ }$11 min). We expect the scalability of the FFSM-based approach to improve if more structural aspects, e.g., hierarchy, are taken into account. We plan to investigate this further in the near future.

Our experiment has been limited mostly to random feature models and (F)FSMs with a given mapping from feature models to FFSMs. We have only included one realistic case-study for comparison. Both of these issues (the actual structure of feature models and of FFSMs) are threats to the validity of our results for real-world cases. We plan to mitigate this threat by analyzing a number of realistic case studies as a benchmark for our future research. Regarding feature models, as our current results suggest, the FFSM-based approach is not very sensitive to the structure of the feature model and hence, our results are not likely to change much for realistic feature models. Regarding realistic FFSMs, it is common that the flat (i.e., non-hierarchical) FFSMs are the result of the composition of parallel features and hence, their number of states grows exponentially with the number of independent non-mandatory features. Hence, for realistic FFSMs, using the hierarchical structure in the validation process is necessary for sustaining scalability.

6   Related Work

There have been several proposals for the behavioural modelling of SPLs in the literature; we refer to [6,11,28] for recent surveys and Thüm et al.'s recent survey [32] for a classification of different SPL analysis techniques. A number of behavioural models proposed in the literature, e.g., these in [1,9,21] are based on Finite State Machines or Labeled Transition Systems. They are mainly used to provide the formal specification of SPLs and their formal verification using model checking.

In Feature-Annotated State Machines, some approaches [10,15] (e.g. the 150% test model) propose a pruning-based approach to UML modelling of SPLs, separating variability from the base models using mapping models. Similar approaches [21,24] use Statecharts to model reusable components and in their approaches, the instances can also be derived syntactically by pruning. Recent approaches [8,17] encode feature annotations into transition guards to project model elements. In [17], the authors use model slicing to generate tests for parts of the model to reduce complexity. In Featured Transition Systems [8], model fragments are annotated with presence conditions, i.e., Boolean expressions that define to which products a fragment belongs. However, in none of these approaches, the authors deal with semantic issues in FSMs/LTSs, such as the validation properties considered in our approach, and only verify the syntactical correctness of possible valid products. Moreover, there is a sizable literature focusing on product-based analysis techniques such as syntactic consistency, type checking and model-checking of SPLs [1,3,32].

Our proposed test model and validation criteria can be classified as a family-based and feature-oriented specification and analysis method. To our knowledge, however, there only a few pieces of research that extend test models, test case generation and test case execution to the family-based level; examples of such work include earlier delta-oriented techniques such as [22,23,33] and feature-oriented approaches [4,5,13]. However, the approach proposed in [4] exploits a non-deterministic test case generation algorithm (with no fault model or finite test suite) and hence, validation of test models is not an issue in their approach. Thus, we are not aware of any prior study one extending the FSM-based test-model validation techniques to the family-based setting.

7   Conclusion

In this paper, we presented the Featured Finite State Machine (FFSM) model as a behavioural test model for software product lines (SPLs). Validation properties were specified for adopting FFSMs as input models for test case generation algorithms and we showed that they coincide with their corresponding properties for the product FSM models. Moreover, a framework for validation of test models using Java and Z3 was implemented.

We conducted an experimental study comparing the validation time of FFSM properties with the accumulated time of validating all FSM product models (both using randomly generated models and a case study for the Body Comfort System). We found that checking collective FFSM models can save significant amount of time for SPLs that have 16 or more independent non-mandatory features.

As future work, we plan to use FFSMs to extend FSM-based test case generation methods to SPLs. Moreover, we plan to extend the FFSM model to Hierarchical FFSMs (using concepts from Statecharts and UML State Machines) to handle the state explosion problem identified in the case study and apply validation (and test case generation) on hierarchical models. Also, in addition to the validation issues, other aspects of the FFSM model can be explored such as applicability, maintainability and the relation between semantic properties such as determinism and minimality.

References

1. Asirelli, P., ter Beek, M.H., Gnesi, S., Fantechi, A.: Formal description of variability in product families. In: Proceedings of the 15th International Software Product Line Conference (SPLC), pp. 130–139. IEEE (2011)
2. Batory, D.: Feature models, grammars, and propositional formulas. In: Proceedings of the 9th International Software Product Line Conference (SPLC), pp. 7–20. IEEE (2005)
3. Benduhn, F., Thüm, T., Lochau, M., Leich, T., Saake, G.: A survey on modeling techniques for formal behavioral verification of software product lines. In: Proceedings of the 9th International Workshop on Variability Modelling of Software-intensive Systems (VaMoS 2015), p. 80. ACM (2015). http://dl.acm.org/citation.cfm?id=2701319
4. Beohar, H., Mousavi, M.R.: Input-output conformance testing based on featured transition systems. In: Proceedings of the Symposium on Applied Computing (SAC 2014), pp. 1272–1278. ACM (2014). http://dl.acm.org/citation.cfm?id=2554850
5. Beohar, H., Mousavi, M.R.: Spinal test suites for software product lines. In: Proceedings of the 9th Workshop on Model-Based Testing (MBT 2014), EPTCS, vol. 141, pp. 44–55 (2014). http://dx.doi.org/10.4204/EPTCS.141
6. Beohar, H., Varshosaz, M., Mousavi, M.R.: Basic behavioral models for software product lines: expressiveness and testing pre-orders. Sci. Comput. Program. **123**, 42–60 (2016). http://dx.doi.org/10.1016/j.scico.2015.06.005
7. Broy, M., Jonsson, B., Katoen, J.-P., Leucker, M., Pretschner, A. (eds.): Model-Based Testing of Reactive Systems. LNCS, vol. 3472. Springer, Heidelberg (2005)
8. Classen, A., Cordy, M., Schobbens, P.Y., Heymans, P., Legay, A., Raskin, J.F.: Featured transition systems: foundations for verifying variability-intensive systems and their application to LTL model checking. IEEE Trans. Softw. Eng. **39**(8), 1069–1089 (2013)
9. Classen, A., Heymans, P., Schobbens, P.Y., Legay, A.: Symbolic model checking of software product lines. In: Proceeding of the 33rd International Conference on Software Engineering (ICSE), p. 321. ACM Press (2011)
10. Czarnecki, K., Antkiewicz, M.: Mapping features to models: a template approach based on superimposed variants. In: Glück, R., Lowry, M. (eds.) GPCE 2005. LNCS, vol. 3676, pp. 422–437. Springer, Heidelberg (2005). doi:10.1007/11561347_28
11. Czarnecki, K., Grünbacher, P., Rabiser, R., Schmid, K., Wasowski, A.: Cool features and tough decisions. In: Proceedings of the Sixth International Workshop on Variability Modeling of Software-Intensive Systems (VaMoS), pp. 173–182. ACM Press (2012)
12. Czarnecki, K., Wasowski, A.: Feature diagrams and logics: there and back again. In: Proceedings of SPLC 2007, pp. 23–34. IEEE (2007)
13. Devroey, X., Perrouin, G., Papadakis, M., Legay, A., Schobbens, P., Heymans, P.: Featured model-based mutation analysis. In: Proceedings of the 38th International Conference on Software Engineering (ICSE 2016), pp. 655–666. ACM (2016). http://doi.acm.org/10.1145/2884781
14. Edwards, S.A.: Languages for Digital Embedded Systems. Springer, New York (2000)
15. Grönninger, H., Krahn, H., Pinkernell, C., Rumpe, B.: Modeling variants of automotive systems using Views. In: Tagungsband Modellierungs-Workshop MBEFF: Modellbasierte Entwicklung von eingebetteten Fahrzeugfunktionen, p. 14. TU Braunschweig (2008)

16. Hierons, R.M., Bogdanov, K., Bowen, J.P., Cleaveland, R., Derrick, J., Dick, J., Gheorghe, M., Harman, M., Kapoor, K., Krause, P., et al.: Using formal specifications to support testing. ACM Comput. Surv. (CSUR) **41**(2), 9 (2009)
17. Kamischke, J., Lochau, M., Baller, H.: Conditioned model slicing of feature-annotated state machines. In: Proceedings of the 4th International Workshop on Feature-Oriented Software Development (FODS), pp. 9–16. ACM (2012)
18. Lee, D., Yannakakis, M.: Principles and methods of testing finite state machines - a survey. Proc. IEEE **84**(8), 1090–1123 (1996)
19. Linden, F., Schmif, K., Rommes, E.: Software Product Lines in Action. Springer, New York (2007)
20. Lity, S., Lachmann, R., Lochau, M., Schaefer, I.: Delta-oriented software product line test models - the body comfort system case study. Technical report (2013)
21. Liu, J., Dehlinger, J., Lutz, R.: Safety analysis of software product lines using state-based modeling. J. Syst. Softw. **80**(11), 1879–1892 (2007)
22. Lochau, M., Lity, S., Lachmann, R., Schaefer, I., Goltz, U.: Delta-oriented model-based integration testing of large-scale systems. J. Syst. Softw. **91**, 63–84 (2014). http://dx.doi.org/10.1016/j.jss.2013.11.1096
23. Lochau, M., Schaefer, I., Kamischke, J., Lity, S.: Incremental model-based testing of delta-oriented software product lines. In: Brucker, A.D., Julliand, J. (eds.) TAP 2012. LNCS, vol. 7305, pp. 67–82. Springer, Heidelberg (2012). doi:10.1007/978-3-642-30473-6_7
24. Luna, C., Gonzalez, A.: Behavior specification of product lines via feature models and UML statecharts with variabilities. In: Chilean Computer Science Society (SCCC), pp. 9–16. IEEE (2008)
25. Moura, L., Bjørner, N.: Z3: an efficient SMT solver. In: Ramakrishnan, C.R., Rehof, J. (eds.) TACAS 2008. LNCS, vol. 4963, pp. 337–340. Springer, Heidelberg (2008). doi:10.1007/978-3-540-78800-3_24
26. Oster, S., Wubbeke, A., Engels, G., Schurr, A.: A survey of model-based software product lines testing. In: Zander, J., Schieferdecker, I., Mosterman, P.J. (eds.) Model-Based Testing for Embedded Systems, pp. 338–381. CRC Press, Boca Raton (2012)
27. Petrenko, A., Bochmann, G.v., Luo, G.: Selecting test sequences for partially specified nondeterministic finite state machines. In: International Workshop on Protocol Test Systems (IWPTS), pp. 95–110. Chapman & Hall (1995)
28. Schaefer, I., Rabiser, R., Clarke, D., Bettini, L., Benavides, D., Botterweck, G., Pathak, A., Trujillo, S., Villela, K.: Software diversity: state of the art and perspectives. Int. J. Softw. Tools. Technol. Transf. **14**(5), 477–495 (2012)
29. Schobbens, P.Y., Heymans, P., Trigaux, J.C.: Feature diagrams: a survey and a formal semantics. In: Proceedings of the 14th IEEE International Requirements Engineering Conference (RE), pp. 139–148. IEEE (2006)
30. SEI: A framework for software product line practice (2011). http://www.sei.cmu.edu/productlines/tools/framework/
31. Simao, A., Petrenko, A.: Fault coverage-driven incremental test generation. Comput. J. **53**(9), 1508–1522 (2010)
32. Thüm, T., Kästner, C., Benduhn, F., Meinicke, J., Saake, G., Leich, T.: Featureide: an extensible framework for feature-oriented software development. Sci. Comput. Program. **79**, 70–85 (2014)
33. Varshosaz, M., Beohar, H., Mousavi, M.R.: Delta-oriented FSM-based testing. In: Butler, M., Conchon, S., Zaïdi, F. (eds.) ICFEM 2015. LNCS, vol. 9407, pp. 366–381. Springer, Cham (2015). doi:10.1007/978-3-319-25423-4_24

Tool Papers

Tool Support for Fuzz Testing of Component-Based System Adaptation Policies

Jean-François Weber[(✉)]

FEMTO-ST UMR 6174 CNRS
and Univ. Bourgogne Franche-Comté, Besançon, France
jfweber@femto-st.fr

Abstract. Self-adaptation enables component-based systems to evolve by means of dynamic reconfigurations that can modify their architecture and/or behaviour at runtime. In this context, we use adaptation policies to trigger reconfigurations that must only happen in suitable circumstances, thus avoiding unwanted behaviours. A tool (*cbsdr*, standing for Component-Based System Dynamic Reconfigurations) supporting both the Fractal and FraSCAti component frameworks was developed, but the testing of the robustness of new adaptation policies was not easy. This is the reason to add to our implementation a new behavioural fuzzing tool. While fuzzing consists of sending invalid data to a system under test to find weaknesses that may cause a crash or an abnormal reaction, behavioural fuzzing sends invalid sequences of valid data. Valid traces are modified using fuzzing techniques to generate test cases that can be replayed on a dummy system using the adaptation policies to be tested while focusing on interesting regions of specific data sequences.

1 Introduction

Component-based systems can evolve at runtime using dynamic reconfigurations that can modify their architecture and/or behaviour. A tool (*cbsdr* [1,2], standing for Component-Based System Dynamic Reconfigurations) supporting both the Fractal [3] and FraSCAti [4] component frameworks was developed. This tool uses adaptation policies based on temporal logic to trigger reconfigurations while enforcing some temporal properties; this means that a specific reconfiguration would only be performed if it does not make the system evolve in a configuration that may violate the properties to be enforced. Reflection polices that would generate a reaction when some properties are violated are also part of this tool. In a nutshell, adaptation policies prevent anything bad to happen at the next configuration, whereas reflection policies trigger a pertinent response when something bad has already happened. Nevertheless, the testing of the robustness of new adaptation policies is complicated and time consuming, especially for large systems that would require tailored settings to test specific policies.

Fuzz testing, or fuzzing [5], is a software testing technique that aims at discovering weaknesses by inputting massive amounts of data (often random and/or invalid). Behavioural fuzzing sends (invalid) sequences of valid data.

© Springer International Publishing AG 2017
O. Kouchnarenko and R. Khosravi (Eds.): FACS 2016, LNCS 10231, pp. 231–237, 2017.
DOI: 10.1007/978-3-319-57666-4_14

These sequences can either be generated from a model, like in [6], or by re-engineering the result of a previous run of the system, namely its log files. By using specificities of our reconfiguration model to generate the data to be injected, we allow the tester to focus on specific regions of the sequence that would enable adaptation policies to be tested.

We will briefly introduce the *cbsdr* project in Sect. 2 before presenting the way we tackle the problem of the test of adaptation policies in Sect. 3. Finally, Sect. 4 presents our conclusion and future work.

2   The *cbsdr* Project

We developed a prototype tool, contained in a java package named *cbsdr*, supporting our reconfiguration model to run component-based systems with dynamic reconfigurations. Using generic java classes, independent of any component-based system framework, we can use our implementation to perform reconfigurations on applications deployed using Fractal [3] or FraSCAti [4]. The Fractal framework is based on a hierarchical and reflective component model. Its goal is to reduce the development, deployment, and maintenance costs of software systems in general[1]. FraSCAti is an open-source implementation of the *Service Component Architecture*[2] (SCA). It can be seen as a framework having a Fractal base with an extra layer implementing SCA specifications. In [4], a smart home scenario illustrates the capabilities and the various reconfigurations of the FraSCAti platform.

Figure 1 shows the *cbsdr* interface displaying a given state of a component-based system developed using Fractal (top frame). The left frame shows the various states of the run under scrutiny, whereas the bottom frame can be used to display various information such as the evolution of parameters of the model, console output, or the outcome of reconfigurations performed.

This interface allows the monitoring of a component-based system and the generation of (external) events during a run of *cbsdr*, but can also be used to analyse the logs of a run already performed.

In addition to the above-mentioned functionalities, adaptation is performed using reconfigurations triggered by temporal properties at runtime, as described in [1]. This works as follows: (*a*) adaptation polices are loaded and applied using a control loop, (*b*) temporal properties are evaluated and candidate reconfigurations (if any) are ordered by priority using fuzzy logic values embedded in adaptation policies, (*c*) these reconfigurations are applied to the component-based system model using our reconfiguration semantics to verify that corresponding target configurations do not violate any of the properties to enforce, and (*d*) the target configuration obtained using the reconfiguration with highest priority that does not violate any of the properties to enforce is applied to the component-based system using a protocol similar to the one described in [7].

---

[1] http://fractal.ow2.org/tutorial/index.html.

[2] http://www.oasis-opencsa.org/sca.

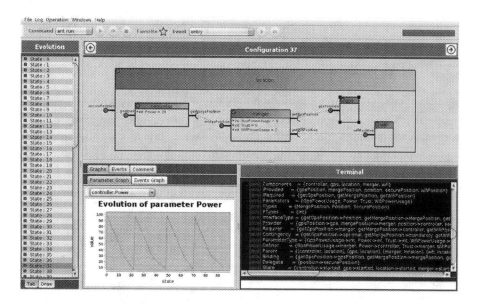

Fig. 1. Model of a component-based system displayed in our interface

The test and implementation of adaptation policies being feasible for small systems can become complex and time consuming for larger ones, and may require specific settings to put the system in the conditions enabling such policies.

3   Fuzz Testing of Adaptation Policies

Fuzz testing or fuzzing [5] is a software testing technique used to discover coding errors and security loopholes in software, operating systems or networks by inputting massive amounts of (random) data, called *fuzz*, to the system in an attempt to make it crash or at least misbehave. Behavioural fuzzing sends invalid sequences of valid data. These sequences can either be generated from a model, like in [6], or by re-engineering the result of a previous run of the system, namely its log files. Since these tests are not performed during but after the run of the system, they consists of *offline* fuzzing, instead of *online* fuzzing that would be performed at runtime.

We chose to use the best of both approaches (model-based and trace-based fuzz generation) by using specificities of our reconfiguration model to generate the fuzz to be injected. In a nutshell, our reconfiguration model is based on configurations that can be seen as a tuple $\langle Elem, Rel \rangle$, where $Elem$ is made of architectural sets containing elements such as components, (required of provided) interfaces, parameters, etc. and Rel contains relations linking architectural elements, e.g., interfaces binding or wiring, components states (*started* or *stopped*), parameters values, etc. We also use a set CP of configuration properties on the architectural elements and the relations between them. These properties are specified using first-order logic formulae [8]. Therefore, the operational semantics of a component-based system is defined by the labelled transition system $S = \langle \mathcal{C}, \mathcal{C}^0, \mathcal{R}_{run}, \rightarrow, l \rangle$ where $\mathcal{C} = \{c, c_1, c_2, \ldots\}$ is a set of configurations, $\mathcal{C}^0 \subseteq \mathcal{C}$ is a set of initial configurations, $\mathcal{R}_{run}$ is a set of reconfigurations, $\rightarrow \subseteq \mathcal{C} \times \mathcal{R}_{run} \times \mathcal{C}$ is the reconfiguration relation, and $l : \mathcal{C} \rightarrow CP$ is a total interpretation function.

The *cbsdr* tool contains controllers using control loops to monitor the evolution of a component-based system under scrutiny by regularly retrieving its configuration. The sequence of all the configurations retrieved during a run constitute a trace that can be modified either manually for the generation of very specific test cases, or automatically for bulk generation of test cases using random shuffling, duplication, and/or deletion of configurations. Such tests cases (called below *fuzzy logs*) are obtained by transformations that can be automated using a sub-package of *cbsdr* called *cbsdr.fuzzy* and referred below as *Fuzzy Engine*.

The Fuzzy Engine tool is integrated in the *cbsdr* development as shows Fig. 2 where light coloured entities are part of the previous developments and the elements of the fuzzing tool are represented in darker colours.

This informal representation of our implementation displays three controllers: (*a*) the *event controller* receives events, stores them, and flushes them after they have been sent to a requester, (*b*) the *reflection controller* sends events to the *event controller* when a property of a reflection policy is violated, and (*c*) the *adaptation policy controller* manages dynamics reconfigurations triggered by adaptation policies.

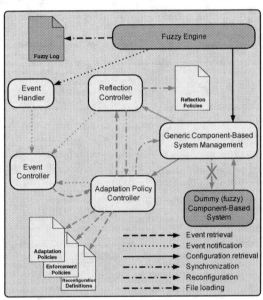

Fig. 2. *cbsdr* fuzzing architecture (Color figure online)

The reader interested by the interactions between these controllers is referred to [1].

In addition, an *event handler* is used to receive events from an external source and to send them to the *event controller*. All interactions with the *component-based system* take place through the *generic component-based system management* entity (*gcbsm*), a set of Java classes developed in such a way that they can be used regardless of the framework used to design the component-based system without modifying its code.

The *gcbsm* is mainly developed using abstract classes that are used for the reification of other classes specially designed for the handling of Fractal [3] or

FraSCAti [4] component frameworks. We just added to the *gcbsm* support for another new component framework that we called *dummy*. This way, each time the *adaptation policy controller* or the *reflection controller* requests the current configuration, the *gcbsm*, when detecting a dummy component, requests the corresponding configuration to the Fuzzy Engine instead of retrieving it from an actual component-based system. Of course, the Fuzzy Engine must always be initialized with a fuzzy log corresponding to the pertinent test case before usage.

We can automatically filter (or put aside for further examination) test cases with an influence on an adaptation policy under test (APUT) by giving unique names to reconfigurations triggered by the APUT. It is also possible to add an additional reflection policy that stops the system (or take any other suitable action) for each success or failure of a reconfiguration triggered by the APUT.

This way, our tool, which can be launched using the interface of Fig. 1, takes fuzzy logs as input to simulate the run of a component-based system using a dummy system. The output consists of a set of trace files containing a subset of traces involving reconfigurations triggered by the APUT. Such traces can be displayed using our interface to verify that the APUT behaves as intended.

As example, we can consider, as in the case study of [1], a component-based system in charge of the location of an autonomous vehicle. To ensure reliability, the position must be computed by using different techniques such as Wi-Fi or GPS signals. When the power level of the vehicle decreases, it may be suitable to remove, for example, the GPS software component to save energy, as long as the other positioning systems keep providing accurate positions. Of course as the batteries can be recharged, when the power level rise above a certain value, the GPS component can be added back using the *addgps* reconfiguration operation. Such a reconfiguration is triggered by an adaptation policy responsible for the management of the GPS component. This policy, among other things, must take into account the low utility of adding back the GPS component to the system when the vehicle is in a tunnel where there is no GPS signal.

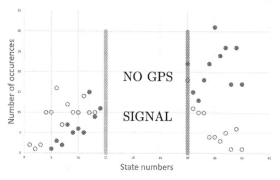

Fig. 3. Occurrences of the *addgps* reconfiguration (Color figure online)

Starting from a trace of a run of the system, we generated with our fuzz test tool 1000 test cases that were used to run the GPS adaptation policy with a dummy component-based system. Among these tests, 203 were selected because they were involving the *addgps* reconfiguration operation. The results are summarised in Fig. 3, where the horizontal and vertical axes represent respectively the states number increasing over time and the cumulated number of occurrences of the *addgps* reconfiguration for each state. Vertical lines symbolise the entrance and exit of a tunnel where there is no GPS signal, plain blue dots represent the successful application of the *addgps* reconfiguration, and hollow red dots show that its application failed[3].

These tests show that none of the *addgps* reconfiguration operations were attempted inside the tunnel where there is no GPS signal, which is the way the GPS adaptation policy was supposed to behave.

Finally, fuzzing makes the test and implementation of adaptation policies easier by allowing the tester to focus on specific regions of the sequence of configurations that would enable these policies. Also, as an interesting secondary benefit, in the early stages of development of the Fuzzy Engine tool, by running fuzz testing against some adaptation polices, we were able to identify and correct several bugs in the *cbsdr* implementation.

4   Conclusion and Future Work

The work presented in [1,2] enables component-based systems dynamic reconfigurations guided by adaptation policies. Whereas the test and implementation of these policies were possible for small systems, this was complicated and time consuming for larger systems as specific settings were required in order to put the system in the conditions that would enable such policies. The usage of fuzzing makes such tests easier by allowing the tester to focus on specific regions of the sequence of configurations that would enable these policies.

As a future work, we are planning to perform more evaluations on various case studies. We are also contemplating the possibility to integrate online fuzzing, as in [9], to the *cbsdr* project. To do so, we would use *fuzzy policies* to generate test cases at runtime, focusing on interesting regions of specific data sequences.

References

1. Kouchnarenko, O., Weber, J.-F.: Adapting component-based systems at runtime via policies with temporal patterns. In: Fiadeiro, J.L., Liu, Z., Xue, J. (eds.) FACS 2013. LNCS, vol. 8348, pp. 234–253. Springer, Cham (2014). doi:10.1007/978-3-319-07602-7_15
2. Kouchnarenko, O., Weber, J.-F.: Practical analysis framework for component systems with dynamic reconfigurations. In: Butler, M., Conchon, S., Zaïdi, F. (eds.) ICFEM 2015. LNCS, vol. 9407, pp. 287–303. Springer, Cham (2015). doi:10.1007/978-3-319-25423-4_18
3. Bruneton, E., Coupaye, T., Leclercq, M., Quéma, V., Stefani, J.B.: The fractal component model and its support in java. Softw. Pract. Experience **36**, 1257–1284 (2006)
4. Seinturier, L., Merle, P., Rouvoy, R., Romero, D., Schiavoni, V., Stefani, J.B.: A component-based middleware platform for reconfigurable service-oriented architectures. Softw. Pract. Experience **42**, 559–583 (2012)

---

[3] Because of the random nature of fuzzing, the configuration following the application the *addgps* reconfiguration may not contain a fully functional GPS component, which leads the reconfiguration to be diagnosed as failed.

5. Takanen, A., Demott, J.D., Miller, C.: Fuzzing for Software Security Testing and Quality Assurance. Artech House, Norwood (2008)
6. Schneider, M., Großmann, J., Tcholtchev, N., Schieferdecker, I., Pietschker, A.: Behavioral fuzzing operators for UML sequence diagrams. In: Haugen, Ø., Reed, R., Gotzhein, R. (eds.) SAM 2012. LNCS, vol. 7744, pp. 88–104. Springer, Heidelberg (2013). doi:10.1007/978-3-642-36757-1_6
7. Boyer, F., Gruber, F., Pous, D.: Robust reconfigurations of component assemblies. In: International Conference on Software Engineering, ICSE 2013, Piscataway, NJ, USA, pp. 13–22. IEEE Press (2013)
8. Hamilton, A.G.: Logic for Mathematicians. Cambridge University Press, Cambridge (1988)
9. Schneider, M., Großmann, J., Schieferdecker, I., Pietschker, A.: Online model-based behavioral fuzzing. In: 2013 IEEE Sixth International Conference on Software Testing, Verification and Validation Workshops (ICSTW 2003), pp. 469–475. IEEE (2013)

Applications and Experiences Papers

Coordinated Actors for Reliable Self-adaptive Systems

Maryam Bagheri[1(✉)], Ilge Akkaya[2], Ehsan Khamespanah[3,4],
Narges Khakpour[5], Marjan Sirjani[4,6], Ali Movaghar[1], and Edward A. Lee[2]

[1] CE Department, Sharif University Of Technology, Tehran, Iran
mbagheri@ce.sharif.ir
[2] EECS Department, University of California at Berkeley, Berkeley, CA, USA
[3] School of ECE, University of Tehran, Tehran, Iran
[4] School of CS and CRESS, Reykjavik University, Reykjavik, Iceland
[5] CS Department, Linnaeus University, Växjö Campus, Växjö, Sweden
[6] School of IDT, Mälardalen University, Västeras, Sweden

Abstract. Self-adaptive systems are systems that automatically adapt in response to environmental and internal changes, such as possible failures and variations in resource availability. Such systems are often realized by a MAPE-K feedback loop, where Monitor, Analyze, Plan and Execute components have access to a runtime model of the system and environment which is kept in the Knowledge component. In order to provide guarantees on the correctness of a self-adaptive system at runtime, the MAPE-K feedback loop needs to be extended with assurance techniques. To address this issue, we propose a coordinated actor-based approach to build a reusable and scalable model@runtime for self-adaptive systems in the domain of track-based traffic control systems. We demonstrate the approach by implementing an automated Air Traffic Control system (ATC) using Ptolemy tool. We compare different adaptation policies on the ATC model based on performance metrics and analyze combination of policies in different configurations of the model. We enriched our framework with runtime performance analysis such that for any unexpected change, subsequent behavior of the model is predicted and results are used for adaptation at the change-point. Moreover, the developed framework enables checking safety properties at runtime.

Keywords: Self-adaptive system · Model@runtime · Performance analysis · Cyber physical system · Air Traffic Control System

1 Introduction

The ubiquitous presence of software systems in everyday life, specially in safety-critical domains like Healthcare and transportation, makes building *reliable* cyber-physical systems (CPS) crucial. Moreover, to guarantee desirable behavior, systems need to evolve in response to environmental and internal changes, such as possible failures and variations in resource availability. Therefore, building reliable self-adaptive systems that are able to adjust their behavior in accordance

© Springer International Publishing AG 2017
O. Kouchnarenko and R. Khosravi (Eds.): FACS 2016, LNCS 10231, pp. 241–259, 2017.
DOI: 10.1007/978-3-319-57666-4_15

with their perception of the environment and the system itself is an important research topic [9, 22].

A self-adaptive system is typically realized through one or a collection of feedback loops that control adaptation of the core system. The MAPE-K feedback loop introduced in [17], is a common approach for realizing control feedback loops where a loop consists of *Monitor, Analyze, Plan* and *Execute* components, together with a *Knowledge* part, which contains information about the system and its environment. To guarantee correctness and quality of the self-adaptive systems, providing quality assurance techniques - in form of verification, validation and performance analysis- is a complicated and important issue. These techniques not only have to be applied in off-line manner, but also need to be used at runtime [8]. For instance, an abstract model of the system and the environment can be kept as the *model@runtime* in the Knowledge component, be updated periodically, and be analyzed for safety assurance, and also be used for runtime optimization and (re-)planning.

In order to design reliable self-adaptive systems, a number of the state of the art approaches benefits from the formal methods at the design time to assure the correct behavior of systems [13, 18, 19, 30, 32] and the behavior of the MAPE-K feedback loops [4, 15]. In contrary, some approaches employ formal methods at runtime [7, 15] or attempt to provide efficient techniques for runtime verification of systems [10–12]. However, a few of approaches have developed an integrated framework for constructing the MAPE-K loops and formal models@runtime, and providing runtime analysis techniques to detect or predict violation of the system's goals.

Here, we propose an actor-based [2, 14, 26] approach augmented with coordination policies for constructing and analyzing self-adaptive track-based traffic control systems. We create a total solution and build the MAPE-K feedback loop together with the model@runtime, but the focus of this paper is on building and analyzing the model@runtime. To this aim, we encapsulate the Analyze and Plan components of the MAPE-K feedback loop as a coordinator, together with the Knowledge component which keeps an updated actor-based model of the system. Monitor and Execute components can smoothly be added using features provided by our proposed implementation platform. It is noteworthy that the presented model@runtime is executable benefiting from java-based definition of the actors in the proposed implementation platform. The actor-based approach is aligned with the structure of distributed self-adaptive systems with behavioral adaptation. Loosely coupled actors as the units of concurrency, with asynchronous message passing, and event-driven computation, are natural candidates for modeling highly dynamic distributed systems. Moreover, in our problem domain, track-based traffic control systems, we have a (multiple) centralized control which is mimicked here as a coordinator. This enhances the properties of our interest (fidelity), and it is easy to understand and build the model with the least needed effort (usability).

The problem domain of the proposed framework, track-based traffic control systems, is a class of traffic control systems in which the traffic is passed through pre-specified tracks and is coordinated by a controller, like railways and some air traffic control systems. These systems follow a common structural and behavioral pattern founded on the track-based configuration. In our model, actors represent the tracks and the moving objects are modeled as messages passing among actors. Our model@runtime has to capture the current configuration which is mainly the placement of messages within the model. The coordinator in our model besides governing message passing between the actors, analyzes the current configuration of the model, predicts the future configuration and makes a plan for adaptation purpose. Modeling a coordinator with mentioned features, separate from functionalities of the actors results in reusability.

To illustrate the applicability of the proposed approach, we model an Air Traffic Control system (ATC), a large scale cyber-physical system, as our real-world case study. Our ATC model is a simplified version of North Atlantic Organized Track System (NAT-OTS) [16], consisting of a set of transatlantic flight routes, and can easily be generalized to other track-based traffic control systems (e.g., railway systems). ATCs are responsible for managing the flow of the air traffic and assuring the safe flight of the aircraft. ATC is a prototypical example where people in charge are constantly dealing with various kinds of changes in the environment and system, such as changes in weather, propagating delays, strikes of the support staff, or unforeseen problems in the aircraft.

Different adaptation policies are implemented to check how changes in environment can affect the performance of the system. Furthermore, we carry out a mechanism in which the performance of the model is predicted using different policies and the prediction results are used for switching between adaptation policies at runtime.

Our proposed framework is implemented in Ptolemy [23], which is an actor-oriented open source platform that provides an extensive actor library for modeling, simulation and analysis of the system feedback loop, provides support for connecting to the physical world and updating the model@runtime, and also offers a graphical design environment that aids in visualization of the system architecture.

Our contributions are summarized as follows.

1. *Coordinated Actor-based model@runtime*: Proposing a modular, reusable, and executable coordinated actor-based model@runtime for track-based traffic control systems,
2. *ATC model@runtime*: Developing executable model@runtime for automated ATC as a real-world large scale cyber-physical system,
3. *Performance Evaluation*: Providing a framework for comparing different adaptation policies and evaluating their impacts on the performance of the system,
4. *Runtime Prediction*: Looking ahead through the model@runtime to explore the future behavior of a model to predict property violations and select appropriate policy at change-points.

The rest of the paper is organized as follows: in Sect. 2, we provide a general overview of track-based traffic control systems and introduce ATCs as our running example. Section 3 presents coordinated actor-based modeling approach and shows how it can be used for building and analyzing model@runtime of track-based traffic control systems, e.g. ATCs. In Sect. 4, Ptolemy platform is introduced briefly and the implementation of an ATC in Ptolemy is explained. Section 5 demonstrates analysis results of the implemented system under different adaptation policies and runtime performance prediction. We describe related work in Sect. 6, and compare the proposed approach with the previous studies. Section 7 concludes the paper and outlines the future work.

2   Track-Based Traffic Control Systems

Transportation systems can be managed in different ways. We focus on those systems where the traffic can only move on certain tracks, like in railways, subways, and even roads. Traffic control for such systems follow a common structural and behavioral pattern. Tracks are generally divided into sub-tracks and the traffic controller uses this structure to guarantee safety and improve performance.

Air traffic is not necessarily guided through predefined tracks, but the ATC system in North Atlantic is based on an Organized Track System (OTS) which follows the same pattern, and is the system we have studied [1]. This pattern can be further generalized, for example a network on chip (NoC) can be considered as a track-based traffic control system in which a packet (moving object) is transferred via a set of routers (sub-tracks).

To have a fully automated traffic control system, we need a control algorithm for managing the traffic, taking into account the environment and congestion conditions. This control algorithm has several decision making capabilities, including accepting or rejecting traffic into a sub-track, and routing and rerouting traffic. Based on the nature of a system, the control algorithm can be distributed or centralized. For example, the control algorithm in NoC is distributed among routers (sub-tracks). In [24], an actor model is used for modeling and analyzing NoCs where each router (sub-track) is mapped into an actor and packets are mapped into messages. Railway systems are examples of centralized traffic control systems. A controller knows the complete map of the traffic network with the details of the current traffic. This knowledge is updated upon any change in the system, and is used for online planning.

In our model, sub-tracks can be augmented with decision making abilities. For example, based on the capacity of a sub-track, it can decide to allow or reject a moving object to enter the sub-track. This way, the safety of a sub-track (mutual exclusion) is wired in at design time. But this property can cause deadlock and fatal problems that has to be avoided. In our framework we use a centralized coordinator to manage the overall traffic and avoid deadlocks. The framework can be customized based on different applications. In our current implementation, the required time for a moving object to pass a sub-track is computed by the controller based on the speed of the object and the length

---

[1] This system is studied in collaboration with Isavia, the air traffic control company in Iceland (http://www.isavia.is).

of the sub-track. Furthermore, at a certain time, a sub-track is reserved as the next sub-track of a moving object by the controller. This way collision is avoided among objects that may request to enter into a sub-track simultaneously. If we encounter a traffic blockage, the controller handles the situation by rerouting the traffic objects, asking for changes in traffic speed, etc. We will show in the next sections how coordinated actor model is used for modeling and analysis of these cases. To this aim, we use ATC as a running example for easier explanation of the modeling and the analysis approach.

Air Traffic Control System: ATC is a system equipped with supervision instruments on the ground and the links for communication, which monitors and controls flights along the airspace routes and operations in the airports [1]. In real-world, each aircraft has a predefined flight plan, which includes its flight route (an ordered sequence of the sub-tracks to be traversed from the source to the destination), speed of flight, and the initial fuel. The aircraft's flight plan is generated prior to its take off, but dynamic changes in the weather conditions, delays in landing and taxiing, etc., requires some modifications in flight plans. For safety concerns, while changing the original flight plan of an aircraft, several parameters are carefully considered, for example loss of separation between two aircraft has to be avoided, and the remaining fuel must be enough for safely arrival to destination. A number of researches in the ATC domain, such as [3,5,6], propose mathematical models and solutions for resolving congestion of air spaces, to achieve the minimum delay and safe movement of the aircraft by taking the rerouting decisions into account. According to [5], modeling rerouting decisions is one of the greatest challenges in this field. The framework presented in this paper (Fig. 3) addresses these challenges by modeling and runtime analysis of ATC. The structure of North Atlantic Organized Track System (NAT-OTS) [16] that we consider as our ATC model consists of a set of nearly parallel tracks, positioned in the light of the prevailing winds to suit the traffic between Europe and North America.

3   A Coordinated Actor Model for Self-adaptive Track-Based Traffic Control Systems

To develop a self-adaptive system using the MAPE-K loop, a model is kept in the Knowledge component, updated by the Monitor component, and analyzed by the Analyze component. Based on the analysis results, the Plan component makes decisions for adapting the system to the new configuration and the decisions are sent to the managed system using the Execute component. To ensure the correct behavior of self-adaptive systems despite the internal and environmental changes, keeping its knowledge model updated at runtime is crucial.

Figure 1 illustrates our overall approach for modeling self-adaptive track-based traffic control systems. As shown in Fig. 1, our proposed *coordinated actor model* realizes three components of the MAPE-K loops, Knowledge, Plan, and Analyze. Using this approach, the model of a self-adaptive system is divided into two different parts, actors and a coordinator. The model@runtime encloses

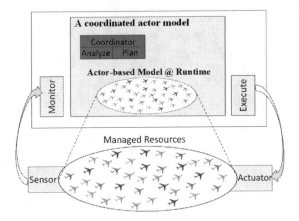

Fig. 1. Modeling self-adaptive track-based traffic control systems with coordinated actor model

the actors in addition to the part of the coordinator which handles the message delivery between the actors; and the Analyze and Plan components are the decision making parts of the coordinator. Actors communicate via asynchronous message passing, but unlike the original (Agha's) actor model, although the sent messages are immediately delivered to their target actors, the target actors do not pick messages. Instead, an event is triggered for the coordinator upon any message sending. The coordinator receives the event related to that message and puts it into its internal buffer. The internal buffer of the coordinator is sorted based on some predefined rules, e.g. an event with the least arrival time has the highest priority. Upon choosing an event with the highest priority, the coordinator can access the target actor, ask about its internal state, change the sent message, drop it, or execute the target actor to pick the message and process it. This way, the message passing among the actors is kept as the basic communication means in the target distributed system but message delivery policies are integrated in the coordinator. This mechanism gives the coordinator the necessary knowledge about the actors which is used in the decision making part. The Analyze part of the coordinator is activated when the updated knowledge shows some pre-specified changes. Analyze is capable of simply analyzing the acquired knowledge or using complicated methods such as executing the model@runtime to obtain new knowledge for predictive analysis (more details in Sect. 3.3). Then, the results of analysis are passed to the Plan part to choose appropriate actions for adapting the system (Managed Resources in Fig. 1).

3.1 Structure of Self-adaptive Track-Based Traffic Control Systems Model

In our proposed model to describe a track-based traffic control system, an actor is associated with each sub-track and the controller is modeled as a coordinator.

Furthermore, the moving objects are modeled as messages, passed by (through) the actors and messages carry the necessary information of moving objects, i.e. traveling route, fuel, and speed. In addition to the track actors and a coordinator, we distinguish the source and destination actors to model the source and the destination of moving objects. The coordinator has a complete map of the track network and current states of the sources and destinations of the traffic. The knowledge of the coordinator is updated by occurrence of events that change the internal state of the actors. These events can be environment changes in sub-tracks, and arrival or departure of moving objects into/from sub-tracks. In other words, upon accessing the actors by the coordinator, it polls their internal states and updates its knowledge.

Using the described structure, different adaptation policies are encapsulated in coordinators. In some traffic control systems, adaptation results in rerouting of traffic, like in ATCs; and in some others it may result in rescheduling, like in train control systems. In the following we will show how the rerouting of moving objects are implemented for our ATC example.

3.2 Adaptation in ATC: Dynamic Reroute Planning

In our ATC model design in Sect. 4, routing an aircraft in the network of track actors is modeled by a sequence of messages which are sent by adjacent track actors. To implement rerouting policies, different algorithms can be considered, affecting the performance of the system in different ways. In the following, three different policies for ATCs are presented. Assume $[T_1, T_2, T_3, \cdots, T_n]$ be a sequence of sub-tracks which shows the flight route associated with the aircraft A. In this sequence, T_1 is the sub-track started from the source airport and T_n is the destination airport. Now, when the aircraft A wants to leave T_1 based on this flight route and the subsequent sub-track on its flight route (sub-track T_2) is unavailable (i.e. it is stormy or is dedicated to another aircraft), the coordinator applies one of the following algorithms to reroute the aircraft A.

- **Safer Route Policy (SRP):** SRP finds the feasible shortest flight route from T_1 to T_n. A feasible flight route is a flight route which does not contain an unavailable sub-track. If there is no such route, the shortest flight route with the least number of unavailable sub-tracks is returned.
- **Blocked Area Avoidance Policy (BAAP):** Similar to the SRP, BAAP tries to find the feasible shortest flight route from T_1 to T_n. If there is no such route, it finds the shortest route which does not pass a blocked area. As shown in Fig. 2, a blocked area is a part of airspace in which all its sub-tracks have been occupied and surrounded by other aircraft at time of rerouting the aircraft A. In other words, an aircraft in a blocked area may hold its current sub-track due to the high traffic around it for a long time. Hence, the aircraft A probably would not be able to pass a sub-track in the blocked area if that sub-track is selected as a part of the aircraft's flight route. We consider three arrangements of the aircraft in the airspace which form the blocked areas. These arrangements are shown in Fig. 2. For instance, if four aircraft hold the

Fig. 2. Three different arrangements of the aircraft in the airspace which form blocked areas. The blocked areas containing unavailable sub-tracks are shown with the dotted-rectangles. The blocked areas are avoided in the BAAP rerouting policy.

sub-tracks such that the left shape of Fig. 2 appears in the airspace, a blocked area, shown by a dotted-rectangle, is formed. Since BAAP avoids areas with higher traffic, it is expected to impose less flight duration comparing to SRP.

- **Shrinking Search Policy (SSP):** This policy employs a multi step searching algorithm. At the first step, SSP tries to find a feasible shortest flight route from T_1 to T_n. If there is no such route, it tries to find a feasible shortest flight route from T_1 to T_{n-1} and so on. If a route is not found, aircraft A holds its position in T_1 for some amount of time, attempts to continue flying based on its initial flight route. Since SSP attempts to find the feasible shortest flight route for the largest possible part of the flight route, it is expected to result in less blocking probability for the aircraft in the airspace.

To improve the adaptation mechanism, one may enrich both planer and analyzer of the coordinator to select a rerouting policy from a pool of policies. For instance, assume that the analyzer is enriched with the ability of detecting blocked area in the whole airspace. This way, planer is able to use SRP as the default rerouting policy but upon increasing the number of blocked areas to a threshold, planer is informed to switch to BAAP to avoid passing the aircraft from the blocked areas.

3.3   Adaptation in ATC: Runtime Performance Prediction

The main purpose of runtime performance prediction is predicting the subsequent behavior of the system after occurrence of any unexpected changes and using the prediction results to adapt the system to the new configuration. To this aim, the required performance metrics and safety issues of the system are defined and a proper adaption takes place to fulfill them.

In the runtime performance prediction, the analyzer looks ahead through the executable model@runtime to explore the future behavior of the model to predict property violations. To this aim, upon detecting any safety violation or crossing the thresholds of the performance metrics, the planner is triggered and tries to adapt the system using its set of predefined prediction based adaptation policies. So, the models@runtime have to be augmented with techniques to record the states of the models at the change points (taking snapshots of models), look ahead and backtrack as follows. In the coordinated actor model, the state of the model is defined as the local states of actors along with the state of the coordinator. The state of each actor is defined as the assigned values to its variables and the coordinator state is defined as the assigned values to its variables, communicated messages between the actors together with the triggered events, and the time. So, when a change happens (based on the coordinator knowledge), state of the model is stored by the analyzer, and model proceeds with its execution to the end. At the final step, the values of performance metrics which are gathered during the execution of the model are gathered by the analyzer. These values are used by the planner part of the coordinator to choose the most suitable adaptation policy for the change.

4   Coordinated Actor Model of ATC in Ptolemy

Ptolemy II is an actor-oriented open-source modeling framework. A Ptolemy model is made up of actors that communicate through ports via message passing. Actors are implemented in Java with a well-defined interface, which includes ports and parameters. Ports are communication points of actors and parameters are used to configure the internal behavior. Parameter values can be changed dynamically during the execution of model. In Ptolemy, the semantics of interactions and communications of actors is defined by a Model of Computation (MoC), implemented by a special component called a *Director*. Different MoCs are implemented in Ptolemy which can be composed to yield heterogeneous models. Ptolemy is open-source and new MoCs can be created by extending or modifying existing MoC implementations. Heterogeneous hierarchical actor-oriented design capabilities in Ptolemy provides a strong modeling and simulation toolkit for CPS design [23]. One of the most widely used MoCs in Ptolemy is Discrete-Event (DE). Actors governed by a DE director communicate via time-stamped events (i.e. time-stamped messages of actors), where events are processed by each actor in time-stamp order. Considering different MoCs in Ptolemy, we choose DE for ATC model, because time-stamped events are natural for representing the decision points in a track-based traffic control system.

Following the coordinated actor model presented in Sect. 3, we model coordinator of ATCs as a new Ptolemy DE director, we call ATCDirector. Here, airports and tracks are modeled using actors of Ptolemy and their interconnections showed by wiring of actors' ports. The model of a simplified ATC model is presented in Fig. 3. In this model traffic is passed from west to east. As shown in Fig. 3, there is a network of tracks where each track is shown by a white aircraft. To present a track which is associated to an aircraft, the distinct color of that aircraft is used for that track. Tracks affected by thunderstorms are highlighted with a red circle around them. As shown in Fig. 3, connections of a track to its neighbors are illustrated as the output ports of the track and ids of its neighbors are set as the parameter of the track. Arrival and departure airports are also modeled by Ptolmey actors, shown by blocks with captions of *Airport* and

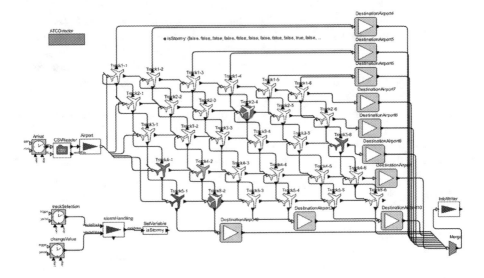

Fig. 3. ATC model in Ptolemy (Color figure online)

Destination Airport in Fig. 3. ATCDirector of this model is shown as a green rectangle with caption of the ATCDirector in Fig. 3.

To execute the ATC model, departure of the aircraft and weather changes are simulated as follows. In this model flights are initialized by Arrival and CSVReader actors. The Arrival actor is a discrete clock that determines the departure time of aircraft. CSVReader reads flight plans and other detailed information of the aircraft from a text file. In Fig. 3 three more actors are implemented for simulating the weather condition changes, called TrackSelection, ChangeValue, and StormHandling. TrackSelection selects a track (with a predetermined probability) and ChangeValue decides about how the weather condition of the selected track must be changed. ChangeValue has the role of both generating and removing storms. StormHandling applies the made decision of ChangeValue on its target track. The ATC model also can be fed by real values from real-world sensors using features of Ptolemy.

5   Safety Check and Performance Analysis

In this section, we study the effectiveness of our approach by evaluating and comparing various performance criteria for rerouting policies described in Sect. 3.2. Our results show that applying runtime performance prediction improves the performance metrics[2].

---

[2] The source code which is used for these experiments is uploaded in http://rebeca.cs.ru.is/files/ATC.zip.

5.1   The Experimental Settings

The performance metrics of the ATC are measured when an aircraft reaches its destination. In our experiments, the performance metrics are the number of aircraft arrived to their destinations, the number of missing aircraft (the aircraft that are stuck in a traffic blockage in the airspace and cannot find a route to their destinations using the rerouting policies), the number of aircraft blocked in their source airports, the average delay of the aircraft in their source airports, the average flight duration of the aircraft, and the throughput. Throughput is defined as the number of aircraft arrived in their destination airports in a specific period of time.

We assumed one unit of time for the takeoff/landing of an aircraft in addition to passing a sub-track. An aircraft sends a request to enter into a sub-track 0.2 unit of time before its planned arrival time. If the aircraft is asked to stay in its current sub-track, it waits for one more unit of time and sends a new request to enter into the same sub-track again. In addition, we assume that each airport has one runway and each sub-track can contain at most one aircraft at a time.

The ATC model in our experiments contains two source airports, eight destination airports and thirty tracks. There are fifty aircraft that intend to fly from a north airport to one of the three south destination airports and the same number of aircraft plan to fly from the west airport to the five destination airports in the east. The initial flight route of an aircraft is the shortest route from its source airport to its destination. For each source airport, twenty batches of flight plans are generated and each batch contains the flight plans for fifty aircraft. The departure times of the aircraft, and the times of the weather changes are produced using Poisson processes with parameters λ in $\{0.5, 2, 3.5\}$ (the mean interval time between two events) and 1 as μ, respectively.

5.2   Safety Checking

In the experiments, we check deadlock-freedom and a few safety issues. Deadlock is detected if none of the aircraft in the airspace change their current sub-tracks within a pre-determined time. This means that the aircraft are stuck in a traffic blockage and cannot find a route to their destinations. As safety issues, the separation between the aircraft, and safe rerouting in stormy weather are checked and guaranteed by the model. A sub-track in our model denotes the minimum separation between two aircraft, so, two aircraft must never be in a sub-track at the same time. The guarantee of this property is built-in in the behavior of the coordinator at design time. The coordinator never triggers a track actor to process a new message (aircraft) while the track actor is handling a message (another aircraft), neither when it is stormy. Also, the remaining fuel level of an aircraft is checked as another safety issue of the ATC. If the fuel level becomes less than a threshold, a notification is raised.

Table 1. Performance metrics in the SRP, BAAP, SSP rerouting policies, Combined Rerouting Policies (CRP), and the Runtime Performance Prediction (RPP)

Policy	λ	Throughput	Number of arrived aircraft	Avg. flight duration	Avg. delay in source airport	Number of missing aircraft	Aircraft blocked in the airport
SRP	0.5	0.65	39.60	10.43	14.39	16.94	43.45
	2	0.60	44.73	9.84	4.59	16.28	38.98
	3.5	0.45	65.52	8.95	1.91	10.26	24.21
BAAP	0.5	0.65	38.05	10.28	13.61	18.02	43.92
	2	0.59	43.54	9.84	4.39	17.21	39.23
	3.5	0.45	63.96	8.88	1.92	10.96	25.06
SSP	0.5	0.68	43.84	10.37	16.49	13.86	42.29
	2	0.62	48.38	9.97	5.04	13.04	38.57
	3.5	0.46	66.03	8.94	1.92	8.21	25.74
CRP	0.5	0.65	41.34	10.08	16.06	7.12	51.52
	2	0.60	45.32	9.81	5.39	6.98	47.69
	3.5	0.46	63.23	8.94	2.01	5.39	31.36
RPP	0.5	0.66	44.72	10.72	17.98	13.09	42.18
	2	0.61	47.67	9.99	5.17	13.04	39.28
	3.5	0.46	67.37	8.96	2.11	7.95	24.67

5.3   Performance Evaluation of Dynamic Reroute Planning

The model mentioned in Sect. 5.1 is executed 150 times per each value of λ and the average of the performance metrics are calculated. Table 1 illustrates the results of executing different rerouting policies under the above-mentioned conditions. Setting the number of departing aircraft to a constant value (100), by increasing the value of λ and increasing the total duration time of the simulation, we expect increasing in the number of arrived aircraft. This is because of the fact that increasing the value of λ results in making the traffic lighter, ends in decreasing delays in the source airports and the flight durations.

Table 1 shows the performance metrics for SSP, BAAP, SRP, CRP and RPP. In the CRP policy, the three basic rerouting policies are combined and used dynamically according to a set of predefined policies. The number of missing aircraft in all policies indicates that in our setting the deadlock is inevitable; the reason is that we increase the crossovers of aircraft intentionally to be able to see the differences among different policies. However, designing rerouting policies without a deadlock is not impossible, but it is beyond the scope of this paper. This table shows that the BAAP rerouting policy performs better than SSP and SRP policies based on the metrics of average delay in the source airports and the average flight duration. The SSP has a better performance in terms of the number of missing aircraft in the sub-tracks and the number of blocked aircraft in the source airports. The cause is that SSP attempts to find the feasible shortest flight route for the longest part of the flight route. However, as SSP is a conservative policy in comparison with the other policies in finding a route, it increases the average delay in the source airport. The reason is that it holds an aircraft in its source airports until it finds a route for the rejected aircraft holding their position in the sub-tracks. The BAAP policy reduces the average flight duration, because if it cannot find a feasible shortest route for a rejected aircraft, it tries to find a route, avoiding to pass the aircraft from the blocked areas. When the aircraft are not allowed to pass from the blocked areas, they rarely need to change their route and also hold the sub-tracks for a fewer time. Consequently the average delay of the aircraft in the source airport decreases.

In our implementation of the CRP, the analyzer continuously monitors the configuration of the model and the planner chooses a suitable rerouting policy to be applied in that configuration. As an example, assume that the coordinator starts rerouting the aircraft using the SRP policy. Upon detecting a blocked area in the airspace, the coordinator switches to BAAP to reduce the flight durations of aircraft by avoiding the blocked area. Moreover, if the number of rejected arrivals to the sub-tracks passes a predefined threshold (that sets to 20 in our experiments), and at least a number of the sub-tracks are occupied (10 in our case), the coordinator will switch to SSP and decreases the airspace load by restricting the number of takeoffs from the source airports. When a predefined percentage of the aircraft arrive to their destinations (50% in our experiments), the coordinator switches to its former policy and the aircraft blocked in the source airport are permitted to takeoff. As shown in Table 1, CRP increases the aircraft delay in ground but decreases the average flight duration and the number of the missing aircraft.

The last row of Table 1, presents the performance evaluation results of rerouting with runtime performance prediction. In our experiments the SSP policy is the default rerouting policy of the coordinator. As shown in Table 1, SSP performs better than BAAP in terms of the number of the missing aircraft but has a higher average flight duration compared to BAAP. If a storm happens, the runtime performance prediction method is applied; if the predicted number of the missing aircraft using SSP exceeds 18 and its average delay in the airport exceeds 13.61, the planner switches its routing policy to BAAP. Furthermore, if the coordinator reroutes the aircraft using the BAAP rerouting policy, the predicted number of the missing aircraft becomes greater than 13.86, and the average delay in an airport becomes greater than 16.49, the coordinator switches to SSP. As a result, the number of the missing aircraft decreases and consequently, the number of the aircraft arrived at the destination airports increases.

6   Related Work

In this section we discuss the most related and recent state of the art in the modeling and analysis of self-adaptive systems. At first, different approaches in modeling feedback control loops are presented and then the applications of formal verification methods in analyzing model@runtime are addressed.

Modeling and analyzing feedback loop: Feedback loops are the most crucial elements of self-adaptive systems which have to be modeled explicitly [27]. The MAPE-K feedback loop is a widely used approach for realizing self-adaptive systems. In order to model the MAPE-K loops, different solutions have been proposed. ActiveFORM is introduced in [15] together with a tool for verifying adaptation goals at runtime as well as the design time. It also provides possibility of changing the system goals at runtime dynamically. ActiveFORM uses timed automata to model each component of the MAPE-K loop and TCTL for specifying properties of the adaptation behavior. To realize self-adaptation, provided models are transformed to codes which are executable on a virtual machine. According to [28], dependencies between the MAPE components and the Knowledge component in ActiveFORM are modeled by signal passing through timed automata; thus, they are only available in an implicit form. Unlike ActiveFORM, our approach does not focus on modeling and verifying MAPE-K loops and does not provide Analyze and Plan components separately. Instead, our focus is on analyzing the models@runtime. Furthermore, encapsulating Analyze and Plan components in a coordinator makes our approach more faithful to the real-world applications in our problem domain comparing to the timed automata.

Vogel et al. [27] presented EUREMA, a model-driven engineering approach to specify and execute multiple feedback loops, runtime models and the dependencies between the feedback loops and the adaptable software. The EUREMA modeling language provides behavioral feedback loop diagram (FLD) to model the feedback loop components and runtime models. It benefits from structural layer diagram (LD) to describe the wiring of FLDs and adaptable software. For executing feedback loops, EUREMA models are interpreted at runtime. Interpretation impacts on the efficiency of the approach but the overhead is negligible. Since our proposed model@runtime is executable, the Analyze activity of the MAPE-K feedback loop is capable of predicting a property violation, while EUREMA has not addressed this feature. EUREMA supports specifying multiple feedback loops which is a part of our future work.

Another approach proposed in [20], introduces Feedback Control Definition Language (FCDL) based on the actor model for modeling adaptable feedback control loops (FCL). In FCL, sensors, actuators, filters, and decision makers are represented by actors. Different FCLs can be organized hierarchically or coordinate with each other. Modeling, structural consistency checking, and code generation using this approach is facilitated by ACTRESS toolkit [21]. ACTRESS transforms FCDL models into Promela models and verifies connectivity and reachability properties of the FCLs using SPIN. As our approach uses the Ptolemy platform, there is no need for more effort to generate executable code, while in ACTRESS an executable application is provided through a set of model-to-model transformation. Furthermore, unlike our approach, there is not model@runtime in ACTRESS.

Multi-agent Abstract State Machine (ASM) is proposed in [4] for modeling and verification of decentralized MAPE-K feedback loops at design time. In this approach, computations of one loop can be distributed over several agents and the behavior of each MAPE-K loop component is specified by ASM transition rules. In the proposed approach, a system exposes a number of MAPE-K loops, one per each adaptation concern. The model is verified using AsmetaSMV tool with the aim of detecting interferences between different feedback loops. This approach models one MAPE-K loop per each adaptation concern, while in our approach for each sub-system a MAPE-K loop is generated. Furthermore, unlike ASM, our approach does not focus on verifying the MAPE-K feedback loops. Instead it focuses on analyzing the model@runtime.

Model@runtime analysis: Forejt et al. [12] proposed an approach for incremental runtime verification of Markov Decision Process (MDP) models which are described in PRISM. In this approach, runtime changes are limited to vary parameters of PRISM models. The MDP of models are constructed incrementally by inferring a set of states, needed to be rebuilt. The constructed MDPs are verified using the incremental verification technique. Besides, QoSMOS is proposed in [7] for the development of adaptive service-based systems. QoSMOS integrates a set of pre-existing tools to model MAPE-K loop. It adapts system in a predictable way by the aim of optimizing quality of service requirements. Model@runtime is expressed in PRISM and is verified in the analysis step. Results of the verification are used to adapt the configuration of systems. Our coordinated actor model is in a higher level of abstract comparing to the state-based model of PRISM. This reduces the semantic gap between the model and the real-world applications in our problem domain and increases the fidelity.

A parametric approach is presented in [10,11] for the runtime verification of Discrete Time Markov Chains (DTMCs). In this method, probabilities of the transitions are given as variables instead of constant values. Then, the model is analyzed and a set of symbolic expressions is reported as the result. This way, the verification at runtime is reduced to calculating the values of the symbolic expressions by substituting real values of variables.

Designing a self-adaptive software as a dynamic software product line (DSPL) is proposed in [13]. In this approach an instance of DSPL is chosen at runtime considering the environmental changes. This approach separately models common behavior of the products and each variation point by the parametric DTMC. So, there is no need for the verification of each configuration separately. In comparison with both of the above approaches, our actor-based model is more reusable and easy to build comparing to the state-based models such as DTMCs.

Wuttke et al. in [31] worked on the effectiveness of developing frameworks to compare and evaluate different adaptation policies, proposed for self-adaptation. To this aim, the authors developed a Java-based simulator for comparing different adaptation policies in automated traffic routing. In addition to it, Weyns et al. in [29] provided an implementation of the Tele Assistance systems and compared the effect of different adaptation policies in this application.

7   Discussion, Conclusion and Future Work

We proposed coordinated actor models for modeling and analyzing self-adaptive track-based traffic control systems. The coordinator encompasses Analyze and Plan components of the MAPE-K loop as well as managing interactions between the actors. The proposed coordinated actor model is augmented with a run-time performance prediction mechanism. Track-based traffic control systems were targeted, as the widely used application domain in cyber-physical systems. We designed an automated adaptive model for these systems which specialized and implemented for ATCs. We used Ptolemy platform to design and analyze model@runtime. Ptolemy enabled our proposed coordinated actor model to be executed at runtime.

In a nutshell, we can describe the highlights of our approach as follows.

- Fidelity and usability of the model@runtime is built-in because of the actor-based modeling. Compared to the analytical state-based models, actor-based modeling decreases the semantic gap between the real-world and the model. This makes the model more understandable and usable and easy to build for software engineers. The level of abstraction can be tuned, and efficient analysis techniques can be used.
- Concurrency, modularity and reusability are provided as the model@runtime is based on actors.
- Scalability results from simplicity, usability and modularity of the approach. In other words, model@runtime can be the model of a large scale self-adaptive system. However, scalability suffers from the bottleneck produced by the coordinator as the message passing between the actors is governed through the coordinator in a centralized way. In our future work we will address this problem by having multiple coordinators.
- As actors in Ptolemy are implemented in Java, the step for transforming the MAPE-K loop and model@runtime to code is already covered.
- The suggested framework allows defining any behavioral adaptation policies which leads to high flexibility.
- The model leads to a correct by construction design because the coordinator performs safety checks (e.g. to avoid collision), and enforces a set of time constraints on handling the messages by the actors that prevent the aircraft to enter a sub-track (and hence lose the safe distance) simultaneously.

The whole air space is divided into multiple air space regions and is controlled by multiple air traffic controllers. As our future work, we will extend our proposed architecture and model@runtime to capture the decentralized nature of ATC when spread over different air space regions. We will develop multiple coordinated actor models (multiple MAPE-K feedback loops) interacting with each other. Moreover, we will define the formal semantics of the coordinated actor model and extend our previous results [25] to provide formal verification of the model@runtime.

Acknowledgment. The work on this paper has been supported in part by the project "Self-Adaptive Actors: SEADA" (nr. 163205-051) of the Icelandic Research Fund.

References

1. Airport and air traffic control system (1982). https://www.princeton.edu/~ota/disk3/1982/8202/8202.PDF
2. Agha, G.: Actors: A Model of Concurrent Computation in Distributed Systems. MIT Press, Cambridge (1986)
3. Agustn, A., Alonso-Ayuso, A., Escudero, L., Pizarro, C.: On air traffic flow management with rerouting. Part II: stochastic case. Eur. J. Oper. Res. **219**(1), 167–177 (2012)
4. Arcaini, P., Riccobene, E., Scandurra, P.: Modeling and analyzing MAPE-K feedback loops for self-adaptation. In: Proceedings of the 10th International Symposium on Software Engineering for Adaptive and Self-Managing Systems, SEAMS 2015, pp. 13–23. IEEE Press (2015)
5. Bertsimas, D., Lulli, G., Odoni, A.: The air traffic flow management problem: an integer optimization approach. In: Lodi, A., Panconesi, A., Rinaldi, G. (eds.) IPCO 2008. LNCS, vol. 5035, pp. 34–46. Springer, Heidelberg (2008). doi:10.1007/978-3-540-68891-4_3
6. Bertsimas, D., Patterson, S.S.: The traffic flow management rerouting problem in air traffic control: a dynamic network flow approach. Transp. Sci. **34**(3), 239–255 (2000)
7. Calinescu, R., Grunske, L., Kwiatkowska, M., Mirandola, R., Tamburrelli, G.: Dynamic QoS management and optimization in service-based systems. IEEE Trans. Softw. Eng. **37**(3), 387–409 (2011)
8. Calinescu, R., Ghezzi, C., Kwiatkowska, M., Mirandola, R.: Self-adaptive software needs quantitative verification at runtime. Commun. ACM **55**(9), 69–77 (2012)
9. Cheng, B.H.C., et al.: Using models at runtime to address assurance for self-adaptive systems. In: Bencomo, N., France, R., Cheng, B.H.C., Aßmann, U. (eds.) Models@run.time. LNCS, vol. 8378, pp. 101–136. Springer, Cham (2014). doi:10.1007/978-3-319-08915-7_4
10. Filieri, A., Ghezzi, C., Tamburrelli, G.: Run-time efficient probabilistic model checking. In: Proceedings of the 33rd International Conference on Software Engineering, ICSE 2011, pp. 341–350. ACM (2011)
11. Filieri, A., Tamburrelli, G.: Probabilistic verification at runtime for self-adaptive systems. In: Cámara, J., de Lemos, R., Ghezzi, C., Lopes, A. (eds.) Assurances for Self-Adaptive Systems. LNCS, vol. 7740, pp. 30–59. Springer, Heidelberg (2013). doi:10.1007/978-3-642-36249-1_2
12. Forejt, V., Kwiatkowska, M., Parker, D., Qu, H., Ujma, M.: Incremental runtime verification of probabilistic systems. In: Qadeer, S., Tasiran, S. (eds.) RV 2012. LNCS, vol. 7687, pp. 314–319. Springer, Heidelberg (2013). doi:10.1007/978-3-642-35632-2_30
13. Ghezzi, C., Molzam Sharifloo, A.: Dealing with non-functional requirements for adaptive systems via dynamic software product-lines. In: de Lemos, R., Giese, H., Müller, H.A., Shaw, M. (eds.) Software Engineering for Self-Adaptive Systems II. LNCS, vol. 7475, pp. 191–213. Springer, Heidelberg (2013). doi:10.1007/978-3-642-35813-5_8

14. Hewitt, C.: Description and theoretical analysis (using schemata) of planner: A language for proving theorems and manipulating models in a robot. Technical report, DTIC Document (1972)
15. Iftikhar, M.U., Weyns, D.: ActivFORMS: active formal models for self-adaptation. In: Proceedings of the 9th International Symposium on Software Engineering for Adaptive and Self-Managing Systems, SEAMS 2014, pp. 125–134 (2014)
16. International Civil Aviation Organization (ICAO): North atlantic operations and airspace manual (2016)
17. Kephart, J., Chess, D.: The vision of autonomic computing. Computer **36**(1), 41–50 (2003)
18. Khakpour, N., Jalili, S., Talcott, C., Sirjani, M., Mousavi, M.: PobSAM: policy-based managing of actors in self-adaptive systems. Electron. Notes Theor. Comput. Sci. **263**, 129–143 (2010). Proceedings of the 6th International Workshop on Formal Aspects of Component Software (FACS 2009)
19. Khakpour, N., Jalili, S., Talcott, C., Sirjani, M., Mousavi, M.: Formal modeling of evolving self-adaptive systems. Sci. Comput. Program. **78**(1), 3–26 (2012). Special Section: Formal Aspects of Component Software (FACS 2009)
20. Křikava, F., Collet, P., France, R.B.: Actor-based runtime model of adaptable feedback control loops. In: Proceedings of the 7th Workshop on Models@Run.Time, MRT 2012, pp. 39–44. ACM (2012)
21. Křikava, F., Collet, P., France, R.B.: ACTRESS: domain-specific modeling of self-adaptive software architectures. In: Proceedings of the 29th Annual ACM Symposium on Applied Computing, SAC 2014, pp. 391–398. ACM (2014)
22. de Lemos, R., et al.: Software engineering for self-adaptive systems: a second research roadmap. In: de Lemos, R., Giese, H., Müller, H.A., Shaw, M. (eds.) Software Engineering for Self-Adaptive Systems II. LNCS, vol. 7475, pp. 1–32. Springer, Heidelberg (2013). doi:10.1007/978-3-642-35813-5_1
23. Ptolemaeus, C.: System Design, Modeling, and Simulation: Using Ptolemy II. Ptolemy. org, Berkeley (2014)
24. Sharifi, Z., Mosaffa, M., Mohammadi, S., Sirjani, M.: Functional and performance analysis of network-on-chips using actor-based modeling and formal verification. ECEASST 66 (2013)
25. Sirjani, M., Jaghoori, M.M.: Ten years of analyzing actors: Rebeca experience. In: Agha, G., Danvy, O., Meseguer, J. (eds.) Formal Modeling: Actors, Open Systems, Biological Systems. LNCS, vol. 7000, pp. 20–56. Springer, Heidelberg (2011). doi:10.1007/978-3-642-24933-4_3
26. Talcott, C.: Composable semantic models for actor theories. Higher-Order Symbolic Comput. **11**(3), 281–343 (1998)
27. Vogel, T., Giese, H.: Model-driven engineering of self-adaptive software with eurema. ACM Trans. Auton. Adapt. Syst. **8**(4), 18:1–18:33 (2014)
28. Wätzoldt, S., Giese, H.: Classifying distributed self-* systems based on runtime models and their coupling. In: Proceedings of the 9th Workshop on Models@ run. time Co-located with 17th International Conference on Model Driven Engineering Languages and Systems, Ceur-WS, pp. 11–20 (2014)
29. Weyns, D., Calinescu, R.: Tele assistance: a self-adaptive service-based system examplar. In: Proceedings of the 10th International Symposium on Software Engineering for Adaptive and Self-Managing Systems, SEAMS 2015, pp. 88–92. IEEE Press (2015)
30. Weyns, D., Malek, S., Andersson, J.: Forms: unifying reference model for formal specification of distributed self-adaptive systems. ACM Trans. Auton. Adapt. Syst. **7**(1), 8:1–8:61 (2012)

31. Wuttke, J., Brun, Y., Gorla, A., Ramaswamy, J.: Traffic routing for evaluating self-adaptation. In: Proceedings of the 7th International Symposium on Software Engineering for Adaptive and Self-Managing Systems, SEAMS 2012, pp. 27–32. IEEE Press (2012)
32. Zhang, J., Goldsby, H.J., Cheng, B.H.: Modular verification of dynamically adaptive systems. In: Proceedings of the 8th ACM International Conference on Aspect-oriented Software Development, AOSD 2009, pp. 161–172 (2009)

Architecture-Based Design: A Satellite On-Board Software Case Study

Anastasia Mavridou[1]([✉]), Emmanouela Stachtiari[2], Simon Bliudze[1], Anton Ivanov[1], Panagiotis Katsaros[2], and Joseph Sifakis[1]

[1] École polytechnique fédérale de Lausanne, Lausanne, Switzerland
{anastasia.mavridou,simon.bliudze,anton.ivanov,joseph.sifakis}@epfl.ch
[2] Aristotle University of Thessaloniki, Thessaloniki, Greece
{emmastac,katsaros}@csd.auth.gr

Abstract. In this case study, we apply the architecture-based design approach to the control software of the CubETH satellite. Architectures are a means for ensuring global coordination properties and thus, achieving correctness of complex systems *by construction*. We illustrate the following three steps of the design approach: (1) definition of a domain-specific taxonomy of architecture styles; (2) design of the software model by applying architectures to enforce the required properties; (3) deadlock-freedom analysis of the resulting model. We provide a taxonomy of architecture styles for satellite on-board software, formally defined by architecture diagrams in the BIP component-based framework. We show how architectures are instantiated from the diagrams and applied to a set of atomic components. Deadlock-freedom of the resulting model is verified using DFinder from the BIP tool-set. We provide additional validation of our approach by using the nuXmv model checker to verify that the properties enforced by the architectures are, indeed, satisfied by the model.

1 Introduction

Satellites and other complex systems become increasingly software-dependent. Even nanosatellites have complexity that can be compared to scientific instruments launched to Mars. Standards exist for hardware parts and designs, and they can be found as commercial off the shelf (COTS) components. On the contrary, software has to be adapted to the payload and, consequently, hardware architecture selected for the satellite. There is not a rigorous and robust way to design software for CubeSats[1] or small satellites yet.

Flight software safety is of paramount importance for satellites. In harsh radiation environments, performance of COTS components is often affected by proton particles. For example, the I2C bus, which is commonly used in CubeSats due to its low energy consumption and wide availability in COTS chips, is well known in space community for its glitches. Although error correcting algorithms

---

[1] CubeSat [15] is a standard for the design of nano- and picosatellites.

© Springer International Publishing AG 2017
O. Kouchnarenko and R. Khosravi (Eds.): FACS 2016, LNCS 10231, pp. 260–279, 2017.
DOI: 10.1007/978-3-319-57666-4_16

are widely implemented across all subsystems and interfaces, the use of the bus by the components requires careful coordination to ensure correct operation. Needless to say, software correctness must be established before launch.

To the best of our knowledge, most flight software for university satellites is written in C or C++, without any architectural thinking. A notable exception is a recent effort at Vermont Tech to use SPARK, a variant of Ada amenable to static analysis [14]. Other projects simply structure their code in C/C++ and then extensively test it, maybe using some analysis tools such as lint [26]. Others use SysML [34] to describe the system as a whole [33] and then check some properties such as energy consumption. SysML can be a valid tool for system engineering as a whole, but it is not rigorous enough to allow automatic verification and validation of software behaviour.

Satellite on-board software and, more generally, all modern software systems are inherently concurrent. They consist of components that—at least on the conceptual level—run simultaneously and share access to resources provided by the execution platform. Embedded control software in various domains commonly comprises, in addition to components responsible for taking the control decisions, a set of components driving the operation of sensing and actuation devices. These components interact through buses, shared memories and message buffers, leading to resource contention and potential deadlocks compromising mission- and safety-critical operations.

The intrinsic concurrent nature of such interactions is the root cause of the sheer complexity of the resulting software. Indeed, in order to analyse the behaviour of such a software system, one has to consider all possible interleavings of the operations executed by its components. Thus, the complexity of software systems is exponential in the number of their components, making a posteriori verification of their correctness practically infeasible. An alternative approach consists in ensuring correctness by construction, through the application of well-defined design principles [4,19], imposing behavioural contracts on individual components [8] or by applying automatic transformations to obtain executable code from formally defined high-level models [32].

Following this latter approach, a notion of *architectures* was proposed in [2] to formalise design patterns for the coordination of concurrent components. Architectures provide means for ensuring correctness by construction by enforcing global properties characterising the coordination between components. An architecture can be defined as an operator $\mathcal{A}$ that, applied to a set of components $\mathcal{B}$, builds a composite component $\mathcal{A}(\mathcal{B})$ meeting a characteristic property Φ. Composability is based on an associative, commutative and idempotent architecture composition operator $\oplus$: architecture composition preserves the safety properties enforced by the individual architectures. *Architecture styles* [22,24] are families of architectures sharing common characteristics such as the type of the involved components and the characteristic properties they enforce. Architecture styles define all architectures for an arbitrary set of components that satisfy some minimal assumptions on their interfaces.

The notion of architectures proposed in [2] is based on the Behaviour-Interaction-Priority (BIP) [6] framework for the component-based design of concurrent software and systems. BIP is supported by a tool-set comprising translators from various programming models into BIP, source-to-source transformers as well as compilers for generating code executable by dedicated engines. Furthermore, the BIP tool-set provides tools for deadlock detection [7], state reachability analysis and an interface with the nuXmv model checker [10]. In the CubETH project [31], BIP was used to design logic for the operation of a satellite, executed on the on-board computer [29]. Although some properties were shown a posteriori to hold by construction, due to the use of a high-level modelling language instead of plain C/C++ code, the BIP model was designed in an ad-hoc manner, without consideration for any particular set of requirements.

In the case study presented in this paper, we have analysed the BIP model obtained in [29] and identified a number of recurring patterns, which we formalised as architecture styles. We have identified a representative sub-system of the CubETH control software, which has a complete set of functional requirements, and redesigned from scratch the corresponding BIP model using the architecture styles to discharge these requirements *by construction*. We have used the DFinder tool to verify that the resulting model is free from deadlocks. Finally, we provide additional validation of our approach by using the nuXmv model checker to verify that the architectures applied in the design process do, indeed, enforce the required properties.

The rest of the paper is structured as follows. Section 2 presents a brief overview of BIP and the architecture-based design approach. Section 3 presents the case study, the identified architecture styles, illustrates our approach through the design of a corresponding BIP model and presents the verification process and results. Section 4 discusses the related work. Section 5 concludes the paper.

2   Architecture-Based Design Approach

Our approach relies on the BIP framework [6] for component-based design of correct-by-construction applications. BIP provides a simple, but powerful mechanism for the coordination of concurrent components by superposing three layers. First, component *behaviour*

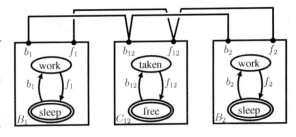

Fig. 1. Mutual exclusion model in BIP

is described by Labelled Transition Systems (LTS) having transitions labelled with *ports*. Ports form the interface of a component and are used to define its interactions with other components. Second, *interaction models*, i.e. sets of interactions, define the component coordination. Interactions are sets of ports that define allowed synchronisations between components. An interaction model is

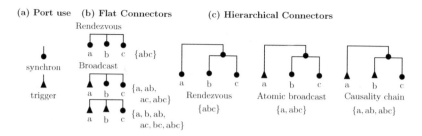

Fig. 2. Flat and hierarchical BIP connectors

defined in a structured manner by using connectors [9]. Third, *priorities* are used to impose scheduling constraints and to resolve conflicts when multiple interactions are enabled simultaneously.

Figure 1 shows a simple BIP model for mutual exclusion between two tasks. It has two components B_1, B_2 modelling the tasks and one coordinator component C_{12}. Initial states of the components are shown with double lines. The four binary connectors synchronise each of the actions b_1, b_2 (resp. f_1, f_2) of the tasks with the action b_{12} (resp. f_{12}) of the coordinator.

Connectors define sets of interactions based on the synchronisation attributes of the connected ports, which may be either *trigger* or *synchron* (Fig. 2a). If all connected ports are synchrons, then synchronisation is by *rendezvous*, i.e. the defined interaction may be executed only if all the connected components allow the transitions of those ports (Fig. 2b). If a connector has at least one trigger, the synchronisation is by *broadcast*, i.e. the allowed interactions are all non-empty subsets of the connected ports comprising at least one of the trigger ports (Fig. 2b). More complex connectors can be built hierarchically (Fig. 2c).

An architecture can be viewed as a BIP model, where some of the atomic components are considered as *coordinators*, while the rest are *parameters*. When an architecture is applied to a set of components, these components are used as *operands* to replace the parameters of the architecture. Clearly, operand components must refine the correspond-

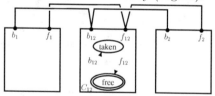

Fig. 3. Mutual exclusion architecture

ing parameter ones—in that sense, parameter components can be considered as *types*.[2] Figure 3 shows an architecture that enforces the mutual exclusion property $AG\neg(cs_1 \wedge cs_2)$ on any two components with interfaces $\{b_1, f_1\}$ and $\{b_2, f_2\}$, satisfying the CTL formula $AG(f_i \rightarrow A[\neg cs_i \ W \ b_i])$, where cs_i is an atomic predicate, true when the component is in the critical section (e.g. in the state work, for B_1, B_2 of Fig. 1). Composition of architectures is based on an associative, commutative and idempotent architecture composition operator '$\oplus$' [2]. If two

---

[2] The precise definition of the refinement relation is beyond the scope of this paper.

architectures $\mathcal{A}_1$ and $\mathcal{A}_2$ enforce respectively safety properties Φ_1 and Φ_2, the composed architecture $\mathcal{A}_1 \oplus \mathcal{A}_2$ enforces the property $\Phi_1 \wedge \Phi_2$, that is both properties are preserved by architecture composition.

Although the architecture in Fig. 3 can only be applied to a set of precisely two components, it is clear that an architecture of the same *style*—with n parameter components and $2n$ connectors—could be applied to any set of operand components satisfying the above CTL formula. We use *architecture diagrams* [24] to specify such *architecture styles*, as described in the next section. (See Fig. 6 in Sect. 3.1 for the diagram of the style generalising the architecture in Fig. 3.)

The architecture-based design approach consists of the three stages illustrated in Fig. 4. First, architecture styles relevant for the application domain—in our case, nano- and picosatellite on-

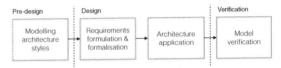

Fig. 4. Architecture-based design flow

board software—are identified and formally modelled. Ideally, this stage is only realised once for each application domain. The remaining stages are applied for each system to be designed. In the second, design stage, requirements to be satisfied by the system are analysed and formalised, atomic components realising the basic functionality of the system are designed (components previously designed for other systems can be reused) and used as operands for the application of architectures instantiated from the styles defined in the first stage. The choice of the architectures to apply is driven by the requirements identified in the second stage. Finally, the resulting system is checked for deadlock-freedom. Properties, which are not enforced by construction through architecture application, must be verified a posteriori. In this case study, we illustrate all steps of this process, except the requirement formalisation.

In the first stage, we use *architecture diagrams* [24] to model the architecture styles identified in the case study. An architecture diagram consists of a set of *component types*, with associated cardinality constraints representing the expected number of instances of each component type and a set of *connector motifs*. Connector motifs, which define sets of BIP connectors, are non-empty sets of *port types*, each labelled as either a trigger or a synchron. Each port type has a *cardinality* constraint representing the expected number of port instances per component instance and two additional constraints: *multiplicity* and *degree*, represented as a pair $m : d$. Multiplicity constrains the number of instances of the port type that must participate in a connector defined by the motif; degree constrains the number of connectors attached to any instance of the port type.

Cardinalities, multiplicities and degrees are either natural numbers or intervals. The interval attributes, 'mc' (multiple choice) or 'sc' (single choice), specify whether these constraints are uniformly applied or not. Let us consider, a port type p with associated intervals defining its multiplicity and degree. We write 'sc$[x,y]$' to mean that the same multiplicity or degree is applied to each port instance of p. We write 'mc$[x,y]$' to mean that different multiplicities or degrees can be applied to different port instances of p, provided they lie in the interval.

For the specification of behavioural properties enforced by architecture styles, as well as those assumed for the parameter components, we use the Computation Tree Logic (CTL). We only provide a brief overview, referring the reader to the classical textbook [3] for a complete and formal presentation. CTL formulas specify properties of execution trees generated by LTSs. The formulas are built from atomic predicates on the states of the LTS, using the several operators, such as EX, AX, EF, AF, EG, AG (unary) and E[·U·], A[·U·], E[·W·], A[·W·] (binary). Each operator consists of a quantifier on the branches of the tree and a temporal modality, which together define when in the execution the operand sub-formulas must hold. The intuition behind the letters is the following: the branch quantifiers are A (for "All") and E (for "Exists"); the temporal modalities are X (for "neXt"), F (for "some time in the Future"), G (for "Globally"), U (for "Until") and W (for "Weak until"). A property is satisfied if it holds in the initial state of the LTS. For instance, the formula $A[p\,W\,q]$ specifies that in *all execution branches* the predicate p must hold *up to the first state* (not including this latter), where the predicate q holds. Since we used the weak until operator W, if q never holds, p must hold forever. As soon as q holds in one state of an execution branch, p need not hold any more, even if q does not hold. On the contrary, the formula $AG\,A[p\,W\,q]$ specifies that the subformula $A[p\,W\,q]$ must hold in *all branches at all times*. Thus, p must hold whenever q does not hold, i.e. $AG\,A[p\,W\,q] = AG\,(p \vee q)$.

3 Case Study

CubETH is a nanosatellite based on the CubeSat standard [15]. It contains the following subsystems: EPS (electrical power subsystem), CDMS (command and data management subsystem), COM (telecommunication subsystem), ADCS (attitude determination and control subsystem), PL (payload) and the mechanical structure including the antenna deployment subsystem.

This case study is focused on the software running on the CDMS subsystem and in particular on the following subcomponents of CDMS: (1) CDMS status that is in charge of resetting internal and external watchdogs; (2) Payload that is in charge of payload operations; (3) three Housekeeping components that are used to recover engineering data from the EPS, PL and COM subsystems; (4) CDMS Housekeeping which is internal to the CDMS; (5) I2C_sat that implements the I^2C protocol; (6) Flash memory management that implements a non-volatile flash memory and its write-read protocol; (7) the s3_5, s3_6, s15_1 and s15_2 services that are in charge of the activation or deactivation of the housekeeping component actions; (8) Error Logging that implements a RAM region that is accessible by many users and (9) the MESSAGE_LIBRARY, MEMORY_LIBRARY and I2C_sat_LIBRARY components that contain auxiliary C/C++ functions.

A high-level BIP model of the case-study is shown in Fig. 5. For the sake of simplicity, we omit some of the connectors. In particular, we show the connectors involving the HK_to_MEM, HK_to_I2C and HK_to_I2C_NOFAIL interfaces of the HK_COM subsystem, but we omit the respective connectors involving the other three Housekeeping subsystems. The MESSAGE_LIBRARY, MEMORY_LIBRARY,

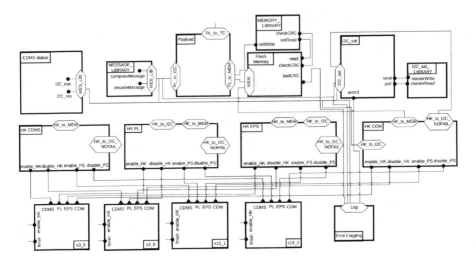

Fig. 5. The high-level interaction model

I2C_sat_LIBRARY, s3_5, s3_6, s15_1 and s15_2 components are atomic. The rest are composite components, i.e. *compounds*.

The full BIP model of the case study can be found in the technical report [23]. It comprises 22 operand components and 27 architectures that were generated from the architecture styles presented in the next subsection.

3.1   A Taxonomy of Architecture Styles for On-Board Software

We have identified 9 architecture styles from the BIP model obtained in [29]. In this section, we present 5 styles (all styles are presented in the technical report [23]). Since the identified architecture styles represent recurring patterns of satellite on-board software, the usage of the presented taxonomy is not limited to this case-study. The identified styles can also be used for the design and development of other satellite on-board systems.

For each architecture style, we have studied two groups of properties: (1) *assumed properties* that the operand components must satisfy so that the architecture can be successfully applied on them and (2) *characteristic properties* that are properties the architecture imposes on the system. In this case study, all characteristic properties are safety properties. Due to space limitations, in the next subsections, for all architecture styles except for Mutual exclusion, we omit their assumed properties. These can be found in the technical report [23].

The styles are specified by using architecture diagrams. Below, for the sake of clarity, we omit the port type cardinality if it is equal to 1. The cardinality of a component type is indicated right next to its name.

The Mutual Exclusion Style (Figure 6) generalises the architecture in Fig. 3. It enforces mutual exclusion on a shared resource (see Sect. 2).

The unique—due to the cardinality being 1—coordinator component, Mutex manager, manages the shared resource, while n parameter components of type B can access it. The multiplicities of all port types are 1, hence, all connectors are binary. The degree

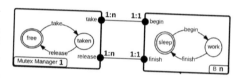

Fig. 6. Mutual exclusion style

constraints require that each port instance of a component of type B be attached to a single connector and each port instance of the coordinator be attached to n connectors. The behaviours of the two component types enforce that once the resource is acquired by a component of type B, it can only be released by the same component. The assumed and characteristic properties of this style were presented in Sect. 2.

The Client-Server Style (Figure 7) ensures that only one client can use a service offered by the server at each time. It consists of two parameter component types Server and Client with 1 and n instances, respectively. In the diagram of Fig. 7, the Server provides two services through port types offer and offer2. The Client has two port types use and use2. Since the cardinalities of offer and offer2 are k and k', respectively, each component instance of type Server has k port instances of type offer and k' port instances of type offer2. Similarly, each component instance of type Client has m port instances of type use and m' port instances of type use2.

Two connector motifs connect use (resp. use2) with offer (resp. offer2). The multiplicity:degree constraints of offer and use are $1 : nm$ and $1 : k$, respectively. Since both multiplicities are 1, all connectors are binary. Because of the degree con-

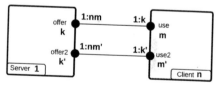

Fig. 7. Client-Server style

straints, each port instance of use must be attached to k connectors, while each port instance of offer must be attached to nm connectors, i.e. all port instances of use are connected to all port instances of offer. An architecture of this style is shown in Fig. 12.

The characteristic property of this style is '*only one client can use a provided service at each time*', formalised by the CTL formula:

$$\forall i, j \leqslant n, \forall p \leqslant k, \ \mathbf{AG}\big(\neg Client[i].use[p] \wedge Client[j].use[p]\big),$$
$$\forall i, j \leqslant n, \forall p \leqslant k, \ \mathbf{AG}\big(\neg Client[i].use2[p] \wedge Client[j].use2[p]\big).$$

The Action Flow Style (Figure 8) enforces a sequence of actions. It has one coordinator component of type Action Flow Manager and n parameter components of type B. The cyclic behaviour of the coordinator enforces an order on the actions of the operands. In the manager's behaviour, abi and aei stand for "action i begin" and "action i end".

Each operand component c of type B provides n_a^c port instances of type `actBegin` and of type `actEnd`. Notice that n_a^c might be different for different operands of type B. The cardinalities of port types `ab` and `ae` are both equal to $N = \sum_{c:B} n_a^c$, where the sum is over all operands of type B. The multiplic-

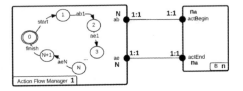

Fig. 8. Action flow style

ity and degree constraints require that there be only binary connectors. An architecture of this style is shown in Fig. 11.

The characteristic property of this style is the conjunction of (a) *'on each action flow's execution, every action begins only after its previous action has ended'* (b) *'on each flow execution, every action occurs at most once'* (c) *'the flow finishes only after the last action has ended'*, formalised by the following CTL formulas, in which the index i denotes the position of an action in the action flow. We consider the following mappings:

- from indices to components $seq_c : [1, N] \to C$, where C is a set containing all operands that execute an action;
- from indices to actions $seq_a : [1, N] \to A$, where A is a set containing all actions of the operands,

such that the action $seq_a(i)$ belongs to the component $seq_c(i)$.

$$\forall 1 < i \leqslant N, \ \texttt{AG}\big(start \to$$
$$\texttt{AX} \ \texttt{A}\big[\neg B[seq_c(i)].actBegin[seq_a(i)] \ \texttt{W} \ B[seq_c(i)].actEnd[seq_a(i-1)]\big]\big) ,$$
$$\forall 1 \leqslant i \leqslant N, \ \texttt{AG}\big(B[seq_c(i)].actBegin[seq_a(i)] \to$$
$$\texttt{AX} \ \texttt{A}\big[\neg B[seq_c(i)].actBegin[seq_a(i)] \ \texttt{W} \ start\big]\big) ,$$
$$\texttt{AG}\big(start \to \texttt{AX} \ \texttt{A}[\neg finish \ \texttt{W} \ B[seq_c(i)].actEnd[N]]\big) .$$

The Failure Monitoring Style (Figure 9) provides monitor components that observe the state of other components. It consists of n coordinator components of type `Failure Monitor` and n parameter components of type `B1`. The cardinality of all port types is 1. Multiplicities and degrees require that each `B1` component instance be connected to its dedicated `Failure monitor` instance.

A `B1` component may enter the following three states: `NOMINAL`, `ANOMALY` and `CRITICAL_FAILURE`. When in `NOMINAL` state, the component is performing correctly. If the component cannot be reached, or if the engineering data is not correct the component enters the `ANOMALY` state. If a fixed

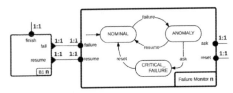

Fig. 9. Failure monitoring style

time has passed in which the component has remained in `ANOMALY`, the component enters the `CRITICAL_FAILURE` state. An architecture of this style is shown in Fig. 13.

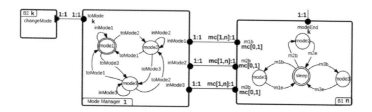

Fig. 10. Mode management style (component behaviour is shown for k=3)

The characteristic property of this style is '*if a failure occurs, a finish happens only after a resume or reset*', formalised by the following CTL formula:

$$\forall c \leqslant n, \ \texttt{AG}\big(B1[c].fail \rightarrow \texttt{AX} \ \texttt{A}\big[\neg B1[c].finish \ \texttt{W} \ (B1[c].resume \vee reset)\big]\big).$$

The Mode Management Style (Figure 10) restricts the set of enabled actions according to a set of predefined modes. It consists of one coordinator of type Mode Manager, n parameter components of type B1 and k parameter components of type B2. Each B2 component *triggers* the transition of the Mode Manager to a specific mode. The coordinator manages which actions of the B1 components can be executed in each mode.

Mode Manager has k states—one state per mode—a port type toMode with cardinality k and k port types inMode with cardinality 1. Each port instance of type toMode must be connected through a binary connector with the changeMode port of a dedicated B2 component. B1 has k port types modeBegin with cardinality mc[0, 1]. In other words, a component instance of B1 might have any number of port instances of types modeBegin from 0 until k. B1 has also a modeEnd port type with cardinality k. mib stands for "mode i begin" and indicates that an action that is enabled in mode i has begun its execution. mie stands for "mode i end" and indicates that an action that is enabled in mode i has finished its execution. Each inMode port instance of the Mode Manager must be connected with the corresponding modeBegin port instances of all B1 components through an n-ary connector. An architecture of this style is shown in Fig. 14.

The characteristic property of this style is '*an action is only performed in a mode where it is allowed*', formalised by the following CTL formula:

$$\forall i \leqslant k, \ \texttt{AG}\big(B1.m[i]b \rightarrow ModeManager.inMode[i]\big).$$

3.2 BIP Model Design by Architecture Application

We illustrate the architecture-based approach on the CDMS status, MESSAGE_ LIBRARY and HK PL components. In particular, we present the application of Action flow, Mode management, Client-Server and Failure monitoring architectures to discharge a subset of CubETH functional requirements (Table 1). We additionally present the result of the composition of Client-Server and Mode management architectures. The full list of requirements is provided in [23].

Table 1. Representative requirements for CDMS status and HK_PL

ID	Description
CDMS-007	The CDMS shall periodically reset both the internal and external watchdogs and contact the EPS subsystem with a "heartbeat"
HK-001	The CDMS shall have a Housekeeping activity dedicated to each subsystem
HK-003	When line-of-sight communication is possible, housekeeping information shall be transmitted through the COM subsystem
HK-004	When line-of-sight communication is not possible, housekeeping information shall be written to the non-volatile flash memory
HK-005	A Housekeeping subsystem shall have the following states: NOMINAL, ANOMALY and CRITICAL_FAILURE

Application of Action Flow Architecture. Requirement CDMS-007, presented in Table 1, describes the functionality of CDMS status. The corresponding BIP model is shown in Fig. 11. Watchdog reset is an operand component, which is responsible for resetting the internal and external watchdogs. CDMS status ACTION FLOW is the coordinator of the architecture applied on Watchdog reset that imposes the following order of actions: (1) internal watchdog reset; (2) external watchdog reset; (3) send heartbeat and (4) receive result.

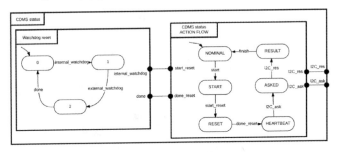

Fig. 11. Application of Action flow architecture

Application of Client-Server Architecture. Requirements HK-001 and HK-003, presented in Table 1, suggest the application of the Client-Server architecture on the HK PL, HK CDMS, HK EPS and HK COM housekeeping compounds (Fig. 5). The four housekeeping compounds are the clients of the architecture. In Fig. 12a, we show how Client-Server is applied on the HK PL process component, which is a subcomponent of HK PL. HK PL process uses the composeMessage and decodeMessage C/C++ functions of the MESSAGE_LIBRARY component to encode and decode information transmitted to and from the COM subsystem. Thus, the MESSAGE_LIBRARY is a server used by the HK PL process client. To enhance readability of figures in Fig. 12a, we use hexagons to group interaction patterns of components. The meaning of these hexagons is explained in Fig. 12b.

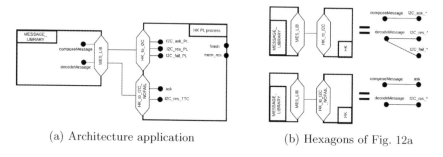

(a) Architecture application   (b) Hexagons of Fig. 12a

Fig. 12. Application of Client-Server architecture

Application of Failure Monitoring Architecture. Requirement HK-005, presented in Table 1, suggests the application of the Failure monitoring architecture as shown in Fig. 13. The BIP model comprises the HK PL process operand and the HK PL FAILURE MONITORING coordinator. The success port of HK PL FAILURE MONITORING is connected with the mem_res and I2C_res_TTC ports of HK PL process. The failure port of HK PL FAILURE MONITORING is connected with the I2C_fail_PL port of HK PL process. The HK PL process component executes 6 actions in the following order: (1) start procedure; (2) ask Payload for engineering data; (3) receive result from Payload or (in case of fail) abort; (4) if line of sight communication is possible send data to COM, if line of sight communication is not possible make a write request to the memory; (5) depending on action 4 either receive COM result or memory result and (6) finish procedure.

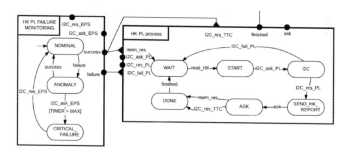

Fig. 13. Application of Failure monitoring architecture

Application of Mode Management Architecture. Requirements HK-003 and HK-004, presented in Table 1, suggest the application of a Mode management architecture with two modes: (1) TTC mode, in which line of sight communication is possible and (2) MEMORY mode, in which line of sight communication is not possible. The corresponding BIP model, shown in Fig. 14, comprises the HK PL process, s15_1 and s15_2 operands and the Packet store MODE MANAGER coordinator. During NOMINAL operation, the Payload subsystem is contacted

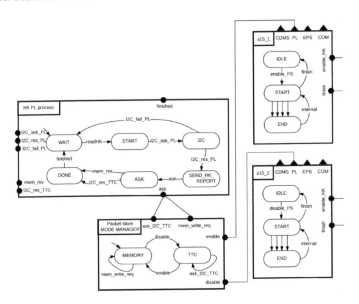

Fig. 14. Application of Mode management architecture

to retrieve engineering data. Depending on the mode of `Packet store MODE MANAGER`, those data is then sent to the non-volatile memory, i.e. `mem_write_req` transition, or directly to the `COM` subsystem, i.e. `ask_I2C_TTC` transition. The mode of `Packet store MODE MANAGER` is triggered by the `s15_1`, `s15_2` services.

Composition of Architectures. The architecture composition was formally defined in [2]. Here, we provide only an illustrative example. Combined application of architectures to a common set of operand components results in merging the connectors that involve ports used by several architectures. For instance, Fig. 15 shows the composition of Client-Server and Mode management architectures. The `HK PL process` component is a sub-component of `HK PL`. The application of the Client-Server architecture (Fig. 12) connects its port `ask` with the port `composeMessage` of `MESSAGE_LIBRARY` through the `MES_LIB-HK_to_I2C` interface with a binary connector. Similarly, the application of the Mode management architecture (Fig. 14) connects the same port with the port `ask_I2C_TTC` of `Packet store MODE MANAGER` with another binary connector. The composition of the two architectures results in the two connectors being merged into the ternary connector `ask-ask_I2C_TTC-composeMessage` (Fig. 15).

3.3   Model Verification

Recall (Sect. 2) that safety properties imposed by architectures are preserved by architecture composition [2]. Thus, all properties that we have associated to the CubETH requirements are satisfied *by construction* by the complete model of the case study example, which is presented in [23].

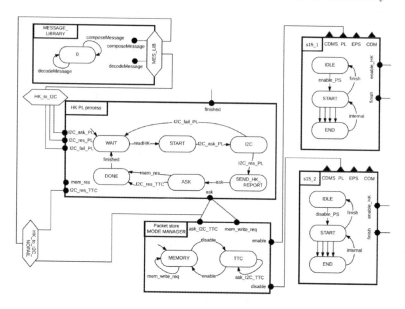

Fig. 15. Composition of Client-Server and Mode management architectures

Architectures enforce properties by restricting the joint behaviour of the operand components. Therefore, combined application of architectures can generate deadlocks. We have used the D-Finder tool [7] to verify deadlock-freedom of the case study model. D-Finder applies compositional verification on BIP models by over-approximating the set of reachable states, which allows it to analyse very large models. The tool is sound, but incomplete: due to the above mentioned over-approximation it can produce false positives, i.e. potential deadlock states that are unreachable in the concrete system. However, our case study model was shown to be deadlock-free without any potential deadlocks. Thus, no additional reachability analysis was needed.

3.4 Validation of the Approach

The key advantage of our architecture-based approach is that the burden of verification is shifted from the final design to architectures, which are considerably smaller in size and can be reused. In particular, all the architecture styles that we have identified for the case study are simple. Their correctness—enforcing the characteristic properties—can be easily proved by inspection of the coordinator behaviour. However, in order to increase the confidence in our approach, we have conducted additional verification, using nuXmv to verify that the characteristic properties of the architectures are, indeed, satisfied. We used the BIP-to-NuSMV tool[3] to translate our BIP models into NuSMV—the nuXmv input language [10].

---

[3] http://risd.epfl.ch/bip2nusmv.

Table 2. Statistics of models and verification

Model	Tool	Components	Connectors	RSS	Deadlocks	Properties
CubETH	D-Finder	49	155	-	0	-
Payload	nuXmv	13	42	8851	0	9
I2C_sat	nuXmv	4	12	52	0	1
HK PL	nuXmv	11	12	77274	0	5
HK EPS	nuXmv	11	12	77274	0	5
HK COM	nuXmv	11	12	77274	0	5
HK CDMS	nuXmv	10	9	12798	0	5
Flash Memory	nuXmv	6	15	44	0	3
CDMS status	nuXmv	3	6	8	0	4
Error Logging	nuXmv	2	2	2	0	1

RSS = Reachable State Space

Verification of the complete model with nuXmv did not succeed, running out of memory after four days of execution. Thus, we repeated the procedure (BIP-to-NuSMV translation and verification using nuXmv) on individual sub-systems. All connectors that crossed sub-system boundaries were replaced by their corresponding sub-connectors. This introduces additional interactions, hence, also additional execution branches. Since no priorities are used in the model, this modification does not suppress any existing behaviour. Notice that the CTL properties enforced by the presented architecture styles use only universal quantification (A) over execution branches. Hence, the above approach is a sound abstraction, i.e. the fact that the properties were shown to hold in the sub-systems immediately entails that they also hold in the complete model. The complete list of CTL formulas is presented in [23]. Table 2 presents the complexity measures of the verification, which was carried out on an Intel Core i7 at 3.50 GHz with 16 GB of RAM. Notice that component count in sub-systems adds up to more than 49, because some components contribute to several sub-systems.

4   Related Work

The European Space Agency (ESA) advocates a model-based design flow rather than a document-centric approach. To this end, a series of funded research initiatives has delivered interesting results that are worth mentioning. The Space Avionics Open Interface Architecture (SAVOIR)[4] project introduces the On-board Software Reference Architecture (OSRA) [20] that imposes certain structural constraints through the definition of the admissible types of software components and patterns of interaction among their instances. The ASSERT Set of Tools for Engineering (TASTE)[5] [30] is more appropriate for the detailed

[4] http://savoir.estec.esa.int/.
[5] http://taste.tuxfamily.org/.

software design and model-based code generation. In TASTE, the architectural design is captured through a graphical editor that generates a model in the Architecture Analysis & Design Language (AADL). However, the AADL semantics is not formally defined, which inhibits it from being used for rigorous design or formal verification purposes. The Correctness, Modeling and Performance of Aerospace Systems (COMPASS)[6] toolset relies on an AADL variant with formally defined semantics called SLIM and provides means for a posteriori formal verification [13]. A formal semantics for the AADL has been defined in BIP, along with a translation of AADL models into the BIP language [16]. The rigorous design approach based on correct-by-construction steps is applied in the Functional Requirements and Verification Techniques for the Software Reference Architecture (FoReVer)[7] and the Catalogue of System and Software Properties (CSSP) projects. The former initiative advocates a top-down design flow by imposing behavioural contracts on individual components [8], while the latter adopts our architecture-based design flow relying on BIP.

Although a number of frameworks exist for the specification of architectures [25,28,35], model design and code generation [1,6,12,34], and verification [11,17,21], we are not aware of any that combine all these features. In particular, to the best of our knowledge, our approach is the first application of requirement-driven correct-by-construction design in the domain of satellite on-board software, which relies on requirements to define a high-level model that can be directly used to generate executable code for the satellite control [29].

BIP has previously been used for the design of control software. The applications closest to ours are the initial design of the CubETH [29] and the DALA robot [5] control software. While the latter design followed a predefined software architecture (in the sense of [4]), the former was purely ad-hoc. Neither was driven by a detailed set of requirements.

In [18], the authors describe the interfacing of Temporal Logic Planning toolbox (TuLiP) with the JPL Statechart Autocoder (SCA) for the automatic generation of control software. The TuLiP toolbox generates from statechart models from high-level specifications expressed as formulas of particular form in the Linear Temporal Logic (LTL). SCA is then used to generate Python, C or C++ code from the obtained statecharts. This approach is grounded in formal semantics, it provides correctness guarantees through the automatic synthesis of control behaviour. Furthermore, the transition through statecharts allows the use of graphical tools to visualise the controller behaviour. However, it also has some limitations. Most notably, it focuses exclusively on the synthesis of one controller component and is not easily amenable to the holistic design of complete software systems involving concurrent components.

---

[6] http://compass.informatik.rwth-aachen.de/.
[7] https://es-static.fbk.eu/projects/forever/.

5   Conclusion and Future Work

Based on previous work [29], we have analysed the command and data management sub-system (CDMS) of the CubETH nanosatellite on-board software (OBSW), concentrating primarily on safety and modularity of the software. Starting from a set of informal requirements, we have used the architecture-based approach [2] to design a BIP model of the CDMS sub-system. We have illustrated the key steps of the BIP model design, discussed and evaluated the verification and validation procedures.

The architecture-based approach consists in the application of a number of architectures starting with a minimal set of atomic components. Each architecture enforces *by construction* a characteristic safety property on the joint behaviour of the operand components. The combined application of architectures is defined by an associative and commutative operator [2], which guarantees the preservation of the enforced properties. Since, architectures enforce properties by restricting the joint behaviour of the operand components, combined application of architectures can lead to deadlocks. Thus, the final step of the design process consists in verifying the deadlock-freedom of the obtained model. The key advantage of this approach is that the burden of verification is shifted from the final design to architectures, which are considerably smaller in size and can be reused. This advantage is illustrated by our verification results: while model-checking of the complete model was inconclusive, verification of deadlock-freedom took only a very short time, using the D-Finder tool.

The main contribution of the presented work is the identification and formal modelling—using architecture diagrams [24]—of 9 architecture styles, whereof 5 are presented in the paper (all styles are presented in the associated technical report [23]). Architecture styles represent recurring coordination patterns: those identified in the case study have been reused in the framework of a collaborative project funded by ESA and can be further reused in other satellite OBSW.

The case study serves as a feasibility proof for the use of architecture-based approach in satellite OBSW design. The modular nature of BIP allows iterative design for satellites in development and component reuse for subsequent missions. The automatic generation of C++ code provided by the BIP tool-set enables early prototyping and validation of software functionality even before the hardware platform is completely defined, also contributing to portability of designs. Indeed, the only non-trivial action required in order to use a different target platform is to recompile the BIP engine.

This case study opens a number of directions for future work. The most immediate consists in studying optimisation techniques, such as [27] to reduce the complexity overhead of the automatically generated models. In the framework of the ESA project, we are currently developing a tool for the automatic application and composition of architectures and a GUI tool for ontology-based specification of user requirements. We plan to integrate these, together with the BIP framework, into a dedicated tool-chain for OBSW design, providing requirement traceability and early validation. We also plan to expand our taxonomy of architecture styles and study the application of parametrised model checking techniques for their formal verification. Finally, it would be interesting to extend the architecture-based approach to real-time systems. Composability of real-time architectures will require a notion of non-interference similar to that used to ensure the preservation of liveness properties in [2].

Acknowledgements. The work presented in this paper was partially funded by the ESA CSSP project (contract no. 4000112344/14/NL/FE). We would like to thank Andreas Jung, Marcel Verhoef and Marco Panunzio for the instructive discussions in the framework of this project, which have contributed to the clarification of some of the ideas realised in this case study. Finally, we are deeply grateful to the anonymous reviewers for their constructive comments.

References

1. Arbab, F.: Reo: a channel-based coordination model for component composition. Math. Struct. Comput. Sci. **14**(3), 329–366 (2004)
2. Attie, P., et al.: A general framework for architecture composability. Formal Aspects Comput. **18**(2), 207–231 (2016)
3. Baier, C., Katoen, J.-P.: Principles of Model Checking. Representation and Mind Series. The MIT Press, Cambridge (2008)
4. Bass, L., Clements, P., Kazman, R.: Software Architecture in Practice. SEI Series in Software Engineering, 3rd edn. Addison-Wesley Professional, New York (2012)
5. Basu, A., et al.: Incremental component-based construction and verification of a robotic system. In: ECAI, pp. 631–635. IOS Press (2008)
6. Basu, A., et al.: Rigorous component-based system design using the BIP framework. IEEE Softw. **28**(3), 41–48 (2011)
7. Bensalem, S., Griesmayer, A., Legay, A., Nguyen, T.-H., Sifakis, J., Yan, R.: D-Finder 2: towards efficient correctness of incremental design. In: Bobaru, M., Havelund, K., Holzmann, G.J., Joshi, R. (eds.) NFM 2011. LNCS, vol. 6617, pp. 453–458. Springer, Heidelberg (2011). doi:10.1007/978-3-642-20398-5_32
8. Benveniste, A., et al.: Contracts for system design. Research report RR-8147, INRIA, November 2012
9. Bliudze, S., Sifakis, J.: The algebra of connectors-structuring interaction in BIP. IEEE Trans. Comput. **57**(10), 1315–1330 (2008)
10. Bliudze, S., Cimatti, A., Jaber, M., Mover, S., Roveri, M., Saab, W., Wang, Q.: Formal verification of infinite-state BIP models. In: Finkbeiner, B., Pu, G., Zhang, L. (eds.) ATVA 2015. LNCS, vol. 9364, pp. 326–343. Springer, Cham (2015). doi:10.1007/978-3-319-24953-7_25
11. Bloem, R., Cimatti, A., Greimel, K., Hofferek, G., Könighofer, R., Roveri, M., Schuppan, V., Seeber, R.: RATSY – a new requirements analysis tool with synthesis. In: Touili, T., Cook, B., Jackson, P. (eds.) CAV 2010. LNCS, vol. 6174, pp. 425–429. Springer, Heidelberg (2010). doi:10.1007/978-3-642-14295-6_37
12. Boulanger, J.-L., et al.: SCADE: Language and Applications, 1st edn. Wiley-IEEE Press, New York (2015)
13. Bozzano, M., et al.: Spacecraft early design validation using formal methods. Reliab. Eng. Syst. Saf. **132**, 20–35 (2014)

14. Brandon, C., Chapin, P.: A SPARK/Ada CubeSat control program. In: Keller, H.B., Plödereder, E., Dencker, P., Klenk, H. (eds.) Ada-Europe 2013. LNCS, vol. 7896, pp. 51–64. Springer, Heidelberg (2013). doi:10.1007/978-3-642-38601-5_4

15. California Polytechnic State University. CubeSat Design Specification Rev. 13 (2014). http://www.cubesat.org/s/cds_rev13_final2.pdf

16. Chkouri, M.Y., Robert, A., Bozga, M., Sifakis, J.: Translating AADL into BIP - application to the verification of real-time systems. In: Chaudron, M.R.V. (ed.) MODELS 2008. LNCS, vol. 5421, pp. 5–19. Springer, Heidelberg (2009). doi:10.1007/978-3-642-01648-6_2

17. Cimatti, A., Dorigatti, M., Tonetta, S.: OCRA: a tool for checking the refinement of temporal contracts. In: ASE 2013, pp. 702–705, November 2013

18. Dathathri, S., et al.: Interfacing TuLiP with the JPL statechart autocoder: initial progress toward synthesis of flight software from formal specifications. In: IEEE AeroSpace (2016)

19. Gamma, E., et al.: Design Patterns: Elements of Reusable Object-Oriented Software. Addison-Wesley Professional, Boston (1994)

20. Jung, A., Panunzio, M., Terraillon, J.-L.: On-board software reference architecture. Technical report TEC-SWE/09-289/AJ, SAVOIR Advisory Group (2010)

21. Kim, J.-S., Garlan, D.: Analyzing architectural styles with Alloy. In: ROSATEA 2006, pp. 70–80. ACM (2006)

22. Mavridou, A., Baranov, E., Bliudze, S., Sifakis, J.: Configuration logics: modelling architecture styles. In: Braga, C., Ölveczky, P.C. (eds.) FACS 2015. LNCS, vol. 9539, pp. 256–274. Springer, Cham (2016). doi:10.1007/978-3-319-28934-2_14

23. Mavridou, A., et al.: Architecture-based Design: A Satellite On-Board Software Case Study. Technical report 221156, EPFL, September 2016. https://infoscience.epfl.ch/record/221156

24. Mavridou, A., et al.: Architecture diagrams: a graphical language for architecture style specification. In: 9th ICE, EPTCS, vol. 223, pp. 83–97 (2016)

25. Medvidovic, N., Taylor, R.N.: A classification and comparison framework for software architecture description languages. IEEE Trans. Softw. Eng. 26(1), 70–93 (2000)

26. Mitchell, C., et al.: Development of a modular command and data handling architecture for the KySat-2 CubeSat. In: 2014 IEEE Aerospace Conference, pp. 1–11. IEEE, March 2014

27. Noureddine, M., Jaber, M., Bliudze, S., Zaraket, F.A.: Reduction and abstraction techniques for BIP. In: Lanese, I., Madelaine, E. (eds.) FACS 2014. LNCS, vol. 8997, pp. 288–305. Springer, Cham (2015). doi:10.1007/978-3-319-15317-9_18

28. Ozkaya, M., Kloukinas, C.: Are we there yet? analyzing architecture description languages for formal analysis, usability, and realizability. In: SEAA 2013, pp. 177–184. IEEE (2013)

29. Pagnamenta, M.: Rigorous software design for nano and micro satellites using BIP framework. Master's thesis, EPFL (2014). https://infoscience.epfl.ch/record/218902

30. Perrotin, M., Conquet, E., Delange, J., Schiele, A., Tsiodras, T.: TASTE: a real-time software engineering tool-chain overview, status, and future. In: Ober, I., Ober, I. (eds.) SDL 2011. LNCS, vol. 7083, pp. 26–37. Springer, Heidelberg (2011). doi:10.1007/978-3-642-25264-8_4

31. Rossi, S., et al.: CubETH magnetotorquers: design and tests for a CubeSat mission. In: Advances in the Astronautical Sciences, vol. 153, pp. 1513–1530 (2015)

32. Sifakis, J.: Rigorous system design. Found. Trends® Electron. Des. Autom. 6(4), 293–362 (2012)

33. Spangelo, S.C., et al.: Model based systems engineering (MBSE) applied to Radio Aurora Explorer (RAX) CubeSat mission operational scenarios. In: 2013 IEEE Aerospace Conference, pp. 1–18. IEEE, March 2013
34. SysML. http://www.sysml.org
35. Woods, E., Hilliard, R.: Architecture description languages in practice session report. In: WICSA 2005, pp. 243–246. IEEE Computer Society (2005)

Author Index